The Genealogist's Guide to Massachusetts
by
Eric J. Ostroff
Volume 1

Historical Framework

&

Barnstable to Bristol

Counties

2026

Dedication

To my beloved wife, Jennifer, whose unwavering love and encouragement have made every journey possible, and to my children—Wesley, Zachary, Hannah, and Christopher—whose curiosity and joy inspire me to uncover the stories of those who came before us. May this work honor our family's past as much as it celebrates our present and future together.

Foreword

Genealogical research in Massachusetts has always required equal parts curiosity, discipline, and historical sensitivity. Few places in the United States offer so deep and complicated a documentary record—nor one rooted in such profound layers of human experience. From thousands of years of Indigenous stewardship, to the earliest English settlements, to the upheavals of revolution, industry, immigration, and modern reform, the Commonwealth's history is inseparable from the paper trail it left behind. To research a Massachusetts family is to enter a landscape defined by overlapping jurisdictions, shifting boundaries, religious and civic experimentation, and more than four centuries of administrators, clerks, ministers, archivists, and neighbors who documented life as they understood it.

This volume, *The Genealogist's Guide to Massachusetts – Volume I*, stands at the intersection of that history and the practical craft of family reconstruction. Rather than offering only a catalog of repositories or a digest of record types, it provides something far more valuable: a guide grounded in historical context, attentive to the lived realities of the people who appear in the records and equipped with a genealogist's eye for the details that matter. It demonstrates—chapter by chapter—that responsible genealogical work is not simply the extraction of names and dates, but the thoughtful interpretation of evidence shaped by political, cultural, and social forces.

Readers will find here a clear and authoritative framework for understanding how Massachusetts towns were formed, how laws evolved, and how particular record sets emerged. The discussions of Indigenous homelands and early European contact remind us that the story of Massachusetts did not begin with colonization, and that the archival silences surrounding Native communities reflect histories of displacement and survival rather than absence. The chapters on Plymouth and Massachusetts Bay illuminate how two distinct colonial experiments created divergent approaches to governance and recordkeeping—differences that still influence where documents reside today. Later sections trace the transformation from provincial colony to industrial commonwealth, revealing how court systems, vital registration, religious life, and civic institutions expanded and adapted over time.

What distinguishes this guide is its commitment to bridging narrative history with the practical needs of genealogists. Each section is written with the researcher in mind: where to look, what to expect, why gaps exist, and how to interpret seemingly ordinary entries in town books, court dockets, land records, or parish registers. This is a manual that teaches researchers **how to think historically**, not just where to search. It encourages reasonably exhaustive investigation, careful source evaluation, and an understanding that every level of Massachusetts government—from town meeting to state legislature—created records for specific reasons that affect their form and completeness.

For newcomers, this volume offers a solid foundation on which to build sound, ethical research practices. For experienced genealogists, it provides a refined map through a landscape that may seem familiar but is rarely straightforward. And for all readers, it restores a sense of depth and humanity to the records we so often treat as static artifacts. Every birth entry, every land transaction, every probate inventory is part of a larger story—of community, conflict, migration, economy, faith, and the constant reinvention of life in Massachusetts.

Table of Contents

Preface 14
   Author's note and purpose 14
   Why Massachusetts matters 14
   How to use this book 15
   Acknowledgements and methodology 15

Part I: The Origins of Massachusetts 17

Chapter 1 18
   Indigenous Homelands Before Colonization 18
   First Contacts and the Shock of Disease (Late 1500s–1630) 21
   Plymouth and Massachusetts Bay: Planting English Colonies (1620–1691) 24
   Puritan Order, Conflict, and the Making of Towns 27
   Empire, Crisis, and the Road to Revolution (1691–1780s) 29
   From Farms to Factories: Industrialization and Reform (1800–1865) 32
   Waves of Newcomers: Immigration and Ethnic Communities (1840s–1920s) 35
   A Modern Commonwealth: Education, Suburbs, and Technology (1900–Present) .. 37
   Bringing It All Together: Using the Timeline in Your Research 39

Chapter 2 44
   Town Governance and Colonial Laws 46
   Religion and Community Structure 54
      Congregational Roots and the Village Church 55
      Religious Diversity and Parallel Communities 59
      Religion, Boundaries, and Social Control 62
   Education and the Rise of Literacy 64
      Early School Laws and Town Responsibilities 67
      The Rise of Common Schools, Normal Schools, and High Schools 68
      Higher Education and New Kinds of Records 70
      Economic Foundations: Agriculture, Fishing, Industry, and Trade 72
      Fishing and Maritime Economy: Salt Cod, Whales, and Global Reach 74
      Trade and Commerce: Merchants, Shops, and Urban Exchange 76
      How Political, Religious, and Social Evolution Shaped Record Creation 78

PART II: The Counties, Cites & Towns 81
of 81

Massachusetts	81
Chapter 3	82
Indigenous Foundations: Wampanoag Stewards of the Land	82
The Ecological and Cultural Landscape	82
Land Use, Stewardship, and Ownership Concepts	83
Early European Contact and Consequences	83
King Philip's War and Its Aftershocks	83
Continuity and Contemporary Presence	84
Genealogical Guidance	84
European Exploration and the Mayflower Moment	84
Colonial Settlement: Towns, Townspeople, and Town Books	86
Provincial Era, Revolution, and Early Republic	88
Maritime Prosperity: Fishing and Whaling	89
Modern Era: Tourism, Preservation, and Governance Shifts	91
Tourism's Ascendancy and Economic Transformation	91
Genealogical Treasures and Research Roadmap	93
City	95
Barnstable	95
Bourne	96
Brewster	98
Chatham	100
Dennis	102
Eastham	104
Falmouth	106
Harwich	108
Mashpee	109
Orleans	111
Provincetown	112
Sandwich	114
Truro	115
Wellfleet	117
Yarmouth	118
Villages	119

Barnstable Village	119
Centerville	121
Cotuit	122
Craigville	123
Hyannis	125
Hyannis Port	126
Marstons Mills	127
North Harwich	128
North Truro	129
Osterville	130
Pleasant Lake	131
South Harwich	132
West Barnstable	133
West Harwich	134
Monument Beach	135
Pocasset	136
Sagamore	137
Sagamore Beach	138
Cataumet	139
Census-Designated Places	140
Buzzards Bay	140
Dennis Port	141
East Falmouth	142
East Harwich	143
East Sandwich	144
Forestdale	145
Harwich Center	146
Harwich Port	147
Mashpee Neck	148
Monomoscoy Island	149
New Seabury	150
North Eastham	151
North Falmouth	152

- Northwest Harwich 153
- Pocasset 154
- Popponesset 154
- Popponesset Island 155
- Seconsett Island 156
- South Dennis 157
- South Yarmouth 158
- Teaticket 159
- West Chatham 159
- West Dennis 160
- West Falmouth 161
- West Yarmouth 162
- Woods Hole 163
- Yarmouth Port 164
- Unincorporated Communities 164
- Bellingsgate 164
- Captains Village 165
- Ferris Fields 166
- Hatchville 166
- Long Point 167
- Monomoy Island 168
- South Brewster 169
- South Chatham 170
- South Sandwich 170
- Waquoit 171
- Wood End 172

Chapter 4 174
- Indigenous Foundations: Mahican Homeland and Continuity 174
- Colonial Settlement and Frontier Life in Berkshire County: A Detailed Examination 175
- Revolutionary Contributions and 19th-Century Transformation in Berkshire County: An Expanded Analysis 177
- Societies, Archives, and Genealogical Resources 179
- Geography, Culture, and Genealogical Context 181

Berkshire County's Enduring Genealogical Legacy	182
City	184
North Adams	184
Pittsfield	185
Towns	187
Adams	187
Alford	188
Becket	190
Cheshire	191
Clarksburg	193
Dalton	194
Egremont	196
Florida	197
Great Barrington	198
Hancock	200
Hinsdale	201
Lanesborough	202
Lee	204
Lenox	205
Monterey	206
Mount Washington	208
New Ashford	209
New Marlborough	210
Otis	212
Peru	213
Richmond	214
Sandisfield	215
Savoy	215
Mahican Highlands and Hathaway Settlement	216
Sheffield	216
Sheffield Resolves and Historical Campus	216
Stockbridge	217
Tyringham	218

Washington	218
West Stockbridge	220
Williamstown	220
Windsor	221
Census-Designated Places	222
Housatonic	222

Chapter 5 223

Bristol County 223

Indigenous Foundations: The Wampanoag Homeland and Survival	223
Colonial Settlement and Maritime Expansion in Bristol County	224
Industry, Immigration, and the 19th-Century Transformation	224
Genealogical Landscape and Archival Resources	225
Geography, Culture, and Genealogical Context	226
Bristol County's Enduring Genealogical Legacy	226
King Philip's War and Colonial Consolidation	226
Maritime Communities and Whaling Genealogies	227
Industrial Immigration and Urban Working-Class Lives	227
Archival Networks and Research Strategies in Bristol County	228
City	229
Attleboro	229
Fall River	231
New Bedford	233
Taunton	235
Towns	238
Acushnet	238
Berkley	239
Dartmouth	241
Dighton	242
Easton	243
Fairhaven	245
Freetown	246
Mansfield	247
North Attleboro	248

Norton	249
Raynham	250
Rehoboth	252
Seekonk	253
Somerset	254
Swansea	255
Westport	256
Census-Designated Places	257
Acushnet Center	257
Bliss Corner	258
Mansfield Center	260
North Seekonk	261
North Westport	262
Norton Center	263
Ocean Grove	264
Raynham Center	265
Smith Mills	266
Villages	267
Assonet	267
Bowensville	268
Britania	269
East Freetown	270
East Taunton	271
Fall River Station	272
Five Corners	273
Flint Village	274
Four Corners	275
Globe Village	276
Gushee Pond	277
Highlands	278
Hixville	279
Hixville	280
Holbrook Village	281

Horbine	282
Hortonville	283
Kingmans Corner	284
Myricks	285
North Attleboro Center	286
North Raynham	287
North Taunton	289
Oakland	290
Padanaram	291
Peck's Corner	292
Perry's Corner	293
Perryville	294
Plesantfield	294
Pleasant Street	295
Pottersville	296
Prattville	297
Ramblewood	298
Rehoboth Village	299
Sassaquin	300
South Attleboro	301
South Rehoboth	302
Squawbetty	303
Steep Brook	304
Titicut	305
Tracy Corner	306
Wade's Corner	307
Weir Village	308
Westerville	309
Whittenton	310
Whittenton Junction	311
Ghost Towns	312
Norton Furnace	312

Preface

This anthology, *The Genealogist's Guide to Massachusetts*, is written for researchers who wish to move beyond isolated names and dates and into the deeper landscape that shaped their ancestors' lives. It is intended equally for those just beginning to explore New England roots and for experienced genealogists seeking a structured overview of Massachusetts resources, history, and research strategies. The goal is to provide a practical, context-rich guide that bridges the gap between historical narrative and hands-on methodology, so that readers can interpret records accurately and place individual families within the wider story of the Commonwealth.

Author's note and purpose

This guide grew out of countless hours spent in town halls, archives, online databases, and local historical societies, puzzling through the quirks of Massachusetts records. Over time, recurring patterns emerged: similar questions from clients and students, similar pitfalls in interpreting town and county jurisdictions, and similar misunderstandings about what records exist, and where. This book responds to those patterns by organizing the essentials of Massachusetts research into a single, coherent reference, with an emphasis on practicality and historical context.

The purpose is not to replace detailed local histories, specialized monographs, or archival finding aids, but to help readers approach them more effectively. The chapters are designed to highlight what records were created, who created them, and how they survived (or did not), so that you can set realistic expectations and construct sound, well-documented conclusions. Throughout, the focus is on helping you ask better questions of the records and to recognize when your evidence is sufficient—and when it is not.

Why Massachusetts matters

Massachusetts occupies a central place in American history, and that prominence is reflected in the richness and complexity of its records. From the early 17th century, when English settlers established Plymouth and Massachusetts Bay, through the American Revolution, industrialization, and waves of immigration, the colony and later Commonwealth exerted outsized influence on politics, religion, education, and social reform. Events associated with Massachusetts—such as the Mayflower migration, Puritan settlement, the Boston Massacre and Boston Tea Party, and the first battles of the Revolution—have drawn genealogists for generations because the families involved left unusually deep documentary footprints.

For genealogists, Massachusetts is both a blessing and a challenge. The blessing lies in the breadth of surviving material: early town records, vital registrations, church books, court and land records, military files, tax lists, newspapers, institutional archives, and extensive published and digital aids. The challenge lies in navigating overlapping jurisdictions, shifting boundaries, evolving record-keeping practices, and the biases and silences in the archive—particularly concerning Indigenous communities, enslaved and free people of African descent, women, the poor, and later immigrant groups. Understanding Massachusetts as a dynamic historical setting, rather than a static backdrop, is essential to responsible research.

How to use this book

This guide is organized to help you move smoothly among three dimensions that shape every Massachusetts research problem: geography, chronology, and record type. The geographic sections outline the development of colonies, counties, and towns, explaining where key records are held today and when jurisdictional changes may affect where you search. Particular attention is given to town-level governance, since so many New England records—including vital registrations and many local decisions affecting residents—were created and preserved at the town, not the county, level.

Chronological chapters highlight major historical periods and legal or administrative changes that altered how and where records were created. For example, shifts from colonial to provincial to state authority, changes in vital registration law, developments in probate and land recording systems, and the arc of industrialization and immigration all affected the documentary trail. Within each period, the guide points you to the core record sets you can expect to find and notes common gaps and pitfalls.

The sections organized by record type—vital, church, town, land, probate, court, military, immigration and naturalization, newspapers, and compiled sources—explain what each category contains, how coverage and content change over time, and how to access them in person and online. Where appropriate, the book offers brief case examples to illustrate how multiple sources can be combined to meet modern standards of proof without reproducing or relying on any single published narrative. An index, cross-references, and suggested reading lists at the close of major chapters are intended to help you jump in at the point most relevant to your current problem and then move outward as your research deepens.

Acknowledgements and methodology

This project rests on the work of generations of record keepers, archivists, librarians, historians, and fellow genealogists who have preserved, described, and interpreted Massachusetts sources. Town clerks who carefully copied births and deaths, ministers who maintained membership rolls, registrars who indexed vital events, and archivists who advocated for preservation and digitization all made this kind of guide possible. The staff and volunteers of state and local archives, historical societies, libraries, and genealogical organizations—public and private—have shaped the landscape described in these pages, as have the authors and editors of prior guides, bibliographies, and histories of Massachusetts.

The methodology underlying this book reflects current best practices in genealogical research and documentation. Each discussion of a record group or repository is informed by direct use of the materials wherever possible, supplemented by institutional guides, catalog records, and scholarly treatments of Massachusetts history and law.

The emphasis throughout is on encouraging reasonably exhaustive research, careful source evaluation, correlation of evidence across multiple record types, and transparent citation of all sources used, while always respecting intellectual property and copyright. Readers are encouraged to adapt the approaches outlined here to their own questions and to remain attentive to voices and communities historically underrepresented in the surviving record.

Part I: The Origins of Massachusetts

Chapter 1

Massachusetts in Time: A Genealogist's Historical Framework

For the genealogist, Massachusetts is not only a jurisdiction; it is a palimpsest of cultures, conflicts, migrations, and reinventions layered across four centuries of written records and thousands of years of human presence. Every deed book, town volume, or census page in this state rests on a much older foundation: Indigenous nations who shaped the land long before Europeans named it, colonists who imposed new laws and institutions, families who moved in and out with war and work, and communities that redefined themselves through immigration, industry, and education.

This chapter traces that long arc from pre-colonial homelands to the modern technological commonwealth, with an eye always on what matters most to genealogists: when people lived where, who governed them, what records were created, and how those records illuminate—or silence—the lives of families.

Because readers approach this book with varying levels of experience, the chapter alternates between broad narrative and concrete, research-focused asides. Period overviews establish the social and political context. Annotated timelines at key junctures highlight turning points that change where records are kept, or which people are most likely to appear in them. Case studies demonstrate how a researcher can move from a single clue—perhaps a line in a town book or a ship list—into a fuller reconstruction of a life. The goal is not only to recount Massachusetts history but to show how that history structures the evidence genealogists use every day.

Indigenous Homelands Before Colonization

Long before anyone called this place "Massachusetts," it was—and remains—Indigenous homeland. For genealogists, this is not a romantic prologue to the "real" story that begins with English settlement; it is the first, essential chapter in understanding why towns were founded where they were, how land was claimed, and why some families are documented while others are not. Archaeological and oral-history evidence indicate that Native peoples have lived in what is now Massachusetts for at least 10,000–12,000 years, moving across a landscape of rivers, coastlines, and uplands that looked different from today yet provided abundant resources for complex, settled societies. When English colonists arrived in the 17th century, they entered a world already deeply ordered by Indigenous laws, alliances, spiritual relationships, and kin networks.

The peoples most often associated with this region include the Wampanoag, Massachuset, Nipmuc, Nauset, Pennacook (or Pawtucket), Pocomtuc, and Mahican, along with more localized groups such as the Naumkeag around the lower North Shore. These names, used in colonial and later sources, can refer to linguistic groups, political confederacies, or specific communities, and their territories overlapped in practice. The Wampanoag held a broad area from southeastern Massachusetts into present-day Rhode Island, including Martha's Vineyard and Cape Cod; the Massachuset confederation extended roughly from Salem to Plymouth along the coast and inland toward present-day Worcester; the Nipmuc occupied much of the central plateau, often forming alliances with neighboring peoples; the Nauset lived along Cape Cod; the Pennacook and related Pawtucket groups centered on riverine systems in the northeast; and the Pocomtuc and Mahican were prominent along the Connecticut and Housatonic River valleys.

Life in these homelands followed seasonal rhythms and ecological knowledge that had developed over millennia. Communities cultivated corn, beans, and squash, supplemented by fishing, shell fishing, hunting, and gathering wild plants, berries, and nuts. They used controlled burns to manage forest undergrowth, improve hunting, and encourage the growth of useful plants. Villages were typically situated near rivers, lakes, or coasts, with semi-permanent structures such as wigwams or longhouses and nearby planting fields; families and bands moved between winter and summer locations in patterns that balanced mobility with deep attachment to particular places.

Political authority was often vested in sachems and councils, but power rested on kinship, reciprocity, and consensus rather than a rigid state; trade routes linked Massachusetts peoples to neighbors throughout what is now New England and beyond. Spiritual life was inseparable from land and water, with sacred places, stories of creation, and ceremonial practices binding communities to their ancestors and to specific features of the landscape.

For genealogists, the most important conceptual shift is to recognize that Indigenous identity and belonging were not defined through European legal categories such as "subject," "citizen," or "landowner." Kinship could be reckoned through both maternal and paternal lines, extended through adoption and alliance, and expressed in naming practices that might change over a person's lifetime. Furthermore, political confederacies such as the Massachuset or Wampanoag encompassed many local communities; individuals might be described in records by a band name, a village name, or simply as "an Indian" connected to a place.

This fluidity complicates efforts to match a single "tribal identifier" from a colonial document to modern categories but more accurately reflects the lived reality of Native people at the time. When a genealogist encounters an Indigenous person in a later land deed, court record, or missionary report, the label attached to that person is often the colonist's shorthand for a much more nuanced identity.

European contact, which intensified in the late 1500s and early 1600s, brought profound disruption even before permanent English colonies were founded. Explorers and fishermen from several European powers began visiting the New England coast, seeking fish, furs, and strategic knowledge. These visitors sometimes traded with Indigenous communities, sometimes kidnapped individuals to serve as guides or enslaved labor and always carried pathogens for which Native peoples had no immunity. Epidemics in the early 1600s, likely involving diseases such as smallpox or other infectious illnesses, killed large portions of the population in many coastal areas, including among the Massachuset and Pennacook, with some estimates suggesting losses of half or more in certain communities. These demographic shocks altered the balance of power, opened vulnerabilities that

English colonists later exploited, and contributed to colonial descriptions of "empty" or "wasted" lands destined for resettlement.

Genealogically, this pre-colonial and immediate contact period presents both challenges and opportunities. There are no parish registers or town vital books in the European sense; written records are almost entirely produced by outsiders—explorers, missionaries, colonial officials, and later historians. Yet names of Indigenous leaders, families, and communities do appear in several types of documents: treaties and land deeds, early colonial histories, missionary and church records, colonial court cases, and later petitions by Native communities seeking recognition, redress, or protection.

For example, some Naumkeag leaders in the Salem area appear as grantors in 17th-century land transactions, and descendants of Massachuset and Naumkeag people later surface in records from "praying towns" such as Natick, where colonial and missionary authorities supervised Indigenous communities who accepted Christian instruction. In western Massachusetts, Mahican and Pocomtuc individuals are recorded in deeds, missionary accounts, and later agreements as they navigated displacement, war, and resettlement.

Because these records are fragmentary and often framed by colonial agendas, reconstructing Indigenous lineages typically requires a different approach than reconstructing colonial settler families. Instead of an unbroken chain of standardized vital records, researchers piece together evidence from multiple, sometimes widely separated sources: a sachem's name embedded in a 17th-century land grant, a Native man listed in a colonial court case, a family group mentioned in an 18th-century guardianship petition, or a 19th-century legislative report describing a community at Mashpee, Hassanamisco, or elsewhere. Oral history and tribal archives are crucial, and collaboration with tribal communities—such as the Mashpee Wampanoag Tribe, the Wampanoag Tribe of Gay Head (Aquinnah), and the Massachuset Tribe at Ponkapoag—provides perspectives and sources not captured in colonial repositories. For non-Native genealogists, this means recognizing the limits of the colonial record, respecting that not all knowledge is public, and being transparent about how evidence is interpreted.

Even for researchers whose ancestors were late-arriving European, African, or other migrants, the story of Indigenous homelands is central to understanding the geography of Massachusetts records. Many later town names echo Indigenous words or communities—Massachusetts itself, Natick, Chicopee, Wareham, Seekonk, and many more—reminding genealogists that every town clerk's book sits on land taken from Indigenous peoples through overlapping processes of treaty, coercion, and outright seizure. Some colonial deeds explicitly acknowledge earlier Indigenous occupation; others are silent but can be linked to prior Native tenure via regional studies and archaeological work. When a family appears in an early 18th-century land record purchasing acreage in what was once a Native planting field or village, that genealogical fact is part of a longer narrative of dispossession and survival.

A short, illustrative case example can show how this context shapes practical research. Imagine a genealogist investigating a 19th-century "Indian" woman listed in a small central Massachusetts town's poor relief record. The entry gives only a single name and a note that she "belongs to Natick." On its face, this could be mistaken for a casual geographic reference. A historically informed approach would link that phrase to the history of the Natick "praying town," a community with deep

Massachuset roots, and to 18th- and 19th-century state oversight of Indigenous lands and property. By consulting legislative reports on "Indians of the Commonwealth," guardianship papers, and local histories of Natick and the Hassanamisco community, as well as tribal histories from the Massachuset Tribe at Ponkapoag, the researcher might uncover a multi-generational story of land loss, guardianship, and the persistence of kinship networks that stretch far beyond the single poor-relief entry. This kind of work shows how a surface-level record, read without context, is radically incomplete.

For genealogists and family historians working in Massachusetts, then, "Indigenous homelands before colonization" is not a static backdrop but an active research domain with its own sources, methods, and ethical obligations. It reminds researchers that all subsequent records—from 17th-century town minutes to 20th-century suburban deeds—are layered over much older claims to place. It underscores that the appearance of an Indigenous person in a colonial document is never just a name to be extracted and slotted into a pedigree, but part of a living community with ongoing history. And it encourages every researcher, regardless of their own ancestry, to situate genealogical questions within a respectful understanding of the Native nations for whom Massachusetts has always been home.

First Contacts and the Shock of Disease (Late 1500s–1630)

By the time permanent English colonies were founded in Massachusetts, Indigenous nations had already endured more than a century of intermittent encounters with Europeans and the devastating diseases that followed those first contacts. To understand why early 17th-century explorers and colonists sometimes described "empty" or "wasted" lands, genealogists must look back to this transitional period, when the long-standing Indigenous world of New England began to intersect with European fishing, trading, and exploratory ventures in ways that would prove catastrophic. This was not yet an age of towns, parishes, or county governments in the English sense, but it was a crucial prelude in which germs, goods, and ideas crossed the Atlantic long before families and formal colonial institutions did.

The earliest documented European visitors to the broader northeast arrived as part of seasonal fishing and trading expeditions rather than organized colonies. Vessels from France, Spain, Portugal, and later England plied the rich cod grounds of the Grand Banks and the Gulf of Maine, sometimes coming ashore along the New England coast to obtain fresh water and wood, dry fish on racks, and trade with nearby Indigenous communities. Although these mariners left few detailed written records about specific villages in what is now Massachusetts, later accounts and tribal histories remember early contact in the 1500s and early 1600s along the coasts used by Wampanoag, Massachuset, and related peoples. For Native communities, these strangers were initially one more set of trade partners moving through an already extensive network of exchange that reached far inland and along the seaboard. For genealogists, this stage rarely yields individual names, but it establishes a critical premise: Europeans and Native peoples were interacting, directly and indirectly, for decades before the Mayflower ever dropped anchor.

As the 16th century turned into the 17th, European interest in the region intensified and diversified. Explorers such as Giovanni da Verrazzano charted stretches of the New England and mid-Atlantic coasts, while later French and English voyages created more sustained impressions on both sides. French expeditions in the early 1600s, including those linked to Samuel de Champlain, mapped harbors, rivers, and islands, and documented encounters with Massachuset-speaking peoples and other Algonquian groups. English figures such as Bartholomew Gosnold led voyages that reached Cape Cod and the Elizabeth Islands, and others probed the Maine and New Hampshire coasts. These exploratory trips were commercial ventures as much as geographic ones: investors sought information on fishing grounds, fur resources, and potential sites for future settlement or trading posts. Although crew lists and logs seldom include individuals who later appear in Massachusetts town records, the narratives produced by explorers provide an invaluable counterpoint to later colonial histories and serve as some of the first written attestations of local Indigenous leaders, place names, and political alliances.

Even at this early stage, however, the asymmetry of power and vulnerability was already evident. Some European crews kidnapped Native men and boys, taking them to Europe as curiosities, guides, or enslaved laborers. Others pressed Indigenous people into service as pilots and interpreters, exploiting their geographic knowledge and multilingual skills. In turn, Native leaders evaluated the newcomers as potential allies or threats, incorporating them into existing rivalries and diplomatic calculations.

For genealogists, these scattered reports hint at individual biographies that were never systematically recorded: a Wampanoag sailor forcibly taken to Europe and later returned to his homeland; a Massachuset or Pennacook mediator who straddled two worlds, remembered only in passing in a European's journal. While most family historians will never be able to trace a direct line to such figures using conventional genealogical methods, being aware of their presence complicates simplistic narratives in which Indigenous people appear only once large-scale colonization begins.

The most consequential "contact" in this period, though, did not involve trade goods or kidnapping but disease. European seafarers and traders carried with them pathogens to which Native communities had no prior exposure. Illnesses that were endemic and often survivable in Europe—such as smallpox and other infectious diseases—could become explosive epidemics when introduced into immunologically naïve populations. Historical and scientific studies converged on the conclusion that between roughly 1616 and 1619, an epidemic—or perhaps a series of epidemics—swept through many Indigenous communities along the southern New England coast, including within Wampanoag and Massachuset territories. Later observers described villages where most of the inhabitants had died and fields left untended. Some colonial chroniclers interpreted this as providential "clearing" of the land, while Indigenous oral histories remember it as a time of profound loss and upheaval.

Demographically, these epidemics shattered communities that had been structured around dense kin networks and reciprocal obligations. Politically, they weakened some nations and altered the balance of power between and within Indigenous confederacies. Socially, they created widows, orphans, and survivors who might be taken in by neighboring groups or forced into new alliances for protection and access to resources. For genealogists trying to reconstruct Indigenous family histories, this means that lineages that seem to "disappear" in one locality may in fact have continued elsewhere under altered circumstances—sometimes recorded under a different group name, sometimes not recorded at all. For researchers focused on settler families, these epidemics form the hidden backdrop to the "vacant" fields and "wilderness" so often mentioned in early colonial land grants. When a 1620s English observer notes that an area is "depopulated" or sees a recently abandoned planting field, that description is the endpoint of a story of disease, grief, and forced reorganization that began years earlier.

The shock of disease also reshaped the conditions under which formal colonization took place. When the Pilgrims arrived at what they would call Plymouth in 1620, they encountered a Wampanoag polity that had been severely weakened by recent epidemics but still retained leadership, territory, and diplomatic capacity. The famous early alliance between Plymouth and the Wampanoag sachem Massasoit must be read against this demographic and political background: it was not an inevitable act of hospitality, but a strategic choice made in a context where European weapons and alliances could be both a threat and a potential counter to rival Indigenous groups.

In the Boston harbor region and along Massachusetts Bay, similar dynamics unfolded as surviving Massachuset communities navigated the arrival of English ships and the establishment of plantations at places like Salem and Charlestown. For the genealogist, these layers of disease, diplomacy, and demographic change explain why, by the 1630s, English colonists perceived "room" for planting new towns in areas that had long been central to Indigenous life.

In terms of sources, the contact-and-disease period is documented primarily through non-genealogical genres: explorers' narratives, missionary and traveler accounts, later colonial histories, and a small number of early legal and commercial documents. These materials rarely follow an individual Indigenous person across multiple life events in the way later parish and town records might, but they do preserve names of leaders, descriptions of specific communities, and sometimes glimpses of family structures, kin terms, or burial practices. They also illustrate how European observers interpreted what they saw—often through religious or economic lenses that obscured Native perspectives. Genealogists working with this period therefore need to be both historically informed and methodologically cautious. Rather than treating a 17th-century description of a depopulated village as a neutral census, researchers should ask: Who wrote this? What did they stand to gain by emphasizing emptiness or chaos? What Indigenous voices, if any, are preserved elsewhere that might complicate this narrative?

For most readers of this guide, the contact and epidemic period will not yield the kind of name-by-name reconstructions that are possible in later centuries. Its value lies instead in framing expectations and sharpening interpretation. A genealogist tracing a family who appears suddenly in a coastal Massachusetts town in the 1620s or 1630s must understand that they are stepping into a landscape already transformed by years of disease and intermittent contact. A researcher trying to follow Indigenous ancestors through colonial documents must recognize that family members may have been lost, displaced, or renamed because of epidemics that pre-date the surviving written record. Even for those without known Native ancestry, appreciating the scale and impact of this demographic catastrophe prevents uncritical acceptance of colonial rhetoric about "empty" land and encourages a more nuanced reading of early deeds, town foundations, and territorial claims.

Finally, this period invites genealogists to think beyond the usual boundaries of their craft. Traditional genealogical practice often begins with surviving written evidence and works backward; in early Massachusetts, that trail quickly runs into the silences created by disease, violence, and cultural misunderstanding. To engage responsibly with the contact era, researchers can draw on interdisciplinary work in archaeology, historical epidemiology, and Native studies, as well as on tribal histories and contemporary Indigenous scholarship. Doing so will not always produce neat pedigrees or fill every gap in a family tree, but it will ground genealogical narratives in a truer understanding of the forces that shaped the region and the lives of the people—Native and newcomer alike—who inhabited it.

Plymouth and Massachusetts Bay: Planting English Colonies (1620–1691)

For genealogists working in Massachusetts, the period from 1620 to 1691 is where many familiar tools and assumptions first take shape: named townships, written town and church records, early land divisions, probate files, and colonial courts. Yet those institutions did not appear all at once, and they did not rise in a vacuum. They were the product of two related but distinct English colonial projects—Plymouth Colony and Massachusetts Bay Colony—built on Indigenous homelands still inhabited by Wampanoag, Massachuset, Nipmuc, and other Native peoples. Understanding how and why these colonies were founded, how they were governed, and how their records were kept is essential to interpreting virtually any seventeenth-century Massachusetts genealogy problem.

Plymouth Colony began as a small, precarious settlement on the shore of what is now Plymouth Harbor. In 1620, a group of English separatists and their associates—later remembered as "the Pilgrims"—sailed on the Mayflower intending to settle within the bounds of the Virginia Company but instead made landfall on Cape Cod and then at a site Patuxet people had used before recent epidemics. Because they were outside the area covered by their original patent, the adult male passengers drafted and signed an agreement now known as the Mayflower Compact, pledging to form a civil body politic and abide by laws and ordinances made for the general good. This was not a full colonial charter but a practical statement of mutual commitment in an ambiguous legal situation. For genealogists, that fact matters. During its early years Plymouth's authority rested on a patchwork of company patents and local consent rather than a royal charter, which influenced how its institutions developed and how its records were framed.

Survival in the first years depended on labor, adaptability, and fragile alliances with neighboring Wampanoag communities. The epidemics of the previous decade had weakened some Native polities, but the Wampanoag remained a significant power and, under leaders such as Ousamequin (often called Massasoit in English sources), negotiated an alliance with Plymouth that included mutual defense and regulated trade. Individuals like Tisquantum (Squanto), who had traveled to Europe and spoke English, acted as cultural and linguistic mediators. These early relationships shaped land use, political expectations, and the flow of information between communities, and they left traces in later documents such as treaties, land deeds, and diplomatic correspondence. When a genealogist encounters a 17th-century Plymouth record naming Native leaders as grantors or signatories, that record is part of this early diplomatic world rather than an isolated transaction.

As Plymouth stabilized, it developed institutions that looked more familiar to genealogists: a governor and assistants elected from among the colonists, a General Court that combined legislative and judicial functions, townships with their own meetings, and, slowly, written records of births, marriages, deaths, land allotments, and court proceedings. Towns emerged as clusters of families petitioned for local autonomy and the right to manage commons, fences, and local disputes. The resulting town books—often a mix of vital entries, land divisions, and minutes—are among the earliest systematic records in New England. However, the quality and completeness of these records vary. Some early events were never written down or were copied into later volumes from memory; spellings of names could shift from one entry to the next; and not every life event was recorded with equal care. Genealogists using published "Plymouth Colony Records" or town vital compilations must keep in mind that these are transcriptions or abstracts of this uneven original record base, not verbatim, comprehensive "lists of everyone who lived there."

While Plymouth was finding its footing, another, larger colonial project took shape to the north. The Massachusetts Bay Company, organized by Puritan investors with a royal charter, secured rights to land around Massachusetts Bay and, crucially, the charter itself remained in the colonists' hands once they emigrated. In 1630, John Winthrop led a substantial fleet of settlers to New England, establishing Boston and nearby towns such as Charlestown, Roxbury, Dorchester, and Watertown. Unlike Plymouth, which grew slowly and never received a full royal charter, Massachusetts Bay arrived with a powerful legal instrument and a determination to build a "godly" commonwealth. Freemen—initially defined as male church members admitted to the franchise—elected a governor, deputy governor, and assistants, and the General Court developed into a representative assembly. Towns were chartered more quickly, and the colony's legal code and court system became more elaborate over time.

For genealogists, Massachusetts Bay's chartered status and larger, more diverse population translate into a broader and more complex paper trail: county courts of different levels, frequent town subdivisions, and a proliferation of church and civil records.

From the 1630s onward, migration to Massachusetts Bay brought not only Puritan families seeking religious refuge but also artisans, laborers, and servants with varying degrees of piety and economic motivation. The colony's leaders promoted settlement in clusters around approved churches, but people moved for opportunities just as often as for theology. New towns like Concord, Dedham, Salem Village, and many others emerged as groups of families received permission to establish congregations and civic structures. Town proprietors divided land among original shareholders, then made further grants as new arrivals were admitted.

These distributions generated the first generation of Massachusetts Bay land records: town-level proprietors' books noting who received which allotment, followed later by county-level land recording systems in which deeds and mortgages were copied into bound volumes. For genealogists, the existence of both proprietary records and formal deed books means that early land research may require checking multiple layers of documentation, some of which remain in town custody while others are in county registries or state archives.

Religious life and recordkeeping in this period were inseparable. Congregational churches formed the heart of most English towns, and ministers-maintained admission lists, baptism registers, and records of disciplinary actions. Admission to full communion and the right to have children baptized could be socially and politically significant, since early in the colony's history church membership was a prerequisite for voting in colony-wide elections. Church records sometimes contain more than basic sacramental information: they may note prior residence in England, reasons for excommunication or reconciliation, or kin relationships within the congregation. For example, a baptism entry might note that the child's parents were "late of" a particular English parish, a clue that can open transatlantic research.

However, survival of these church books is uneven; some congregations preserved their earliest volumes, while others lost or discarded them during schisms, relocations, or later reorganizations. Genealogists must therefore treat any surviving church register from this era as a partial, precious window, not a complete roster.

The existence of two parallel colonies—Plymouth and Massachusetts Bay—complicates the map of early New England research. Plymouth's jurisdiction covered much of what is now southeastern Massachusetts, including the south shore, Cape Cod, and parts of present-day Bristol County, while Massachusetts Bay's authority extended north and west from Boston, eventually overlapping with areas claimed by neighboring colonies and Indigenous nations. Each colony had its own legal traditions, record-keeping habits, and patterns of town formation.

In practice, families often moved across these boundaries, especially as new land opened in interior regions and along the frontier with Native territories. A family might appear in Plymouth town records in the 1640s, then in Massachusetts Bay court files in the 1650s after resettling. Genealogists must therefore resist the temptation to treat "Massachusetts" as a single, uniform jurisdiction during this period; instead, they should ask, at any given moment, which colony claimed authority over a place and where that colony's records are now held.

By the later 17th century, both colonies were drawn into wider imperial and regional conflicts. Religious dissent and political disagreements with the Crown culminated, for Massachusetts Bay, in challenges to its charter and periods of royal intervention. At the same time, wars with Indigenous nations, particularly the conflict known as King Philip's War (1675–1676), deeply affected both Plymouth and Massachusetts Bay. Plymouth, which had long-standing ties and tensions with the Wampanoag, was at the heart of that war, and many of its towns were attacked or abandoned.

Casualty lists, relief petitions, and post-war land reassignments related to this conflict and to other imperial wars are critical sources for genealogists. They record where families resided, who served in militia companies, who suffered losses of property or life, and how communities reconstituted themselves afterward. For Native families, these same events often mark moments of forced removal, enslavement, or dispersal, which are more difficult to track in the surviving colonial record but can sometimes be glimpsed in court cases, captivity narratives, and later petitions.

Administratively, the story of Plymouth and Massachusetts Bay as separate entities ends in the 1690s, when a new royal charter created the Province of Massachusetts Bay by merging Plymouth, Massachusetts Bay, and additional territories. For genealogists, however, the legacies of this dual-colony period persist in how records are arranged and cataloged. Transcripts of Plymouth Colony records are curated as a distinct corpus, and references to "Old Plymouth Colony" in secondary literature signal materials that pre-date the provincial consolidation. Similarly, early Massachusetts Bay laws, court records, and town grants are often organized under colonial headings that differ from later county structures.

When planning research, it is helpful to think in layers: first, which colony (Plymouth, Massachusetts Bay, or later the Province) had authority at the time of interest; second, which town or proprietors were responsible for local records; third, which court or registry handled land and probate; and finally, which institution (state archives, county registry, town office, or historical society) now houses those materials.

For the genealogist or family historian, the "planting" of Plymouth and Massachusetts Bay thus represents much more than a cluster of iconic stories about the Mayflower, first winters, or famous sermons. It marks the creation of overlapping systems of governance, recordkeeping, and religious life that still structure how evidence is preserved and accessed today. Appreciating the differences between these colonies, their uneven legal foundations, their entanglements with Indigenous polities, and their evolving institutions allows researchers to ask sharper questions: why is a particular family present in one record set but absent in another; what does it mean when a person appears in both Plymouth and Massachusetts Bay sources; how do town boundaries and colonial jurisdictions interact? Answering those questions with care is central to turning names in a record book into grounded, historically informed family narratives.

Puritan Order, Conflict, and the Making of Towns

When genealogists imagine seventeenth-century Massachusetts, they are often picturing the world created by the Puritans of Massachusetts Bay: tight-knit towns clustered around meetinghouses, ministers preaching long sermons to watchful congregations, and lay leaders running a government that insisted it was answerable first to God and only secondarily to any distant king. This social order was not accidental. It was the deliberate project of men and women who believed that by ordering their churches, families, and towns according to their reading of scripture, they could build a "godly commonwealth" that would stand as a model to the world. For genealogists, this Puritan project matters because it structured almost every record that survives from the period: who could vote, who could own land, who appeared in town minutes or court cases, and who was disciplined—or banished—when they stepped outside of accepted norms.

The basic principle of Puritan social order was covenant. Congregations formed by mutual promises between members and God; families were bound by promises between husband and wife and by parental responsibilities toward children; towns and the colony framed their charters, laws, and oaths in covenantal language. In practice, this meant that status and belonging were always being negotiated and recorded. Men who could convincingly testify to an inner "work of grace" were admitted as full church members and, in Massachusetts Bay, could then become "freemen" with the right to vote in colony-wide elections.

Church admission lists and freeman rolls therefore overlap but are not identical: a man might attend worship without ever seeking full membership; another might be admitted as a freeman after moving between towns. From a research perspective, these lists are invaluable because they fix individuals in time and place and sometimes note former residences, but they also reveal the colony's exclusions: women, servants, non-Puritan Christians, and people of African or Indigenous descent did not share the same political rights, even though they were very much part of the communities where they lived.

Towns were the core building blocks of Puritan Massachusetts. As population grew, groups of settlers petitioned the General Court for permission to establish new towns, often specifying where they would meet for worship and how they would support a minister. Once granted, towns held their own meetings, elected selectmen and other officers, and took responsibility for local concerns: laying out roads and house lots, managing common fields, appointing constables, caring for the poor, and enforcing moral regulations.

Town clerks recorded decisions and transactions in books that mixed minutes, vital events, land distributions, and bylaws. For genealogists, these town records are among the richest sources for the period because they capture both the ordinary routines of community life—fines for letting pigs wander, votes to repair bridges—and the milestones of individual lives, such as the recording of a child's birth or a vote assigning land to a newly arrived householder. However, the form and content of town books varied widely; some clerks were meticulous, others were brief or haphazard, and some early volumes have been lost or damaged. Knowing that a town existed in the 1640s does not guarantee that a continuous, legible record survives from that date, so genealogists must be ready to work with gaps, partial copies, and later reconstructions.

The Puritan drive for order extended to the courts. Massachusetts Bay developed a tiered system in which local magistrates and county courts heard civil and criminal cases, while the General Court acted as the highest legislative and judicial authority. Court records from this era are invaluable not only because they mention individuals but because they illuminate how people interacted across lines of class, gender, and belief. Debt disputes show who borrowed from whom; slander suits reveal what neighbors said about each other; cases of fornication, adultery, and "disorderly conduct" lay bare the moral expectations placed on men and women.

For genealogists, a single court case can provide a wealth of detail about dates, relationships, property, and even personality. A woman accused of "slandering her neighbor" may be identified as the wife or daughter of a particular man; witnesses might include her brothers, in-laws, or former employers. Yet these records also show the limits of Puritan tolerance. Those whose religious views diverged too far from the colony's norms—such as Roger Williams, Anne Hutchinson, Baptists, and later Quakers—were subjected to hearings and, in many cases, banished or persecuted. When a genealogist discovers that an ancestor disappears from Massachusetts records around the time of a notable religious controversy, it is worth asking whether they might have relocated to Rhode Island, Connecticut, or elsewhere under pressure.

Conflict, in fact, was woven throughout Puritan Massachusetts. Internally, the colony wrestled with disputes over theology, gender roles, and the distribution of authority between magistrates and deputies. Externally, towns and colonial leaders were constantly negotiating—and frequently fighting—with neighboring Indigenous nations over land, resources, and sovereignty. Missionary efforts to establish "praying towns" for Indigenous converts created new communities under heavy colonial control, such as Natick and Hassanamesit, whose residents appear in both town-style records and special reports to the General Court.

At the same time, wars like the Pequot War and, later, King Philip's War profoundly disrupted both Native and English communities, destroying some settlements and reshaping where survivors lived, worked, and appeared in the record. For genealogists, this means that sudden clusters of probate inventories or guardianship appointments in a particular year can reflect not just ordinary mortality but the impact of war or epidemic; towns that vanish from one period's records may reappear later, reconstituted by returning inhabitants or newcomers.

All these elements—the covenant theology, church-filtered political rights, town-based governance, active courts, and enduring conflicts—shaped how towns were created and how people lived within them. When a genealogist looks at an early Massachusetts town, it is useful to think in layers. At the surface is the recognizable structure: a name, a date of incorporation, a meetinghouse, a clerk's book where births and marriages might be recorded.

Beneath that lies the proprietary layer: a group of initial grantees parceling out land among themselves and reserving common resources. Below that still are the prior Indigenous land uses and claims. And binding all of it together is a Puritan vision of a disciplined, godly community in which relationships and obligations were supposed to be legible—to neighbors, to magistrates, and to God. Appreciating that vision, and the ways people conformed to or pushed against it, allows genealogists to read the surviving records not just as lists of facts but as artifacts of an often-tense social order.

Empire, Crisis, and the Road to Revolution (1691–1780s)

When Plymouth and Massachusetts Bay were combined under the 1691 charter into the Royal Province of Massachusetts Bay, the colony entered a new political world. The charter of William and Mary broadened the geographic scope of the province—folding in former Plymouth territory and much of what is now Maine—while also tightening imperial control by providing for a royally appointed governor with expanded powers. This was a profound change for a society that had grown accustomed to electing its own governors and running its own affairs under a Puritan-dominated franchise.

Yet at the local level, town meetings, selectmen, and congregations continued to operate much as they had before, sustaining a strong culture of self-government that would later become a crucible for resistance. For genealogists, this era marks the transition from "colonies" to "province" in legal language and record series; it is also the point at which a growing imperial presence begins to leave more structured and voluminous documentation in the form of royal instructions, provincial legislation, and correspondence between Boston and London.

Throughout the early 18th century, Massachusetts remained simultaneously a local, agrarian society and a key node in the British Atlantic world. The provincial government regulated trade in accordance with the Navigation Acts, mapped and disputed boundaries with neighboring colonies, and gradually extended its claimed authority north and west. Frontier settlements in what is now western Massachusetts and Maine coexisted uneasily with Indigenous nations and with French imperial interests to the north.

Wars such as Queen Anne's War, King George's War, and the French and Indian War drew Massachusetts men into imperial campaigns from Canada to the Caribbean, generating muster rolls, pay lists, and disability or widow's claims that often prefigure the more familiar Revolutionary War records. At the same time, Boston grew into a major New England port with a cosmopolitan mercantile community, a vibrant print culture, and widening economic inequalities. Town, county, and provincial records from this period therefore document both the routines of rural life—land transfers, probate inventories, church membership—and the increasingly dense web of commercial and legal obligations that bound Massachusetts to the larger empire.

The seeds of crisis lay in tensions over authority and identity. On one side, imperial officials expected the province to conform more closely to metropolitan norms: governors were instructed to enforce trade regulations, veto legislation that conflicted with British policy, and ensure that the Church of England had space to operate alongside Congregationalism. On the other side, Massachusetts residents, long used to robust local autonomy, insisted that their assemblies retained the traditional rights of English subjects, especially the right to tax themselves through their own representatives.

Disputes over the governor's salary, the issuance of paper money, and compliance with trade laws filled the correspondence between Boston and London and periodically stalled provincial government. For genealogists, these policy fights surface in surprising places: tax assessments that reflected new revenue schemes, town resolutions protesting particular acts, and occasionally in court cases where merchants or mariners were prosecuted for smuggling or violating customs regulations, which can place named individuals at the heart of imperial controversy.

By the 1760s, these underlying tensions erupted into open conflict. In the wake of the expensive French and Indian War, the British government sought to increase revenue and tighten control over colonial trade and governance. Measures such as the Sugar Act, Stamp Act, Townshend Duties, and Tea Act were perceived in Massachusetts not just as fiscal policies but as assaults on established rights.

Boston became a focal point of resistance: crowds protested the Stamp Act, harassed customs officials, and used town meetings and pamphlets to organize opposition. The Boston Massacre in 1770, when British soldiers fired into a crowd, and the Boston Tea Party in 1773, when colonists destroyed East India Company tea, became iconic moments in a widening imperial crisis. Each of these events left a paper trail: depositions from eyewitnesses, broadsides and newspaper reports, records of town meetings convened to respond, and private correspondence among leading figures. For genealogists, those sources can reveal not only the famous names but also the rank-and-file residents drawn into protests, juries, or militia musters.

Imperial retaliation deepened the crisis. In 1774, Parliament passed the Coercive (or Intolerable) Acts, partly aimed at punishing Massachusetts for the Tea Party and reasserting control. Among other measures, these acts curtailed town meetings, altered the Massachusetts charter to concentrate more power in the royal governor, and allowed royal officials accused of capital offenses to be tried outside the colony. General Thomas Gage arrived as military governor with troops to enforce the new regime, but the attempt to clamp down on Massachusetts instead galvanized resistance.

Provincial institutions effectively split: while the royal government clung to authority in Boston, an extralegal Provincial Congress convened in the countryside, supported by county conventions and local committees of correspondence that coordinated boycotts, musters, and supplies. In this environment, town records and county convention minutes become crucial genealogical sources, capturing the names of men appointed to committees of safety, delegates chosen for extralegal assemblies, and residents who signed association tests or local resolves declaring opposition to British measures.

The outbreak of fighting in Massachusetts in 1775—at Lexington and Concord in April, followed by the siege of Boston and the Battle of Bunker Hill—moved the conflict from politics to war. Massachusetts men poured into provincial regiments and, later, Continental Army units, while local militias continued to guard towns and frontiers. Muster rolls, pay abstracts, orderly books, and later pension applications document their service, sometimes with rich biographical detail.

These military records are some of the best-known Revolutionary sources for genealogists, but they are complemented by civilian records that reveal how the war affected families and communities: town votes to provide for soldiers' families, tax lists that record wartime levies, committee reports on suspected Loyalists, and petitions from widows or disabled veterans seeking relief. The war also intensified preexisting social divides. Loyalists—those who remained attached to the Crown—might face confiscation of property, harassment, or exile; some left for Canada, Britain, or other colonies, leaving behind probate disputes, confiscation proceedings, and scattered clues in parish and legal records abroad.

By the time Massachusetts adopted its state constitution in 1780, the province had effectively transformed itself into a commonwealth, claiming sovereignty within a new federal structure. The 1780 constitution, drafted in part by John Adams, entrenched town-based representation and laid out a more formal separation of powers between executive, legislative, and judicial branches, while preserving many continuities in local governance.

For genealogists, the Revolutionary and immediate post-Revolutionary years mark a hinge point: some record series, such as provincial court dockets and legislative journals, come to an end or are renamed; new state institutions, like higher courts under the constitution, begin their own runs of documentation. Yet from the perspective of ordinary families, the transition could be subtle—town clerks continued to record births, marriages, and deaths; county registers continued to copy deeds; probate courts continued to oversee estates.

What changed more visibly were patterns of migration and allegiance. Veterans and their families might move to new lands in Maine, Vermont, or the "western" territories; Loyalist departures and confiscations could abruptly sever local lineages; Black and Indigenous residents who served or supported the patriot cause might gain or be denied new opportunities in the shifting legal landscape.

For the family historian, the "empire, crisis, and road to revolution" period is thus a dense knot of continuity and change. It requires moving comfortably between local and imperial perspectives: reading a town's meeting minutes alongside the text of a parliamentary act; linking a name on a muster roll to a tax list and then to a postwar land grant on a new frontier. It calls for attention to language in the records—are people described as "inhabitants" of the province, "subjects" of the king, "friends of the government," or "enemies of the state"? —and to the ways political conflict reshaped who appears in which kinds of documents.

Above all, this era invites genealogists to situate individual ancestors within the broader story of a society that moved, over less than a century, from being a sometimes-restive part of a transatlantic empire to a state within a new republic. Understanding that trajectory, and the records it generated at every level, can turn Revolutionary-era research from a search for a lone soldier into a full exploration of how entire families and communities lived through the age of crisis.

From Farms to Factories: Industrialization and Reform (1800–1865)

Between 1800 and the end of the Civil War, Massachusetts moved from being a landscape of small farms, coastal trade, and handicraft shops to one of mills, railroads, and dense factory towns. This shift did not happen overnight, nor did it affect all communities equally, but its cumulative effect was to transform where people lived, how they worked, and how their lives were documented. For genealogists, this period opens an entirely new documentary world: city directories, factory employment records, expanded vital registration, and an explosion of newspapers and organizational records, all layered on top of older town, church, probate, and land sources.

Understanding the social and economic changes that drove industrialization and reform helps explain why a farm family suddenly appears in an urban census, why a daughter vanishes into a boardinghouse register, or why a mid-century ancestor turns up in the minutes of an abolitionist society or on a Civil War monument.

At the turn of the nineteenth century, most Massachusetts residents still lived on farms or in small villages, combining subsistence agriculture with local trades and periodic market exchange. Town economies were diverse but modest: blacksmiths, coopers, shoemakers, and weavers supplied nearby households, and coastal communities outfitted ships for fishing or Atlantic commerce. Yet the seeds of industrial change were already present.

Since colonial times, the region had experimented with ironworks and small manufactories, especially in places like Saugus and Springfield, and water-powered sawmills, gristmills, and fulling mills dotted streams and rivers. What changed after 1800 was the scale and integration of production. Entrepreneurs and merchants began to harness river power systematically to drive mechanized textile machinery, concentrating labor and capital in mills rather than dispersing production among households.

Early American industrialization in New England drew on technological and organizational models that had developed in Britain and in Rhode Island. In the 1810s and 1820s, Boston-area merchants—often called the Boston Associates—adapted and expanded these models, launching fully integrated textile operations that combined spinning, weaving, and finishing under one roof and built entire factory towns to house and control the workforce. Waltham, and soon after Lowell, became symbols of this new order: brick mills straddling canals, rows of company-owned boardinghouses, and large workforces composed initially of young New England women recruited from rural farms.

For genealogists, these developments matter in several ways. First, they generated records that simply did not exist before: company account books, worker registers, boardinghouse rolls, and corporate minutes that can place individuals in specific mills at specific times. Second, they rearranged populations.

A daughter who left a Hampshire County farm in 1835 to work in Lowell might appear in the 1840 federal census not in her parents' household but as a nameless tick mark in a block of young women classified under her boardinghouse head. Third, they created a paper and print culture—factory rules, employee publications, reform tracts—that sometimes-preserved workers' experiences in their own words.

As mills proliferated—from Waltham and Lowell to Chicopee, Lawrence, Holyoke, and beyond—transportation infrastructure followed. Canals and, increasingly, railroads connected inland towns to Boston and to markets across the United States. The Granite Railway (charted in 1826) and lines such as the Boston and Lowell, Boston and Worcester, and Western Railroad were early milestones; by the 1850s, rail networks laced the state. For family historians, these developments both explain and document migration.

Railroads made it easier for farm families to send members to work seasonally in mills or to relocate entirely; they also generated their own records—corporate charters and reports, occasionally payrolls and accident logs, and indirect traces such as new stations that appear as landmarks in deeds or village descriptions. The growth of rail and industrial hubs also spurred the emergence of city directories and urban tax lists, which list heads of households, occupations, and addresses, effectively bridging the gap between decennial censuses.

Industrialization did not simply add factories to an otherwise static society; it reshaped daily life. In rural areas, many families adapted by combining traditional farming with wage labor, sending sons and daughters to mills for a few years to earn cash or dowries while retaining ties to the land. In cities and mill towns, work became increasingly regimented by the clock, and cash wages replaced barter or in-kind exchanges.

Gender roles and household dynamics shifted as young women lived away from home in company boardinghouses and young men navigated new forms of wage labor and urban association. These changes are visible in the records: patterns of marriage (often later or in new locales), more frequent moves, and occupational descriptions ("operative," "spinner," "machinist") that reflect new kinds of work. For genealogists, careful reading of repeated directory entries and census occupations can reveal a family's movement up, down, or sideways in an evolving industrial hierarchy.

At the same time, Massachusetts emerged as a center of reform movements that responded to or were amplified by these social changes. The early nineteenth century saw waves of religious revival and experimentation—Calvinist revivals, Unitarianism, Transcendentalism—alongside practical reform campaigns for temperance, public education, prison and asylum reform, women's rights, and, centrally, the abolition of slavery. Boston and other Massachusetts towns hosted antislavery societies, women's organizations, labor associations, and benevolent groups, many of which kept minutes, membership lists, subscription records, and printed annual reports. Free Black communities in Boston, New Bedford, and other towns organized churches, schools, mutual aid societies, and antislavery activity that are documented in both mainstream and Black-run newspapers, in church records, and in institutional archives.

For genealogists working on Black ancestors, these institutional and print sources are often more informative than standard town records, which might list individuals simply as "colored" laborers or omit them entirely from some civic roles.

Public education and legal reforms also changed the documentary landscape. Under the influence of reformers such as Horace Mann, Massachusetts expanded common schooling, standardized curricula, and invested in teacher training, making the state a national model. School district records—committee reports, teacher contracts, attendance registers—can, where they survive, locate children in a specific neighborhood and hint at family circumstances (for instance, irregular attendance during planting or harvest seasons).

At the state level, a crucial change for genealogists was the adoption of statewide civil registration of births, marriages, and deaths beginning in 1841, with returns submitted by town clerks to a central authority and later published in annual volumes. These state-level vital records supplement and sometimes correct local town books, providing more uniform coverage and, over time, more detailed information, such as parents' birthplaces or causes of death. The mid-century thus marks a transition from patchy, town-by-town vital registration to a more standardized state system.

Beneath these cultural and institutional developments lay persistent economic and social tensions. While mill owners and merchants amassed considerable wealth, workers and small farmers often faced precarious conditions and periodic economic downturns. Labor protests occurred in Lowell and other mill towns as early as the 1830s and 1840s, with "mill girls" organizing strikes and petition campaigns against wage cuts and speed-ups. These activities can surface in local newspapers, legislative petition files, and, in some cases, in the private papers of reformers or company officials. Small farmers confronted shifting markets and competition from western lands, prompting some to intensify production (for example, in dairy or market gardening) and others to migrate westward.

A genealogist tracing a Massachusetts family line in this era must therefore be alert not only to moves within the state—from hill towns to mill cities—but also to chains that lead into upstate New York, Ohio, and beyond, often documented in land sales, probate distributions, and the appearance of familiar surnames in distant county histories.

The decades leading up to the Civil War further entangled industrial Massachusetts with national conflicts over slavery and union. As a hub of abolitionism, the state sent speakers, literature, and money into the wider antislavery movement, and its Black and white residents helped sustain networks of escape and resistance often referred to as the Underground Railroad. Meanwhile, the state's factories turned out textiles, shoes, and arms that fueled the national economy and, during the war, supplied the Union army. When war came in 1861, Massachusetts responded quickly, raising regiments that included not only white volunteers but, later, famous Black units such as the 54th Massachusetts.

Military enlistment rolls, regimental histories, draft records, and pension files from this period are some of the richest genealogical sources for male ancestors; they often include age, birthplace, occupation, physical description, and postwar residence, and pension applications can contain affidavits from relatives and neighbors that illuminate family structure and migration. War also widened existing documentary coverage of women and children as states and towns tracked dependent families of soldiers and distributed relief, leaving lists and correspondence in municipal and state archives.

For genealogists, "From Farms to Factories" is best approached as a period where older and newer record systems overlap. Town meetings, deed books, and probate files continue, but they now coexist with company archives, city directories, railroad records, organizational minutes, and state-level vital registration. The core task is to read across these layers: to see how a single individual might appear, in different guises, as a farmer in an 1820 census, a laborer in a railroad town in 1835, a "weaver" in a Lowell directory in 1845, a signatory on a temperance petition in 1850, and a Union private in a Civil War regiment in 1862. By grounding those appearances in the broader history of industrialization and reform, genealogists and family historians can turn what might otherwise be a series of disconnected notices into a coherent, context-rich life story.

Waves of Newcomers: Immigration and Ethnic Communities (1840s–1920s)

From the Irish Famine of the 1840s through the quotas of the 1920s, Massachusetts absorbed successive waves of immigrants that fundamentally reshaped its cities, mill towns, and rural enclaves, turning a predominantly Yankee Protestant society into a mosaic of ethnic neighborhoods, parishes, and mutual aid networks. These newcomers—Irish laborers, French Canadian mill workers, Portuguese fishermen and factory hands, Italians, Eastern European Jews, Poles, Lithuanians, and others—filled the jobs created by industrialization, built vibrant subcultures amid often-hostile nativism, and generated a parallel universe of records alongside the established town, church, and court systems.

For genealogists, this era demands a shift in strategy: from assuming uniform English-language vital records to navigating multilingual church books, naturalization petitions with variant spellings, ethnic fraternal ledgers, and federal censuses that finally ask about birthplace and immigration year.

The first major surge began with the Irish, driven by the potato blight that ravaged their homeland from 1845 to 1852, killing about a million and prompting another million to emigrate. Tens of thousands landed in Boston, often arriving malnourished and penniless at Castle Island or other quarantine stations before fanning out to construction sites, factories, and domestic service in Boston, Lowell, Worcester, Lawrence, and Springfield.

By the 1850s, Irish-born residents comprised over 90% of Boston's foreign-born population, settling initially in the North End, Fort Hill, and East Boston before moving to South Boston and Charlestown as earlier Yankee residents departed. They faced fierce anti-Catholic prejudice—epitomized by the 1834 Ursuline Convent burning in Charlestown and nativist riots—but built resilient institutions: Catholic parishes with baptismal registers in Latin, the Charitable Irish Society for aid to newcomers, and fraternal groups like the Ancient Order of Hibernians whose membership rolls can reveal kin networks and prior residences in specific Irish counties.

For genealogists, Irish ancestors often first appear in ship passenger lists at Boston or New York (many walked or took coastal packets from Canada), then in city directories as laborers or servants, poor farm records, or hospital admissions during famine-related epidemics. Chain migration meant siblings and cousins followed, sometimes documented in letters preserved in family papers or parish sponsorship notations.

Hot on the heels of the Irish came French-Canadians, or "Canucks," who crossed the border overland from Quebec starting in the 1860s and peaking around 1900, drawn to textile mills in Lowell, Lawrence, Holyoke, and Woonsocket (though the latter is now Rhode Island). Unlike transatlantic arrivals, they often migrated seasonally or in family groups, retaining ties to Canadian farms and returning home during off-seasons, which can make them elusive in U.S. censuses—appearing one decade in Massachusetts, the next back across the border.

They formed tight-knit enclaves with French-language Catholic parishes (registres paroissiaux) recording baptisms, marriages, and burials in French or Latin, often noting parents' Quebec origins; mutual benefit societies like the Union Saint-Jean-Baptiste provided insurance and burial plots, with ledgers listing dues-payers and beneficiaries; and newspapers such as Le Travailleur preserved community news and obituaries.

Genealogical challenges include phonetic spellings (e.g., Tremblay as "Tramblay"), dit names (aliases like "dit Lajeunesse"), and dual residency; researchers must correlate U.S. federal censuses (post-1880 birthplace columns), Massachusetts vital records (post-1841), and Quebec Drouin Collection church extracts to reconstruct families split by the border.

Portuguese immigrants, primarily from the Azores and Cape Verde Islands, arrived from the 1870s onward, initially as whalers and fishermen in New Bedford, Provincetown, and Gloucester, later shifting to factories in Fall River and Cambridge. Cape Verdeans, often of mixed African, Portuguese, and Indigenous descent, faced additional racial barriers but built resilient communities around Catholic parishes, Cape Verdean social clubs, and the bilingual Cape Verdean News.

Italians followed in the 1880s–1910s, peaking just before World War I, with southern Italians (Sicilians, Neapolitans) dominating; they filled the North End after the Irish moved out, worked in construction and factories in East Boston, Brockton, and Worcester, and relied on paesani networks, feste patronali (saint's day societies), and parish records from churches like Saint Leonard's. Eastern European Jews, fleeing pogroms from the 1880s, settled in Boston's West End, Roxbury, and Dorchester, founding synagogues, landsmanshaften (hometown mutual aid societies), and Yiddish newspapers whose archives hold membership lists, burial records, and naturalization aids. Poles, Lithuanians, and other Slavs clustered in mill towns like Chicopee and Southbridge, with Polish parishes and fraternal orders like the Polish Falcons providing similar documentation.

Federal records explode in utility during this era. Post-1850 censuses list foreign-born individuals by birthplace, by 1880 adding parents' birthplaces, immigration year, citizenship status, and occupation; 1900 and 1910 add years in U.S., naturalization, and children born/living—goldmines for pinpointing arrival windows and family completeness.

Passenger lists from Boston, New York, and Providence (post-1820, digitized on Ancestry and FamilySearch) note ship names, last residence, and contacts in old/new countries. Naturalization records (post-1906 federalized, earlier at county courts) include declarations with birthplaces, arrival ports/dates, and witness affidavits from relatives; Massachusetts Supreme Judicial Court papers (1802–1906) hold early petitions.

State vital records (1841+) standardize but vary by ethnicity—Irish in English/Latin parish books, French Canadian in French—while city directories track addresses and jobs ("puddler," "scowman"). Ethnic newspapers (e.g., Boston Pilot for Irish, L'Italo-Americano for Italians) carry marriage notices, deaths, and arrival announcements.

Nativism peaked with the 1882 Chinese Exclusion Act (few Chinese in MA but affected Cape Verdeans), 1917 Asiatic Barred Zone, and 1924 quotas slashing southern/eastern European entries based on 1890 census (favoring Nordics). This scattered families—some returned home, others Americanized names/surnames—and created alien registration lists (1917–18, WWI draft). World War I and 1918 influenza further thinned communities, visible in spike-year death records and military draft cards (1917–18) listing exact birthdates, occupations, nearest relatives (often overseas).

Case Study: Tracing an 1880s Italian from Palermo in Boston's North End starts with 1900 census ("Gioachino Russo," arrived 1885, naturalized), cross-referenced to Saint Leonard's baptism for his U.S.-born child (godparents from same Sicilian town), a 1906 naturalization petition naming wife/arrival ship, and L'Italo-Americano obituary linking to feste society burial plot. Chain migration reveals siblings in 1910 Fall River directory; WWI draft card confirms WW1 service. Without ethnic context—regionalism (palermitani vs. abruzzesi), reliance on paesani—lines dead-end in manifests.

For genealogists, these waves demand multilingual persistence, cross-border chasing, and institution-hunting beyond town halls. Immigrants clustered by origin, creating record silos: Irish in Boston Pilot ads, French Canadians in Quebec parish hops, Jews in synagogue minute books. Yet common threads—mill payroll stubs, tenement house censuses, poor relief ledgers—tie them. By reading against nativist silences (e.g., "pauper alien" labels), researchers reconstruct not just pedigrees but lives of adaptation amid prejudice, turning "faceless laborers" into named patriarchs of enduring communities.

A Modern Commonwealth: Education, Suburbs, and Technology (1900–Present)

The twentieth century and beyond transformed Massachusetts from an industrial state grappling with mill closures and labor strife into a global leader in education, suburban living, and high technology, reshaping where families lived, how children were schooled, and what jobs sustained them. This evolution generated unprecedented documentation—standardized vital records, school registers, zoning boards, corporate personnel files, and digital archives—but also introduced access barriers through privacy laws and the sheer volume of material.

For genealogists, this era bridges the gap between public records and living memory: ancestors who appear in 1920 censuses as factory workers may resurface as suburban homeowners in 1950 city directories, tech engineers in 1970s employment rolls, or recent retirees in online obituary databases, all while navigating school systems that increasingly tracked academic paths and community ties.

Education expanded dramatically as a cornerstone of Massachusetts identity, building on Horace Mann's 19th-century reforms with progressive experiments, vocational training, and higher standards. By 1900, compulsory attendance laws extended schooling to age 14 (later 16), high schools proliferated with classical, commercial, and manual training tracks, and normal schools (teacher-training institutions like Westfield and Framingham) professionalized instruction amid debates over "tracking" by class or ability.

The 1917 Smith-Hughes Act funded vocational education, reflecting industrial needs, while the 1920s saw junior high schools and IQ testing influence placements. Post-World War II, the GI Bill fueled college access, state universities grew (e.g., UMass system), and METCO (1966) addressed desegregation via busing.

By the 1993 Education Reform Act and 1998 MCAS standards (removed as graduation requirement in 2024), Massachusetts led national rankings, with records evolving from district reports to digitized student transcripts. For family historians, school sources—yearbooks, alumni lists, attendance rolls, report cards—pinpoint residences, siblings, and social circles; normal school catalogs name teacher-trainees (often women pursuing careers before marriage); and reform debates surface in newspapers, revealing family involvement in PTA or union activities.

Suburbanization accelerated after World War II, fueled by the GI Bill's low-interest mortgages, interstate highways (I-95, Mass Pike), and white flight from deindustrializing cities. Levittown-style developments sprouted in Metrowest (Framingham, Natick), North Shore (Peabody), and Route 128 suburbs, while zoning laws preserved rural character in places like Concord and Lincoln. By 1970, suburbs housed over half the state's population, with commuter rail and automobiles enabling "bedroom communities" tied to Boston jobs.

This shift is traceable in records: subdivision plats and building permits in town assessors' offices, FHA mortgage files, school overcrowding reports prompting bond issues, and Little League rosters or PTA minutes reflecting new family arrivals. Black and Latino families, often excluded from suburbs by redlining, clustered in urban Roxbury, Dorchester, and Springfield, appearing in housing authority tenant lists, busing-related court cases (e.g., Morgan v. Hennigan, 1974), and community center records. Genealogists must cross-reference 1940 urban censuses with 1950 suburban directories to track these migrations, noting how women's paid work (as teachers, nurses) or men's defense jobs enabled homeownership.

Technology redefined the economy from the 1940s onward, with Route 128 (I-95 corridor) emerging as "America's Technology Highway." Raytheon (1940s radar), Digital Equipment Corporation (1957 minicomputers), and later biotech/biopharma hubs drew engineers from MIT, Harvard, and abroad, spawning suburbs like Lexington and Bedford.

The 1970s "Massachusetts Miracle" (software, semiconductors) collapsed in the 1989 recession but rebounded with life sciences (Genzyme, Biogen). Records include corporate personnel files (union contracts, pension rolls), patent applications naming inventors, company newsletters with employee photos, and "tech town" school expansions funded by property taxes.

Defense work during WWII and Cold War generated selective service cards, shipyard payrolls (Fore River, Quincy), and Hanford Project rosters for women in computing. For recent research, privacy laws (HIPAA, FERPA) restrict post-1920 vital records (75-year seal on births), but workarounds abound: voter rolls, property cards, online alumni networks, and DNA matches linking tech migrants.

Social movements added layers: civil rights (NAACP branches, Freedom Summer volunteers), women's lib (NOW chapters, ERA petitions), antiwar protests (Moratorium records), and LGBTQ+ organizing (Glad Day Bookshop logs). Deindustrialization hit mill towns (Lowell, Holyoke) with unemployment rolls, urban renewal razings (West End evictions), and welfare caseloads.

Pandemics (1918 flu, COVID-19) spike death certificates; economic booms/busts prompt migration waves.

Practical genealogy thrives on integration: a 1930 teacher from Westfield Normal (catalog) marries a Raytheon engineer (1940 census), buys a Lexington Cape (1950 deed), joins PTA (yearbook), and retires amid biotech boom (2000 obituary). Access tips: Mass. Archives for state censuses (1855–1865, 1875–1885), NEHGS for digitized directories, town websites for PDFs. Living relatives fill gaps via interviews, photos yielding school/classmate clues. This era demands ethical navigation—recent records protect privacy—but rewards with vivid stories of adaptation in the "education state" that birthed modern America.

Bringing It All Together: Using the Timeline in Your Research

The historical timeline outlined in this chapter is not meant to be memorized as a string of dates but to be used as a working tool—a kind of mental map you consult every time you pose a research question in Massachusetts. The central idea is simple: every ancestor lived inside a specific legal, social, and economic environment, and that environment determined what kinds of records were created about them, who created those records, and why.

Once you know roughly *when* and *where* a person lived, you can predict which record sets are most likely to mention them and how those records will tend to describe them. From a genealogist's point of view, the timeline and the record system are inseparable; learning to move back and forth between the two is what turns scattered discoveries into coherent, well-supported family histories.

Thinking in Eras, Not Just in Dates

A good starting habit is to stop thinking of an ancestor as "born in 1740, married in 1765, died in 1810" and start thinking of them as "born in the imperial province, came of age during the pre-Revolutionary crisis, married while Massachusetts was at war, died in the early national period." Each of those phases carries predictable record consequences. Someone born in 1740 in rural Massachusetts is likely to appear first in a town birth record or church baptism, to be taxed as a young adult in the 1760s when imperial tensions rose, and to show up in militia or Revolutionary War records if he served.

His death in 1810 may be recorded in a town death register that is still fairly minimal (often lacking parents' names), but his probate may be part of a more mature county court system, with inventories and distributions that reveal his household's economic life. Seen this way, the timeline becomes a scaffold: you attach each life event to its surrounding era and ask, "What was happening in Massachusetts at this moment, and what paper did that moment tend to produce?"

This same logic applies in more complex scenarios. A woman who appears in an 1850 census as the Irish-born wife of a Lowell mill operative did not simply "arrive in Massachusetts" at some unspecified point; she arrived into the intersection of industrialization and mass immigration, which means she may leave a trail in passenger manifests, in early Catholic parish registers catering to Irish newcomers, in city directories that track boardinghouse addresses, and possibly in reform or benevolent society records if she or her children needed assistance. By anchoring her to the 1840s–1860s portion of the timeline, you immediately narrow your search: you know to look for famine-era ships, early Irish neighborhoods, and mill-adjacent record sets, not for scattered references in colonial-era town votes. When an ancestor seems elusive, it is often because the researcher has not yet matched their life span to the right segment of the timeline and the right bundle of record behaviors.

Using the Timeline to Predict Record Types

The timeline also acts as a predictive engine. Each era in Massachusetts history tends to generate particular kinds of records while phasing others in or out. In the early colonial period, the key sources cluster around town governance, church life, and a small suite of colonial courts: town meeting minutes, proprietors' land grants, freeman lists, church admission and baptism registers, and early probate and county or colony-level court records. Knowing that, you can predict that a man described in a 1670 deed as "of Roxbury" should be sought in Roxbury's town books, church rolls, and the pertinent county court and probate volumes.

In the imperial and Revolutionary periods, you expect to add provincial legislative proceedings, tax valuations, and militia or Continental service records to your search list. In the early industrial era, you bring in city directories, factory employment rosters, and expanded newspapers. In the immigration wave, you add passenger lists, naturalization files, ethnic parish registers, and fraternal society ledgers. In the modern commonwealth, you overlay standardized state-level vital registration, school records, zoning and property files, corporate personnel records, and an ever-expanding body of digitized local history.

This predictive use of the timeline is especially helpful when you hit gaps. If you know that statewide civil registration in Massachusetts begins in 1841, a missing town death record from 1855 does not necessarily end your search; it alerts you to check the state copy of that year's vital returns, which might include entries that were never recopied into the town's book. Similarly, if you know that a particular county's land records begin at a certain date, but your ancestor held property earlier, you know to look for town proprietors' allotment books or for colonial patent records rather than assuming "no deeds exist." The timeline tells you not just what *should* be there, but also what's *too early* or *too late* for a given record type.

Mapping Jurisdiction on Top of Time

Chronology and jurisdiction are intertwined in Massachusetts. The same patch of ground that lay in an Indigenous homeland, then Plymouth Colony, then the Province of Massachusetts Bay, might eventually be in a new county, a re-incorporated town, or even another state (as with territories that became Maine). From the genealogist's point of view, this means that a single family line can be documented under several different governmental arrangements across the generations, each with its own record-keeping practices.

A person living in 1670 in what is now western Massachusetts may appear in a different county's court records than their descendant living on the same land in 1770, simply because county boundaries and court jurisdictions have shifted.

Using the timeline, you can layer jurisdiction on top of era. First, identify the time period of the event you're investigating. Second, determine which colony or state structure was in place at that moment (Plymouth vs. Massachusetts Bay vs. Province vs. Commonwealth). Third, identify the county—or pre-county—jurisdiction that handled land, probate, and higher court matters for that town at that time. Fourth, locate where those records have been deposited in the present—state archives, county registry, town hall, historical society, or digitized collection. This approach prevents common mistakes, such as looking for a 1730 probate in a county that did not yet exist, or assuming that a 1660 land transaction will be in a modern registry rather than in a colonial grant or town proprietors' book.

Building Multi-Era Case Studies

One of the most powerful ways to internalize the timeline is to build multi-era case studies for your own families. Instead of treating each record as an isolated "find," you can consciously plot a family's movement across historical phases. For example, imagine a family whose earliest known ancestor is a man listed as a Revolutionary War private in a small Berkshire County town. A careful case study might proceed like this:

- In the pre-war imperial era, locate him as a young man in provincial tax lists, perhaps as a son under an older head of household, and in a town meeting record where he is admitted to commonage or allowed to settle.
- In the Revolutionary period, find him in muster rolls and, later, in a pension application that describes his service, movements, and perhaps his place of birth.
- In the early national era, track him through deeds as he acquires or sells land, and in a probate file that names his widow and children.
- In the early industrial era, follow his children or grandchildren as they leave the original farm, surface in village directories or mill employment lists, and appear in the 1850 and 1860 censuses with changing occupations.
- In the immigration and modern eras, watch as later generations intermarry with newcomers, move into or out of cities, and eventually appear in twentieth-century school yearbooks, WWI or WWII draft cards, and suburban deeds.

By deliberately tying each record to its era, you become more alert to context-dependent clues. A sudden change of occupation from "farmer" to "operative" in an 1840s directory is not just a quirk of language; it marks entry into the factory world, with all the attendant record possibilities. A move from a central city ward to a new subdivision in the 1950s is not merely a change of street; it is part of suburbanization, which has its own documentation (planning board minutes, subdivision plans, school building campaigns). Multi-era case studies teach you to see each life as threaded through the larger history you have just read, rather than floating above it.

Using the Timeline to Anticipate Bias and Silence

Equally important, the timeline reminds you that not all people are documented equally at all times. In Puritan town records, women, servants, enslaved Africans, and Indigenous people often appear only when they intersect with the legal or church disciplinary system; in early industrial records, factory operatives may be nameless in company reports but vivid in reformers' tracts or in the minutes of mutual aid societies; in immigration-era sources, naturalization and passenger lists may privilege male heads of household, leaving wives and children less clearly described.

By aligning your research with the timeline, you can anticipate these patterns and compensate for them. If you are tracing a woman in the 17th century, you know to look for her in her father's and husband's records—dowry arrangements, dower rights in deeds, mentions as "relict" in probate—more than in standalone entries.

If you are working on Black families in antebellum Boston, you know to extend your search into church minutes, abolitionist papers, and city directories that may identify occupations and addresses even when town vital entries are scant.

For Indigenous ancestors, you know that early mentions are likely to appear in land negotiations, missionary records, and legislative reports rather than in the classic trio of birth-marriage-death registers. The timeline thus becomes a lens for recognizing whose stories are more likely to be muted in each era's standard records and a prompt to seek out supplementary source types.

Bringing Modern Tools into an Era-Aware Framework

Modern technology—digitized databases, online finding aids, DNA analysis—can tempt any researcher into ahistorical searching: typing a name into a search box and following whatever hits appear. Used thoughtfully, however, these tools mesh beautifully with a timeline strategy. Before you search, you identify the probable era(s) in which an event occurred and the likely jurisdictions; that tells you which digital collections to prioritize.

If you are seeking a marriage in the 1860s, you know to search both town and state copies of vital records; if you are hunting a deed from the 1720s, you look for county-level registrations or colonial land grants, not for town-based grantor indexes that begin later. Online guides maintained by state archives, major libraries, and genealogical societies can be read as era-specific: they often group collections by period or record type, which you can map directly onto your mental timeline.

DNA, likewise, benefits from a timeline perspective. Clusters of matches who all trace back to a specific mill town or immigrant neighborhood in the late 19th century can be interpreted in light of that era's social history: endogamy in French Canadian communities, tight Irish parish networks, or shared origins in a single Italian village. Clusters that center on early colonial surnames may reflect deep New England intermarriage and long-standing local roots; understanding the historical window in which those ancestors lived can guide your documentary search toward specific towns, churches, and court records.

From Timeline to Narrative

Ultimately, the value of this timeline for genealogists lies in its ability to transform data into story. A well-constructed family history is not simply a collection of dates and record citations; it is an account of how particular people navigated the constraints and possibilities of their time and place. By grounding your research in the eras outlined here—Indigenous homelands, first contact and disease, colonial planting, Puritan order, imperial crisis, industrial expansion, immigration waves, and modern transformations—you give yourself a structure within which each ancestor's choices and circumstances become legible.

For a beginning researcher, this might mean starting every project with a worksheet that lists an ancestor's life events down one side and the relevant historical phases across the top, filling in which record types to pursue at each intersection. For an experienced genealogist, it might mean revisiting older conclusions, asking whether an overlooked era-specific source—say, a set of 19th-century school district reports or 20th-century zoning board minutes—might resolve a longstanding puzzle.

For all researchers, it means approaching Massachusetts not as a static backdrop but as a living, changing context that needs to be understood on its own terms. In that sense, the timeline is less a finished chart and more an invitation: to keep learning about the Commonwealth's evolving history and to let that understanding guide every research plan, every search, and every narrative you write.

Chapter 2

Political, Religious, and Social Evolution

Massachusetts has always been more than a collection of towns and dates; it is a landscape built and rebuilt through decisions about *who* holds power, *what* a good community should look like, and *how* people ought to live together. Political structures—not just governors and legislatures, but town meetings, selectmen, and local courts—defined who counted as an inhabitant, who could vote or hold office, and who bore the burden of taxes and militia service. Religious ideas shaped where settlements were planted, how villages were laid out, and who was welcome or unwelcome within them. Social expectations, reinforced by education and economic opportunity, marked off lines of class, gender, race, and ethnicity that affected every aspect of daily life. For genealogists and family historians, these overlapping forces are not mere background; they explain why some ancestors appear repeatedly in the records while others surface only briefly or not at all.

From the first decades of English settlement, Massachusetts was imagined as a deliberate project. Puritan leaders in Massachusetts Bay hoped to build a "godly commonwealth" ordered according to their understanding of scripture and English law, while Plymouth's separatists tried to craft a stable society on the edge of empire.

Over time, that project changed: royal authorities imposed new charters and governors; revolutionaries remade the colony into a commonwealth; industrialists and reformers refashioned towns into factory centers and later into suburbs; immigrants built parallel institutions alongside older Yankee structures. At each stage, new laws were passed, new churches and schools were founded, new economic arrangements were tried, and new kinds of records were created. If you trace a single Massachusetts family across several generations, you can see them moving through these changing frameworks: a 17th-century freeman voting in town meeting, his great-grandson signing a Revolutionary War muster roll, his descendant sending children to a 19th-century common school, and a 20th-century great-grandchild commuting from a suburb to a technology job along Route 128.

Understanding these shifts matters because records do not spring up randomly; they are byproducts of power and purpose. Town meeting minutes exist because colonial law required towns to manage their own local affairs and account for their decisions. Court records exist because disputes were required to be resolved and punishments documented. Church registers exist because congregations believed membership and sacraments should be carefully recorded.

School reports and examination lists exist because communities and state authorities wanted to measure attendance, attainment, and the success of reforms. Tax rolls, land deeds, and probate files exist because governments and families wanted to allocate property, extract revenue, and avoid (or win) legal battles. When you open a town book, a church volume, or a court docket, you are looking directly at the practical outcome of a particular political or religious choice about how society should be organized.

At the same time, every one of these systems carried exclusions and biases. Early voting rights were restricted to male property-holders, often further limited to church members. Women's lives were usually recorded in relation to fathers, husbands, or children. Enslaved and free people of African descent, Indigenous families, and the poor were documented mainly when they were taxed, punished, hired out, or made the subject of charity. Later, Catholic immigrants might find their family's most detailed records in parish registers rather than town books; factory workers might be better documented in company employment lists, union minutes, or benevolent society records than in land deeds. By placing your research within a clear understanding of Massachusetts' political and social evolution, you learn to expect these patterns—not as personal oversights, but as structural realities—and to compensate for them by seeking out alternative record groups or reading familiar sources "against the grain."

For that reason, this chapter does not treat politics, religion, education, and the economy as separate, abstract topics. Instead, it follows four intertwined threads—town governance and colonial law, the role of religion in settlement and community structure, education and the rise of literacy, and the economic foundations of agriculture, fishing, industry, and trade—and shows how each one operated on the ground and in the record books.

In the section on town governance and law, you will see how authority flowed from colony and province into counties and towns, how meetings and courts were organized, and how that structure created minutes, tax lists, warnings out, and case files that still anchor 17th- and 18th-century research.

In the section on religion, you will move from the early Congregational meetinghouse through the proliferation of denominations and the arrival of Catholic, Jewish, and Orthodox communities, learning how to navigate an increasingly diverse and multilingual set of church and synagogue records.

The discussion of education will trace the development from early laws requiring basic schooling, through the common school movement and teacher training, to the rise of high schools and universities, highlighting the many points where students and teachers leave traces in catalogs, yearbooks, and administrative reports.

The section on economic foundations will tie these political and religious worlds to the work people performed—on farms, on fishing vessels, in shops and factories, and later in offices and research labs—and will show how land deeds, maritime records, business ledgers, and corporate personnel files can be read alongside traditional genealogical sources.

Each major section will include case examples that follow real-world research paths: a colonial widow asserting her dower rights through town and court records; an Irish Catholic family navigating both civil and parish systems in an industrial city; a French-Canadian mill worker's descendants moving from factory neighborhoods into suburban schools and white-collar jobs.

The aim of this chapter, then, is twofold. First, it offers an interpretive framework: a way of thinking about Massachusetts communities as evolving political, religious, and social projects rather than static backdrops. Second, it provides practical guidance: pointing you to the kinds of records each phase produced and suggesting how to integrate them into your research. Whether you are tracing a single line from the 1600s to the 2000s or jumping into a newly discovered branch in the 19th century, this chapter is designed to help you ask sharper questions—about jurisdiction, about belonging, about who held power over your ancestors at a given moment—and to use the answers to those questions to find, interpret, and correlate the records that tell their stories.

Town Governance and Colonial Laws

Town government is the backbone of Massachusetts genealogy. From the earliest English settlements forward, most of the records genealogists rely on—vital entries, tax lists, poor relief, land divisions, warnings out, school decisions—were created not in some distant capital but in town meetings chaired by neighbors. Towns were the primary units of governance and identity: people thought of themselves as "of Salem," "of Dedham," or "of Springfield" long before they thought of themselves as "of Massachusetts." Understanding how towns were organized, what the law expects them, and how those expectations changed over time is essential to knowing where to look for your ancestors and how to interpret what you find.

The Town as a Corporate Community

When a new town was established in colonial Massachusetts, the governing authority—first a colonial General Court, later provincial and state legislatures—was essentially creating a public corporation. The town as a legal person could hold common lands, sue and be sued, raise taxes, and make local regulations. In return, towns accepted responsibilities: maintaining roads and bridges, supporting the poor, organizing the militia, and, over time, providing schools and enforcing public order.

This corporate nature meant that town meetings mattered. In most places, eligible male inhabitants gathered at least annually, often more frequently, to elect officers and vote on local business. The town clerk recorded these decisions in a town book, and those books are among the earliest systematic records in Massachusetts. Entries might include:

- Election of officers (selectmen, constables, fence viewers, hog reeves, school committee).
- Votes to divide or fence common lands; grants of house lots and meadow to named residents.
- Orders about roads: where to lay out new ways, who must provide labor or materials.
- Contracts with individuals to maintain bridges, keep the pound, or "warn out" newcomers.
- Instructions on poor relief: assigning families to board paupers or children, approving reimbursement.

For genealogists, each of those categories is a research doorway. A vote granting land "unto John Smith, inhabitant" may be the earliest evidence of a man's arrival in the town. An order paying a widow to keep the town's poor may reveal both her economic situation and her standing in the community. Seeing the same surname elected as selectmen generation after generation signals a family's enduring prominence; seeing a cluster of names in a single year's warnings out may indicate an influx of migrants or economic crisis pushing marginal residents out.

Inhabitants, Settlement, and Poor Law

Colonial and provincial laws drew sharp distinctions between "inhabitants" (legally settled residents) and those merely dwelling in a place. Settlement had critical consequences: a town was liable for the support of its settled poor, widows, and orphans, but could attempt to shift responsibility for unsettled newcomers back to their last place of legal settlement. To control these obligations, the law evolved procedures for warning and removal. Newcomers might be formally "admitted" by a town vote, sometimes with conditions, or implicitly accepted by long residence. Others were visited by the constable or a selectman and given a warning to depart; the warning did not necessarily force them to leave, but it preserved the town's right to deny future poor relief.

These settlement rules generated a distinctive set of records:

- Warning-out books or entries in town minutes naming individuals and families warned, often with previous places of residence.
- Settlement examinations, recorded in town or county records, where a person was questioned about their birthplace, apprenticeship, marriage, and residence history.
- Overseers of the poor account books listing who received relief, who boarded paupers or children, and which towns were charged for reimbursement.

For genealogists, such records can be unexpectedly rich. A settlement examination might recount decades of a laborer's movements; a poor relief ledger may name widows and their children otherwise absent from land and tax lists. A warning entry "to depart to Weston, where last legally settled" can identify an earlier residence that does not appear in vital records. These documents also reveal the social geography of a town: who was precarious, who was stable, and how local authorities managed people on the margins.

Selectmen, Clerks, and Local Officers

Town officers were the hands and eyes of local government, and their roles intersect with genealogical evidence at many points. Selectmen functioned as an executive board, implementing town votes, overseeing the poor, and managing day-to-day affairs between meetings. The town clerk recorded vital events (at least in theory), copied deeds and votes into the town book, and sometimes kept copies of state vital returns. Constables collected taxes and served warrants; fence viewers inspected boundary fences; surveyors of highways oversaw labor on roads.

Because these offices involved trust and contact with higher authorities, their holders often appear in multiple record sets. A man serving as town clerk is almost certain to leave his name in nearly every volume of local records; his distinctive handwriting may be the one you pore over for hours. A selectman's name will show up in overseers' accounts, settlement examinations, and correspondence with the county or colony. Even seemingly humble roles—like "hog reeve"—can mark a young man's first step into public life and help distinguish him from older relatives with the same name.

From a methodological standpoint, genealogists should always note when an ancestor appears as a town officer and then look "sideways" into the related series: overseers' books if he was an overseer of the poor, highway records if he was a surveyor, school committee reports if he served in that capacity. These lateral sources can reveal how he thought, what issues mattered in his community, and with whom he collaborated or clashed.

County and Colonial Courts: Law in Practice

Above the town level, colonial and provincial Massachusetts relied on county courts, higher appellate tribunals, and a legislative body that also exercised judicial functions in some eras. The structure and names of these courts shifted with charters and constitutions, but their function remained broadly similar: adjudicating disputes, enforcing criminal law, and recording the outcomes.

Court records are often organized by county, term, and case type (civil vs. criminal). In civil cases, genealogists may find:

- Debt suits, where shopkeepers or neighbors sued for unpaid accounts, listing items sold and sometimes the debtor's circumstances.

- Ejectment and trespass cases over land boundaries and property rights, assisting in reconstructing landholding when deeds are incomplete.

- Appeals from probate decisions, highlighting intra-family disputes over inheritance.

In criminal cases, records may include:

- Indictments for offenses ranging from Sabbath-breaking and drunkenness to assault, theft, and more serious crimes.

- Depositions from witnesses, giving vivid narratives and naming kin, neighbors, and employers.

- Sentences that might involve fines, whipping, imprisonment, or public penance.

For family historians, these cases can be startlingly revealing. A slander suit might include verbatim quotes of accusations, revealing community standards and conflicts. A fornication case naming a father of an illegitimate child can establish paternity otherwise unstated in any birth record. A prosecution for selling liquor without a license might show how a family supplemented its income.

Legal context matters here. Knowing what the law prescribed for inheritance, for example, helps you understand why a widow received a one-third dower interest and sons and daughters shared the balance in a certain way. Recognizing that certain religious offenses reflected not just personal morality, but enforcement of a community covenant explains why church members and town officials often appear together in the same case. When using court records, think not only about what they say explicitly but also about what they imply about economic status, social networks, and power.

Colonial Charters, Provincial Reforms, and the Massachusetts Constitution

Over the 17th and 18th centuries, the legal framework in which towns and courts operated changed significantly. The original Massachusetts Bay charter gave wide latitude to local authorities, but the 1691 provincial charter reconstituted Massachusetts as a royal province with a governor appointed by the Crown. This introduced new layers of imperial oversight: royal instructions, appeals to London, and periodic disputes over the reach of provincial legislation.

Despite these changes, town government remained robust, and local political culture continued to emphasize participation and autonomy. Nevertheless, genealogists should be aware that some legal and administrative records from the provincial period are preserved centrally (e.g., legislative journals, gubernatorial correspondence, provincial tax rolls), while others stay at the county or town level. Statutes concerning land titles, religious toleration, and voting qualifications all evolved under this provincial regime and can affect how you interpret an ancestor's legal status—whether they could vote, hold land, or serve on a jury.

The adoption of the Massachusetts Constitution in 1780 created the Commonwealth as a state with a clearer separation of powers among executive, legislative, and judicial branches. New courts were established, some old ones renamed or reorganized, and the structure of town representation in the legislature was codified. For genealogists, the main practical effect is a shift in terminology and series: after 1780, you will find cases in "Supreme Judicial Court" and "Court of Common Pleas" records rather than in colonial-style General Court dockets, and state-level printed session laws supplant some older compilations. Yet the everyday experience of town government changed slowly; clerks continued to record vital events, selectmen continued to manage local affairs, and county registries continued to copy deeds.

Annotating Time: Using Legal Change as a Research Aid

Seeing town governance and colonial law as evolving systems rather than fixed backdrops helps you in several concrete ways:

- It sharpens your sense of *when* to look for certain kinds of records. For example, formal state-level vital registration begins in 1841; before then, town records are primary. County land registration has become more standardized over the 18th century; earlier landholding may rely more on town proprietors' books or colonial grants.

- It teaches you to expect jurisdictional shifts. A town that starts out in one county may later be assigned to another; over time, court structures change, so you must know which court had jurisdiction at the date in question.

- It prepares you for gaps and overlaps. Some towns kept meticulous minutes but lost early vital books; others preserved vital records but have scattered or missing town meeting volumes. Court records may survive for some counties and periods but be fragmentary for others.

When you begin a Massachusetts research problem, one of the most powerful things you can do is sketch a quick legal timeline for the place involved: date of town incorporation; county formation and any later changes; relevant colonial or state constitutional shifts; dates when key record-keeping laws (like vital registration or poor law reforms) were enacted. That annotated timeline becomes your roadmap. It tells you which town, county, and state offices to investigate, which record series should exist, and how likely it is that your ancestor's name will appear in a given source.

In the chapters that follow, the legal and governmental structures described here will be woven repeatedly into case studies and source discussions. Whenever you encounter a town book, a court file, or a legislative petition, you can return to this framework and ask: Which officers created this? What law required or motivated its creation? Whose interests did it serve—and whose did it ignore? Answering those questions will not only make you a more efficient researcher; it will also help you see your Massachusetts ancestors as actors within a living legal and political world, not just as names on a page.

The Town as a Legal Person

When English colonists used the word "town" in early Massachusetts, they did not mean simply a cluster of houses on a map. They were talking about a legal entity with rights, responsibilities, and a continuing existence beyond the lives of any individual inhabitant. The town could own land collectively, enter contracts, sue and be sued, levy taxes, and make local regulations within the bounds set by higher authorities. This "corporate" character is what makes town records so valuable for genealogists: because the town had to act and account as a legal person, it left a remarkably continuous paper trail in which individual residents appear as officers, taxpayers, landholders, petitioners, and beneficiaries of public decisions.

From the earliest settlements in Plymouth and Massachusetts Bay, the process of creating a town followed a recognizably legal script. A group of settlers petitioned the colonial or provincial legislature (the General Court) for recognition as a town, often after an earlier phase as a "plantation" or district. If granted, the act of incorporation named the place, specified its boundaries, and conferred the basic powers shared by other towns: to hold meetings, elect officers, raise and expend money for local purposes, and regulate matters such as roads, commons, and poor relief.

Once incorporated, the town did not dissolve when founding families died or moved away. It persisted, a fictional "person" that could sue for unpaid rates, be sued for failing to maintain a bridge, and be called to account by the colony or state—ensuring that its clerks kept minutes, its treasurers kept accounts, and its selectmen documented their decisions.

The 'Town Meeting' was the principal way this legal person acted. In most communities, eligible male inhabitants gathered at set times (often annually in March and at other points as needed) to elect officers and vote on warrants listing the business to be transacted. The warrant—essentially the town's agenda—was itself a legal instrument, warning inhabitants of the meeting and specifying what could be decided there. Votes to "choose selectmen," "raise a sum" for schools or poor relief, "lay out a highway," "grant" a parcel of common land to a named individual, or "admit" someone as an inhabitant all became part of the permanent record when the town clerk entered them in the town book.

Genealogically, these entries do three things: they place named people in a specific community at a specific date; they indicate their civic status (whether as officers, ratepayers, or recipients of town action); and they reveal how the town's collective decisions shaped individual lives, for example by assigning a widow support from the town treasury or granting a newcomer permission to build on the common.

Because the town was responsible for core public functions, the law bound it to keep certain kinds of records and to act through specific officers. Statutes required towns to choose clerks, constables, and later school committees, to maintain vital event registers, to keep accounts of money raised and spent, and to report periodically to colonial, provincial, or state authorities. The town clerk's vital record volumes exist because the town, as a legal person, had a duty to record births, marriages, and deaths reported to it; overseers' books exist because the town had a legal obligation to support its settled poor and account for that support; tax lists exist because the town had to demonstrate how it apportioned and collected rates for colony, province, or state levies. For genealogists, recognizing that these registers and lists are byproducts of the town's legal responsibilities helps in two ways: it explains why certain events are recorded more reliably than others (taxation and landholding often more systematically than, say, stillbirths or informal marriages), and it suggests where to look when a record seems missing (for example, in town copies versus state copies of vital returns).

The town's corporate status also shaped how families interacted with higher levels of government. When the colony or province needed soldiers, it called on towns to supply quotas; muster and bounty records are often organized by town, listing the men each corporate body furnished. When new counties were formed or court systems reorganized, towns were reassigned, but their internal structure persisted: the town as a legal person simply found itself under a different county umbrella, continuing to produce the same kinds of local records while sending its representatives to different courts and legislatures.

Even in the modern era, as cities and regional authorities took on more functions, Massachusetts towns retained substantial corporate powers, with select boards (or city councils) and town meetings still making decisions on zoning, schools, and local services. Contemporary records—planning board minutes, conservation commission filings, school committee reports—are the latest manifestations of the town's long legal life and can be just as useful for genealogists tracing 20th-century families as 17th-century town books are for colonial lines.

For researchers, thinking of the town as a legal person encourages a shift in perspective. Instead of seeing "the town records" as a single monolithic source, you can ask: what duties did the town have at this time, and which officers carried them out? That question points you to specific series: town meeting minutes when looking for civic participation, selectmen or overseers' books when tracing pauper support or settlement disputes, treasurer's accounts when following tax burdens, vital registers when documenting family events, and returns sent up to the province or state when tracking how local decisions were reported outward.

It also reminds you that when your ancestor appears in a town record, they are interacting with the town as a corporate entity—petitioning it, serving it, being regulated or supported by it—and that each such interaction may leave traces in more than one place, from the town book to county court dockets and even to legislative petitions at the state level.

Courts, Counties, and the Law in Action
If the town meeting was the everyday face of local power in Massachusetts, the courts were where conflicts crystalized into paper. From the 1600s onward, county and higher courts translated quarrels over debt, land, reputation, morality, and crime into formal proceedings, leaving behind narratives, judgments, and supporting documents that are among the richest sources a genealogist can use. These records show people under pressure—suing, defending, testifying, petitioning, appealing—and in the process they reveal relationships, occupations, migrations, and social hierarchies that rarely appear as clearly anywhere else. Understanding how courts and counties

were structured, how they changed over time, and what kinds of cases they handled allows you to mine these materials effectively and to avoid missing crucial evidence that sits just beyond the familiar realm of vitals and deeds.

From the colonial period through the provincial era and into statehood, Massachusetts organized its courts hierarchically. In the 17th century, the General Court at the colony level initially combined legislative and judicial functions, while lower courts in counties or shires handled routine civil and criminal matters. Over time, as population grew and legal business multiplied, a more differentiated structure emerged: county-level courts of general sessions for criminal and administrative matters, courts of common pleas for most civil suits, and higher appellate or superior courts (later the Supreme Judicial Court) for serious cases and appeals. Each court met on a regular circuit—terms were held a certain number of times per year in each county—and clerks kept dockets, minute books, and files for individual cases.

For genealogists, the key point is that, at any given time, a particular kind of dispute (say, a land boundary fight or an assault charge) will have been heard in a specific level of court, usually tied to a particular county. Knowing the era and residence of your ancestor lets you identify which court's records to search and which repository—state archives, county courthouse, or historical society—is likely to hold them.

Civil cases form a large portion of surviving material and are especially fruitful for reconstructing lives. Debt suits were ubiquitous: shopkeepers sued customers for unpaid accounts, craftsmen sued for wages, landlords sued tenants for rent in arrears. These actions often include itemized accounts listing what was bought (fabric, tools, foodstuffs, rum), when it was purchased, and sometimes why payment was delayed.

For a genealogist, such an account can illuminate a household's consumption patterns, economic strain, and occupational links (for example, a blacksmith repeatedly supplying a particular farmer). Land-related suits—ejectment, trespass, partition—arose when deeds were unclear, boundaries disputed, or heirs at odds over division. These cases often recapitulate property histories, recite earlier conveyances, and bring in witnesses who testify to long-term occupation ("he has possessed the said farm these thirty years") or to previous family agreements. Even when land records themselves are patchy, such litigation can help reconstruct who owned which parcel when, and how it passed through a family.

Criminal and quasi-criminal cases add another dimension, revealing the enforcement of community norms and the public handling of behavior deemed unacceptable. In the colonial and provincial eras, prosecutions for Sabbath-breaking, drunkenness, fornication, adultery, and "disorderly conduct" mingle with indictments for theft, assault, counterfeiting, and occasionally more serious offenses. Depositions in these cases reproduce conversations, describe gatherings, and name participants, often situating people in taverns, fields, or private homes at specific dates and times. For example, a fornication case involving an out-of-wedlock birth may record the mother's sworn statement about paternity; witnesses might testify about courtship behavior, promises of marriage, or admissions made by the alleged father.

For a genealogist, such material can provide elusive linkages—identifying fathers of illegitimate children, clarifying the timeline of a relationship, or revealing family tensions that led to estrangement or migration.

County and higher courts also served administrative roles that generate records of direct genealogical interest. They appointed guardians for minors and "persons non compos mentis," overseeing the management of their property; they licensed innholders, shopkeepers, and certain trades; and they heard appeals from local decisions about roads or town boundaries. Guardianship files name minors, their deceased parents, and chosen guardians, sometimes with extended kin detailed; licensing records list occupations and can tie an ancestor to a specific tavern or shop; road cases may map a neighborhood, name abutters and describe landmarks that can be correlated with later surveys. When you encounter a vague reference in a town record to "as the court hath ordered," it is often worthwhile to look for an associated case in the relevant county's docket.

The relationship between town and court records is symbiotic, and genealogists get the best results when they read across the two. A dispute that surfaces in a town meeting—say, about a delinquent taxpayer or an unruly pauper—might escalate into a court case if local remedies fail, creating a richer narrative in the court file. Conversely, a court judgment ordering a town to support a particular individual will likely be reflected in overseers' accounts, showing ongoing payments or boarding arrangements.

This back-and-forth is especially important for understanding poor law and settlement disputes, where towns argued over which community was legally responsible for a person's support. Settlement examinations recorded by justices of the peace (often preserved in county or state archives) can read like miniature autobiographies, as individuals recount where they were born, apprenticed, married, and employed to establish their legal settlement. These are invaluable for tracking migrants, servants, and others who leave few other traces.

Over the long term, changes in charters and constitutions reshaped the court system, and genealogists must be sensitive to these shifts when planning research. After the 1691 charter made Massachusetts a royal province, imperial authorities expected more formal adherence to English legal norms, and provincial statutes standardized some procedures. After independence and the 1780 constitution, the Commonwealth created a clearer judiciary with named courts (Supreme Judicial Court, Court of Common Pleas, later Probate Courts as distinct entities), each with its own record series. In the 19th and 20th centuries, reform and specialization produced new courts—police courts, district courts, juvenile courts—whose records may still be in local custody or partially restricted.

What this means in practice is that a theft case in 1740, a similar case in 1840, and one in 1940 will likely be found in different types of records in different institutions, even if all occurred in the same town. Consulting guides from the Massachusetts Archives, county registries, and major libraries can help you align the date and type of case with the correct court and surviving documentation.

For the family historian, court and county records also help correct overreliance on "respectable" sources. Published town and church compilations tend to highlight births, marriages, and deaths among stable residents; court records draw in the whole spectrum—from prominent merchants litigating complex contracts to marginalized people charged with vagrancy or petty theft. Enslaved and free Black individuals, Indigenous people, women, servants, and the poor often appear more distinctly here than in town vital records, precisely because the law intervened in their lives more visibly. A woman seeking a divorce, a Black sailor resisting impressment, an Indigenous man contesting land or guardianship—all may leave detailed testimony in court files. Reading these cases with care and empathy allows genealogists to recover stories that might otherwise be invisible.

In using these materials, it is wise to proceed systematically. Start by identifying the relevant county and time frame, then consult docket books or indexes (many now digitized or abstracted) to locate cases involving your surnames or towns. Once you have case numbers, seek out the underlying papers: not just the summary judgment, but the declarations, depositions, accounts, and exhibits. As you read, annotate names, places, dates, relationships, and economic details, and then cross-check these against town records, land deeds, probate files, and church registers.

The goal is not to treat a court case as an isolated curiosity, but to integrate it into a broader reconstruction of a person's life and community. When approached this way, "courts, counties, and the law in action" become less an intimidating legal archive and more a powerful narrative resource—one that can turn a bare name on a vital record into a fully contextualized human story.

Religion and Community Structure

Religion has shaped Massachusetts communities from the very beginning, not only as a matter of belief but as a framework for where people settled, how they organized themselves, and which events in their lives were written down. Congregations determined where meetinghouses and churches were placed; doctrines influenced who was admitted as a full member of the community and who remained on its margins; religious conflicts created migrations, schisms, and new institutions.

For genealogists and family historians, understanding this religious landscape is essential because so many core sources—baptismal registers, marriage records, burial entries, membership lists, minutes of discipline, and even some early "vital" records—were created and kept by religious bodies. Knowing how religion structured community life in a given era helps you predict which records exist, where they are likely to be found, and what biases they may carry.

In the 17th and early 18th centuries, especially in Massachusetts Bay, the organizing force was the Congregational church rooted in Puritan theology. English settlers often arrived as organized church groups or quickly formed congregations on arrival, drafting covenants and calling ministers before or as they established towns. Church admission was not simply a matter of attendance; it required a public profession of faith and approval by existing members. In the earliest decades, only male church members could become "freemen" with voting rights in colony-wide elections, further intertwining religious commitment and political power. The meetinghouse served as both church and civic hall: Sabbath services, town meetings, militia musters, and public punishments all took place in or around the same building.

For genealogists, this means that a 17th-century New England town is best understood as a covenant community: church membership rolls, baptism lists, and records of discipline are not ancillary—they are central evidence of belonging and status.

Congregational Roots and the Village Church

For the first century and a half of English settlement, the typical Massachusetts town was, at its core, a Congregational village: a meetinghouse at or near the town center, a minister called and supported by the inhabitants, and a church covenant that bound members together in what they understood as a spiritual and social compact. The Congregational way that developed in Massachusetts Bay took English Reformed theology and married it to a distinctive form of church government in which each congregation was largely autonomous, choosing its own minister and officers and disciplining its own members, while still maintaining fellowship with sister churches. In practice, this meant that religious and civic life were deeply entangled. Sabbath worship, town meetings, militia musters, and even public punishments took place in or around the same building; the men who guided the church often guided the town, and vice versa.

Membership in these early churches was not automatic. Attendance at public worship was expected of all, but "full communion" membership required a credible profession of faith and acceptance by existing members. In the 1630s and 1640s, only such male church members could be admitted as freemen of the Massachusetts Bay Colony, with the right to vote in colony-wide elections and hold certain offices, though town governance quickly broadened participation somewhat.

This linkage between church membership and political privilege created a layered community structure: at the center, full communicants; around them, regular attenders who might have their children baptized but lacked full voting rights in early years; at the edges, dissenters, servants, enslaved people, and Native neighbors who were present in town life but variably included or excluded in church practice. For genealogists, recognizing these layers helps explain why some early men show up on lists of freemen and communicants while others, equally present in land and tax records, do not.

The church book in a Congregational village was as central to record-keeping as the town book. Typically kept by the minister or church clerk, it often began with the covenant, followed by lists of members, admissions, dismissions, baptisms, marriages, and records of discipline. Admissions might note when an individual "owned the covenant" or joined by confession or by recommendation from another church, sometimes stating the previous place of residence ("lately from London," "from Ipswich").

Dismissions tracked people who transferred to new congregations, often indicating their destination town, a crucial clue for tracing migration. Baptism entries, especially in the 17th and early 18th centuries, might name only the father and child, but many also name the mother; some later entries add her maiden surname or note her former town. Although civil marriage registration improved over time, early church records may be the only surviving documentation of a marriage, particularly when the ceremony was purely ecclesiastical.

Discipline and pastoral oversight were also recorded in detail. Congregational churches took seriously their responsibility to maintain the purity of the covenant community. Members could be "admonished" for various offenses—drunkenness, neglect of worship, sexual sin, dishonesty in business, or slander—and, in more serious cases, "cast out" (excommunicated) if they did not repent. The minutes of such proceedings often include confessions, the names of offended parties, and the steps taken toward reconciliation. A modern genealogist might discover, for example, that an ancestor was cited for fathering a child before marriage, or for striking a neighbor, or for "disorderly carriage," with the narrative naming spouses, witnesses, and sometimes children.

These incidents, read carefully and sensitively, can explain later moves (families leaving after conflict), sudden changes in standing (a man no longer chosen to town office), or estrangements hinted at in wills and land divisions.

The physical and social centrality of the village church also makes it a key to understanding geography. Early meetinghouses were often placed near the geographic center of a town as then conceived. As population spread and outlying districts felt distant from worship, they sometimes petitioned to be set off as separate precincts or parishes with their own churches, a prelude to later town divisions.

These petitions and the resulting parish records are essential for genealogists because they show how a single original town fractured into multiple ecclesiastical and, eventually, civil units. A family living in a distant part of an old town may appear first in the mother church's records, then in a new precinct's register after it forms, then in a separate town's vital records once civil incorporation follows. Without awareness of these ecclesiastical subdivisions, it is easy to think a family has "disappeared" when, in fact, they simply began attending and being recorded in a nearer meetinghouse.

Over time, the Congregational system itself evolved. The Half-Way Covenant (mid-17th century) allowed the baptism of children whose parents had been baptized but were not themselves full communicants, an attempt to preserve church influence as explicit conversion experiences seemed less common among later generations. The Great Awakening in the 1730s–1740s brought waves of revival preaching that split some congregations into "Old Lights" and "New Lights," with new churches organized by those favoring or resisting the new piety.

In the late 18th and early 19th centuries, theological divisions over the Trinity and human nature led many long-standing Congregational churches, especially in eastern Massachusetts, to adopt Unitarian beliefs, while orthodox Trinitarians formed separate congregations. This history has direct implications for research: an ancestor might be baptized in a Congregational church that later became Unitarian, while their descendants join the orthodox "second church" in town, with separate records in different repositories today. Consulting local histories, denominational guides, and archival finding aids helps untangle these threads and ensures that you do not overlook a branch of records created when a parish split.

Case work with Congregational records benefits from a methodical approach. Start by establishing which Congregational (and related) churches existed in your town of interest at the time your ancestor lived there. Use town histories, denominational directories, and major research guides (such as those from FamilySearch, American Ancestors, or state and local archives) to learn what records survive and where they are held—local church custody, town vaults, regional archives, or microfilm and digital collections. Then, work through the registers chronologically, noting every occurrence of your surnames, but also paying attention to patterns: clusters of admissions around migration waves, bursts of baptisms following revivals, or sudden disappearances of families after a disciplinary conflict. Cross-reference what you find with town vital records, land deeds, probate files, and court records, bearing in mind that church books were often maintained by the same men who served in civic offices, and that theological and social disputes in the meetinghouse rarely stayed there.

For many Massachusetts families with deep local roots, the village church is where the paper trail truly begins—sometimes decades before civil registration becomes reliable. Even for those whose ancestors arrived later and joined other denominations, understanding these Congregational roots clarifies how New England towns were originally structured and why their records look the way they do.

The meetinghouse on the hill was more than a place of worship; it was the institutional heart of the early community. Its covenants and controversies, baptisms and burials, admissions and excommunications all contributed to the web of documentation that genealogists now painstakingly reconstruct, one entry at a time.

Congregational church books from this era typically include multiple layers of information. Admission lists name those accepted into membership, sometimes noting prior residence ("of London," "from Rowley") or familial relationships. Baptismal entries may identify parents, sponsors, and occasionally the mother's maiden name. Discipline minutes outline cases of drunkenness, sexual misconduct, doctrinal error, or other "scandals," and record not only the accused but also family members and neighbors who testified or were affected.

Dismissal and recommendation letters document people moving between congregations and towns. When read in sequence, these records allow genealogists to trace migrations, reconstruct family structures, and understand the social standing of particular individuals within their communities. However, coverage and survival vary widely: some churches kept meticulous records from their founding; others lost early volumes or recorded only sparse details. Researchers must therefore treat surviving church books as precious but partial, supplementing them with town, court, and land records.

Religious life in Massachusetts was never static. The 17th-century ideal of a uniform Congregational commonwealth quickly encountered dissent. Figures like Roger Williams and Anne Hutchinson challenged prevailing doctrines and church–state relationships, leading to banishments and new settlements in Rhode Island and elsewhere. Quakers and Baptists faced persecution before toleration expanded in the late 17th and early 18th centuries. The Great Awakening in the 1730s–1740s introduced new forms of evangelical piety, splitting some Congregational churches into "Old Lights" and "New Lights."

Each wave of controversy, revival, and schism resulted in new congregations, secessions, and sometimes duplicate church structures in a single town. For genealogists, this religious fragmentation creates both challenges and opportunities. A family that appears in one church's baptismal register in the 1720s may reappear in the records of a "separates" congregation in the

1740s, then in a Baptist church a decade later. Failing to recognize that a town had multiple contemporaneous congregations can lead to false assumptions that a family "disappeared" when, in reality, they simply changed pews and record-keepers.

The 19th century brought a dramatic broadening of Massachusetts' religious landscape through both theological evolution and mass immigration. Within old Congregational strongholds, the rise of Unitarianism led many historic churches—especially in eastern Massachusetts—to adopt more liberal theology, while orthodox members formed new Trinitarian Congregational churches. Meanwhile, Methodists, Baptists, Universalists, and other Protestant groups expanded, often appealing to working-class and rural populations.

At the same time, large numbers of Irish Catholics arrived in the mid-19th century, followed by French Canadians, Italians, Portuguese, Eastern European Jews, and others. These immigrant communities created their own religious institutions: Irish, French, and Italian Catholic parishes; synagogues catering to specific Jewish traditions; Eastern Orthodox churches; and ethnic Protestant congregations. Each institution kept its own registers, usually separate from town vital records.

For genealogists, this diversification means that civil records alone seldom tell the full story. Catholic parish registers, often in Latin or the community's vernacular, record baptisms, marriages, and burials that might not be registered—or might be registered with less detail—in town or state vital records. They frequently include the maiden names of mothers, the names of godparents (who are often relatives or close associates), and the precise place of origin in Ireland, Quebec, Italy, the Azores, or elsewhere. Jewish congregational records—membership lists, circumcision ledgers, marriage registers, burial society records—may reveal Hebrew names, patronymics, and links to specific European towns. Protestant immigrant congregations (e.g., Swedish Lutherans, German Reformed) leave similar footprints.

Successfully reconstructing immigrant families in Massachusetts almost always requires integrating these religious records with civil sources, recognizing that denominational and ethnic boundaries often mattered more than town lines in determining where events were recorded.

Religion also played a powerful role in shaping community structure and social boundaries. In Puritan Massachusetts, religious dissent could lead to banishment, fines, or loss of civic rights; in the 19th century, Catholic and Jewish communities faced nativist hostility, which influenced where they could live, work, and worship. Anti-Catholic movements like the Know-Nothings left traces in political records and newspapers; anti-Semitic housing covenants and social exclusions appear indirectly in real estate patterns and club memberships.

Within communities, religious institutions provided mutual aid: church poor funds, Catholic sodalities, Jewish landsmanshaften, and fraternal orders affiliated with parishes or synagogues offered sickness and burial benefits, job placement, and social support. Membership rolls, benefit ledgers, and minutes from these organizations are often preserved in denominational archives or local historical societies and can be extraordinarily helpful for identifying kin networks and tracking internal migrations.

Case studies illustrate how religion and community structure intersect in practice. A 17th-century Congregational church discipline case might reveal that a woman "of Boston, formerly of Salem" was excommunicated for "disorderly carriage," naming her husband and neighbors and hinting at why the family later appears in a different town. An 1850s Boston Catholic baptism entry might record the Irish parish in County Kerry from which both parents came, with godparents whose surnames later appear as neighbors in a South Boston ward. A 1920s Jewish burial in a Chelsea cemetery, recorded by a landsmanshaft society, might give a precise shtetl in Lithuania and list surviving relatives in New York and Montreal. In each instance, religious records anchor the family in a specific community structure that is not visible in civil registration alone.

For family historians, the key is to treat religion as a structural element of research, not just a biographical detail. At the outset of any project, ask: what religious tradition did this family likely belong to at this time and place, how did that tradition organize congregations and communities locally, and where are those institutions' records now kept?

In early New England, that means identifying which Congregational (or later Baptist, Methodist, or other) churches existed in the town at the relevant time and checking published and archival finding aids for their extant registers. In the immigrant era, it means learning which Catholic parishes served specific neighborhoods or ethnic groups, which synagogues catered to which immigrant cohorts, and which denominational archives or online collections have filmed their books. Across all periods, it means recognizing that religious institutions were often the first and strongest points of attachment for newcomers, and that their records—like the communities they served—reflected both inclusion and exclusion.

By embedding your genealogical work in this religious and communal context, you gain more than additional sources; you gain a deeper understanding of how your ancestors fit into the moral and social universe of their time. You see why a family might uproot after a church split, why a widow might lean on a parish benevolent society, why a factory worker might join a Catholic temperance group or a Jewish mutual aid lodge. Those choices, in turn, left the records you now rely on. Reading them with an awareness of religion and community structure will make your reconstructions not only more accurate, but also more humane and historically grounded.

Religious Diversity and Parallel Communities

By the mid-19th century, Massachusetts had shifted from a largely Congregational landscape to a patchwork of religious worlds that overlapped yet often operated in parallel. This diversity arose from both internal theological change and the arrival of large immigrant populations who brought their own traditions. For genealogists, the result is a complex but record-rich environment: instead of relying on a single parish or meetinghouse, researchers must navigate multiple denominations, languages, and institutional cultures, each maintaining its own registers, minutes, and membership lists. Understanding how these religious communities were organized on the ground—often by ethnicity and neighborhood as much as theology—helps explain where families chose to worship, how they interacted with civic structures, and where their most detailed records may be preserved.

The first major shift came from within New England Protestantism itself. As Enlightenment ideas and new approaches to Bible interpretation spread in the late 18th and early 19th centuries, many historic Congregational churches, especially in eastern Massachusetts, adopted more liberal,

Unitarian theology, emphasizing the moral teachings of Jesus and human perfectibility over Calvinist doctrines of predestination. Orthodox members who wished to retain traditional Trinitarian beliefs formed separate Congregational churches, often known as "orthodox" or "Trinitarian" societies. At the same time, Baptists, Methodists, Universalists, and other denominations grew rapidly, planting new churches in towns that had once known only a single meetinghouse. Each of these congregations generated its own records—membership rolls, baptism and marriage registers, minutes, pew deeds—and sometimes inherited or contested the buildings and endowments of older churches. For genealogists, this means that tracing a single family through the 19th century may require checking multiple Protestant church books as theological and social affiliations shift.

Mass immigration layered new religious communities onto this already changing Protestant field. The Irish, arriving in large numbers from the 1840s famine onward, brought Roman Catholicism as a central marker of identity and solidarity. They initially worshiped in shared urban parishes but soon founded distinctly Irish churches in Boston, Lowell, Worcester, Springfield, and many mill towns. These parishes kept sacramental registers—baptisms, marriages, confirmations, burials—in Latin or English, often recording parents' birthplaces in Ireland and naming godparents who were frequently relatives or close friends. French Canadians followed, settling heavily in textile centers such as Lowell, Lawrence, Holyoke, and Fall River; they established French-language Catholic parishes that maintained separate registers, parish schools, and mutual aid societies. Portuguese and Cape Verdean Catholics formed yet more parishes in New Bedford, Fall River, and other coastal communities, some of which kept records that distinguish between island origins and track complex naming practices.

These Catholic communities often existed as parallel worlds within the same civil town. A city might have multiple Catholic parishes within walking distance of each other, each serving a specific ethnic group or neighborhood, alongside older Protestant churches and, later, synagogues. Civil vital records might list a child's birth with an anglicized version of an Irish or French-Canadian name, while the corresponding baptism appears in a parish register with the original spelling and a note of the parents' home county or village. Marriages may be recorded in both civil and ecclesiastical registers, sometimes on different dates (civil for the license, church for the sacrament). Genealogists who rely only on civil records risk missing this richer layer of identity and connection; integrating parish registers into research can reveal parents' places of origin, maiden names, godparent networks, and patterns of chain migration that civil records alone cannot show.

Jewish communities added further complexity starting in the mid-19th century, with small numbers of German Jews arriving first and larger waves of Eastern European Jews following from the 1880s onward. They established synagogues in Boston's West End, South End, Roxbury, Dorchester, Chelsea, and other cities and towns, often organized by place of origin (landsman associations) or ritual tradition (Hasidic vs. non-Hasidic, Sephardic vs. Ashkenazi). Synagogue records might include membership rolls, marriage registers, minutes of boards of trustees, and burial records tied to specific plots in Jewish cemeteries. Chevra Kadisha (burial societies) maintained their own ledgers, listing members, dues, and funerals. For genealogists, these sources can supply Hebrew names, patronymics, exact shtetl origins, and connections to relatives in other cities that do not appear in civil vital records or city directories.

Other immigrant groups built their own religious infrastructures: Greek Orthodox churches in cities like Boston and Lowell; Armenian Apostolic churches in Worcester and Watertown; Russian Orthodox and later Ukrainian and other Eastern Christian congregations. Scandinavian Lutherans, German Evangelicals, and other Protestant immigrants also founded churches where services, minutes, and records were kept in their native languages for decades. Each congregation tended to cluster in particular neighborhoods, shaping and reflecting patterns of residential settlement. When a genealogist identifies an ancestor's address in a census or directory, knowing the nearest likely ethnic parish or synagogue can guide which religious records to consult.

Religious diversity also produced distinct social and institutional ecosystems that functioned in parallel to civic structures. Catholic parishes sponsored schools, temperance societies, and sodalities; Jewish synagogues and benevolent societies operated loan funds, hospitals, and orphanages; Protestant churches ran Sunday schools, missionary societies, and charitable associations.

These organizations kept membership lists, minutes, financial records, and often published newsletters or annual reports, many of which survive in parish or denominational archives, local historical societies, or specialized repositories. For working-class or marginalized families who owned little property and seldom appear in probate, such records may offer the most detailed glimpses of their lives: a widow receiving aid from a parish conference, a young man listed as a choir member or Sunday school teacher, a family recorded as charter members of a new ethnic congregation.

At the same time, religious diversity intersected with social boundaries and discrimination. Irish Catholics in the 19th century, and later Italians and Polish immigrants, faced nativist hostility that limited employment opportunities and led to residential segregation. Jewish families encountered restrictive housing covenants and social exclusion from certain clubs and universities well into the 20th century. Black congregations—both historically Black Protestant churches and later Catholic parishes with predominantly Black memberships—had to fight for resources and recognition and often served as hubs for civil rights activism. These dynamics are visible in the historical record: in newspapers debating "foreign" schools, in city planning documents that site highways through ethnic or minority neighborhoods, in court cases over discrimination. For genealogists, being aware of these patterns is crucial not only for understanding why a family lived where it did, but also for locating their records in institutions that may sit outside the mainstream denominational or civic archive.

Practically, working in this environment requires a deliberate, community-aware approach. Once you know when and where your ancestors lived, ask: what congregations, of what traditions, were active in that neighborhood and period? Local histories, diocesan or denominational guides, and specialized projects such as Global Boston's "Eras of Migration" can help identify likely parishes or synagogues and point to archival locations. Then, seek out their registers and ancillary records, paying attention to language, naming conventions, and the social role of godparents, sponsors, or witnesses. Cross-reference these findings with civil vital records, censuses, and city directories, noting when the religious source provides additional or conflicting detail—and always respecting both the sensitivities of the communities involved and any access restrictions on recent records.

Seeing Massachusetts as a tapestry of religiously defined and overlapping communities rather than a single monolithic culture enriches genealogical research in two ways. It broadens the range of sources you consult, pushing you beyond town halls into parish basements, denominational archives, and specialized collections. And it deepens your interpretation of the records you find, prompting questions about why an ancestor chose a particular congregation, what that choice meant for their social and economic opportunities, and how their religious community supported or constrained them. In this way, "religious diversity and parallel communities" becomes not just a stylistic description of the modern commonwealth, but a practical guide to understanding—and finding—the people whose lives you seek to reconstruct.

Case study sketch: consider a French-Canadian family living in Holyoke around 1900. The parents married in a parish in Quebec, migrated with their first two children, and had four more in Massachusetts. Town vital records capture the Massachusetts-born children with anglicized surnames; the French parish registers record all baptisms with original surname and parents' place of origin; a later move to a different neighborhood leads them to attend an English-speaking parish that spells the surname differently again. Only by understanding that parishes were ethnic as well as geographic, and by recognizing that families might cross parish lines, can a genealogist reconcile these fragmented identities into a single, coherent family.

Religion, Boundaries, and Social Control

Religion in Massachusetts has never been only a matter of private conviction. From the earliest Puritan settlements through the immigration waves of the 19th and 20th centuries, religious institutions helped draw—and enforce—boundaries about who belonged, who led, and who was pushed to the edges of community life. For genealogists, this matters because those boundaries shaped which ancestors are well documented in church and civic records, which appear mainly when they ran afoul of norms, and which are visible only in traces left by conflict, reform, or charity.

In the 17th century, Massachusetts Bay's leaders openly envisioned a "godly commonwealth" in which civil and religious authority worked together to promote what they saw as right belief and behavior. Church membership and political rights overlapped; enforcing religious conformity was seen as essential to the health of the whole. Dissenters—whether over doctrine, church–state relations, or ecclesiastical discipline—could face admonition, fines, disarmament, or banishment.

The banishments of Roger Williams and Anne Hutchinson, the persecution of Quakers, and restrictions on Baptists all illustrate how religious disagreement mapped onto civic penalties. Genealogically, this means that people who challenged prevailing norms may surface in a distinct cluster of sources: church discipline minutes, General Court proceedings, town votes "not to entertain" certain ministers or practices, and, in some cases, records from new towns founded by dissenters just over the border in more tolerant jurisdictions.

Even for those who stayed within the formal bounds of Congregational orthodoxy, religion structured social control. Churches exercised discipline over members for infractions ranging from drunkenness and sexual misconduct to absenteeism from worship and slander. Towns, drawing on both religious and civil law, prosecuted "Sabbath-breaking," profane speech, and "disorderly behavior." In practical terms, this means that some of the most detailed accounts of everyday life— arguments in taverns, premarital relationships, neighborhood feuds—are preserved in church and court records precisely because the community responded to them as moral or religious problems. For family historians, a fornication case naming the father of an illegitimate child, or a church censure that led a family to relocate, can fundamentally alter the understanding of relationships in a pedigree.

As the formal legal bonds between church and state loosened in the late 18th and early 19th centuries, other forms of religiously inflected boundary-making took shape. The disestablishment of Congregationalism (completed in Massachusetts in 1833) ended tax support for a single "standing order," but it did not eliminate religious influence in civic life. Local elites continued to be drawn disproportionately from certain churches; town decisions about school funding, licensing of entertainments, and regulation of alcohol often reflected the preferences of dominant religious groups.

New evangelical movements, temperance societies, and Sabbatarian campaigns used moral suasion and social pressure to enforce norms, leaving their own documentary footprints in society minutes, pledge books, and petition campaigns. When genealogists encounter ancestors listed as officers of a temperance lodge or signers of an anti-slavery petition circulated through a church, they see individuals positioned at specific points along these moral and social boundaries.

For immigrant and minority communities, religion could serve both as a shield and as a marker of difference. Irish and later Italian Catholics, Eastern European Jews, and others relied on parishes and synagogues as primary sources of support—providing schools, mutual aid, and social services in the face of nativist hostility and economic discrimination. At the same time, their religious identities made them targets for exclusionary practices: anti-Catholic political movements, restrictive housing covenants that quietly barred Jews and sometimes Catholics from certain neighborhoods, and college or club quotas that limited access to elite institutions.

These dynamics influenced where families could live, which schools their children attended, what jobs they could obtain, and how quickly they could accumulate property—all factors that show up in records such as deeds, tax lists, school reports, employment files, and organization rosters. A genealogist tracing an Italian Catholic family's slow movement from a crowded North End tenement to a post-war suburb can read that trajectory against the background of changing religious and social boundaries.

Black and Indigenous communities experienced religious boundaries in particularly sharp ways. Black worshipers in Boston and other cities founded independent churches—such as African Meeting House congregations—partly in response to segregation and discrimination in white churches. Their church records, membership lists, and denominational reports document not only spiritual life but also activism around abolition, education, and civil rights. Indigenous people encountered missionary efforts that aimed to reshape their spiritual and social worlds, creating "praying towns" and later mission churches where acceptance of Christianity was tied to oversight of land and governance. In both cases, religious institutions could be instruments of control, but also vehicles for community resilience and self-definition. For genealogists, this means that in addition to colonial town and court records, mission records, denominational archives, and the minutes of Black and Native churches are key—and that these sources must be read critically, recognizing the power dynamics embedded in them.

In a practical sense, thinking about "religion, boundaries, and social control" gives genealogists a set of questions to apply to every era and locality:

- Which religious groups held most civic influence here at this time, and which were marginalized?
- How did those groups use formal power (laws, offices) and informal pressure (discipline, patronage, prejudice) to enforce norms?
- Which institutions—church courts, town authorities, reform societies—responded when people crossed those boundaries, and what records did they create?

Answering those questions for a particular ancestor's time and place helps you predict where to find evidence of conflict or conformity. A 17th-century Baptist in a predominantly Congregational town might appear in both town fines and a separate meeting's minutes; a 19th-century Irish Catholic laborer might show up in a city directory but be absent from Yankee church rolls, with his fuller story preserved instead in parish registers and Hibernian society minutes; a 20th-century Jewish shopkeeper may appear in business directories and tax rolls, but his communal life is better documented in synagogue records and landsmanshaft bulletins.

Ultimately, recognizing the role of religion in drawing and policing boundaries encourages more nuanced, humane readings of the record. Names in a church censure or a court case are not merely "troublemakers"; they are people caught at fault lines where personal choices, communal expectations, and larger power structures met. By situating such records within the broader religious and social context of Massachusetts history, genealogists can avoid anachronistic judgments and instead reconstruct how families navigated a world in which religious institutions and ideas played a central role in defining who belonged, who led, and who was left out.

Education and the Rise of Literacy

From the earliest decades of English settlement, Massachusetts leaders understood that reading and writing were not luxuries but tools of governance, religious life, and social order. Laws requiring towns to hire schoolmasters and later to maintain "grammar schools" grew out of a conviction that people who could not read scripture or laws were vulnerable to error and disorder. Over time, this conviction expanded into the common school movement, the rise of high schools, the growth of normal schools and universities, and ultimately a highly developed educational system that has become central to the state's identity.

For genealogists and family historians, education and literacy matter not only as context for ancestors' opportunities but also because schooling created its own records: committee minutes, teacher contracts, attendance registers, examination lists, yearbooks, alumni directories, and institutional histories. These sources can locate children in a particular neighborhood at specific dates, document women's and men's careers as teachers, and connect families to broader social and economic change.

The story begins in the 17th century, when Massachusetts enacted laws that made it a town's responsibility to provide basic education. The famous "Old Deluder Satan" law of 1647 required towns of a certain size to appoint a teacher to instruct children in reading and writing, and larger towns to establish grammar schools to prepare boys for college and the ministry. The language of the law framed education as a defense against ignorance and false doctrine, underscoring the link between literacy and religious as well as civic health. Practically, this meant that towns had to raise money, hire and oversee schoolmasters, and sometimes build schoolhouses or arrange for instruction to rotate among districts.

Some towns complied diligently; others struggled to meet the letter or spirit of the law, particularly in scattered rural areas where farm work competed with schooling. The records that survive from this early period are uneven—some school committee notes, occasional teacher contracts, town meeting entries authorizing wages—but where they exist, they can reveal names of teachers, the length of school terms, and sometimes lists of families whose children were expected to attend.

By the early 19th century, Massachusetts was at the forefront of the "common school" movement that sought to create a more universal, tax-supported system of elementary education. Reformers such as Horace Mann argued that publicly funded schools, staffed by trained teachers and governed by state standards, were essential for an informed citizenry and social cohesion. The state created a Board of Education in 1837, expanded teacher training through "normal schools" (beginning in Lexington, then in places like Westfield and Framingham), and promoted graded schools and longer terms.

Towns were required to submit annual school reports, listing expenditures, number of students, attendance, and sometimes naming teachers and their qualifications. For genealogists, these printed town reports—often bound with other municipal reports—are a valuable but underused source: they can place an ancestor as a teacher in a specific district, show when a new schoolhouse was built in a neighborhood, and indicate when a town first offered higher grades or specialized instruction.

At the same time, high schools emerged as an important new tier in the educational ladder. Initially, only a few larger or wealthier towns established high schools, often offering classical curricula aimed at college preparation. Over the course of the 19th century, high schools spread, added commercial and scientific tracks, and began to serve a wider range of students. The expansion of secondary education generated new record types: high school catalogs listing students and teachers, examination lists for admittance or graduation, and, eventually, yearbooks that included photographs, personal notes, and accounts of clubs, sports, and activities. For a genealogist, a high school yearbook can provide a rare visual image of an ancestor, as well as hints about their interests, peer group, and aspirations.

Teacher training and employment also produced significant documentation. Normal schools kept detailed catalogs of students, with names, hometowns, and sometimes prior schooling and later appointments. Graduates often taught in multiple towns before marriage or changing careers, and school committee reports, town meeting minutes, and local newspapers can trace their movements.

A woman listed in a census simply as "teacher" might have a much richer paper trail: an entry in a normal school alumni list, a mention in a town report as "Miss X. engaged for the winter term," a photograph in a faculty group in a high school yearbook. Linking these pieces allows family historians to reconstruct not only where an ancestor lived, but how they contributed to their communities and what kinds of education they themselves received.

Education, of course, intersected with class, gender, race, and immigration. In early periods, formal schooling often favored boys and families with enough means to forgo labor or pay tuition for advanced study. Over the 19th century, girls gained greater access to schooling, and teaching became a major occupation for young women—one of the few socially acceptable ways to earn an independent income before marriage.

For genealogists, this means that daughters who otherwise leave a faint trace in property and civic records may be found as teachers in school documents. At the same time, Black and Indigenous children, as well as children of recent immigrants, often faced segregated or inferior education, or were steered toward vocational tracks. Local histories, school committee reports, and sometimes court cases (especially in the 20th century desegregation era) reveal these disparities and can help explain why some ancestors had limited schooling or were tracked into particular kinds of work.

The 20th century saw further expansion and differentiation. Compulsory attendance laws grew stricter, junior high and middle schools appeared, and high school attendance became the norm rather than the exception. After World War II, the GI Bill dramatically increased college attendance, and Massachusetts' network of public universities, private colleges, and community colleges expanded.

Each of these institutions generated records: matriculation registers, transcripts, alumni directories, yearbooks, student newspapers, and, later, digital footprints on institutional websites. While many detailed student records from the mid-20th century onward are protected by privacy laws, alumni publications, graduation lists, and commemorative histories remain accessible and can confirm family stories about "he went to Boston College" or "she trained as a nurse at X hospital school."

For genealogists, working with educational records requires awareness of both their potential and their limits. Many school records are local and fragile: attendance books and grade registers might remain in town vaults, be transferred to historical societies, or be discarded altogether. Some have been microfilmed or digitized, but access often depends on knowing they exist and where they were deposited.

State-level guides and library or archive research guides—such as those maintained by the Massachusetts Archives, State Library, Boston Public Library, and major universities—can point to collections of school reports, normal school records, and college archives. As with church records, the key is to identify the institutions that would have served your ancestor given their time, place, and likely social position, then systematically explore their surviving documentation.

Finally, education and literacy shaped how ancestors interacted with other records. Individuals who could read and write were more likely to generate letters, diaries, account books, and signatures on legal documents. Even when such personal writings have not survived in family hands, their existence can sometimes be inferred: from notations that a person "signed" rather than made a mark; from references in probate inventories to "books" or "papers"; from newspaper advertisements placed by tradespeople or professionals. Conversely, noting when an ancestor consistently marks with an "X" or leaves no written trail can prompt questions about access to schooling and the barriers they faced.

Seeing "education and the rise of literacy" as a genealogical theme thus does more than add color to family stories. It provides a structured way to think about where and how people learned, which institutions shaped their opportunities, and what records those institutions left behind. By incorporating school and educational records into your research, and by reading other sources with an eye to literacy, you can more fully understand both the individual paths your ancestors took and the broader social transformations that framed their lives.

Early School Laws and Town Responsibilities

Massachusetts' early school laws are foundational for understanding how and why ordinary people learned to read and write—and why their lives begin to appear differently in the records. From the mid-17th century onward, colonial leaders treated basic education as a civic and religious duty, not merely a private family matter. Towns, not parents alone, were charged by law with ensuring that children could read scripture and understand the colony's laws, and over time those statutes created administrative routines and records that genealogists can still use.

The best-known milestone is the 1647 "Old Deluder Satan" law, which ordered towns of 50 or more householders to appoint a teacher to instruct children in reading and writing, and towns of 100 or more to establish a grammar school preparing boys for the university. The preamble warned that ignorance of the Scriptures left people vulnerable to deception, making literacy a spiritual safeguard as well as a civic necessity. In practice, the law shifted responsibility upward: instead of relying solely on parents or churches, town governments now had to vote funds, hire and supervise schoolmasters, and sometimes build or maintain schoolhouses.

Town meeting minutes from the late 17th and 18th centuries frequently include articles "to agree with a schoolmaster," "to provide a school for the winter," or "to divide the town into school districts," each naming individuals and sometimes specifying where classes would be held.

Compliance varied by community. Some wealthier or more compact towns quickly met or exceeded the minimum requirements, supporting year-round schools and reporting proudly on them in local histories and later town reports. Others, especially small or scattered agricultural towns, struggled to afford a full-time schoolmaster or to persuade families to spare children from farm labor.

These pressures led to compromises that themselves produced records useful to genealogists. Many towns adopted a "moving school," rotating the teacher among different neighborhoods so that children did not have to travel far; town votes and school committee minutes sometimes specify that the school "be kept one quarter at the north end, one quarter at the south," and so on, revealing intra-town geography and settlement patterns. When towns failed to comply, colonial and later provincial authorities occasionally intervened, and fines or admonitions appear in legislative and court records, showing which places lagged behind.

To manage the growing complexity, towns began appointing dedicated school committees or assigning school oversight to selectmen. These local officials negotiated contracts with teachers—documents that might specify wages, length of term, boarding arrangements, and expectations about curriculum and discipline—and then reported back to town meeting. Surviving contracts and committee reports, preserved in town files or reprinted in 19th-century town histories, often name teachers who may otherwise appear only anonymously in census entries as "schoolmaster" or "schoolmistress." For genealogists, this is a vital connection: if a census or directory lists an ancestor as a teacher, early school records can tie that occupation to a specific district and term, clarifying where they lived and whom they served.

The laws also linked schooling to taxation and thus to the broader machinery of town finance. Money for teachers' wages, fuel, and buildings was raised through local rates, and tax lists sometimes include special "school rates" or note appropriations voted for schools in town meeting. Disputes over the fairness of school funding—between village and outlying districts, or among ratepayers with and without children—occasionally surfaced in town or even county records, leaving behind petitions and protests that can shed light on family interests and alignments.

A farmer who signs a petition complaining that his remote neighborhood receives too few months of schooling for its share of taxes might also be one of the men who later spearheads creating a new district or, in time, a separate town.

For researchers, the key insight is that early school laws wove education into town government in a way that generated three main kinds of sources: town-level deliberations (meeting minutes and school committee reports), financial records (appropriations and special school rates), and personnel documents (teacher contracts and hiring decisions). These records are rarely indexed under individual children's names, but they contextualize an ancestor's access to education and can directly name adult ancestors as teachers, committee members, or prominent advocates for or against particular school arrangements.

When you know that a town was above the statutory threshold for a grammar school in a given decade, you also know that there *should* have been provision for Latin and advanced studies—and that sons from families with the means and ambition to pursue further schooling could have used that pathway to Harvard or other colleges.

By anchoring your research in the framework of these early laws, you not only uncover new record sets but also gain a sharper sense of what literacy and schooling likely looked like in your ancestors' daily lives. A signature "by mark" on an early deed may be less surprising in a town repeatedly fined for neglecting its school obligations; a cluster of teachers and ministers emerging from a particular village can be seen as the fruit of a long-standing local commitment to education recorded in generations of town meeting votes. In this way, "early school laws and town responsibilities" becomes a practical research lens: every time you identify a time and place for your ancestor, you can ask what the law then required of the town, what the town actually did, and where the resulting traces might still be found.

The Rise of Common Schools, Normal Schools, and High Schools

The 19th century marked a remarkable transformation in Massachusetts education, as the early colonial commitments to rudimentary schooling evolved into a robust, tax-supported system aimed at educating all children. This transformation was driven largely by the common school movement, which sought to make public education accessible, universal, and increasingly standardized—a vision championed by leaders like Horace Mann, who earned the state the nickname "the Mother of American Public Education." For genealogists, records from common schools, normal schools (teacher-training institutions), and high schools open new avenues for placing ancestors in educational contexts while revealing broader social changes affecting families and communities.

The Common School Movement and Public Education

The common school idea spread widely after Horace Mann's appointment as Secretary of the Massachusetts Board of Education in 1837. Mann's annual reports not only documented the state of education but advocated longer terms, better-trained teachers, compulsory attendance laws, and endowed school funds funded by local taxes. Common schools emphasized the "three Rs" alongside moral education, viewed as essential for preparing informed voters and responsible citizens in a republic.

Massachusetts towns responded to these reforms by appointing school committees with explicit authority to oversee multiple districts or grades, hire teachers, and manage financial appropriations. Town reports often include school sections documenting expenditures on books, salaries, and schoolhouse maintenance. Registers of enrolled pupils, attendance books, and teacher contracts—the archives of many towns preserve at least some of these—place children and young adults squarely in an educational setting. These records are invaluable for genealogists, especially when other vital records may be missing or sparse. Extended attendance over multiple years can provide a chronological anchor; teacher names might link to other towns if the teacher moved; disagreements or petitions recorded in meeting minutes, or court records reflect local debates that affected schooling access.

Normal Schools: Professionalizing Teaching

One of the radical innovations in Massachusetts education was the establishment of normal schools—institutions dedicated to training teachers. The first normal school opened in Lexington in 1839, soon followed by others in Framingham, Westfield, and Bridgewater. These schools offered rigorous coursework in pedagogy, moral philosophy, and subject-area preparation, elevating teaching from a transient or informal job to a professional career for many women and men. Normal school catalogs and graduation lists document course enrollments and teaching placements afterward, offering rich genealogical data rarely found in civil records. They may list students' birthplaces, prior schools, and employment histories, enabling researchers to trace teacher migration and career trajectories across towns and decades.

Marriage often ended or altered women's teaching careers—reflecting social norms of the era—and normal school records sometimes capture this transition, either directly (noting a graduate's resignation or marriage) or indirectly by showing graduates disappear from teaching registers. For genealogists, these documents help fill the common gap where daughters vanish from census enumerations after marrying, offering insights into education, work, and mobility that complement family narratives.

High Schools and Secondary Education

By the mid-19th century, regional and urban high schools began to appear, fueling upward mobility for many Massachusetts families. Unlike common schools, which provided basic literacy and numeracy, high schools offered classical curriculums with Latin and Greek, sciences, commercial subjects, and later vocational training. Attendance was selective—limited by geography, social class, and gender—but rapidly expanded, especially in larger cities and towns.

High school records include entrance registers, graduation lists, and yearbooks—by the late 19th century, yearbooks became common and are now invaluable for their photographs, club and sports rosters, and short biographical notes. Because high schools often served as communal centers, especially in immigrant neighborhoods, these records link education with social networks, helping genealogists understand connections among peers, siblings, and neighbors beyond mere household listings. Tracking a family's presence in these records illuminates educational attainment and, by extension, economic opportunity.

Education as a Social Index and Mobility Marker

Cumulatively, the rise of common schools, normal schools, and high schools reflects deeper social changes in Massachusetts: expansion of tax-based public services, increased expectation of female and male education, urbanization and immigration pressures, and the democratization of knowledge. School attendance became a key marker of social status and opportunity, shaping family decisions about child labor, marriage, and migration.

Genealogically, these educational records allow researchers to pinpoint children's whereabouts and ages more accurately when census data is ambiguous, to verify parent-child relationships through school registers, and to identify educators who played roles beyond the classroom, such as local clerks or civic leaders. Furthermore, when integrated with church, town, and employment records, educational documentation enriches narratives about efforts toward upward mobility, cultural assimilation, and community investment.

Massachusetts education records from the common school movement onward thus provide genealogists with layers of detail not only about when and where people learned but how schooling intersected with family, community, and economic history. These nuanced records help family historians trace ancestors' paths through the evolving opportunities of a transformative era.

Case study sketch: a young woman born in 1885 in a Berkshire town appears as "teacher" in the 1910 census. By locating her in the Westfield State Normal School catalog, a genealogist can confirm her training, see her listed among graduates with her hometown, and then track school committee reports showing where she taught. A high school yearbook from a town where she later worked may include her photograph and a brief description. These educational records, integrated with vital records and census entries, turn a one-word occupational label into a clear career trajectory.

Higher Education and New Kinds of Records

Massachusetts has long been a national leader in higher education, from Harvard College (founded 1636) through the expansion of liberal arts colleges, technical institutes, professional schools, and public universities that defined the state's 20th-century identity. These institutions not only trained ministers, lawyers, and professionals but also generated distinctive records—matriculation registers, alumni directories, commencement programs, student newspapers, fraternity and club rosters, and faculty catalogs—that offer genealogists unparalleled insights into ancestors' networks, aspirations, and life transitions. Unlike K-12 records, which focus on basic attendance and discipline, higher education documentation often captures personality, achievements, and future trajectories, turning a census occupation like "student" or "clerk" into a fuller portrait of ambition and connection.

Colonial Foundations: Harvard and Early Colleges

Higher education in Massachusetts began with Harvard College, chartered to train a learned clergy and civil leadership for the new settlements. Admission required Latin proficiency (typically from grammar schools), and students—almost exclusively young men from established families—pursued a classical curriculum. Harvard's records from the 17th and 18th centuries include entrance books (noting preparation and guarantors), class lists, demerit books (detailing infractions from tardiness to gambling), commencement records naming degrees and sometimes hometowns, and alumni association materials. For genealogists, these sources anchor early colonial elites: a Harvard graduate listed as "of Ipswich" might lead back to town records confirming family origins, while demerit entries reveal youthful scrapes or associations that surface later in court files.

Other early colleges—Williams (1793), Amherst (1821), Bowdoin (Maine, but with Massachusetts ties)—followed similar models, preserving class rolls, oration lists from commencements, and alumni sketches. These records often note students' preparatory academies, family connections, and postwar careers (ministry, law, medicine), helping researchers trace paths from rural grammar schools to urban professions. Women were excluded until the 19th century, but some early women's seminaries (e.g., Mount Holyoke Seminary, 1837) kept parallel documentation, listing pupils, sponsors, and later teaching placements—crucial for daughters who pursued education as a profession.

19th-Century Expansion: Liberal Arts, Technical Institutes, and Professional Schools

The 19th century saw explosive growth. Liberal arts colleges like Tufts (1852), Boston University (1869), and Wellesley (1870, women's) democratized access somewhat, admitting students from merchant and professional families. Technical education emerged with MIT (1861), Rensselaer ties, and Worcester Polytechnic, reflecting industrial demands. Theological seminaries (Andover, Newton) and professional schools (Harvard Law 1817, Harvard Medical 1782, Boston College Law) proliferated, each generating specialized records: law school moot court results, medical theses, seminary ordination rolls.

Key genealogical sources include:

- Entrance and matriculation registers: Names, ages, birthplaces, parents' occupations/residences, preparatory schools—gold for verifying parentage and prior locations.

- Class catalogs and annuals: Roommates, club memberships (debating societies, literary groups), academic standing.

- Student newspapers and yearbooks: Articles on pranks, elections, athletics; photos by the 1880s; "prophecies" predicting futures.

- Alumni directories: Career summaries, marriages, deaths, often with hometowns and relatives listed.

- Fraternity/sorority records: Pledge lists, events, blackball votes revealing social networks.

For example, a Tufts yearbook might show an ancestor as "class orator" with roommates from the same mill town, explaining later business partnerships; an MIT catalog could list a father's engineering firm as sponsor, linking education to family enterprise.

20th-Century Boom: Public Universities, Community Colleges, and Access

Post-WWII, the GI Bill supercharged enrollment at UMass (system expanded), state colleges (Bridgewater, Framingham), and community colleges (50+ by 2000s). Catholic institutions like Boston College (1863), Holy Cross (1843), and Notre Dame-affiliated schools served immigrant-descended students; women's colleges like Radcliffe (Harvard affiliate) and Simmons preserved women's paths amid coeducation debates.

Records evolved: ROTC rosters (WWII/Cold War), veterans' lists, diversity initiatives (1960s+). Privacy laws (FERPA post-1974) restrict recent transcripts, but alumni magazines, reunion books, digitized newspapers, and online databases (e.g., Ancestry's college yearbooks) remain open. Black students at historically white schools appear in NAACP files or affirmative action reports, women in sorority rushes or dean's lists.

Practical Research: Navigating Higher Ed Records

Start with era/institution fit: Harvard for 17th-19th elites; state normals/community colleges for mid-20th working-class. Key repositories: university archives (Harvard's Pusey Library, MIT's), NEHGS/AmericanAncestors (yearbooks), FamilySearch (catalogs). Cross-reference: a "college student" in 1920 census matches a Brown University annual; alumni notes confirm marriage/job.

Case sketch: 1890 MIT freshman from Lowell (entrance book notes textile-engineer father) joins engineering club (yearbook photo); alumni directory lists 1920s Raytheon job, 1950s suburb. Links family migration, career, Route 128 rise.

Higher education records thus illuminate ambition, networks, and mobility, complementing vital/deed trails with personal/social data. They humanize ancestors as students, debaters, athletes—bridging "name on a list" to an individual who lived university life.

Economic Foundations: Agriculture, Fishing, Industry, and Trade

Massachusetts' economy evolved from subsistence farming and coastal fishing through maritime trade and early manufacturing to industrial dominance and modern innovation, each phase creating distinct records that reveal ancestors' occupations, wealth, mobility, and networks. These economic activities did not exist in isolation from political or religious structures; town meetings voted on fences and fisheries, churches hosted trade guilds, courts resolved merchant disputes. For genealogists, economic records—deeds, tax valuations, customs ledgers, payrolls, account books—complement vital and church sources by showing *how* families sustained themselves, *where* they worked, and *why* they moved, often providing physical descriptions, associates, and asset inventories absent elsewhere.

Agriculture: Land, Labor, and Rural Persistence

Agriculture formed the economic bedrock of Massachusetts for over two centuries, sustaining inland towns, supporting coastal fisheries, and even persisting amid industrial growth in places like the Connecticut Valley and Berkshire hills. Farms were rarely monocultures; mixed operations—grain, livestock, dairy, orchards, vegetables—fed families, supplied local markets, and fueled exports like cheese and hay. For genealogists, agricultural records reveal not just wealth and status but daily realities: who tilled which fields, how families divided inheritances, and why some stayed rural while kin sought factory wages. Land deeds, tax lists, probate inventories, and farm censuses create a dense web of evidence that anchors rural ancestors in specific places and economic roles.

Land as the Core Asset: Deeds, Grants, and Divisions

Ownership of farmland was the primary measure of security and influence. Early colonial towns allocated "house lots," meadow rights, and upland via proprietors' records or town grants, often specifying acreage, boundaries by neighbors' lands ("east of John Smith's barn"), and conditions like improvements within years. These entries in town books place newcomers precisely: "Granted unto Thomas Hale 20 acres near the great pond, 1648." As generations passed, deeds in county registries formalized sales, mortgages, and partitions, with wives often releasing dower rights—revealing marriages otherwise unrecorded.

Sequential deed analysis reconstructs farm histories. A 1720s purchase of "40 acres improved" might expand via 1750s acquisitions from neighbors or heirs, peak in a 1780s valuation, then fragment through 19th-century divisions among sons (or daughters if no sons survived). Quitclaims among siblings clarify inheritance without probate; mortgages signal hard times, foreclosures economic distress. Women appear as grantors (post-widowhood), witnesses (kin networks), or in dower clauses; Indigenous land losses surface in colonial patents referencing prior Native use.

Taxation: Valuations and Rates Revealing Prosperity

Colonial "country rates" and provincial "valuations" (e.g., 1754, 1771, 1780, 1784) apportioned taxes by real estate (acres, buildings), personal property (horses, cattle, swine), and trade goods, creating snapshots of rural economies. A prosperous yeoman might list "150 acres, barn 30x20, 8 oxen, 12 cows"; a marginal tenant "no real, 2 cows." Printed or manuscript lists, often town-organized, distinguish freeholders from laborers and track changes over decades—vital for differentiating same-name families.

State and federal agricultural schedules (1840s–1880s) deepen this: 1850/1860 federal censuses detail farm values, acreage improved/unimproved, livestock numbers, yields (bushels corn, tons hay), machinery. Massachusetts state censuses (1855, 1865) add similar data. These quantify success: a farm growing from 50 to 120 acres suggests thrift; dairy specialization (cows-to-milk ratio) hints at market ties to Boston. Paupers or "farm laborers" in censuses rarely own land but board with owners, explaining boardinghouse-like households.

Labor: Family, Hired Hands, Enslaved, and Indentured

Farm work relied on family labor, supplemented by hires, apprentices, and bound people. Probate inventories list "Negro man Jack" valued at £50 alongside oxen, confirming enslaved presence even in small farms; manumissions or bills of sale appear in deeds/courts. Indentures bind orphans or poor children "until 21" for farm chores, naming guardians/masters—key for non-vital parentage proofs. Hired hands surface in overseers' accounts (town poor farm labor), daybooks (hours/weeds hoed), or 1850+ census "farm laborers" with boarder status.

Women contributed via dairying, poultry, gardens; widows often continue farms, appearing as "administratrix" in probate or tax ratables. Town records note contracts: "Widow Hale to keep town oxen, £5 annum." Seasonal hires (haymakers, shearers) cluster in account books of general stores doubling as farm suppliers.

Town Governance and Agricultural Regulation

Towns regulated farming via bylaws: fence viewers inspected boundaries (fines for "insufficient"), hog reeves controlled swine, pound keepers impounded strays—all elected offices naming locals. Votes on wolf bounties, seed distributions, or "commons" grazing list claimants. Poor farms (town-owned) generated ledgers: inmates' labor, overseers' auctions of produce, binding out children—revealing indigent farmers' fates.

Persistence Amid Change: 19th–20th Century Rural Life

Industrialization drew youth to mills, but farms adapted: truck gardening near cities, tobacco/nursery in valleys, dairies on rail lines. 1880s Grange records (Patrons of Husbandry) list members petitioning rail rates; 20th-century milk cooperatives, USDA censuses track survivors. Suburbanization preserved some via zoning; conservation restrictions now protect heirlooms.

Research Strategies for Agricultural Ancestors

1. Start with place/time: Town incorporation date → proprietors' grants; county formation → deeds.
2. Layer valuations/censuses: Track acreage/livestock changes across decades.
3. Probe probate/deeds: Inventories for assets/labor; sequences for expansions/divisions.
4. Mine town minutiae: Fence viewers, poor farm ledgers for marginal names.
5. Digitize/cross-reference: AmericanAncestors (valuations), FamilySearch (ag schedules), local societies (daybooks).

Case Study: 1754 valuation shows Josiah Smith (120 acres, 10 cattle, Northampton); 1784 deed partitions to sons; 1850 census grandson (80 acres dairy, 15 cows). Links generations, explains stability vs. mill migration.

Agriculture records humanize rural persistence: petitions against wolf depredations, dower fights over meadows, inventories blending plowshares with family Bibles. They show families as economic units navigating soil, markets, kin—core to Massachusetts' enduring rural thread.

Fishing and Maritime Economy: Salt Cod, Whales, and Global Reach

Massachusetts' coastal communities—such as Gloucester, New Bedford, Marblehead, and Provincetown—built a globally influential maritime economy anchored in fishing, whaling, and international trade. Rooted in the abundant cod fisheries of the Grand Banks, the colonial and early American fishing industry evolved into a complex network of seafaring ventures with far-reaching economic and genealogical significance. The industry left behind an array of maritime records—crew lists, ship registries, customs logs, insurance policies, whaling voyage accounts—that provide genealogists with detailed evidence of ancestors' occupations, residences, voyages, networks, and sometimes physical descriptions, often absent elsewhere in the documentation landscape.

Salt Cod Fishing and Coastal Communities

The cod fishery was the economic lifeblood of many Massachusetts fishing towns from early colonial times. Fishermen ventured seasonally to the Grand Banks, drying and salting cod for export to the Caribbean, Europe, and American colonies, fueling an export trade that underpinned local prosperity. Crew lists from fishing vessels include names, ages, places of residence, and sometimes births or occupations, enabling genealogists to track individual mariners across voyages and towns. Ship registration records and customs logs provide technical details about vessels, owners, and cargoes—offering clues to family economic standing and business connections.

Coastal town records complement marine sources, documenting fishing-related occupations in city directories, tax lists, and census enumerations. Shore-based roles—shipbuilders, coopers, merchants, fish processors—appear in local business directories or guild records. Mutual aid societies and maritime benevolent funds, such as the Gloucester Fishermen's Widow and Orphan Fund, generated membership lists, petitions, and financial assistance ledgers that are invaluable for reconstructing family and community support networks among seafarers and their dependents.

Whaling: Nantucket and New Bedford's Global Industry

From the late 18th into the 19th century, Massachusetts towns like Nantucket and New Bedford rose to dominance as centers of the American whaling industry, exploiting whales for oil, baleen, and other products. Whaling voyage logs, held in maritime museums and archives, detail crew rosters, ship movements, kills, and cargo returns. The "lay system" recorded the shares of profits allotted to captains, mates, harpooners, and crew, often including detailed lists of expenses, contracts, and payments; such financial documents connect individual labor to family income and community status.

Maritime insurance records from societies like the Salem Marine Insurance Company or Boston Marine Insurance Company include policies, claims, and surveys describing vessels and losses, highlighting risks faced by families that were dependent on whaling. Crew lists sometimes include physical descriptions, helping distinguish men with common names. Widows' pension records provide genealogists the names of deceased sailors, birthplaces, and proof of service, complementing census and vital records.

Maritime Trade, Shipping, and Port Records

Massachusetts' ports functioned as hubs of international trade, importing goods—from sugar, molasses, and rum to textiles and hardware—and exporting fish, timber, and manufactured goods. Customs house records, starting in the colonial period and expanding post-1789 under federal law, document ship arrivals and departures, cargo manifests, duties paid, and owners and captains' identities. These documents allow genealogists to trace family members' participation in trade, ownership stakes, and even transatlantic family movements.

Shipping company ledgers and merchant account books chronicle business dealings, store credit, loans, and ship outfitting expenses. Surviving retail and wholesale ledgers reveal consumer patterns tied to maritime income, illuminating how families balanced maritime work with shore-based economies. Port registries record pilots, harbor masters, and customs officials, individuals often active in town governance and social institutions.

Labor, Diversity, and Maritime Communities

Maritime economies were multicultural and layered. Free and enslaved Black sailors were significant in fishing and whaling crews; Native Americans served as guides, pilots, or crewmen. Immigrant communities, particularly the Irish in the 19th century, populated waterfront neighborhoods and maritime professions. Church and benevolent association records linked to maritime professions provide additional genealogical clues about ethnicity, religion, and social networks.

Women played crucial roles as merchants, boardinghouse keepers, fish processors, or fundraisers for widows and orphans. Widows of fishermen often appeared in town welfare records or fishing benevolent societies' ledgers. Court cases over wage disputes, contracts, or salvage captures supplement marine source narratives and may include testimony from family members.

Integrating Maritime Records into Family Research

Genealogists approaching maritime ancestors should:

- Identify the home port or residence, then locate crew lists, ship registries, and customs documents linked to that place and period.
- Consult local historical societies or maritime museums holding whaling logs, insurance policies, and benevolent fund records.
- Use city directories and tax lists to place shore-based roles—merchants, coopers, shipwrights.
- Explore court records for labor disputes or probate inventories noting maritime tools or shares.

Cross-referencing helps resolve common issues with common names or sporadic service. A fisherman "John Brown" in a Gloucester crew list gains context with a matching Boston customs clearance and a probate inventory listing fishing gear. A whaler missing from census records might be found in pension files or marine insurance claims.

Massachusetts's maritime economy shaped lives not only through employment and wealth but by connecting coastal families to global currents—routes to the Caribbean, Europe, Africa, and the Pacific. Its records allow genealogists to trace these complex journeys in impressive depth, moving beyond abstract economic history to lived family experience across oceans and generations.

Trade and Commerce: Merchants, Shops, and Urban Exchange

Massachusetts' towns and cities flourished as centers of commerce from the colonial era onward, with merchants, shopkeepers, artisans, and transporters creating vibrant economies that linked local consumers with global markets. Trade networks spanned the Atlantic world, while local shops supplied daily needs and built complex credit relationships. For genealogists, records of trade and commerce—merchant account books, customs entries, city directories, probate inventories, court suit files—offer crucial insights into ancestors' occupations, social standing, and community ties.

These sources complement vital records and land transactions by documenting the economic fabric that sustained families and neighborhoods.

Merchants and Maritime Trade

Boston, Salem, Newburyport, and other port cities exported fish, lumber, and manufactured goods while importing sugar, rum, textiles, and hardware, fueling both local consumption and wider colonial economies. Merchants generated customs house records, shipping registers, and insurance policies. Customs entries detailed voyages, cargo manifests, tonnage, and duties, allowing genealogists to link surnames to specific ships and trade routes. Marine insurance records documented vessel ownership and losses; these records sometimes survive in company or maritime museum archives, revealing business relationships and risks traders managed. Probate records often included merchant inventories of goods and receivables, illustrating balance sheets that shaped family fortunes and economic influence.

Shops and Credit Networks

Within towns and cities, general stores and specialized shops formed economic lifelines. Storekeepers maintained ledgers documenting credit extended to customers, often local families, recording purchases of essentials like flour, sugar, cloth, tools, and rum. These account books, some preserved in historical society collections, illuminate household economies, consumption preferences, and payment patterns. They may mention kinship ties, apprenticeships, or migration stories embedded in transactions, such as a widow charged for "yard goods" who later entered relief registers or probate files.

City directories, starting in Boston in 1789 and spreading to other towns, become key sources as indexes of merchants, tradesmen, and shopkeepers, listing occupations and addresses. These directories help pinpoint when families moved uptown, down to waterfront streets, or into new commercial districts. Before directories, newspapers' trade advertisements provide limited but useful snapshots, often naming merchants, product lines, and business partnerships.

Artisans, Guilds, and Trade Societies

Artisans and craftsmen—blacksmiths, coopers, shoemakers, tailors—populated towns in significant numbers, creating a network of producers whose products fed both local and export markets. Record types include apprenticeship indentures, guild or trade association membership lists, and petitions for trade licenses. These documents often name both master and apprentice, apprenticeship length, and sometimes fees paid, which helps document informal education and skills transmission outside formal schooling. Trade society minutes and benefit fund ledgers (e.g., Mechanics' Associations) illustrate community among workers, strike actions, and welfare efforts during industrial transitions.

Courts and Commerce: Suits and Debt

Commercial life generated frequent disputes resolved in courts: debt suits involving unpaid accounts, contracts over shipments, land or property leases, and partnership disagreements. Court docket books and suit files detail claims, witnesses, counterclaims, and verdicts. Debt suits, in particular, often itemize goods sold and purchased, revealing what households consumed and the financial pressures they faced.

A court case where a shoemaker sues a customer for unpaid boots may name material suppliers and pattern sources; a merchant's suit over a lost cargo shipment explains risks shared among investors. Probate disputes sometimes arose over unfinished business, such as ongoing store credit balances or unsold merchandise inventories, adding complex layers to family financial histories.

Genealogical Applications and Research Strategies

To incorporate trade and commerce records into family histories, genealogists should:

- Search customs records and vessel registries for involvement in maritime commerce.

- Explore merchant account books or store ledgers in local historical societies or archives to track household consumption and credit ties.

- Use city directories to place ancestors by occupation and location over time.

- Investigate guild and trade association records to document apprenticeships and social networks.

- Examine court and probate files for commercial conflicts and business inventories that reveal asset distribution and family involvement.

By integrating these economic records, researchers gain insight not only into what ancestors did for a living but how their economic activities shaped family fortunes, social relationships, and migration patterns. The layers of trade and commerce connect household economies to broader regional and global markets, turning the genealogical story from isolated names to dynamic participants in Massachusetts' economic development.

How Political, Religious, and Social Evolution Shaped Record Creation

The intertwining of political authority, religious institutions, and social structures in Massachusetts played a defining role in shaping the documentary landscape genealogists now navigate. These evolving forces determined not only which records were created but also what they contained, who was included or excluded, and how long the records were preserved. Understanding this dynamic is essential for interpreting sources accurately and for recognizing both the silences and the emphases within the archival record.

Political Authority and Legal Mandates

From the earliest colonial period, Massachusetts authorities—whether town governments, colonial legislatures, or later state bodies—mandated the creation and maintenance of specific record types to enforce law, taxation, and governance. Town meeting minutes, tax lists, vital records, court dockets, and militia rolls reflect the jurisdiction and priorities of local and higher authorities. For example, the statutory requirement instituted in 1841 for state-level vital registration centralized birth, marriage, and death records, standardizing data collection but also creating parallel documentation alongside town registers. Courts needed records to adjudicate disputes, collect debts, and enforce contracts, generating files rich in narrative detail. Political reforms—such as expanding suffrage, establishing public schools, or enacting poor relief laws—prompted new administrative records, including school committee minutes, welfare rolls, and voter lists.

However, political imperatives also led to exclusions. Voting was restricted initially to property-owning male church members; enslaved and Indigenous peoples appeared selectively or under duress in legal records; marginalized populations were less likely to generate stable property or tax records. When jurisdictions changed—due to county realignments, town incorporations, or shifting legislative frameworks—records were scattered or duplicated, demanding careful tracking from genealogists.

Religious Institutions and Social Boundaries

Religious organizations were both record creators and social boundary enforcers. Puritan congregations kept membership rolls, baptismal and marriage registers, and discipline minutes, documenting spiritual and social inclusion or exclusion. Over time, pluralism and immigration introduced Catholic, Jewish, Orthodox, and diverse Protestant denominational records, often multilingual and maintained independently from civil authorities. These religious records preserve not only vital events but also social networks—godparents, sponsoring families, fraternal affiliations—that transcend civil boundaries.

Religiously motivated social control influenced record creation by prompting documentation of conformity and deviance: church discipline records, court cases against heresy or immorality, temperance society rosters, and charity rolls all surface in the archives. At the same time, religious groups provided welfare and education, creating records such as parish poor relief accounts and school registers that supplement and sometimes supplant official municipal documents.

Social Structures and Evolving Record Types

Class, ethnicity, gender, and race shaped both who was recorded and how. Elite families appear in property deeds, legislative petitions, probate inventories, and college matriculation lists. Working-class and immigrant families often surface in labor contracts, factory payrolls, fraternal society rolls, and parish records. Women's records are often relational—appearing as daughters, wives, widows—while institutional expansions over the 19th and 20th centuries gradually increased the visibility of women as individuals in education and civic documents.

The rise of public education introduced an array of new record types—from school attendance rolls to high school yearbooks—providing granular detail on youth, literacy, and social mobility. Industrialization and urbanization produced business records, union minutes, and directories that track occupational shifts and migrations. These records embody demographic and social change yet also reflect biases; for example, many minorities have "silent" periods in vital registrations but appear in church or mutual aid society records.

Integration and Interpretation

The genealogist's task is to interpret records not only as isolated documents but as products of these overlapping forces. A birth record exists because the town clerk was required to keep it; a church admission roll records both spiritual belonging and civic standing; a court file reflects the intersection of law, moral norms, and economic relations. Recognizing the political and religious contexts clarifies why certain documents emphasize property and lineage, others community membership or conformity, and still others economic transactions or social conflict.

Moreover, this understanding guides a genealogist's research strategies: knowing that a non-church member might be absent from early church registers but appear in town poor relief accounts; that a millworker's family might be traced through factory records and union documents as well as census and vital records; or that a family's religious affiliation shifts across generations, creating multiple parallel record trails.

In the Massachusetts genealogical landscape, political, religious, and social evolution is not just background—it is the framework that explains the existence, the content, and the interrelation of records. By situating ancestors within their evolving legal and social worlds, researchers can navigate these sources more confidently, overcome gaps and silences, and reconstruct lives with greater depth and accuracy.

PART II: The Counties, Cites & Towns of Massachusetts

Chapter 3
Barnstable County

Nestled at the southeastern tip of Massachusetts, Barnstable County forms the crooked arm of Cape Cod—a landscape of shifting dunes, tidal marshes, kettle ponds, and windswept beaches that has captivated explorers, settlers, and modern visitors alike. Spanning from the bustling gateway town of Sandwich in the west to the bohemian outpost of Provincetown at the northern tip, this county of roughly 400 square miles embodies the resilience of New England's coastal frontier. Established on June 2, 1685, by the Plymouth Colony General Court as one of its original three counties (alongside Plymouth and Bristol), Barnstable initially encompassed the towns of Sandwich (incorporated 1637), Yarmouth (1639), Barnstable (1639), and Eastham (1646), with the village of Barnstable designated as the shire town for its central location and emerging prominence. For genealogists and family historians, this history is more than a backdrop; it is the key to unlocking records shaped by isolation, maritime necessity, and layered Indigenous and European legacies, from proprietors' land grants to whaling logs and Wampanoag deeds.

Indigenous Foundations: Wampanoag Stewards of the Land

Long before the arrival of European settlers, the lands that now comprise Barnstable County were home to a vibrant and sophisticated Indigenous people—the Wampanoag Nation—whose relationship to the environment and each other reflects centuries of complex social, cultural, and economic systems. The Wampanoag, part of a broader confederation of Algonquian-speaking peoples across southeastern Massachusetts, Rhode Island, and parts of Connecticut, managed the Cape Cod peninsula's rich but challenging landscape with an intricate balance of seasonal resource use, spiritual stewardship, and communal governance. Understanding these Indigenous foundations is essential for genealogists seeking to trace Native ancestors, interpret early colonial records, and appreciate the enduring cultural presence influencing the region's history.

The Ecological and Cultural Landscape

The geography of Barnstable County presented diverse micro-environments: fertile salt marshes, dense pine and oak forests, sandy dunes, kettle ponds, and an extensive coastline abundant in shellfish, fish, and migratory birds. The Wampanoag adapted to this mosaic through seasonal movements carefully designed to optimize food gathering and social interaction. During the warmer months, families and extended kin groups dispersed to coastal villages such as Nantucket, Martha's Vineyard, and Eastham (part of the Wampanoag homeland), fishing, harvesting shellfish, and cultivating native crops like maize, beans, and squash. In autumn and winter, they moved inland to more protected areas, hunting deer, small game, and trading with neighboring groups.

Their villages were not mere temporary encampments but well-established, semi-permanent settlements with wooden longhouses, wigwams, and communal facilities. Archaeological finds, oral traditions, and early colonial accounts reveal a people skilled in crafting toolsets from stone, bone, and wood; practicing spiritual ceremonies tied to the cycles of nature; and organizing leadership around sachems (tribal chiefs) and councils who made decisions for the welfare of their communities. The exercise of sovereignty was embedded in cultural practices linking land, spirituality, and diplomacy.

Land Use, Stewardship, and Ownership Concepts

Contrasting sharply with later European notions of land as commodity, the Wampanoag viewed land through a lens of stewardship and communal benefit. Seasonal open hunting, fishing, and planting rights were distributed among families or clans, with clear understandings regarding access and use shaped by customary law enforced through community consensus and sachem authority. Important sites such as shellfish beds, freshwater springs, and sacred groves were protected and managed appropriately.

The arrival of English settlers upset these delicate balances. Initial relationships involved reciprocal gift-giving and trade—deer hides for metal tools, for example—but misunderstandings over property rights grew acute. English legal frameworks failed to recognize Indigenous stewardship models, treating land as alienable property to be purchased or seized. The 1658 and 1670 Mashpee deeds, in which the Wampanoag secured or reaffirmed reserves recognized by colonial authorities, represent critical moments of negotiation and struggle over territory and autonomy amid pressure from expanding European settlement.

Early European Contact and Consequences

The first sustained European contact began with Bartholomew Gosnold's 1602 exploration and was solidified with the Pilgrims' landing in 1620 at Provincetown Harbor. Wampanoag leaders such as Massasoit met Plymouth settlers, forming alliances that were essential for early colonial survival. However, European diseases—smallpox, measles, influenza—devastated Indigenous populations, with mortality rates exceeding 90% in some estimates, fracturing social structures before large-scale settlement.

The Wampanoag town of Mashpee, an inland community within Barnstable County borders, became a site of concerted Indigenous resilience, maintaining land and cultural identity through petitioning colonial authorities and adapting to missionary efforts. The establishment of "praying towns," including Mashpee, represented attempts by English missionaries to convert Native people to Christianity, often linked to regulation of Indigenous governance and lifestyles. While these missions brought new religious practices and schooling, they were also tools for cultural transformation and assimilation.

King Philip's War and Its Aftershocks

From 1675 to 1676, King Philip's War wrenched the region, pitting Wampanoag and allied tribes under Metacom (King Philip) against English settlers striving to assert dominance. The conflict devastated Indigenous communities and led to widespread loss of life, displacement, and loss of lands. Survivors faced imprisonment, enslavement, or forced relocation, yet maintained cultural identity in remnant communities such as Mashpee and Aquinnah (on Martha's Vineyard).

For genealogists, this period complicates research: Indigenous families may appear sporadically in town, court, and colonial records, sometimes under anglicized names or as wards of the state. Land deeds, guardianship records, and colonial petitions documenting Mashpee Wampanoag land tenure are critical but must be approached with sensitivity to Indigenous protocols and oral histories.

Continuity and Contemporary Presence

Despite centuries of dispossession and marginalization, the Wampanoag persist culturally and politically. Modern Mashpee Wampanoag Tribe federal recognition struggles (achieved in 2007 amid contestation) attest to ongoing sovereignty claims rooted in historical documents and traditional knowledge. Contemporary genealogical research increasingly incorporates Indigenous perspectives, seeking to reconstruct family histories through mixed sources, including missionary records, census enumerations, Indian allotment rolls, and DNA evidence, complemented by tribal archives and community collaboration.

Genealogical Guidance

Researchers should approach Wampanoag and broader Indigenous genealogy with attention to:

- Early and mid-colonial deeds recognizing reservations, such as the 1670 Mashpee deed, held at Massachusetts Archives.
- Missionary records, noting baptism, marriage, and membership within praying towns.
- Colonial court and guardianship records reflecting Indigenous legal encounters.
- Oral histories and tribal genealogies, engaging respectfully with contemporary tribal programs.
- Integration with DNA and community-based methods to supplement fragmentary written records.

This multifaceted approach respects the Wampanoag's enduring relationship with Cape Cod while revealing the rich, though often shadowy, genealogical trail left by the earliest stewards of Barnstable County lands.

European Exploration and the Mayflower Moment

The story of Barnstable County's European heritage begins not with permanent settlement but with exploration—voyages that carried English ships along the jagged edges of Cape Cod, setting the stage for some of the earliest sustained contact between Native peoples and European settlers in New England. Among these voyages, the most historically resonant is the Mayflower's landing in Provincetown Harbor in November 1620, an event that shaped not only Massachusetts' colonial development but also the genealogical identity of countless families who trace their roots to this crucible of American history.

Bartholomew Gosnold's 1602 Voyage: Naming and Navigating Cape Cod

Before the Pilgrims, Bartholomew Gosnold sailed the *Concord* in 1602 along the Massachusetts coast in search of fishing grounds and potential settlement sites. His expedition was among the first English ventures to the region and coined the familiar name "Cape Cod," drawn from the abundant fish harvested by the crew. Gosnold's brief landing on Cuttyhunk and exploration of Martha's Vineyard and the mainland coast revealed a landscape rich in resources, with expansive salt marshes and numerous estuaries. The expedition's observations helped set early English expectations about North America's potential, and its charts guided later explorers.

This voyage marked the first recorded English encounters with the Indigenous peoples of the region, including the Wampanoag and Nauset, who greeted the explorers cautiously but participated in exchanges of goods such as furs and corn. Though Gosnold's mission did not establish a colony, it carved a place for Cape Cod in English colonial imagination and provided critical geographical and ethnographic knowledge that informed subsequent ventures.

The Mayflower's Arrival: November 1620 in Provincetown Harbor

Nearly two decades after Gosnold's reconnaissance, the Pilgrims on the *Mayflower* faced treacherous storms that forced them to anchor not at their intended destination in the Hudson River region but in Provincetown Harbor on November 11, 1620 (Old Style calendar). The bay presented a daunting and unfamiliar landscape of narrow harbors, dunes, and dense forests, with Indigenous settlements nearby that were both sources of aid and potential threat.

Impelled by the necessity of survival and governance, the Pilgrim leaders convened a gathering aboard ship, during which 41 male passengers signed the Mayflower Compact. This seminal document established a self-governing "civil body politic," committing signatories to enact just laws for the colony's welfare and laying foundational principles for American democracy. Genealogists track this moment with reverence, knowing that many family legends begin here, while recognizing that the Compact also overlooked the rights and sovereignty of local Native peoples.

The Pilgrims' brief stay in Provincetown involved reconnaissance and difficult interactions with the Nauset tribe. While negotiations and gift exchanges occurred, early clashes were frequent; historical records note that Nauset warriors climbed aboard the *Mayflower*, smoking the ship's lower decks and challenging the newcomers' presence. The pilgrims' exploration eventually led them across Cape Cod Bay to establish Plymouth Colony in December 1620.

Early Interactions and Land Negotiations

Following the establishment of Plymouth Colony, exploratory parties ventured back to Cape Cod, charting land and seeking suitable sites for settlement. Early agreements, such as the 1621 Nauset deed, represent some of the earliest formal land transactions between Native peoples and English colonists in the region. These deeds documented the cession of territory on terms that colonists believed legitimized settlement, though Indigenous understandings of land use and ownership diverged substantially.

These nascent interactions set patterns of trade, alliance, and conflict. Pilgrims relied on Native knowledge for survival, while the Wampanoag engaged in diplomacy to protect their homelands. Yet rising tensions over land, culture, and disease culminated decades later in violent confrontations such as King Philip's War.

Genealogical Implications and Research

For genealogists, this period's records are complex and rich. The Mayflower Compact and its signatories compose a core pillar in many family histories, yet researchers must move beyond hagiography to explore the broader indigenous context, less documented but ever crucial. Documents such as land deeds, colonial court petitions, town records, missionary accounts, and oral histories provide paths to reconstruct the lives of Native people who shaped—and were shaped by—European settlement.

Understanding Cape Cod's early colonial encounters involves tracing intertwined English and Indigenous genealogies, acknowledging cultural transformations wrought by colonization, missionization, and conflict. Early settlers' arrival marked a pivotal moment of contact and change that continues to resonate as genealogical, cultural, and historical touchstones for Barnstable County and Massachusetts as a whole.

Colonial Settlement: Towns, Townspeople, and Town Books

The colonial settlement of Barnstable County reflects a story of religious conviction, economic adaptation, and evolving self-governance in a challenging maritime frontier. Beginning in the 1630s, English settlers—many fleeing religious strife in the Massachusetts Bay Colony or seeking new opportunities—established towns that would become the enduring heart of Cape Cod's social and economic life. These settlements created intricate local governments, church communities, and property systems that produced detailed records essential for genealogists tracing families across centuries of change.

Founding of Cape Cod Towns

The first permanent English town in the region was Sandwich, incorporated in 1637 amid a wave of migration from Plymouth and Massachusetts Bay. Sandwich's settlers included religious dissenters and artisans, such as Richard Warren, who helped introduce ironworking and glass manufacturing to New England. Soon after, Barnstable and Yarmouth were planted (1639), with Eastham (1646) following on the cape's northern shore. These towns were legal entities responsible for organizing settlement, land distribution, defense, and moral oversight. Each incorporated under a colonial charter—a blend of religious covenant and English legal tradition—granting the town the power to hold meetings, elect officers, levy taxes, and maintain order.

Town Governance and Civic Life

Town meetings quickly became the cradle of community governance. Adult male inhabitants attended regular meetings to elect selectmen, constables, fence viewers, and other officials. They voted on budgets for communal projects: road maintenance, poor relief, militia equipment, and school funding. These votes, recorded by town clerks in minutes, document not only political activity but social hierarchies: prominent families often dominated elections, captains and ministers held leadership, and newcomers petitioned for "freemen" status—affording voting rights and land grants.

The town clerk's books are genealogical goldmines. They contain not only vital event entries from infancy through deaths but land grants, common land divisions, highway layouts, and records of disputes like "warnings out" issued to unsettled migrant families. Town books also preserved petitions to higher governments, petitions for the release of persons from the poorhouse, and militia rolls. The survival of such records varies but is often richer in Barnstable and Sandwich than in some other counties, reflecting the early establishment and relative affluence of these communities.

Religion and Social Cohesion

Congregational churches, integral to these towns, served both spiritual and civic functions. Church membership lists and baptismal registers constituted some of the earliest vital records, often predating town birth registries. Ministers influenced not only morality but civic participation, and church discipline records detail social conflicts, including excommunications, marital separations, and indenture arrangements. Dissenting sects such as Quakers and Baptists appeared, sometimes meeting persecution, their records reflecting religious diversity and social tensions.

Economy and Settlement Patterns

Early Barnstable settlers balanced farming with maritime resources—fishing, salt works, small-scale shipbuilding. Town records often note who held which "proprietors' lots," granted meadows, or had rights to plank houses or wharves. Deeds and tax lists trace the rise of family wealth or decline, migration to other Cape towns or mainland Massachusetts, and occasional divisions of property among heirs. The aggregation of these records allows genealogists to trace genealogical families as they grew from founders to multi-generational residents tied to the Cape's unique economy and landscape.

Challenges and Record Preservation

Despite early growth, Barnstable towns faced hardships: harsh winters, poor soil, and conflicts with Native peoples. Wars such as King Philip's War disrupted communities, resulting in property loss and displacement recorded in court and town records. Records also suffered from fires; notably, the 1827 Barnstable courthouse fire destroyed many early documents. Surviving materials are scattered across town halls, Massachusetts Archives, and regional historical societies, underscoring the importance of cross-referencing multiple sources.

Genealogical Application

For genealogists, colonial settlement records of Barnstable County demand a multi-source approach:

- Town books supply vital events, land transactions, and civic participation evidence.
- Church records offer baptismal, marriage, and social discipline data.
- Court and probate records reveal disputes, guardianships, and property divisions.
- Town meeting minutes uncover political roles and community disputes.

Together, they reveal the fabric of early Barnstable life—families forged in a crucible of faith, industry, and governance—and provide a rich foundation for reconstructing lineages tied to Cape Cod's uniquely enduring colonial heritage.

Provincial Era, Revolution, and Early Republic

The transition of Barnstable County from Plymouth Colony into the Province of Massachusetts Bay in 1691 marked the beginning of profound political, economic, and social transformations that reverberated through the 18th and early 19th centuries. This provincial era brought new governance structures, intensified maritime commerce, complex interactions with Indigenous peoples, revolutionary upheavals, and early American nation-building efforts that shaped both the region's identity and the genealogical records ancestors left behind. Understanding this period illuminates how familiar colonial communities adapted to imperial reforms, resisted British control, and engaged in republican experimentations foundational to Massachusetts and the United States.

The 1691 Charter and Provincial Integration

The 1691 royal charter merged the Plymouth Colony, Massachusetts Bay, Nantucket, and Martha's Vineyard into the Province of Massachusetts Bay, imposing a stronger royal governor and council atop colonial self-government. For Barnstable County, this shift meant more formalized courts, new colonial taxes, and expanded bureaucracies, though local town meetings and courts retained significant autonomy. Officials like the royal-appointed judges sometimes clashed with Cape residents, who guarded town prerogatives and religious freedoms rooted in Congregational traditions. Town records from this time show petitions, militia musters, and tax assessments reflecting these layered authorities.

Maritime and Agricultural Economies in Transition

Throughout the 18th century, Barnstable's economy flourished with diversified activities. Salt cod fishing remained vital, with crews sailing seasonally to rich offshore grounds; records of crews, ship logs, and customs entries illustrate the global scope of trade, linking Cape Cod to Caribbean and European markets. Agriculture sustained inland communities, with land deeds and tax valuations depicting farm expansions, partition disputes, and rural persistence.

The mid-century wars—King George's War, French and Indian War—imposed military demands, with muster rolls documenting local militia service. Naval privateering during conflicts provided economic windfalls, reflected in letters of marque, prize court records, and personal papers naming participants and their ventures.

Revolutionary Turmoil and Resistance

Barnstable County played an active role in revolutionary politics. Tensions over British taxes and regulations culminated in local acts of defiance, such as the 1774 confrontation when townspeople barricaded the county courthouse to prevent royal judges from holding court, symbolizing widespread colonial resistance. Men from Barnstable towns enlisted in militia and Continental forces, with rosters, pension applications, and bounty lists preserved in state archives.

The war disrupted maritime and agricultural production; British naval raids burned coastal properties, including villages in Falmouth (now Woods Hole). Post-war, veterans received land grants or pensions, recorded in county documents that enrich genealogical research.

Early Republic: Constitution, Governance, and Social Change

With the 1780 Massachusetts Constitution, Barnstable transitioned into the new Commonwealth framework, establishing elected local offices and state courts that further defined political life. Town meetings persisted as centers of community decision-making, shaping schools, roads, and poor relief. County courts evolved to handle probate, land disputes, and minor criminal matters, producing extensive records.

The early Republic also saw demographic shifts: increased immigration from Ireland and later England, the rise of small towns like Hyannis as maritime and commercial hubs, and gradual industrialization with shipbuilding, whaling, and saltworks prospering. Deeds, directories, vital records, and school registers from this period document expanding family networks and social stratification within Barnstable.

Genealogical Implications

Genealogists researching Barnstable families in the provincial and early American eras benefit from a rich patchwork of sources. Provincial legislative journals, town meeting records, militia rolls, and court files illuminate political loyalties and local governance. Religious dissent and toleration debates may surface in church minutes and disciplinary records, especially with the late 18th-century rise of denominational diversity. Military service records and pension applications connect families to the Revolutionary cause and place ancestors in broader national narratives.

Understanding shifts in jurisdiction and record-keeping—such as town versus county responsibilities, excepted court types, and state centralized vital records initiation in 1841—helps navigate gaps and locate documents. The period's upheavals also produced widow's petitions, indenture contracts, and occasionally orphan guardianships, offering humanizing details of family resilience amid change.

Through the provincial era, revolution, and early Republic, Barnstable County's communities endured and adapted, leaving layered records that tell stories of governance, loyalty, conflict, and renewal critical to reconstructing the genealogical fabric of Cape Cod.

Maritime Golden Age and Industrial Diversification

The 19th century ushered in a maritime golden age for Barnstable County, anchored by the thriving fisheries, whaling expeditions, and expanding coastal trade that connected Cape Cod to the world's oceans. These industries fueled local prosperity, shaped migration patterns, and created rich documentary legacies that remain vital to genealogists studying families bound to the sea. Concurrently, the century saw the beginnings of industrial diversification as some towns laid foundations for manufacturing, artisanal crafts, and new economic ventures, marking transitions from purely maritime economies to mixed industrial societies reflective of broader American transformations.

Maritime Prosperity: Fishing and Whaling

Barnstable County's coastal towns, especially Provincetown, Chatham, and Harwich, became world-renowned for their fishing fleets, which harvested cod, mackerel, and other species from the Grand Banks and beyond. The salt cod industry was the backbone of the economy, with crews working months at sea, producing internationally traded goods essential to the Atlantic economy.

Detailed crew lists, shipping manifests, fishery licenses, and customs house records survive in local archives and federal repositories, naming tens of thousands of fishermen, captains, and merchants. Whaling, although centered in Nantucket and New Bedford just beyond Barnstable's jurisdiction, intersected significantly with Cape Cod's mariners, provisioning their voyages and sustaining local boatyards.

Ship registries and insurance records provide genealogists with information on vessel ownership, construction dates, shipmasters, and losses, revealing economic risk and reward in perilous ocean enterprises. Mutual aid societies and benevolent funds founded by fishing communities granted assistance to widows and orphans, their minutes and membership rolls shedding light on family ties and social solidarity. Pension files for sailors and whalers offer personal descriptions and narratives absent from standard vital records.

Industrial Beginnings: Beyond the Sea

While much of Barnstable County's economy remained maritime, the 19th century saw towns exploring industrial diversification. Limited textile manufacturing emerged around places like Hyannis and Barnstable Village, taking advantage of tidal streams and proximity to raw materials. Small shoe factories, shipbuilding yards, and barrel-making shops supplemented farming and fishing incomes. This transition is preserved in tax records noting new industrial properties, employment censuses capturing factory operatives, and city directories listing burgeoning trades and manufacturers.

The cranberry industry, flourishing in bogs across towns like Harwich and Carver, added a unique agricultural-industrial blend to the county's economy. Cranberry harvests, processing, and shipping generated seasonal employment and economic diversification documented in agricultural censuses, cooperative association minutes, and commercial ledgers.

Transportation and Infrastructure

The construction of railroads and, later, bridges such as the Sagamore and Bourne (1935), began integrating Barnstable more tightly with the mainland economy, enabling easier export of goods and influx of tourists. This infrastructural expansion is reflected in town meeting records authorizing bonds, railroad company files, and road and bridge commission reports — sources that genealogists can use to understand shifting economic landscapes and family mobility.

Impact on Family Life and Records

The maritime golden age and industrial diversification reshaped social structures and genealogical footprints. Families involved in fishing and industry often spread across multiple towns and occupations, their records scattered among maritime logs, factory payrolls, town vital records, and church membership rolls. Migration from purely rural or maritime livelihoods into factory jobs or service roles is traceable through census occupational data, apprenticeship indentures, and union membership lists.

Industrial labor strikes, workers' cooperatives, and fraternal organizations proliferated, generating minutes, rosters, and correspondence that enrich family narratives beyond traditional sources. These layers reveal not only economic activities but social affiliations, ethnic identity, religious commitments, and political leanings.

Genealogical Research Strategies

To navigate this complex economic tapestry, genealogists should:

- Explore maritime logs, customs records, and insurance files for seafaring ancestors.
- Consult tax lists and census schedules for industrial employment patterns.
- Investigate town meeting minutes for authorizations of infrastructure projects affecting economic opportunities.
- Seek labor organization archives and mutual aid society records for working-class family networks.
- Utilize local historical society collections, digitized local newspapers, and cooperation with maritime museums.

Collectively, Barnstable County's maritime golden age and early industrial diversification reflect adaptive economies that sustained and transformed communities. Their records offer genealogists lenses into the hazards and hopes of oceans and factories, weaving family histories into a broader narrative of innovation, resilience, and regional identity along Cape Cod's storied shores.

Modern Era: Tourism, Preservation, and Governance Shifts

Barnstable County's trajectory into the modern era reveals a dynamic adaptation of its coastal legacy, balancing economic diversification, burgeoning tourism, historic preservation, and shifts in governance that have collectively reshaped both the county's communities and its genealogical record landscape. From the early 20th century onward, the rise of automobile travel, the expansion of state infrastructure, and evolving local government structures converged to position Barnstable County not only as a historical bastion of Cape Cod culture but also as a contemporary hub of seasonal migration, conservation, and regional administration.

Tourism's Ascendancy and Economic Transformation

Automobiles and improved bridges, especially the Sagamore and Bourne Bridges completed in 1935, connected Cape Cod more securely to the mainland, triggering a tourism boom that transformed many Barnstable towns into seasonal resorts. Towns like Hyannis, Falmouth, and Chatham experienced sprawling summer populations, leading to the construction of hotels, beaches access points, and cultural attractions. This influx diversified the local economy, promoting retail, hospitality, and real estate development alongside traditional fishing and cranberry farming.

Genealogically, the tourism era introduced new record types: property and tax records reflecting seasonal and vacation home ownership, hotel registers documenting visitors and sometimes seasonal workers, city directories noting temporary residents, and local newspapers chronicling community events and social registers. Tracking ancestors through these materials requires sensitivity to the seasonal nature of residence and an understanding of the dual identities many Cape Codders held as year-round residents and hosts to summer populations.

Historic Preservation and Cultural Identity

As tourism grew, so too did awareness of Barnstable County's distinctive cultural and architectural heritage. The mid-20th century witnessed increased efforts to preserve historic sites, including the 1690 Barnstable jail, colonial meetinghouses, maritime museums, and colonial-era cemeteries. Local historical societies and preservation groups produced extensive documentation—photographs, oral histories, property surveys—that enrich genealogical research with broader context on community identity, family homesteads, and settlement patterns.

Preservation efforts often emphasized the continuity of families and neighborhoods, encouraging the collection and archiving of private papers, diaries, and genealogical manuscripts. These materials bridge the gap between formal government records and personal memory, offering genealogists deep, nuanced insights into Barnstable's social fabric.

Shifts in Governance: Courts, County Administration, and Regional Services

Governance in Barnstable evolved significantly in the 20th century. While town meetings and select boards remained central to local decision-making, many services consolidated at the county level or shifted to state control. The Barnstable Superior Court lost some local authority following statewide judicial reforms in the 1970s, centralizing judicial functions in state-run facilities. The relocation of correctional institutions to Bourne and the development of regional planning commissions reflect a broader trend toward regional governance addressing modern infrastructure, health, and environmental challenges.

These governance shifts impacted record keeping and accessibility. Many court records, once held locally, were transferred or centralized, requiring genealogists to navigate multiple repositories including the Massachusetts Archives and state judiciary records offices. County government files, minutes from county commissioners, and regional service agency reports also became important documents for tracing family interactions with local institutions over the 20th and 21st centuries.

Environmental Conservation and Land Use

Simultaneously, environmental conservation became a hallmark of the Cape region. State and local initiatives protected fragile coastal and wetland ecosystems, influencing land use policies and limiting development in certain areas. Conservation commission records, zoning board minutes, and environmental impact statements document these tensions between growth and preservation, providing genealogists with insights into property transactions, family disputes over land use, and shifting community landscapes.

Genealogical Approaches to the Modern Era

Navigating modern Barnstable County records requires understanding the complexity of seasonal population changes, the overlay of multiple jurisdictions, and expanding types of documentation. Researchers should consult:

- Town and county property and tax records for year-round and seasonal interests.
- Court and state judicial records for 20th-century legal proceedings.
- Local historical society holdings for personal papers and preservation archives.
- Planning board, conservation commission, and zoning files for land use history.

- Newspapers, directories, and membership lists that cover an active tourism and summer resident population.

The modern era highlights the ongoing evolution of Barnstable County as a region rooted in a deep historical legacy but adapting to new economic and social realities. For genealogists, these transformations add layers of documentation and context that illuminate the lives of ancestors navigating rapid change—residents, seasonal visitors, working families, and community leaders alike—in one of Massachusetts' most iconic counties.

Genealogical Treasures and Research Roadmap

Barnstable County, with its distinctive blend of Indigenous heritage, colonial roots, maritime economy, and modern transformations, offers genealogists a rich, albeit complex, tapestry of records and research avenues. Its genealogical landscape mirrors the layered history of Cape Cod—from Wampanoag stewardship through Pilgrim settlement, colonial municipal governance, revolutionary fervor, maritime golden ages, and ongoing adaptation to 20th- and 21st-century socio-economic shifts. By understanding the variety and provenance of surviving documents, researchers can develop effective roadmaps to reconstruct family histories that are both deeply tied to place and open to new interpretations.

Primary Record Types and Their Repositories

- Town Vital Records and Town Books: Barnstable's sixteenth and seventeenth-century town records include baptismal, marriage, and burial entries predating state-wide vital registration (1841), recorded by town clerks and ministers. Meeting minutes, land grant records, and tax lists document civic participation and property ownership. These are housed largely in Town Halls, Massachusetts Archives, and digitized repositories such as FamilySearch and AmericanAncestors.

- Proprietors' and Land Records: Early proprietors' book grants and town lot allocations clarify initial settlement patterns. County deed registries track property transfers, mortgages, and partition deeds. Important for genealogists are abstracts and indexes due to historical courthouse fires and scattered documentation.

- Maritime Records: Crew lists, customs manifests, ship registers, insurance records, and pension files document the central role of fishing and whaling in local economies. Maritime museum archives and federal repositories provide extensive sources.

- Court and Probate Records: County courts managed estate inventories, guardianships, lawsuits, and criminal prosecutions. Probate files humansize ancestors through assets, kin, and legal disputes.

- Church and Religious Records: Congregational, Catholic, Quaker, and other denominational registers cover vital events, membership, and discipline, revealing social standings and religious affiliations. These are found in church archives, town collections, and denominational libraries.

- Census and Census Substitutes: Federal and state censuses (esp. agriculture, industry, and mortality cohorts) complement vital records, offering household details, occupations, and migration insights.
- 20th-century Records: Include school registers, yearbooks, directories, county administration reports, property and zoning records, and digitalized news media, illuminating modern residential and occupational patterns.

Research Roadmap: Strategies and Considerations

1. Establish Place and Era: Start by pinpointing the ancestor's town and estimate dates of residence. Use town incorporation and county boundary data to avoid jurisdictional pitfalls.
2. Consult Vital Records: Town birth, marriage, and death records offer foundational data. If gaps or fires that occurred, look to church registers and probate files.
3. Explore Land and Probate: Deeds and wills clarify family relationships and economic status. Recognize name variations and cross-check land locations with town maps and proprietors' books.
4. Utilize Maritime and Occupational Records: For coastal families, consult crew lists, customs files, and whaling logs; for inland families, tax valuations and labor rolls reveal economic roles.
5. Incorporate Religious and Community Records: Church disciplinary records, membership roles, and benevolent society minutes add social context.
6. Broaden to Modern Records: School records, directories, and county archives track family dispersal and evolving community ties into the 20th century.
7. Work Collaboratively: Engage with local historical and genealogical societies, tribal archives, maritime museums, and digitization projects to access lesser-known sources and benefit from community expertise.

Challenges and Opportunities

Researchers face challenges including record losses (notably the 1827 courthouse fire), variant spellings, overlapping jurisdictions, and Indigenous families recorded under European names or as wards. However, Barnstable's historical preservation efforts and digitization initiatives facilitate unprecedented access. Integration of traditional records with DNA testing, oral histories, and tribal collaboration offers richer reconstructions of ancestral narratives.

Barnstable County's genealogical treasures reflect its storied past: the intertwining of Wampanoag stewardship, colonial settlements, maritime enterprise, and modern adaptation. A careful, layered research approach leveraging varied archival collections will unlock family histories embedded in this distinctive Cape Cod landscape, transforming names in records into lived stories spanning centuries.

The Cities & Towns of Barnstable County

City

Barnstable

The Town of Barnstable stands as one of New England's oldest continuously inhabited communities, a place where colonial grit, maritime enterprise, and modern reinvention converge. Incorporated on September 4, 1639, alongside Sandwich and Yarmouth, Barnstable emerged from the Plymouth Colony's expansionist vision, drawing religious dissenters, farmers, and fishermen to its fertile marshes and sheltered harbors. Spanning seven distinct villages—Barnstable Village, Centerville, Cotuit, Hyannis, Marstons Mills, Osterville, and West Barnstable—the town covers 76 square miles of undulating terrain, tidal creeks, and cranberry bogs, embodying Cape Cod's resilient spirit. For genealogists, Barnstable's history yields a profound documentary legacy: town books predating state vital registration, proprietors' grants revealing founding families, maritime logs tracing seafaring kin, and modern zoning records charting suburban growth.

Indigenous Presence and Early European Contact

Before English settlement, the area sustained Nauset and Wampanoag communities, who harvested quahogs from Great Marshes, hunted deer in oak stands, and navigated coastal waters in dugout canoes. Archaeological sites reveal seasonal villages tied to shellfish beds and maize plots, with sachems negotiating early trades. Bartholomew Gosnold's 1602 *Concord* voyage skirted these shores, naming Cape Cod for its fisheries and exchanging goods with Nauset people, foreshadowing deeper encounters.

The Mayflower's 1620 anchorage in nearby Provincetown Harbor initiated sustained contact, with Pilgrims crossing Cape Cod Bay amid Nauset resistance. These interactions—trade, skirmishes, and the 1621 Nauset deed—set patterns of uneasy coexistence, decimated by epidemics that halved Indigenous populations before formal settlement.

Founding and Early Settlement (1639–1700)

Barnstable's founding stemmed from religious schisms in Scituate. Rev. John Lothrop, chafing under rigid church oversight, led ~70 parishioners south in 1639, securing a patent from Plymouth Colony for "Mattakeese" (Great Marshes). They erected a meetinghouse, allocated house lots via proprietors' books, and named their shire town Barnstable after Devon, England. Early settlers—Lothrop, Thomas Lothrop, Henry Rowley, James Cudworth—cleared meadows for cattle, built saltworks, and fished offshore, their town book logging grants, freemen oaths, and "warnings out."

Life blended Puritan piety with frontier pragmatism: Congregational discipline censured Sabbath-breakers; town meetings regulated fences and wolves; Quakers faced fines by 1658. By 1685 Barnstable County formation, the town hosted courts in a 1690 wooden jail (America's oldest surviving), its records anchoring vital events absent statewide until 1841.

Provincial Era and Wars (1700–1775)

The 1691 Province charter integrated Barnstable into royal Massachusetts, imposing taxes amid salt cod booms and privateering. King Philip's War (1675–1676) echoes lingered in Nauset petitions;

French & Indian Wars muster rolls list Cape men. Town books detail militia quotas, poor relief, and commons divisions, with women prominent as widows farming meadows.

Revolution and Early Republic (1775–1820)

Patriot fervor peaked in 1774: residents barricaded the courthouse against royal Chief Justice Peter Oliver, predating Lexington. Militia companies from Hyannis drilled; privateers raided British shipping. Post-1780 Constitution, Barnstable thrived on shipbuilding, fisheries, and taverns along King's Highway. The 1827 courthouse fire destroyed deeds, but abstracts endure in registries.

Maritime Zenith and Industrial Stirrings (1820–1900)

By mid-century, Barnstable harbored 804 vessels, its harbors buzzing with schooners carrying fish to Boston. Hyannis emerged as a packet hub; Cotuit oysters graced markets. Cranberry bogs revolutionized agriculture: small mills dotted streams. Civil War enlistments swelled, pensions naming kin. Railroads (1854) and bridges spurred growth, town reports logging schools and poor farms.

20th Century: Tourism, Suburbs, and Renewal (1900–Present)

Sagamore/Bourne Bridges (1935) unleashed tourism: Hyannis hosted Kennedys; Osterville yachts gleamed. WWII radar bases dotted dunes; post-war suburbs sprawled. Judicial reforms (1978) centralized courts; conservation protected marshes. Today, Barnstable (pop. ~45,000) balances seven villages, with Hyannis as "Hub," its records digitized for global access.

Genealogical Roadmap

- Town/Clerk Records: Vitals (1639+), meetings, grants—FamilySearch/AmericanAncestors.
- Probate/Deeds: Superior Court (post-1827 abstracts).
- Maritime: Customs, crew lists.
- Churches: Lothrop's Congregational (NEHGS).
- Modern: Directories, yearbooks, zoning.

Barnstable's saga—from Nauset stewards to Lothrop's flock, privateers to presidents' playgrounds—invites researchers to unearth families etched in salt marshes and ship logs.

Towns

Bourne

Situated at the western gateway of Cape Cod, Bourne, Massachusetts, holds a unique place in the region's history as both a rural town and a critical transportation hub connecting the peninsula with the Massachusetts mainland. Incorporated in 1884, Bourne emerged from parts of Sandwich and Falmouth towns, developing a distinctive identity shaped by maritime commerce, bridges, cranberry agriculture, and military installations. The town's evolution from a farming and fishing community to a corridor of railroads, highways, and naval facilities generates rich records spanning colonial grants, town meeting minutes, agricultural censuses, and 20th-century governmental archives vital for genealogical research.

Indigenous and Early European Context

Before European settlement, the area that would become Bourne was part of the traditional territory of the Wampanoag people, whose fishing and shell fishing villages thrived along the shores of Buzzards Bay and the Cape Cod Canal area. Early English explorers and settlers encountered these well-established communities during the 17th century, but with the displacement brought by colonial expansion, Native presence diminished significantly by the 18th century, though descendants remain active in regional history and genealogical records.

Colonial and Early American Settlement

For much of the colonial period and early republic, the lands now within Bourne were administered as parts of the towns of Sandwich and Falmouth. Sandwich, founded in 1637, is the oldest town on Cape Cod and an early center of colonial governance, maritime trade, and industry. Falmouth, incorporated in 1686, developed as an agricultural and maritime community. Bourne's territory reflects the gradual settlement and economic diversification characteristic of these parent towns, with farming, shellfishing, and sloop-building prominent livelihoods recorded in town meeting records, tax lists, and probate inventories.

Incorporation and Growth as Bourne (1884)

Bourne was officially incorporated on April 11, 1884, carving out its own municipal governance from Sandwich and Falmouth. The town's creation responded partly to population growth, transportation developments, and regional needs for administration closer to the Cape's western end. Early town records, including meeting minutes, land grants, and school committee reports from the 1880s onward, illustrate community priorities: maintaining roads, expanding schools, and managing burgeoning cranberry bogs.

The Cape Cod Canal and Infrastructure Developments

A defining feature of Bourne's history is the Cape Cod Canal, authorized by Congress and completed in 1916, providing a strategic maritime shortcut and economic stimulus. As the canal sliced the Cape from the mainland, Bourne became a transportation nexus, with bridges such as the Bourne Bridge (opened 1935) linking the cape to Buzzards Bay and the mainland road network. These infrastructure projects spurred commercial growth, tourism, and regional integration, producing planning commission records, bridge construction documents, and transportation maps valuable to genealogists tracing ancestral movements or property ownership near these key sites.

Military Presence and Modern Economic Shifts

Throughout the 20th century, Bourne hosted several U.S. military installations, including Camp Edwards, part of the Massachusetts National Guard training grounds, and the now-closed Otis Air National Guard Base. Military records, federal land use documents, and veterans' archives intersect with local histories, reflecting the town's role in national defense and the impact on families connected to service personnel.

The economy diversified into manufacturing, service industries, and cottage tourism. Agricultural records document the continuing importance of cranberry farming, with cooperative association minutes and agricultural censuses reflecting crop production cycles and labor sources.

Genealogical Records and Research Resources

Researchers investigating Bourne families will find a variety of records held across local and state repositories:

- Town Records: Vital records post-1884, town meeting minutes, school and cemetery records.

- Parent Towns' Archives: Pre-1884 Sandwich and Falmouth civil and church records are essential.

- Land and Probate: Barnstable County deed registries and probate files.

- Military Archives: National Guard and federal military records, pension applications.

- Agricultural and Industrial Reports: Cranberry cooperative documents, manufacturing censuses.

- Transportation Records: Cape Cod Canal authority documents, bridge engineering plans.

Digitization efforts by the Massachusetts Archives, FamilySearch, and local historical societies facilitate access, while regional genealogical groups offer expertise on local families and migration patterns.

Bourne's story intertwines threads of Cape Cod's indigenous heritage, colonial farming and fishing, infrastructure innovation, and 20th-century defense. Its records bridge centuries and sectors of life, inviting genealogists to assemble narratives of families shaped by water, land, and community resilience.

Brewster

Located on the scenic upper Cape within Barnstable County, Brewster, Massachusetts, boasts a rich heritage deeply tied to its coastal geography, maritime economy, and enduring rural character. Incorporated in 1803 from lands formerly parts of Harwich and Orleans, Brewster developed as a community centered on salt marsh farming, shell fishing, and whaling-related industries, while preserving its small-town charm amid evolving tourism and residential development. Its historical trajectory, anchored by early English settlement and continued reliance on natural resources, offers genealogists a wealth of records ranging from proprietors' deeds to church registers, town reports, and seasonal population accounts.

Indigenous Presence and Early Settlement

Prior to European arrival, the area now known as Brewster was used seasonally by Nauset and Wampanoag peoples for shell fishing, hunting, and cultivation of native crops. Archaeological evidence reveals complex seasonal patterns of resource use, with enduring cultural and spiritual connections to the salt marshes and bays. The advent of English settlers in the 17th century followed patterns of gradual expansion from established towns, with land transactions formalizing colonization, often at the expense of Indigenous landholdings.

Founding and Incorporation

Brewster was officially incorporated in 1803, emerging from portions of Harwich and Orleans as settlement intensified in what was initially called the Little Commons. The town's name honors Elder William Brewster, the Pilgrim spiritual leader, reflecting a pride in its colonial ancestry. Early town records, including proprietors' books, land grants, and meeting minutes, reveal a community emphatically tied to salt marsh agriculture, particularly cranberry cultivation, and shellfish harvesting, which supplemented farming in the sandy soils less suited for large-scale crops.

Maritime Economy and Industry

Though not a major whaling port like nearby Barnstable or Provincetown, Brewster participated significantly in regional maritime commerce. Residents engaged in fishing, shipbuilding, and provisioning whaling vessels, with family connections crossing Cape Cod towns. Local records include fishing licenses, cooperative shellfish management documents, and shipyard logs, highlighting the persistence of traditional maritime livelihoods well into the 19th century.

Social and Religious Life

Brewster's social fabric coalesced around congregational churches, with early meetinghouses serving as loci of worship and town governance. Church registers provide baptism, marriage, and membership records essential to tracing families over generations, while town meeting minutes document civic affairs, school funding, and local infrastructure. Disciplinary records capture social norms and community control, shedding light on family reputations and neighborly relations.

Modern Development and Tourism

In the 20th century, Brewster, like much of Cape Cod, experienced growth as a summer destination. The preservation of open spaces, salt marshes, and historic village centers fostered a balance between tourism and local resilience. Property records note the proliferation of summer cottages, while town zoning documents and school reports reflect demographic shifts, including seasonal residency patterns.

Genealogical Resources

Genealogists researching Brewster families may consult:

- Early town records (incorporation papers, proprietors' grants).
- Baptismal, marriage, and death registers from local churches pre- and post-civil registration start in 1841.
- Land deeds and probate files accessible through Barnstable County Registries.
- Military service records linked to residents, preserved in state and federal archives.
- 19th-century and later school and census records documenting occupational shifts and migration.
- Cooperative shellfish documents and maritime logs for ancestors engaged in related industries.

Brewster's history, from its Indigenous roots through colonial settlement and maritime economy to modern recreational hub, offers a well-preserved record trail. The town's modest scale and strong community identity make it a fertile ground for genealogical exploration rooted in the rhythms of Cape Cod's seasons and seas.

Chatham

Chatham, perched at the southeastern elbow of Cape Cod, has long been one of Massachusetts' most maritime-oriented towns. Incorporated as a town in 1712, after earlier years as the "Monomoit" precinct of Eastham, it developed around a series of harbors and inlets that opened directly onto the Atlantic and Nantucket Sound, shaping a community whose fortunes have always been tied to the sea. For genealogists, Chatham's history yields unusually rich documentation of fishermen, mariners, lifesavers, and their families, alongside town, church, and land records that trace the transition from a remote fishing village to a premier resort and retirement town.

Indigenous roots and early English settlement

Before English colonization, the Chatham area was home to Indigenous Monomoyick (Monomoy/Monomoit) people within the broader Wampanoag sphere, who exploited rich shellfish beds, inshore fisheries, and cranberry bogs along what is now Pleasant Bay, Stage Harbor, and Monomoy Island. Seasonal villages, fish weirs, and burial sites predate European arrival by centuries, and early colonial land transactions refer to Native leaders conveying or confirming tracts under mounting pressure from disease and encroachment.

English settlement at Monomoit began in the 1660s as families pushing south and east from Eastham and other Plymouth Colony towns took up land near today's Old Village. For several decades the area remained a precinct of Eastham, with local inhabitants attending church there or in small local gatherings and appearing in Eastham's town and church records under the name Monomoit. In 1712, the Massachusetts General Court incorporated Chatham as a separate town, taking its new name from Chatham in Kent, England, reflecting both maritime aspirations and transatlantic roots.

A town built on fishing, salt, and the sea

Through the 18th and early 19th centuries, Chatham's economy centered on inshore and offshore fishing, coastal trading, and saltworks. Harbors like Stage and Old Harbor offered anchorage for small schooners and shallops that worked Georges Bank and the offshore grounds, bringing in cod, mackerel, and other species for local use and export. Families combined small-plot agriculture and livestock with boat ownership or crewing, and many households included multiple active mariners—fathers, sons, and sons-in-law—whose names recur in crew lists, customs records, and town meeting minutes dealing with wharf maintenance or harbor regulations.

By the early 1800s, Chatham residents operated saltworks along the shoreline, using wind-driven pumps and solar evaporation to produce salt for preserving fish, an industry that left traces in town tax valuations and land descriptions mentioning "salt vats" and "salt meadows." The town also supplied men and smaller vessels into the wider New England whaling and merchant fleets based in Nantucket, New Bedford, Boston, and beyond, so that a Chatham mariner may appear as a crewman or officer in whaling voyage records or merchant ship registers even when he owned no large vessel at home.

Dangers and lifesaving on a shifting coast

Chatham's location at the confluence of strong currents, shifting bars, and fog-prone waters made it one of the most perilous stretches of the Atlantic coast. Shoals off Monomoy and the South Beach area caused frequent shipwrecks, prompting early establishment of lighthouses, life-saving stations, and eventually Coast Guard facilities. The construction of a lighthouse at Chatham in 1808 and the later development of U.S. Life-Saving Service stations brought new types of federal and local records—keeper's logs, wreck reports, payrolls, and commendations that list local men serving as surfmen, keepers, or volunteers. These sources provide genealogists with detailed accounts of rescues, storms, and community participation in maritime disasters.

The dynamic coastline also produced periodic land loss and new inlets, affecting property records and settlement patterns. Changes in the course of Chatham Harbor and breaches through Nauset Beach or South Beach altered access to the sea, sometimes isolating or erasing parts of Monomoy Island. Deeds and town plans, as well as 19th- and 20th-century coastal surveys, help researchers reconcile place-names that no longer match the modern map.

Social, religious, and civic life

Like other Cape towns, Chatham organized around its meetinghouse, with Congregationalism as the established church through the 18th and early 19th centuries. Early town and church records, originally linked to Eastham and later kept locally, include baptisms, marriages, membership lists, and minutes of ecclesiastical councils that document both conformity and conflict. Over time, Methodists, Baptists, and other denominations established congregations, especially in the 19th century as evangelical movements spread and maritime families sought differing forms of worship.

Town governance followed the typical New England pattern of open town meetings and elected boards (selectmen, school committee, overseers of the poor). Minutes and annual reports record decisions on schools, road building, wharf repair, poor relief, and, later, zoning and conservation—each decision naming individuals who served in office or petitioned for or against particular measures.

From working port to resort and retirement town

While fishing remained important into the 20th century, especially weir fishing and later scalloping and shell fishing, Chatham gradually shifted toward tourism and seasonal residency. Rail connections (19th century) and improved roads made the town more accessible, leading Boston and New York families to build summer houses and, later, retirees to settle year-round. The town preserved much of its historic character, with 18th- and 19th-century houses, churches, and windmills becoming focal points of a growing heritage tourism economy.

This transformation generated new records valuable for genealogists: subdivision plans; planning board and zoning board minutes; hotel and boarding-house advertisements in local newspapers; street and house-numbering changes recorded in town directories; and the activities of historical societies documenting "old Chatham" families and properties. Property valuation lists and tax rolls trace the transition from primarily local ownership to a mix of long-time families, in-migrants, and absentee owners.

Genealogical sources and strategies for Chatham

For family historians, Chatham offers a deep but sometimes scattered record set, reflecting its shifts in jurisdiction and economy:

- Town and vital records: Births, marriages, and deaths from 1712 onward are recorded in town volumes and in the state vital records system after 1841, with 19th-century entries often republished in "Vital Records of Chatham" compilations.

- Church records: Congregational and later Methodist, Baptist, and other congregational registers preserve baptisms, marriages, memberships, and dismissals, often filling gaps or extending earlier than civil vital records.

- Maritime records: Federal customs records, ship registers, crew lists, and Life-Saving Service / Coast Guard logs provide rich detail on mariners, surfmen, and wrecks, frequently including ages, places of residence, and sometimes physical descriptions.

- Land and probate: Deeds in the Barnstable County Registry and probate files in county court collections document property ownership, inheritance, and economic standing, especially important where coastal change makes landscape interpretation tricky.

- Census, directories, and local reports: Federal and state censuses, school reports, town annual reports, and 20th-century directories trace occupational shifts from fishing and boatbuilding to tourism, trades, and professional work.

- Historical society and preservation materials: The Chatham Historical Society and regional institutions hold photographs, family files, diaries, and house histories that bring texture to names found in formal records.

Taken together, Chatham's history illustrates a community repeatedly renegotiating its relationship with the sea—from Indigenous fisheries and colonial shallops to 19th-century cod fleets and modern Coast Guard operations—while evolving into a town that markets its maritime past as part of its present identity. For genealogists, the town's layered record trail makes it possible to follow families as they adapt to storms, shifting inlets, changing economies, and the arrival of visitors drawn, as their ancestors once were, to the edge of the open Atlantic.

Dennis

Situated centrally on Cape Cod's southern shoreline and nestled within Barnstable County, Dennis, Massachusetts, is a town of rich colonial roots, thriving maritime heritage, and evolving residential and tourist appeal. Incorporated in 1793 from portions of Yarmouth and Harwich, Dennis developed as a community whose landscape and livelihood have been shaped by proximity to the Atlantic Ocean, Cape Cod Bay, and vibrant salt marshes. Over centuries, its economic profile evolved from agriculture and fishing to summer tourism and real estate, producing a broad documentary footprint crucial for genealogical research, including colonial land grants, town records, church registers, and modern civic documentation.

Indigenous and Early Colonial Context

Long before English settlers arrived, Dennis' lands were occupied by Wampanoag peoples, whose seasonal harvest of shellfish, fish, and game sustained semi-permanent villages along the bayshores and interior woods. Indigenous stewardship profoundly influenced the natural environment with managed burns and fish weirs, shaping the landscape into which colonists entered in the 17th century. Colonial settlements expanded gradually from Yarmouth and Harwich, with English settlers laying out farms, saltworks, and fish processing sites along what became Dennis' seven villages: Dennis, Dennis Port, East Dennis, South Dennis, West Dennis, and the twin villages of Harwich Port and South Harwich.

Incorporation and Early Development

Dennis was incorporated as a separate town in 1793, reflecting growth in population and economic importance. Early settlement focused on mixed agriculture—grain, livestock, cranberry bogs—and offshore fisheries. Town meeting records from the late 18th and early 19th centuries detail public projects such as school funding, road maintenance, and harbor improvements, many naming elected officers who served as local leaders across generations. Proprietors' grants and early land deeds document initial lot allocations, often reflecting kinship ties and migration from earlier Cape towns.

Maritime Economy and Shipping

Fishing remained vital into the 19th century, especially in villages like Dennis Port and Sesuit Harbor, with harbors supporting small schooners and fishing fleets working the cod-rich Grand Banks. Wharf records, fishery licenses, and crew lists document seafarers' occupations and vessels. Local shipyards built fishing boats and small merchant ships, an industry recorded in town histories and tax valuation rolls. Later crab and shell fishing industries contributed to the economic diversification and influenced family occupations and local histories.

Social and Religious Life

Congregational churches anchored Dennis' early spiritual and social life, with registers recording baptisms, marriages, and church membership stretching back into the 18th century. Methodist and Baptist congregations emerged in the 19th century, reflecting religious diversification. Church disciplinary records and vestry minutes, often kept alongside town records, provide genealogical insight into community dynamics, family disputes, and neighborhood ties.

Transition to Tourism and Suburban Growth

The 20th century saw Dennis emerge as a premier summer resort, its beaches popularized by improved roads and vacationers from Boston, New York, and beyond. Summer homes, hotels, and yacht clubs proliferated, changing the social fabric and generating new property records, municipal planning documents, and social event listings. Town directories and school records show shifts in permanent and seasonal populations. Efforts to preserve Dennis' salt marshes and historic architecture catalyzed local heritage movements, adding photo archives, oral histories, and genealogical collections to research resources.

Genealogical Resources and Research Strategies

Researchers tracing Dennis ancestors should explore:

- Colonial and town vital records, including town meeting minutes, school committee reports, and property tax lists.
- Deeds and probate records in Barnstable County, supplemented by proprietors' records.
- Church baptismal, marriage, and death records for multiple denominations.
- Maritime and fisheries documentation highlighting occupations and migrations.
- 19th and 20th-century directories, school registers, and tourism archives that reflect demographic shifts.

Dennis' history—from Indigenous stewardship to colonial farms, from fishing fleets to summer retreats—offers genealogists a nuanced record set to explore the lives of families shaped by the rhythms of land and sea

Eastham

Eastham, situated on the outer fringe of Cape Cod along the Atlantic coast within Barnstable County, is one of the earliest English settlements on the Cape, incorporated in 1651 as the "Naumkeit" district before formal town status. With a landscape characterized by beaches, dunes, salt marshes, and pine forests, Eastham developed from Indigenous Wampanoag lands into a thriving maritime and agricultural community, later evolving into a destination for tourism and conservation. Its rich history produces a diverse array of genealogical records, including early town and church registers, maritime documents, land deeds, and shrine archives, all vital for researchers tracing families rooted in this historic Cape Cod town.

Indigenous Heritage and Early European Contact

Eastham lies in the heart of traditional Nauset territory, part of the broader Wampanoag Nation. Indigenous communities established seasonal camps and villages exploiting abundant shellfish, fish, and wild flora. Long before English colonists arrived, Nauset people maintained trade networks and spiritual traditions tethered to this coastal environment. Colonial-era deeds and missionary records reflect initial land transfers, missionary efforts, and complex cultural interactions that continue to inform genealogical reconstruction.

Colonial Settlement and Town Incorporation

Settlement began with English colonists in the early 1640s, initially as a precinct of Eastham's parent town, including settlers like Thomas Paine and William Shiverick. The area's incorporation as a separate town in 1651 under the name Naumkeit formalized governance structures and community institutions. Early town meetings and proprietors' records chart land distributions, common holdings, and governance. Town books document the appointment of constables, selectmen, and school committees, indicating community priorities such as road maintenance, poor relief, and militia organization.

Maritime Economy and Fisheries

Eastham's economy long relied on fishing, saltworks, and boatbuilding. Fishing boats staged from Wellfleet and Eastham harbors captured cod, mackerel, and shellfish, reflected in port records, crew lists, and fishery licenses. Salt extraction utilized coastal marshes producing essential goods for fish preservation and trade. Maritime activities generated extensive records, including marine insurance policies, customs house entries, and wharf appropriation documents vital to genealogical inquiries into maritime family histories.

Social and Religious Life

Congregationalism dominated early Eastham, with meetinghouses doubling as church and civic center. Church records, including membership rolls, baptismal, and marriage registers, provide foundational genealogical data often predating civil registration. The history includes periods of religious dissent and alternative worship groups like Quakers, reflected in court cases and town minutes. Town governance evolved with increased school funding and infrastructure projects, documented in detailed town meeting records, enhanced by 19th-century educational reports.

Modern Era: Conservation and Tourism

Eastham's Cape Cod National Seashore, established in 1961, conserved extensive lands including Nauset Light, Coast Guard Station, and ocean beaches, transforming the town into a protected area balancing tourism and preservation. Seasonal population surges led to growth in service industries and real estate developments, documented in zoning files, property tax records, and town reports. Tourism-created records include guest registries, historical society collections, and oral histories.

Genealogical Resources and Research Approaches

Research in Eastham leverages:

- Early town and church records for vital events and governance.
- Deeds, plats, and probate for land ownership and family dynamics.
- Maritime documents for sailor and fisherman ancestors.
- Conservation and tourism archives for recent demographic influences.
- Local repositories and digitized collections for comprehensive coverage.

Tracing Eastham families reveals lives shaped by Atlantic tides, shifting sands, and centuries of community resilience—memories etched in indigenous pathways and colonial town books alike.

Falmouth

Falmouth, occupying the southwestern corner of Cape Cod in Barnstable County, is a seacoast town rich with colonial heritage, maritime commerce, and cultural transformation. Incorporated in 1686, Falmouth grew from early English settlements along Buzzards Bay into a prosperous community centered on agriculture, fishing, shipbuilding, and later, tourism. The town's historical evolution is reflected in a wealth of genealogical records—including early town books, vital records, church registers, maritime documentation, and land deeds—providing diverse sources for family historians seeking to unravel ancestral stories from the colonial era to the present day.

Indigenous Heritage and Early Settlement

The territory of present-day Falmouth was originally the homeland of the Wampanoag people, whose seasonal movements and resource management shaped the landscape. Coastal villages, shellfish harvesting, and farming practices were carefully attuned to the local environment, which included harbors, salt marshes, and forested uplands. Early colonial settlers arrived in the mid-17th century, displacing indigenous inhabitants through epidemics, land purchases, and colonial expansion. Wampanoag deeds, missionary records, and early colonial correspondences document these complex interactions that have genealogical relevance for tracing Native and mixed-heritage ancestors.

Colonial Founding and Early Community Life

Falmouth was settled as part of the Plymouth Colony expansion, with incorporation as a town formalized in 1686. Early settlers established farms, saltworks, and fishing enterprises, reflected in proprietors' land grants and town meeting records. Governance depended on annual town meetings, electing selectmen, constables, and schoolmasters, who oversaw town affairs such as road maintenance, militia muster, and poor relief.

The town book archives contain vital event entries, real estate transactions, and minutes recording civic disputes and community initiatives. Early church establishment centered on Congregationalism, with records of baptisms, marriages, and membership critical for genealogists filling gaps left by civil records.

Maritime Economy and Shipbuilding

Falmouth's position on Buzzards Bay fostered a robust maritime economy. Fishing, whaling, and coastal trade thrived, with shipyards building schooners and merchant vessels documented in town records and regional maritime archives. Crew lists and customs documents illuminate seafarers' livelihoods, while local insurance company records capture vessel ownership and marine incidents. Lighthouses, pilots, and the Coast Guard stationed at Nobska Point added to the town's nautical legacy, and related records provide further genealogical opportunities.

Agriculture and Industry

Agriculture complemented maritime pursuits, with farms producing grains, vegetables, and livestock. Saltworks and cranberry bogs leveraged Falmouth's natural environment, generating tax rolls, agricultural censuses, and cooperative records that document production and labor. Small-scale industries including milling and boatbuilding further diversified the economy.

Social and Religious Developments

Religious life centered on Congregational churches, which evolved over time to accommodate Baptist, Methodist, and Catholic congregations reflecting immigration and denominational diversification. Church registers, discipline records, and vestry minutes offer insight into community values and familial relationships. Educational development expanded with common schools and later higher education institutions, whose records document rising literacy and social mobility.

Modern Growth, Tourism, and Conservation

The 20th century brought significant change, as improved transportation—including the construction of bridges connecting Falmouth to Martha's Vineyard—and railroads fostered tourism, real estate development, and summer residency. Preservation of historical sites, open spaces, and beaches emerged as priorities, recorded in municipal planning documents, conservation commission minutes, and heritage society archives.

Genealogical materials from this period include property tax records, school enrollment lists, business directories, and newspaper archives documenting active community life and seasonal population shifts.

Genealogical Research Resources

For those researching ancestors in Falmouth, key records include:

- Early town books and vital records (baptisms, marriages, deaths).
- Land deeds and probate documents within Barnstable County archives.
- Maritime crew lists, customs logs, and shipbuilding contracts.
- Church registers across multiple denominations.
- 19th and 20th-century censuses, school records, and directories reflecting demographic changes.

Falmouth's layered history—from Indigenous stewardship to colonial maritime hub, from agricultural community to modern tourist destination—provides genealogists with a rich archival terrain. This landscape offers not only vital statistics but also narratives of families shaped by wind, wave, soil, and evolving community institutions along the shores of Buzzards Bay.

Harwich

Harwich, located on Cape Cod's south shore in Barnstable County, is a town rich in colonial heritage, maritime economy, and traditional New England charm. Incorporated in 1694, it developed as a woodworking, fishing, and agricultural community, with early settlers carving farms from the rocky sands and earning livelihoods from the sea. Today, Harwich balances vibrant year-round neighborhoods with a bustling summer tourism economy, making it a focal point for genealogists researching families whose roots run deep in the Cape's history. The town's extensive records—including town meeting minutes, vital registers, church records, maritime logs, and land deeds—offer numerous pathways to reconstruct ancestral narratives tied to shifting economic and social landscapes.

Indigenous Stewardship and Early Settlement

Long before English colonization, the area that is now Harwich was inhabited by the Nauset and Wampanoag peoples, who sustained themselves through fishing, shellfish harvesting, and seasonal agriculture along Cape Cod's bays and coastal marshlands. These Indigenous communities managed resources through communal customs and maintained sophisticated social structures, which colonial settlers encountered and ultimately overlaid with competing land claims and European legal frameworks documented in early deeds and court records.

Colonial Foundation and Growth

Harwich established its identity as a distinct township in 1694, having previously been part of the broader Eastham settlement. Early English settlers focused on agriculture and maritime trades, developing from small farmsteads into a community with multiple village centers. Proprietor's records and town meeting volumes capture land allocations, common field divisions, roadway construction, and militia organization, reflecting both the practical challenges and communal governance central to early colonial life.

Maritime Economy and Wooden Shipbuilding

Vital to the town's economy was fishing and shipbuilding. Harwich waters supported cod and mackerel fisheries, with fish houses, drying racks, and wharfs lining villages such as Harwich Center and Harwich Port. Shipyards constructed schooners and smaller vessels, serving not only local needs but also regional trade routes extending to Boston and beyond. Maritime records—ship registries, crew lists, licensure, and customs logs—document the lives and careers of Harwich mariners, while insurance records and harbor master files enrich understanding of the economic networks in which they operated.

Religious and Civic Institutions

Congregationalism formed the religious backbone during the colonial and early American periods, with church records offering essential genealogical data including baptisms, marriages, and church censures. The 19th century saw diversification with the rise of Methodism and other denominations, alongside robust town governance structures documented in selectmen records, school committee minutes, and poor relief registers.

Transition to Tourism and Modern Economy

By the 20th century, Harwich evolved into a popular summer destination, strengthening its economy with tourism-related services and preserving its historic character. Town zoning reports, building permits, and civic planning documents from this era reflect these shifts and are valuable for genealogists tracking property ownership, family relocations, and community development. Beachfront neighborhoods and summer colonies added layers to demographic patterns captured in municipal and school records.

Genealogical Resources and Research Strategies

Effective research in Harwich draws upon:

- Early town vital records and town meeting books.
- Proprietors' land grants and Barnstable County deed registries.
- Church baptismal and marriage registers from multiple denominations.
- Maritime crew lists, ship registries, and customs records.
- Census, school records, and town directories that illustrate shifts in population and occupation.
- Preservation society collections holding manuscripts, photographs, and family histories.

Harwich's layered history—from Indigenous roots through its maritime heyday to present-day community—offers genealogists a diverse record corpus for reconstructing lives shaped by sea, soil, and society across centuries on Cape Cod.

Mashpee

Mashpee, set in the heart of Cape Cod's southwestern reaches within Barnstable County, is a town with a unique historical trajectory deeply intertwined with the Wampanoag people, whose continued presence distinguishes it as a center of Indigenous cultural and political resilience. Incorporated in 1870, Mashpee's boundaries encompass vast salt marshes, oak forests, and coastal shores that have shaped both Native communities and English colonial settlement patterns. For genealogists, Mashpee offers a particular challenge and opportunity: the interplay of tribal records, colonial deeds, missionary archives, and civil documents form a complex patchwork essential to tracing Native and mixed-heritage family histories while understanding the wider Cape Cod context.

Indigenous Homelands and Early Colonial Relations

Mashpee was historically a core part of the Mashpee Wampanoag territory. As one of Massachusetts' last federated Indigenous communities maintaining traditional government and land rights, Mashpee's early history encompasses a continuum of Indigenous stewardship and colonial challenge. Throughout the 17th and 18th centuries, Mashpee was recognized as a self-governing "praying town" where Wampanoag peoples were subjected to missionary efforts aiming at Christianization and colonial governance overlays.

The 1670 deed from Plymouth Colony reaffirmed Mashpee's possession of approximately 25 square miles of land, a rare document of Indigenous land tenure during a century of colonial expansion. Subsequent legal battles throughout the 18th and 19th centuries revolved around protecting Mashpee lands from encroachments by settlers and speculators, creating a large body of petitions, court rulings, and legislative acts that serve as a rich genealogical repository.

Incorporation and Governance

Unlike other Barnstable towns, Mashpee remained unincorporated for centuries, governed under tribal councils and colonial-appointed overseers. It was formally incorporated in 1870, after long struggles for municipal recognition reflecting its distinct status as a Wampanoag enclave. This late incorporation means that much early vital information is found in church and missionary records, Wampanoag tribal documents, and colonial court records rather than standard town registries typical elsewhere in Barnstable County.

Religious and Missionary Influence

Christian missionary activity, especially under the Society for the Propagation of the Gospel and later Congregational and Catholic missionaries, left extensive baptismal and marriage registers that record Native families alongside settlers. These records are frequently multilingual and include Indigenous naming conventions, valuable but requiring cultural and linguistic contextualization. Church archives of Mashpee's earliest congregations provide baptism, marriage, and burial records crucial for genealogical research, often complemented by missionary correspondence and school records.

Land Disputes and Legal Records

Throughout the 18th and 19th centuries, Mashpee's land was the focus of intense legal controversy, as colonial settlers sought to claim parts of the reservation. Court cases, legislative petitions, and land surveys document property disputes, transfers, and Wampanoag resistance. Probate and guardianship files often name Indigenous heirs and families, offering genealogical details where vital records may be sparse.

Modern Developments and Tribal Recognition

In the 20th century, Mashpee faced challenges of federal and state policies toward Indigenous lands, culminating in the 2007 federal recognition of the Mashpee Wampanoag Tribe—a milestone restoring certain self-governance rights and spurring record digitization and preservation. Contemporary tribal offices maintain extensive genealogical and cultural documentation, accessible to researchers in partnership with tribal authorities. This blend of historical and modern records underscores Mashpee's unique place as both a town and a living Native nation.

Genealogical Resources and Research Guidance

Researching Mashpee families entails combining:

- Colonial and missionary church registers with Indigenous oral histories.
- Land deeds and court petitions involving tribal territory claims.
- Probate, guardianship, and census records noting Native households.
- Tribal archives and federal recognition documents.

- Collaborative research with Mashpee tribal genealogists and historians.

Mashpee's enduring legacy as a Wampanoag homeland and evolving municipality offers genealogists a distinct yet deeply interconnected record network. Its story—spanning pre-contact cultures, colonial pressures, religious missions, legal battles, and tribal renewal—invites respectful, nuanced research into families who shaped and were shaped by the living traditions of Cape Cod.

Orleans

Orleans, located on the northeast side of Cape Cod facing the Atlantic Ocean and converted into Barnstable County from addresses historically tied to Eastham and Chatham, is a coastal town defined by its storied maritime legacy, agricultural heritage, and development as a resort community. Incorporated as a town in 1797, Orleans maintains a landscape of pristine beaches, marshes, and forests that have deeply influenced the economic and social lives of its residents. For genealogists, Orleans boasts rich repositories spanning early town records, church registers, maritime documentation, and land deeds, making it a key area for exploring Cape Cod family histories anchored in both sea and soil.

Indigenous Presence and Early European Encounters

Long before colonial settlement, Orleans was within the domain of the Nauset and Wampanoag peoples, whose sophisticated seasonal subsistence patterns leveraged the region's rich marine and terrestrial resources. Indigenous villages and seasonal camps along Pleasant Bay, Nauset Marsh, and nearby shores attest to longstanding occupancy. Early English explorers and settlers entered a landscape shaped by these Indigenous cultural practices, whose complexities resonate through early deed transactions and missionary records.

Colonial Establishment and Town Formation

Orleans evolved from parts of Eastham and Harwich precincts, with English settlement beginning in the mid-17th century. The town was formally incorporated in 1797, reflecting growing population and the desire for local self-governance. The town's early administration followed the New England tradition of town meetings, electing selectmen and other officers, regulating communal lands and resources, and managing militia obligations. Proprietors' land grants and town meeting minutes provide genealogists with detailed accounts of settlement patterns, land ownership, and community concerns.

Maritime Economy and Fishing Traditions

With several harbors such as Nauset and Stage Harbors, Orleans developed a maritime economy rooted in fishing, coastal trade, and shell fishing. Local fleets worked the Grand Banks and bays, captured cod and lobsters, and helped supply regional markets. Maritime records including crew lists, customs manifests, fishery licenses, and ship registries document these activities in detail, offering genealogical insights into fishermen's careers, vessel ownership, and wharfage.

Religious and Social Life

Congregational churches dominated Orleans' early religious landscape, with local parish registers documenting baptisms, marriages, and church membership essential for family history research. Over time, denominational diversity increased with Methodist and Episcopal churches serving expanding populations. Town meeting records reflect the civic roles taken by residents in education, infrastructure, and social welfare, including school establishment and maintenance of burial grounds.

Transformation Into a Resort and Retirement Community

The late 19th and 20th centuries saw Orleans develop as a popular summer destination for urban vacationers drawn to Cape Cod's natural beauty. This seasonal influx stimulated the construction of hotels, cottages, and cultural institutions, which are documented in town zoning, property transfer records, and tourism-oriented publications. The town preserved its historic architecture and natural landscapes, encouraging a balance of growth and conservation that produced extensive planning documents and photographic archives useful for genealogists tracking property and family relocations.

Genealogical Resources and Research Strategies

Key records for genealogists include:

- Early town meeting minutes and vital records (births, marriages, deaths) predating state registration.
- Land deeds, mortgage records, and probate filings housed at Barnstable County Archives.
- Church registers from Congregational, Methodist, and Episcopal parishes.
- Federal and state census records detailing demographic shifts and occupations.
- Maritime documentation, including customs records and fishery licenses.
- Local historical society collections with family papers, photographs, and maps.

By integrating these records, researchers can reconstruct Orleans families navigating the dual tides of maritime enterprise and seasonal tourism, generating rich genealogies rooted in Cape Cod's dynamic history.

Provincetown

Provincetown, located at the extreme tip of Cape Cod, is a small town with an outsized historical and cultural significance. Founded in 1620 as the first landing site of the Pilgrims aboard the Mayflower, it quickly evolved from an isolated fishing village into a bustling maritime center and, later, a haven for artists and tourists. Incorporated in 1727, Provincetown's unique geographical location fostered a distinctive community tied intimately to the sea, with a rich genealogical record that reflects the confluence of Indigenous presence, early European settlement, fishing and whaling industries, and modern cultural diversity.

Indigenous Roots and Early Contact

Prior to European arrival, Provincetown was part of the homeland of the Nauset people, a subgroup of the Wampanoag Nation, whose seasonal presence focused on fishing, shellfish harvesting, and small-scale agriculture along the harbor and dunes. The Nauset engaged in early interactions with European explorers, including Bartholomew Gosnold's 1602 voyage, and with the Pilgrims who landed in 1620. Early deeds, missionary records, and colonial documents provide limited but vital information about Native inhabitants during the early contact period.

The Mayflower Landing and Colonial Foundations

On November 11, 1620, the Pilgrims arrived in Provincetown Harbor, where they crafted the Mayflower Compact, establishing a civil government for the new colony. Although the settlement quickly moved across Cape Cod Bay to Plymouth, Provincetown remained a seasonal fishing and whaling port. Over the 17th and 18th centuries, the town grew as fishermen, shipbuilders, and merchants established a community supportive of the wider Cape Cod maritime economy.

Maritime Economy and Whaling

Provincetown's economy has been embedded in fishing, whaling, and maritime trades. By the 19th century, it was a leading whaling port with hundreds of vessels outfitting voyages worldwide. Whaling ship logs, crew lists, customs records, and insurance policies filed in local and federal archives document these enterprises. Fishermen's families are well represented in town tax lists, probate inventories, and maritime guilds, providing genealogists rich context for occupational and familial connections.

Social and Religious Life

Provincetown's early Congregational church records contain vital events and community discipline, often reflecting tensions within the population and fluctuating demographics due to maritime occupations. Over time, Protestant dissenters, Catholics, and other denominations established places of worship, preserving registers of baptisms, marriages, and deaths. Town meeting minutes offer insights into local governance, infrastructure, and social welfare, while the 20th century introduced a vibrant artistic and LGBTQ+ cultural scene, generating newspapers and archival material relevant to modern genealogical narratives.

Modern Developments and Cultural Renaissance

The 20th century transformed Provincetown into a popular tourist destination and artist colony, with records reflecting this shift including real estate transfers, civic planning documents, and cultural event archives. The town's recognition of its heritage as Mayflower landing site established a strong preservation ethic that supports genealogical research through maintained cemeteries, historical societies, and digital collections.

Genealogical Resources and Research Strategies

Key sources include:

- Early town vital and meeting records reflecting community origins.
- Maritime archives containing whaling logs, crew lists, and customs files.
- Church registers across multiple denominations documenting vital and social histories.

- Probate and land records from Barnstable County Archives detailing family estates.
- Cultural archives and newspapers that reflect 20th-century societal shifts.

Provincetown's layered history—from Nauset stewardship through Pilgrim landing and whaling prosperity, to artistic renaissance and inclusive community—offers genealogists diverse and dynamic records to explore families connected to one of New England's most iconic towns.

Sandwich

Sandwich, located on the west side of Cape Cod in Barnstable County, is the oldest town on the Cape and one of the earliest settlements in New England, incorporated in 1637. Known for its rich maritime heritage, early industry, and cultural contributions, Sandwich has served as both a gateway and anchor for Cape Cod's historical development. Its varied landscape, encompassing harbors, forests, and the forebays of Cape Cod Bay, has influenced its economic and social trajectory, leaving an extensive and diverse array of genealogical records crucial for researching families in the region.

Early Settlement and Indigenous Context

Before European colonization, Sandwich was part of the traditional lands of the Wampanoag people, who engaged in seasonal fishing, planting, and social activities revolving around the area's rich coastal and riverine resources. Early colonial accounts and land deeds document interactions, land transactions, and conflicts with Indigenous inhabitants during the early 17th century, providing critical context for genealogists researching mixed heritage lines and the dynamics of early settlement.

Incorporation and Colonial Development

Founded in 1637, Sandwich quickly became a focal point for settlers arriving from Plymouth Colony and Massachusetts Bay. The town was laid out with a system of home lots and common fields, documented in proprietors' records and town meeting minutes that detail land grants, road construction, and local governance practices. Selectmen, clerks, and clergy wielded significant influence, with town books recording vital events, militia organization, and taxation essential for tracing family involvement in civic life.

Economic Foundations: Shipbuilding, Glassworks, and Agriculture

Sandwich developed an early reputation for craftsmanship and industry. Notably, it was home to New England's first successful glassworks established in 1637, which produced glass for export and local use until its closure in the late 17th century. The town's shipyards and maritime trades supported fishing fleets and commercial vessels, with town records, customs documents, and insurance policies chronicling this economic vitality. Agricultural activities included mixed farming and salt marsh haying, documented through land deeds, tax rolls, and agricultural censuses.

Religious and Social Institutions

Early Sandwich was predominantly Congregationalist, with church records covering baptisms, marriages, and church discipline providing a key genealogical resource. The town witnessed religious dissent and diversity over time, accommodating Baptists, Methodists, and, eventually, Catholic congregations, reflected in church archives and town records. Social history is enriched by school committee minutes, poor relief accounts, and minutes of fraternal organizations that reveal community dynamics.

Modern Growth and Tourism

In the 19th and 20th centuries, Sandwich adapted to waves of change as tourism expanded, becoming a cultural center with historic preservation efforts and a thriving arts scene. Town planning, historic district documentation, and property records chronicle shifts toward a service economy. Opportunities for genealogists include directories, yearbooks, newspapers, and archives maintained by local historical societies.

Genealogical Resources and Research Approaches

Key genealogical sources for Sandwich include:

- Town meeting records, vital registers, and proprietors' grants documenting early settlement and local governance.
- Probate and land transaction records held at Barnstable County registries.
- Maritime documents like customs manifests and ship registers for nautical ancestors.
- Church scarcities, school and poor relief records revealing social relations.
- 19th- and 20th-century directories, newspapers, and preservation archives offering social and demographic context.

Sandwich's deep layers of history, from Indigenous lifeways through colonial enterprise to modern cultural vitality, create a broad archival landscape. This offers genealogists diverse entry points to explore familial ties bound to one of Cape Cod's most historically significant and resilient towns.

Truro

Truro, occupying the northernmost tip of Cape Cod in Barnstable County, offers a compelling history marked by its remote geography, maritime economy, and strong ties to Indigenous Wampanoag heritage. Incorporated in 1709 from parts of neighboring Eastham, Truro developed as a small fishing and farming community, surviving the challenges posed by its exposed location on the Atlantic Coast and its relatively isolated position. For genealogists, Truro provides a rich array of records—from early town and church documents to maritime logs and land deeds—that illuminate the lives of families adapting to coastal living in New England's maritime frontier.

Indigenous Heritage and Early Contact

Before English settlers arrived, the area now known as Truro was part of the Wampanoag Nation's territory. Indigenous peoples engaged in seasonal fishing, hunting, and gathering, utilizing the abundant coastal and inland resources. Early European explorers and settlers encountered these Native communities, whose presence is documented in colonial deeds, missionary accounts, and oral traditions, offering essential context for genealogical research involving Native or mixed-heritage ancestry.

Colonial Origins and Town Formation

Truro was initially settled in the late 17th century as part of Eastham but was incorporated as an independent town in 1709. Early settlers established farms with small-scale agriculture complemented by fishing ventures. The town grew slowly due to its challenging terrain and exposure, with proprietors' records, town meeting minutes, and early court documents chronicling land allocations, governance, and communal concerns such as road building and poor relief.

Maritime Economy: Fishing, Whaling, and Shipbuilding

Fishing was central to Truro's economy, with local harbors providing staging areas for cod, haddock, and mackerel fisheries. Community members participated in the broader New England whaling industry, often boarding vessels out of Nantucket or Provincetown. Maritime records—crew lists, customs logs, ship registries, and insurance documents—detail these activities and the individuals involved, enabling genealogists to map livelihoods tied to the sea.

Shipbuilding, though limited compared to other Cape towns, had a presence, with records of small craft construction and harbor maintenance appearing in town and county archives.

Religious and Social Fabric

Truro's early religious life centered on a Congregational church established in the early 18th century, whose registers record baptisms, marriages, and community membership. The town's isolation contributed both to close-knit social relations and to challenges in sustaining educational and other institutions, documented in school committee minutes and town meeting records.

Modern Development and Preservation

Today, Truro is known for its conservation efforts, historic preservation, and as a seasonal tourist destination. The establishment of Cape Cod National Seashore in 1961 protected much of the town's natural landscape, shaping land use and property records. Local historical societies preserve photographs, diaries, and manuscripts that enrich genealogical research by capturing personal narratives and community histories.

Genealogical Resources and Research Tips

Research in Truro entails consulting:

- Town vital records and meeting minutes dating to early incorporation.
- Church baptismal, marriage, and membership registers.
- Maritime records that detail fishery participation and vessel ownership.
- Land deeds and probate records housed at the Barnstable County Registry.
- Conservation and preservation archives for insights into more recent history.

Truro's history—shaped by Indigenous stewardship, colonial challenges, maritime enterprise, and modern conservation—provides a multidimensional context for genealogical studies. The town's records invite exploration of families anchored in the rugged beauty and enduring traditions of Cape Cod's northernmost shores.

Wellfleet

Wellfleet, occupying a striking coastal position on the outer Cape within Barnstable County, has a history deeply shaped by its rich maritime resources, expansive shellfish beds, and a resilient community balancing fishing traditions with modern conservation and tourism. Incorporated in 1763 from portions of Eastham and Truro, Wellfleet's unique geography—marked by ocean beaches, salt marshes, and bay shores—fostered a reliance on shell fishing, fishing, and small-scale agriculture. This history has produced a diverse set of genealogical records encompassing town and church registers, maritime logs, land deeds, and environmental and recreational archives, serving as vital resources for family historians.

Indigenous Background and Early Settlements

Long before colonial occupation, the area was integral to the seasonal rounds of Nauset and Wampanoag peoples, offering abundant oysters, clams, and fish. Indigenous use of the shellfish beds, and coastal resources was extensive, forming the economic and cultural fabric of native communities. Early colonial records and missionary reports provide intermittent documentation of Native peoples, their land rights, and interactions with European settlers.

Colonial Origins and Municipal Development

Wellfleet was carved from the lands of Eastham and Truro, reflecting growing population density and local governance needs. The town's early records—petition documents, proprietors' grants, and town meeting minutes—chart land disputes, road creation, and maritime regulations, indicating a community deeply engaged with both land and sea.

Maritime Economy and Shell Fishing

The town became famed for its thriving shellfish industry, particularly oysters and clams harvested from Wellfleet Harbor and adjacent marshes. Shellfish licenses, cooperative documents, and fisheries management records trace the evolving regulation and economic importance of these resources. Fishing vessels operated in nearby offshore waters, with maritime logs and customs records chronicling fish catches and crew details. Shipbuilding, albeit limited, appears in local records alongside saltworks and small-scale farming, reflecting a diversified rural maritime economy.

Religious and Social History

Congregationalism initially dominated religious life, with early church records offering genealogical data on baptisms, marriages, and membership. Later denominational diversity included Methodist and Baptist congregations, reflected in registers and meeting minutes. Social cohesion was maintained through town meetings, education committees, and benevolent societies documented in municipal and archival collections.

Modern Era: Conservation and Tourism

Wellfleet is a cornerstone of Cape Cod's conservation movement, largely due to establishment of the Cape Cod National Seashore, which protects much of its natural and cultural heritage. This designation spurred tourism focused on natural beauty, with a growth in seasonal residences and related property records, zoning files, and local publications documenting demographic and economic changes.

Genealogical Resources and Research Strategies

Researchers tracing Wellfleet families should consult:

- Town vital and meeting records dating from incorporation.
- Church baptismal, marriage, and membership registers.
- Maritime crew lists, fishery licenses, and ship registries.
- Land deeds and probate files archived at Barnstable County.
- Conservation and tourism records highlight modern social dynamics.

Wellfleet's layered narrative—from Indigenous homelands through colonial maritime enterprise to modern stewardship and tourism—offers genealogists a rich archival landscape to explore families shaped by sea, marsh, and community on Cape Cod's eastern shore.

Yarmouth

Yarmouth, a coastal town located on the southwestern part of Cape Cod within Barnstable County, boasts a rich history dating back to its incorporation in 1639. As one of the earliest settled towns on Cape Cod, Yarmouth developed as a farming and fishing community that leveraged its natural coastal harbor and fertile lands, evolving over centuries into a blend of maritime heritage and modern residential and tourism hub. Genealogists exploring family roots in Yarmouth benefit from extensive town records, church registers, land deeds, and maritime documents that provide insights into the town's development, population shifts, and socio-economic patterns.

Indigenous Heritage and Early Settlement

Long before English settlers arrived, the region was inhabited by the Wampanoag people, whose seasonal activities—fish and shellfish harvesting, hunting, and cultivation—sustained vibrant Indigenous communities along Cape Cod's shores. The English established their earliest permanent settlements in Yarmouth in the 1630s, with families from Plymouth and the nearby settlements seeking fertile lands and maritime resources. Early interactions, described within colonial deeds and missionary records, laid the foundation for Yarmouth's colonial identity while reflecting the profound changes imposed on Indigenous land use and governance.

Town Incorporation and Colonial Governance

Yarmouth was officially incorporated in 1639, establishing local government with town meetings, selectmen, and church elders shaping civic and religious life. Proprietors' records from the early period document distribution of land grants, while town meeting minutes reveal decisions regarding infrastructure, taxation, and militia duties. The establishment of churches further integrated religious authority into communal governance, with congregational records preserving vital genealogical data.

Maritime Economy and Agricultural Foundations

The town's economy historically hinged upon maritime endeavors—particularly fishing, whaling support, and coastal trade—while agricultural activities, including farming and cranberries cultivation, sustained the population. Commercial fishing fleets operated from Yarmouth harbors, with crew lists, customs documents, and licensing records providing valuable direct information on mariners and vessel owners. Agricultural censuses and tax rolls reflect the importance of landholding, crop production, and livestock in household economies.

Religious Life and Community Institutions

Originally dominated by Congregationalism, Yarmouth's religious landscape expanded with Methodists, Baptists, and Catholics establishing churches in the 18th and 19th centuries. These institutions-maintained registers of baptisms, marriages, and deaths essential for family historians. Church disciplinary records and town governance materials illuminate social values, community disputes, and public responsibilities.

Transition to Tourism and Modern Developments

The late 19th and 20th centuries saw Yarmouth transform as railroads and roadways improved access, spurring summer tourism and growth of seasonal residences. Real estate transactions, zoning board minutes, and town reports detail this shift, providing researchers with documentation of residential expansion, economic diversification, and demographic changes.

Genealogical Resources and Strategies

Genealogists tracing ancestors in Yarmouth should consult:

- Early town vital records and proprietors' archives for birth, marriage, death, and land ownership.
- Church registers across denominations for additional family event data.
- Maritime and customs records to track fishing and shipping activities.
- Agricultural censuses and tax lists for economic status examinations.
- 19th- and 20th-century directories, newspaper archives, and planning documents reflecting community growth.

Yarmouth's layered history—from Indigenous lands through colonial enterprise and maritime economy to modern tourism nucleus—provides genealogists with a well-rounded archive, tracing familial ties bound to the ebb and flow of Cape Cod's coastal life.

Villages

Barnstable Village

Barnstable Village, the shire town within the Town of Barnstable in Barnstable County, Massachusetts, serves as the historical and administrative heart of the region. As one of the earliest settlements on Cape Cod, its origins date back to the early 17th century and are closely tied to the founding and governance of Barnstable Town itself, incorporated in 1639. The village grew as the site of county courts, town hall, churches, and commercial activity, functioning as the focal point for political, religious, and economic life. For genealogists, Barnstable Village holds a wealth of primary source materials—court records, vital registers, land deeds, church documents, and town archives—that document the lives of families central to Cape Cod's development.

Early Settlement and Role as County Seat

Barnstable Village was established soon after the founding of Barnstable Town and was selected as the shire town (county seat) upon the creation of Barnstable County in 1685. This designation brought the county courthouse, jail (built in 1690 and noted as the oldest wooden jail in the United States), and administrative offices to the village, anchoring its centrality within local government. Early settlers cleared forests and established farms between Pleasant Bay and Cape Cod Bay, with town meeting records and proprietors' grant books detailing land allotments and communal regulations.

Religious Institutions and Civic Life

As the early spiritual center, Barnstable Village housed the main Congregational church, with surviving church records providing vital genealogical data including baptisms, weddings, deaths, and membership rolls. Over time, additional denominations established churches in the village, enriching the religious landscape. Town meetings held in the village's meetinghouse documented civic deliberation on school construction, road maintenance, tax levies, and poor relief, naming residents who constituted town leadership and participated in community governance.

Economic Development and Maritime Connections

While primarily agrarian in its early history, Barnstable Village's location near harbors and transport routes fostered maritime engagement including fishing, shipbuilding, and coastal trade. Ship registries, customs records, and port logbooks, often housed in local and state archives, reflect the village's commercial activity and residents' maritime occupations. Market days and annual fairs centered in the village as commercial hubs, recorded in newspapers and town minutes, provide additional insights into daily economic life.

Modern Growth and Historical Preservation

The village retains a well-preserved historic core, protected through zoning and historical commissions. Preservation efforts have safeguarded colonial-era homes, public buildings, and cemeteries, which, along with archives and local histories curated by the Barnstable Historical Society, provide genealogists with rich contextual materials. Modern municipal records, including property assessments, census enumerations, and school reports, continue to track demographic changes and family continuities in the village.

Genealogical Resources and Research Recommendations

Research in Barnstable Village is facilitated by access to:

- Early town records that include vital statistics predating state registration.
- County court records, probate files, and deed transactions that reflect legal and property histories.
- Congregational and other church registers for family vital events.
- Maritime and commercial records documenting occupational and economic ties.
- Historical society collections with family papers, photographs, and oral histories.

Barnstable Village's rich archival heritage embodies the political, religious, and economic nucleus of Cape Cod's Barnstable County, offering genealogists ample resources to explore family histories rooted in this historic New England village.

Centerville

Centerville, a village within the Town of Barnstable in Barnstable County, Massachusetts, has a history that reflects the broader Cape Cod experience of rural development, maritime enterprise, and suburban transformation. While officially part of Barnstable since its founding in 1639, Centerville emerged as a distinct community over time, situated at a crossroads of inland and coastal activities between Barnstable Village and the southern bays. Its evolving economy—rooted in farming, fishing, and later summer tourism—produced diverse records creating rich opportunities for genealogical research. Documents held in local archives and libraries reveal family connections, social structures, and economic life unique to this Cape Cod village.

Early Settlement and Land Development

Centerville's origins date to the 17th and 18th centuries as settlers expanded from established Barnstable Village into outlying lands. Proprietors' books and town land grant records document initial settlement patterns, with families clearing forests, establishing farms, and laying out roads. The village's geography along the journey towards Nantucket Sound positioned it as an important waypoint for transport and trade.

Agricultural and Maritime Economy

Centerville's economy historically blended agriculture with maritime activities. Farms produced mixed crops and livestock suited to the sandy soils, while residents engaged in fishing, clam digging, and maritime trades associated with nearby coves and harbors. Tax valuations, agricultural censuses, and probate files document farm sizes, property values, and inventories of tools reflecting rural livelihoods.

Maritime records, including crew lists and fishery licenses, demonstrate the village's connection to coastal fishing economies, while local wharfs featured in town meeting discussions highlight infrastructural priorities.

Religious and Social Institutions

Centerville's social life was centered around Congregational churches, with early church registers preserving vital records. As denominational diversity grew, Methodist and Baptist congregations expanded influence, leaving additional documentary trails recording baptisms, marriages, and memberships. Town meeting minutes and school reports reveal community governance, educational development, and social welfare activities reflecting evolving public priorities.

Modern Growth and Tourism Impact

In the 20th century, Centerville, like much of Cape Cod, experienced suburban expansion and tourism-driven growth. Residential developments, summer cottages, and recreational facilities altered demographic patterns, documented through property records, building permits, and local directories. The village balanced preservation of historic structures with accommodating modern residential needs, producing planning commission and conservation records invaluable for tracing 20th-century family movements.

Genealogical Research Considerations

Researchers investigating Centerville families should explore:

- Town vital records and land grants for early settlement data.
- Church registers from established and emerging denominations.
- Agricultural censuses, probate, and tax lists that document economic status.
- Maritime and fishery records connecting families to coastal livelihoods.
- Modern property, school, and civic documents reflecting social changes.

Centerville offers genealogists a microcosm of Cape Cod's layered history, its records reflecting the complex interweaving of rural, maritime, and suburban family lives over four centuries along the shores and hills south of Barnstable Village.

Cotuit

Cotuit is a picturesque village within the Town of Barnstable in Barnstable County, Massachusetts, enjoys a rich historical heritage deeply intertwined with Cape Cod's maritime economy, agricultural tradition, and coastal culture. Known for its charming harbor, historic homes, and active boating community, Cotuit developed from a primarily farming and fishing settlement into a cherished summer retreat while retaining its historic character. Genealogists exploring Cotuit's past benefit from extensive town and church records, maritime logs, land grants, and 19th- and 20th-century civic documents that reveal familial ties rooted in the land and sea of Cape Cod.

Early Settlement and Land Use

Cotuit's colonial origins date back to the 17th century as part of Barnstable's proprietors' grants and land divisions. Early settlers established farms, woods, and salt marshes, utilizing the fertile pockets of sandy soil and coastal resources. Proprietors' records and town land grant books detail the original divisions of land among families, enabling genealogists to track early residency and property succession.

Maritime and Agricultural Economy

Cotuit's economy balanced agriculture—including mixed farming and cranberry cultivation—with an active maritime presence. Its protected harbor on Cotuit Bay supported boatbuilding, fishing, and coastal trade, with residents participating in the broader New England fisheries economy. Ship registries, customs documents, crew lists, and fishery licenses provide detailed insights on seafaring ancestors and local maritime commerce.

Cranberry bogs and small-scale farming supplemented this maritime focus, with agricultural censuses and tax assessments tracing land use changes and economic diversification over the 18th and 19th centuries.

Religious and Community Life

Religious institutions played a central role in Cotuit's communal life. Congregational churches that provide church membership rolls, baptismal, and marriage registers essential for genealogical research. By the 19th century, other denominations including Methodists and Baptists established congregations, adding complexity and breadth to the religious and social landscape. Town meetings and school committee records document governance, educational development, and community initiatives reflecting the priorities of Cotuit's residents over time.

Transition to a Summer Colony and Modern Identity

In the late 19th and 20th centuries, Cotuit evolved into a sought-after summer destination, attracting seasonal residents and boaters. Property records, regional planning documents, and local archives reveal the growth of vacation homes, yacht clubs, and cultural activities that shaped Cotuit's modern identity.

Historic preservation efforts have documented and conserved many colonial and Victorian-era buildings, while local historical society archives offer photographs, family histories, and oral traditions.

Genealogical Resources and Research Tips

Genealogists researching Cotuit families will find valuable sources in:

- Early proprietary and town land grant records.
- Church baptismal and marriage records from various denominations.
- Maritime and fishing-related documentation, including customs and ship registries.
- Agricultural censuses, tax records, and probate files showing property details.
- 19th- and 20th-century directories and municipal records tracing demographic and economic changes.

Cotuit's combination of maritime heritage and rural charm offers genealogists a well-documented community to explore family histories deeply connected with Cape Cod's waters and woodlands across centuries.

Craigville

Craigville, a historic village within the Town of Barnstable in Barnstable County, Massachusetts, is renowned for its role as a religious camp meeting ground and summer colony, evolving from 17th-century Indigenous land into a 19th-century Christian retreat center. Named after J. Austin Craig (1824–1903), who purchased land in the area in the mid-19th century, Craigville developed around the Craigville Conference Grounds, established in 1871 as a site for the New England Convention of Christian Churches. This unique heritage blends colonial settlement patterns with evangelical gatherings, producing specialized records like camp meeting registers, conference minutes, and property deeds that enrich genealogical research alongside standard Barnstable town documents.

Indigenous Foundations and Colonial Settlement

The land comprising Craigville was originally part of a 1644 tract sold by Wampanoag sachem Iyannough to early English settlers, marking one of Cape Cod's initial land transfers amid broader Nauset and Wampanoag presence. As part of Barnstable Town (incorporated 1639), the area saw gradual settlement by farmers and mariners, with proprietors' grants and town land records allocating parcels for agriculture and salt marsh haying. These early documents, preserved in

Barnstable town books, trace family landholdings from colonial times through divisions among heirs.

Emergence of the Religious Camp Meeting Tradition

Craigville's distinct identity crystallized in 1871 with the founding of the Craigville Conference Grounds by Methodist and Congregational leaders seeking a summer venue for revivals, Bible studies, and denominational assemblies. Cottages, tabernacles, and communal facilities sprang up, attracting clergy, missionaries, and families from across New England. Conference records, attendee lists, and cottage ownership deeds from the Craigville Methodist Association (later Craigville Conferences) provide rare insights into seasonal residents, ministerial networks, and family spiritual affiliations often absent from civil vital records.

The site hosted annual events through the 20th century, including youth programs and interdenominational gatherings, with surviving programs, photographs, and membership rolls documenting participants amid events like the 1944 Great Atlantic Hurricane recovery efforts.

Economic and Social Evolution

Agriculturally rooted in Barnstable's farming economy, Craigville supplemented this with small-scale maritime ties to nearby harbors for fishing and oystering, reflected in town tax valuations and crew lists. By the 20th century, it transitioned into a summer colony, with beach houses and tourism boosting property development. Zoning records, building permits, and directories capture this shift, highlighting families who owned "cottages" across generations.

Socially, the village fostered tight-knit evangelical communities, with church minutes and temperance society rolls revealing moral and charitable activities.

Modern Preservation and Cultural Significance

Today, the Craigville Historic District preserves over 100 cottages and structures from the camp meeting era, listed on the National Register of Historic Places. Local archives, including James Buffington's "Craigville Historical Fragments," offer annotated histories, photos, and genealogies tied to conference leaders and attendees. Conservation efforts protect beaches and wetlands, generating environmental records useful for recent property research.

Genealogical Resources and Strategies

Genealogists targeting Craigville ancestors should prioritize:

- Barnstable town vital records and proprietors' grants for baseline settlement data.
- Craigville Conference Grounds archives: attendee lists, cottage deeds, and programs for 1871–present.
- Church registers from Methodist/Congregational assemblies, supplemented by Sturgis Library's Cape Cod collections.
- Maritime and tax records for early economic ties.
- Historic district surveys, photos, and family papers at Centerville Library or Cape Cod Genealogical Society.

Craigville's arc—from sachem's tract to evangelical haven—yields a specialized record set blending Barnstable's colonial depth with unique camp meeting documentation, ideal for tracing families drawn to faith, sea, and seasonal shores.

Hyannis

Hyannis, the largest village and commercial hub within the Town of Barnstable in Barnstable County, Massachusetts, has evolved from a modest 17th-century farming outpost into Cape Cod's bustling "Hub"—a center of transportation, retail, tourism, and regional services. Emerging as a distinct population center by the mid-19th century amid Barnstable Town's (incorporated 1639) expansion, Hyannis gained prominence through railroads (1850s), steamship packets, and modern airports, fostering economic diversification from maritime trades to hospitality. Genealogists value Hyannis for its layered records: town-wide Barnstable archives supplemented by village-specific directories, business ledgers, and passenger manifests that illuminate family migrations, occupations, and social mobility.

Colonial Roots and Early Development

Hyannis originated within Barnstable's colonial land grants, with early settlers farming meadows along the Centerville-Hyannis River and engaging in coastal fishing via nearby coves. Proprietors' records and town meeting minutes from the 1640s document lot allocations, commons divisions, and "warnings out" for newcomers, placing Hyannis families within broader Cape networks. By the 18th century, it served as a stagecoach stop on the Old King's Highway, with taverns and inns noted in tax valuations and probate inventories.

Maritime and Commercial Rise

Hyannis Harbor emerged as a packet boat hub in the early 19th century, linking Cape Cod to Boston, Nantucket, and Martha's Vineyard via steamers like the *Massachusetts*. Customs records, crew lists, and wharfage logs capture mariners' voyages, while shipbuilding and oystering thrived, reflected in fishery licenses and insurance policies. The 1854 Cape Cod Branch Railroad terminus spurred warehouses, hotels, and shops, with business directories listing merchants, ship captains, and boardinghouse keepers.

Social and Religious Foundations

Congregational churches anchored early life, their registers logging baptisms, marriages, and memberships predating state vital records (1841). Methodist and Baptist congregations proliferated by mid-century, alongside fraternal societies like Odd Fellows, whose minutes reveal mutual aid networks. School committee reports and poor farm ledgers detail education and welfare, often naming Hyannis residents.

Modern Boom: Rail, Roads, and Tourism

Rail expansion solidified Hyannis as the Cape's gateway, with the 1935 Sagamore Bridge accelerating automobile tourism. Steamship companies like the New England Steamship Co. generated passenger lists, while WWII-era naval air stations (now Barnstable Municipal Airport) produced military rosters. Post-war suburbs, Kennedy family associations (JFK's summer White House), and resorts boomed, documented in zoning files, hotel registers, and yearbooks. Today, it's a retail epicenter with Cape Cod Hospital and ferry terminals.

Genealogical Resources and Strategies

Key sources for Hyannis research include:

- Barnstable town records: vitals, meetings, proprietors' grants (1640–1855).
- Maritime/customs logs and passenger manifests for packets/ferries.
- Church registers (Congregational/Methodist) and society minutes.
- Directories, censuses, and business ledgers for 19th–20th-century occupations.
- Airport/military files, zoning, and Sturgis Library collections for modern ties.

Hyannis embodies Cape Cod's transformation—from colonial farmstead to transit nexus—offering genealogists dynamic records of families propelled by ships, rails, and tourists across centuries.

Hyannis Port

Hyannis Port, an affluent village within the Town of Barnstable in Barnstable County, Massachusetts, emerged as a prestigious summer enclave in the late 19th and early 20th centuries, building on colonial maritime roots to become synonymous with elite vacationing and political legacy. Distinct from bustling Hyannis proper, this waterfront community along Nantucket Sound developed around grand estates, yacht clubs, and private beaches, most famously as the Kennedy Compound—a National Historic Landmark purchased by Joseph P. Kennedy Sr. in 1928. Genealogists researching Hyannis Port uncover layered records: Barnstable town archives for early settlement, plus unique 20th-century property deeds, social registers, and Kennedy-era documents revealing elite family networks and seasonal migrations.

Colonial Foundations and Maritime Origins

Hyannis Port's land traces to 17th-century Barnstable proprietors' grants, with early settlers like the Nye family farming meadows and fishing coastal waters. Descendants of Benjamin Nye (arr. 1635 Sandwich) dominated, as seen in deeds and town books; Charles H. Nye (1821–1907), railroad superintendent, exemplifies mid-19th-century prominence, his genealogy linking to English roots via the Nye Family Association (formed ~1880). By the 18th century, it served as a shipping point, with customs logs noting captains and merchants amid Hyannis Harbor's packet boats.

Rise as an Elite Summer Colony

Improved rail (1850s) and roads drew Boston/NY elites post-Civil War, transforming farms into estates. The Hyannis Port Yacht Club (founded 1914) and golf courses catered to seasonal residents, documented in club rosters, invitation lists, and society pages. Property records capture estate sales, like Kennedy's 1928 purchases (50 Marchant Ave. main house; expansions for RFK/Ethel), hosting family gatherings until JFK's 1963 death—photographs and correspondence preserved at JFK Library enrich elite lineages.

Social and Economic Shifts

Churches (Congregational/Universalist) logged baptisms/marriages for year-rounders, while Methodist camp influences lingered nearby. 20th-century censuses/directories distinguish permanent fishers/merchants from summer folk, with tax rolls noting "cottages" owned by industrialists/politicians. WWII naval activity and post-war suburbs spurred growth, zoning files tracking waterfront developments.

Preservation and Modern Legacy

The Hyannis Port Historic District safeguards Shingle-style mansions and Kennedy sites, with surveys/house histories at Sturgis Library aiding property research. Hyannis Historical Society PDFs detail local evolution.

Genealogical Resources and Strategies

Key sources include:

- Barnstable town vitals/proprietors' records (1640s+).
- Nye/Kennedy genealogies; family association proceedings.
- Maritime customs/crew lists for early captains.
- Yacht club/social registers; estate deeds for elites.
- JFK Library photos/correspondence; directories/censuses.

Hyannis Port's saga—from Nye farms to Kennedy compound—offers genealogists elite contrasts to Cape working-class histories, via deeds, clubs, and compounds etching seasonal sojourns into enduring archives.

Marstons Mills

Marstons Mills, an inland village within the Town of Barnstable in Barnstable County, Massachusetts, traces its origins to mid-17th-century settlement amid Cape Cod's rural heartland, evolving from farming hamlets and mills into a suburban community preserving its historic mills and homesteads. First settled before 1653 by Roger Goodspeed from Barnstable Village, the area gained its name from Benjamin Marston (arr. 1738 from Salem), whose marriage to Goodspeed's granddaughter Lydia spurred development of a fulling mill (built 1689) and grist mills that dominated local economy for over a century. Genealogists prize Marstons Mills for its deep family continuity—Crocker, Goodspeed, Jones, Marston lineages documented across deeds, probate, and mill records—offering insights into inland Cape Cod life distinct from coastal maritime hubs.

Indigenous Context and Early Settlement

The land was part of Wampanoag territory, with Paupmunnock sachem's sites like Prince's Cove (Broad Nook) yielding 10,000-year archaeological records of Native fishing camps. Goodspeed's arrival initiated English farming, with proprietors' grants allocating meadows for hay and crops; Ebenezer Goodspeed's pre-1708 house endures as the village's oldest.

Mill Economy and Family Dominance

Marstons powered economic life: fulling/grist mills ground corn for Plymouth settlers, run by Marstons (Nymphas I civic leader; Nymphas II probate judge 1828–1854; Charles state senator). Nathaniel Hinckley controlled grocery/mills in the 19th century. Crockers (Isaac 1725 farm; Wilson 1805–1885 inheritance) and Joneses (Deacon Thomas pre-1857 homestead) held properties for generations, per deeds/probate (e.g., Shubael Crocker's 1847 will; Bethuel Crocker's 1853 bequest).

Oyster shacks (Cyrus Jones, Hinckleys, Hamblins) dotted coves, blending inland/rural pursuits.

Social and Religious Fabric

Congregational churches logged vitals; Quaker Joneses and civic Marstons shaped governance via town meetings/school committees. 19th-century newspapers (Barnstable Patriot) note farm continuity; mills ceased ~1920–1930.

Modern Suburbanization and Preservation

20th-century roads/bridges spurred growth; Marstons Mills Historical Society (active today) preserves images/documents/artifacts, including George W. Pierce family photos and 1920s river/bridge shots. Digital Commonwealth hosts collections; Crockers span villages.

Genealogical Resources and Strategies

Vital sources:

- Barnstable town/proprietors' records (Goodspeed/Marston grants).
- Probate/deeds (Crocker wills 1847/1853; Marston estates).
- Mill accounts/church registers for occupations/vitals.
- Historical Society photos/maps (Digital Commonwealth).
- Family associations (Crocker/Goodspeed).

Marstons Mills' mill-centric saga—from Goodspeed settler to Marston industrialists—yields probate-rich trails of enduring Cape families, preserved via society's vigilant archiving.

North Harwich

North Harwich, a remote rural village straddling the borders of Harwich, Dennis, and Brewster in Barnstable County, Massachusetts, emerged as a 17th-18th century mill hamlet and later a 19th-century transportation/immigrant hub, deeply intertwined with Cape Cod's cranberry economy and Baptist heritage. Pre-1700 settlement centered on Samuel Hall's mill at Herring River headwaters, evolving into a bustling depot village bisected by modern Route 6 (mid-Cape Highway), with underpass linking historic cores. Its genealogy reflects family migrations across Mid-Cape towns—Doane, Kelley, Nickerson, Cape Verdeans—documented in church records, depot logs, and bog ownership files.

Indigenous and Colonial Origins

Wampanoag territory sustained seasonal fishing/hunting camps; early English expansion yielded Hall's Mill (pre-1700), powering grain/fulling amid Herring River ponds/lakes. Baptist roots trace to 1757 North Harwich Baptist Church (one of MA's first), splitting from Separate Church; Elder Richard Chase pastored 1757–1777 (records lost), succeeded by Revs. Samuel Nickerson, Enoch Eldredge, Abner Lewis (1794–1809, parsonage built ~1795–1798). Church relocated 1828 to West Harwich (rebuilt 1841), parsonage moved to Harwichport by Elbridge Gerry Doane Sr. (b.1813).

19th-Century Boom: Mills, Rails, Cranberries

Village thrived on mills, cranberry bogs, and North Harwich Railroad Depot (sole freight/passenger for West/South Dennis, Harwich Port pre-Chatham spur). Families like Doane (Capt. Nathaniel 1781–1866; Elbridge m. Temperance Kelley 1835), Kelley (Patrick 1753–1834 variants Killey/O'Kelley), and Paine/Knowles populated homes (150–200 yrs old south of Rt.6). Cape Verdeans arrived turn-of-century, working/owning bogs in North Harwich/Pleasant Lake.

Social/Religious Networks

Baptist church fostered ties; Kelley Cemetery (hidden) holds early graves. Depot/incubator role dispersed offspring to Dennis/Harwich villages via genealogy. 20th-century Rt.6 bifurcation isolated cores, but bogs endure.

Genealogical Resources and Strategies

Key sources:

- Harwich/Dennis vital/town records (births/marriages post-1841; pre-church).
- Baptist church registers/minutes (post-1777 Nickerson/Eldredge/Lewis).
- Probate/deeds (Doane/Kelley estates; Barnstable Registry).
- Railroad depot logs/cranberry co-op files (Cape Verdean bog owners).
- Harwich Historical Society/Cape Cod Genealogical Society (family files, Paine's Harwich history).

North Harwich's mill-depot-bog nexus—bridging Wampanoag waters, Baptist dissent, rail migrants, Cape Verdean resilience—yields cross-town family trails via churches, bogs, and buried Kelleys.

North Truro

North Truro, the northernmost village of Truro in Barnstable County, Massachusetts, embodies Cape Cod's rugged maritime frontier—a landscape of towering dunes, historic lighthouses, and WWII-era relics that evolved from 18th-century fishing outposts to a hub for lifesaving stations and military installations. Incorporated within Truro (1709), North Truro's exposed Atlantic position fostered resilient seafaring families (Dyer, Small, Lewis, Farnsworth-Sawyer) documented extensively in Cobb Archive materials: sea charts, family memorabilia, and 2,000+ photos spanning people, buildings, and livelihoods.

Indigenous Foundations and Colonial Settlement

Wampanoag Nauset/Pamet people called the area home, their Algonquian name "Pamet" (adopted for Pamet River/Harbor) reflecting seasonal fishing camps amid dunes. English settlement post-1709 Truro incorporation focused on whaling/fishing; vital records to 1849 (Bowman transcription) log births/marriages/deaths, with town clerks preserving 1709–1783/1844–1870 entries.

Maritime Lifesaving and Lighthouse Era

North Truro's cliffs hosted vital Coast Guard/Lifesaving Service stations (est. 1873), with logs/wreck reports naming surfmen amid frequent shipwrecks. Highland Light (1797, relocated 1996) and sea charts (Capt. Atkins Hughes, early 1800s) detail mariners; U.S. Coastal Survey maps (19th c.) chart hazards. Railroad era (1873–1960) spurred freight/passenger ties, per Truro Historical Society exhibits.

20th-Century Military and Preservation

WWII radar bases dotted dunes; post-war Cape Cod National Seashore (1961) conserved landscapes. Cobb Archive (1912 Arts & Crafts library) holds Dyer/Small/Lewis/Farnsworth-Sawyer papers, merchant letters, Bibles, and oral histories—volunteer-assisted research (free 30min/day). Highland House Museum (seasonal) displays artifacts.

Genealogical Resources and Strategies

Prime sources:

- Truro vital records (1709–1849 Bowman; FamilySearch images).
- Cobb Archive: family memorabilia, photos (2,000+), sea charts/maps (Dyer surveys 1925–1957).
- Church registers/gravestones (Old North Cemetery inscriptions).
- Maritime/Coast Guard logs; railroad exhibits.
- Truro Historical Society (Cobb 508-349-0200; research@trurohistoricalsociety.org).

North Truro's dune sentinel saga—from Pamet camps through lifesavers' vigils to archived legacies—unlocks seafaring kin via Cobb's treasures and Truro's resilient records.

Osterville

Osterville, a prestigious village within the Town of Barnstable in Barnstable County, Massachusetts, traces its origins to Cotochese (Wampanoag) oyster-rich bays, evolving through colonial oystering into a renowned boatbuilding center and elite summer enclave on Nantucket Sound. Named from "Oyster Island Village" (evolved to Oysterville by 1815), its three bays (Wianno, Seapuit, Oyster Harbors) sustained Native trade before Capt. Miles Standish's 1648 Plymouth deed. The Crosby Yacht Yard (1850, est. by Horace S. & C. Worthington Crosby) built iconic Wianno catboats—including JFK's Wianno Senior—cementing maritime fame, while mid-19th-century Boston elites spawned summer colonies. Genealogists access Barnstable records plus Osterville-specific yacht rosters, estate deeds, and Historical Society archives revealing seafaring/wealthy lineages.

Indigenous Oyster Heritage and Colonial Transition

Cotochese tribe (Wampanoag subtribe) named bays chunkoo/chunkomuck for prolific oysters, central to diet/trade. 1639 English arrival dubbed it Oyster Island Village; Standish's deed formalized transfer. Early Barnstable proprietors' grants allocated oyster beds/salt marshes to families farming alongside harvesting, per town books/deeds.

Maritime Boatbuilding and Economic Core

Crosby Yard's wooden masterpieces (catboats, Wianno Seniors) drew international acclaim; family records/rosters detail builders/captains. Oystering persisted, with fisheries licenses/customs logs naming crews amid coastal schooners. Tax valuations/probate inventories trace estate wealth from boats/oysters to land.

Rise of Summer Colonies and Social Elites

Mid-1800s influx built Wianno/Seapuit/Oyster Harbors enclaves: grand homes/guesthouses for Bostonians/NYers. Yacht clubs/golf courses solidified status; social registers/directories log seasonal residents. Kennedy ties amplified prestige, though not genealogically central.

Preservation and Cultural Legacy

Osterville Historical Society (1931, Capt. Jonathan Parker House) curates wooden boats (MA's largest collection), Cammett House (oldest structure), gardens; Alys/Bob Bownes Cape Cod History Room at Village Library holds rare books/*Village View* articles (1970–1984 digitized). History Walks/self-guided monument tours by Paul Chesbro/Cathy Wright enrich context.

Genealogical Resources and Strategies

Key holdings:

- Barnstable vitals/proprietors' deeds (Cotochese transfers/oyster lots).
- Crosby Yacht records/rosters (builders/captains).
- Church registers (Congregational/Methodist vitals).
- Ancestry/HeritageQuest (library-only); *Village View*/society files.
- Probate/tax rolls for estates; Digital Commonwealth photos.

Osterville's oyster-to-yacht arc—from Cotochese bays to Crosby craft/elites—delivers maritime/affluent trails via society archives and Barnstable depths.

Pleasant Lake

Pleasant Lake (also Hinckley's Pond/Herring Pond), a rural hamlet in Harwich (Barnstable County) near the Dennis/Brewster borders, centers on its namesake kettle pond sustaining cranberry bogs, mills, and Cape Verdean communities amid Wampanoag roots and 18th-century settler farms. Emerging as "Indian Range" tracts sold by sachem Mattaquason's heirs (1730s Edward Kenwrick purchase), it evolved via railroads (benefiting from Harwich depot) into a bog-centric enclave blending English (Kenwrick, Brooks/Broadbrooks) and Portuguese immigrant lineages like Gomes (Manuel B. Gomes, 1920s widower). Genealogists leverage Harwich records plus bog ownership/depot logs tracing Native-settler intermarriages and labor migrations.

Indigenous Land and Early Purchases

Mattaquason (Monomoyick sachem aiding Pilgrims) descendants sold tracts to Edward Kenwrick (1730s), passed to son Solomon (early whaler) and explorer grandson John Kendrick—chain traceable via deeds measuring "history in lifetimes." Paths/tribal boundaries fenced into lots reflect Native-settler shifts, with Anglicized names signaling adaptation.

Mill and Bog Economy

Thomas Hinckley farmed east side (naming pond); Bell's Neck disputes (1700s Paine/Thatcher/Gorham arbitration) involved John Bell (d. pre-1700, Sandwich orig., admin. Samuel Berry). Mills powered grain; cranberries dominated 19th–20th c., Cape Verdeans owning/working bogs (Gomes family: Manuel B. to Onset).

Rail spurred growth; Broadbrooks-to-Brooks family act renamed via legislature.

Genealogical Resources and Strategies

Core sources:

- Harwich vitals/probate/deeds (Kenwrick/Kendrick chains; Bell/Berry admin.).
- Bog co-op/rail depot logs (Cape Verdean owners/laborers).
- FamilySearch/NEHGR (Mattaquason descendants; Portuguese intermarriages).
- Harwich Historical Society (Paine's 1620–1800 history).

Pleasant Lake's bog-pond saga—from sachem sales to immigrant bogs—unfurls Native/English/Portuguese kin via deeds and depot echoes

South Harwich

South Harwich, a rustic southern village within Harwich in Barnstable County, Massachusetts, retains its 18th-19th century rural charm amid Cape Cod's development pressures, characterized by scattered farms, cranberry bogs, and isolation from deeper harbors that shaped Harwich's maritime core. Part of Harwich's original 1694 incorporation (encompassing pre-1803 Brewster as North Parish), South Harwich featured small-scale agriculture, saltworks, and post-Civil War railroad spurs connecting to Chatham, fostering bog labor and family continuity among Nickerson, Paine, and Cape Verdean descendants. Genealogists access Harwich-wide records enriched by Paine's 1620–1800 history and society collections tracing inland lineages distinct from port-centric Harwich Port/West Harwich.

Indigenous Lands and Colonial Settlement

Wampanoag Monomoitick territory sustained seasonal shellfish/maize camps; post-1620 Plymouth purchases divided tracts into Harwich commons. Early South Harwich farms emerged mid-1700s, proprietors' grants/town meetings allocating meadows for hay/livestock amid sandy soils ill-suited for grains.

Rural Economy: Bogs, Salt, and Rails

Lacking deep ports, villagers pursued saltworks (evaporating seawater for fish preservation), cranberry cultivation (post-1840 boom), and small mills. Civil War-era railroad extension spurred bog freight; Cape Verdeans settled/worked bogs (late 1800s–1900s), intermarrying locals per censuses/directories. Tax rolls/probate detail bog ownership shifts (e.g., Brooks family influences nearby).

Social and Religious Ties

Congregational/Baptist churches (linked to North Harwich origins) logged vitals/discipline; Paine family (Josiah, author of Harwich history) anchored civic life via meetings/schools. Isolation preserved "rustic charm," per society notes.

Modern Retention of Rural Identity

Despite Rt.6/28 pressures, South Harwich resists overdevelopment; Harwich Historical Society/Brooks Academy Museum preserves artifacts/Paine Collection (documents 1620–1800).

Genealogical Resources and Strategies

Essential holdings:

- Harwich vitals/town reports (1843+ births/marriages/deaths).
- Paine's *History of Harwich* (1620–1800 families/Indians).
- Probate/deeds (Barnstable Registry; bog estates).
- Cape Verdean censuses/directories (labor migrations).
- Historical Society (John H. Paine docs; family files).

South Harwich's bog-bound saga—from Monomoyick meadows to rail-freighted cranberries—unveils resilient inland kin via Paine's tome and Harwich's enduring archives.

West Barnstable

West Barnstable, the westernmost village within the Town of Barnstable in Barnstable County, Massachusetts, represents the rural agricultural backbone of Cape Cod's founding settlement, anchored by the Crockers—one of Barnstable's premier families since 1639. Centered around Route 149 and the 1717 Meetinghouse (West Parish Congregational Church), this inland hamlet evolved from salt marsh farms and deacon estates to a quiet commuter suburb preserving colonial homes and family graveyards. Genealogists uncover deep Crocker lineages (Deacon William/Alice, "questionable" John/Joan) via Amos Otis's *Genealogical Notes of Barnstable Families*, town records, and West Parish archives tracing 17th-century Scituate migrants led by Rev. John Lothrop.

Colonial Settlement and Crocker Dominance

Rev. Lothrop's 1639 exodus from Scituate brought Deacon William Crocker (wealthy church leader/large estate) and brother John (childless, "questionable" per Otis) to West Barnstable's salt marshes. William's 2-mile strip (1643) from bay to meadows housed descendants; Experience Crocker (b. ~1660s) owned 13 15/16ths of family home (325 Willow St., adjacent "stone fort"). Blue Crocker resided 1710–1790 before Nye transfer. All Crockers descend from pious William/Alice; 17 Crocker-Crocker marriages noted.

Agricultural and Civic Life

Villagers farmed hay/cattle, saltworks aiding preservation; 1717 Meetinghouse hosted town meetings/schools. Crockers led as deacons/senators (e.g., Nymphas II probate judge). Gustavus A. Hinckley transcribed church/town records (donated NEHGS 1905; searchable CDs).

Social Networks and Preservation

West Parish links trace Lothrop congregants (1616 London origins via Henry Jacob/Jessey Baptist offshoot); NEHGS databases include "Barnstable Church 1639–1892"/"Town 1640–1793." Sturgis Library/Cape Cod Genealogical Society hold Crocker sites (270+).

Genealogical Resources and Strategies

Prime access:

- Barnstable vitals/proprietors (FamilySearch; Lothrop/Crocker grants).

- Otis *Genealogical Notes*/Hinckley transcripts (NEHGS americanancestors.org).
- West Parish church records (1639–1892; Scituate/Barnstable).
- Crocker videos/files (YouTube/1717 Meetinghouse; 400+ individuals).
- Sturgis/CCGS (Crocker estates/probate).

West Barnstable's Crocker meadow realm—from Lothrop deacons to enduring farms—unlocks Scituate exiles via Otis/Hinckley treasures and parish depths.

West Harwich

West Harwich, a vibrant southern village in Harwich (Barnstable County, Massachusetts), emerged as a 19th-century maritime and agricultural hub along the Herring River, famed for the Chase family's multi-generational sea captains and global traders who shaped its economy and Baptist heritage. Straddling Yarmouth/Harwich lines since William Chase's 1630 arrival (Roxbury/Yarmouth settler relocating post-indenture), the village hosted Job Chase Sr. (1736–1833, 15 vessels) and Jr. (fleet of 48 square-riggers), culminating in Caleb Chase (1831–1908, Chase & Sanborn Coffee empire). Its Baptist church (relocated 1828 from North Harwich, rebuilt 1841) and cemetery cenotaph (Chase-Chace Association, 1899) anchor Revolutionary lineage—John Chase dying crossing Delaware (1776), kin in French/Indian/War of 1812/Civil Wars. Genealogists mine Harwich records, Paine histories, and Chase-specific archives tracing 400-year density of Mayflower-descended families.

Indigenous and Colonial Foundations

Wampanoag Herring River basin (Gosnold 1602/Bradford 1622 noted) sustained fertile settlements; Winthrop Fleet families (Bradford/Hopkins) divided tracts post-Mayflower. William Chase (1595–1659, constable/Yarmouth) centered business here despite Yarmouth residence, quelling Narragansett 1644; buried overlooking lake, cenotaph honors descendants.

Maritime Empire and Baptist Anchor

Job Sr.'s Georgian dwelling (still standing) launched schooners from felled timber; Jr.'s riverbank home (1792, extant) sired 16, fueling abolitionist Baptist hotbed (Rev. Richard Chase, cousin). 1841 church replacement served shifting congregants (West/South Dennis/Harwich Port).

Economic and Social Density

Blue-water captains imported culture/finance to village; Chase & Sanborn achieved national brand pre-1893 Chicago Expo. Density of old lines (Doane/Kelley/Paine) exemplifies republic-building via heroism/patriotism.

Preservation Legacy

Harwich Historical Society/Brooks Academy preserve Paine Collection (1620–1800 docs); Chase cenotaph/West Harwich Baptist Cemetery hold keys.

Genealogical Resources and Strategies

Vital holdings:

- Harwich vitals/town reports (1600s+ lineage).

- Paine *History of Harwich* (1620–1800 families).
- Chase-Chace Association *Chronicle* (Vols.1–14, 1910–1924); NEHGR Chase articles (1933–34).
- Probate/deeds (Barnstable; Job Sr./Jr. estates).
- Society files (Paine Collection; Cape Verdean ties).

West Harwich's Chase River realm—from Winthrop captains to coffee moguls—epitomizes Cape lineage density via Paine/Chase tomes and Baptist stones.

Monument Beach

Monument Beach, a coastal census-designated place (CDP) within Bourne (Barnstable County, Massachusetts), marks the western Cape Cod gateway where Buzzards Bay meets the Cape Cod Canal, evolving from 17th-century Sandwich farms into a 19th-century rail/shipping depot and modern summer enclave. Named for its beachfront monument (likely WWII or canal-related), the village boomed post-1914 canal opening (first ship *Rose Standish*, FDR aboard destroyer *McDougall*) and 1872 Woods Hole rail branch, fostering merchants like Perez H. Phinney (lifelong resident/store owner). Genealogists tap Bourne/Sandwich records, canal archives, and cemetery surveys revealing Phinney, Bourne, and maritime kin amid transportation revolutions.

Indigenous and Colonial Farming Roots

Wampanoag shores sustained shellfish camps; Sandwich (1637) proprietors granted Monument Neck tracts for meadows/hay. Pre-1884 Bourne incorporation, farms dotted County Road; Bourne Archives hold family collections/photos/oral histories tracing Sandwich splits.

Rail, Canal, and Commercial Surge

Old Colony Railroad (1872 Woods Hole spur) anchored Phinney's Monument Beach store; 1909–1914 canal excavation (Monument River dredging, Collins Farm) drew laborers, with dam breaches/parades documented in Bourne photos. Post-canal, boat lines/parades boosted inns/shops; treacherous Hog Island/Mashnee currents spurred lifesaving stations.

Social and Maritime Ties

Congregational churches logged vitals; Civil War vets/enslaved ties surface in Pemberton Collection (Ayer/Farwell papers, James Ayer MD practiced here). WWII monuments/cemeteries (Monument Beach Cemetery, surveyed 2002 by Carlson to 1870) hold Phinney/Bourne graves.

Modern Preservation

Bourne Historical Commission preserves canal ties/fire dept histories; CDP status (pop. 2,790) balances beaches/resorts.

Genealogical Resources and Strategies

Core access:

- Bourne/Sandwich vitals (pre-1884 Sandwich; FamilySearch).
- Cemetery surveys (Monument Beach/Neck, Carlson 2002).

- Canal photos/archives (Bourne slideshows; first ship/parades).
- Phinney family/business records (rail merchants).
- Pemberton/Ayer papers (MHS; MD practices).

Monument Beach's canal-rail nexus—from Wampanoag shores to FDR's parade—unlocks gateway kin via Bourne digs and beach stones.

Pocasset

Pocasset, a serene bayside village within Bourne (Barnstable County, Massachusetts), embodies Cape Cod's transition from 17th-century Wampanoag oyster beds to colonial farms, 20th-century social clubs, and modern harbor preservation amid Buzzards Bay. Named from Algonquian "where a strait widens out" (distinct from RI's historic Pocasset village), its shores drew Native shellfish camps before Sandwich proprietors' grants (pre-1884 Bourne split). The 1905 Pocasset Improvement Club (charter members: Barlows, Bliss, Lumbert sisters, Phinney) fought pollution/mini-malls via ancient ways research, evolving into Pocasset Village Association (1980s Barlows Landing Assoc.). Genealogists access Bourne/Sandwich vitals, cemetery catalogs, and club minutes tracing Nye, Barlow, Phinney, Tobey kin alongside Cape Verdean laborers.

Indigenous Bays and Colonial Farms

Wampanoag (Cotuit-related) harvested oysters; post-1620 Plymouth deeds formalized transfers. Sandwich farms (pre-Bourne 1884) dotted County/Barlows Landing Roads; Nye lineage (Benjamin Sandwich progenitor) farmed here, per Hyannis Nye genealogy. 1905 club origins reflect year-round/summer divides (Bliss hoteliers building beach homes).

Social Clubs and Preservation Fights

Pocasset Improvement Club (1905–) battled beach closures (1980s pollution task force), mini-mall threats (Village Way ancient way saved), and McMansions; plaques ("POCASSET VILLAGE 1694"), community building rentals, scholarships ensued. Barlows Landing Assoc. (1960s social club) preceded; Tobey family (Ben/Rhoda/Malcolm County Rd.) noted in Bourne history posts.

Maritime and Modern Harbor Life

Canal proximity spurred boating; WWII murders (Davis family 1901, unrelated Phinney girl) surface in local lore. Pocasset Cemetery (catalogued alphabetically w/genealogy links) holds keys.

Genealogical Resources and Strategies

Essential sources:

- Bourne/Sandwich vitals (FamilySearch; pre-1884 Sandwich).
- Pocasset Cemetery catalog (alphabetical w/links).
- Club minutes/archives (PVA; Barlow/Phinney/Lumbert).
- Nye genealogy (Sandwich-Hyannis progenitors).
- Bourne Archives/Library (Ancestry in-library; Tobey/Davis photos).

Pocasset's bay-club saga—from Wampanoag oysters to pollution warriors—unveils harbor kin via cemetery catalogs and Barlows' ancient ways.

Sagamore

Sagamore, a village within the Town of Bourne in Barnstable County, Massachusetts, carries a name rooted in the Algonquian term "sagamore," meaning chief or leader, reflecting its Indigenous and colonial heritage. Sagamore developed from early 17th-century Wampanoag territories into an industrial and residential community shaped by its proximity to the Cape Cod Canal, railroads, and maritime commerce. Today, the village balances historical preservation with modern growth, offering genealogists a rich record base spanning Indigenous land deeds, colonial town activities, canal construction documents, and 19th-20th century census and church registers.

Indigenous Background and Early Settlement

The area around Sagamore was traditionally occupied by Wampanoag peoples, including the leaders who held councils on Sagamore Hill. The early 1600s saw conflict and negotiations between Indigenous groups and English settlers. Important early sachems such as Nanepashemet, Sagamore John, and Sagamore George governed the region before colonists expanded into these lands. Several deeds and colonial records document land transfers from Native owners to English proprietors, framing genealogical inquiry into Native-descended families and settler pioneers.

Colonial and Industrial Development

Initially part of Sandwich and Plymouth Colony land grants, Sagamore began as a farming and fishing settlement, with early proprietors' records showing family landholdings. The construction of the Cape Cod Canal (1914) transformed Sagamore into a transportation hub, spurring industrial growth, rail connections, and harbor development. Shipbuilding and fishing industries flourished, documented through customs rolls, insurance policies, and town meeting minutes. Census records reflect demographic shifts including immigrant labor involvement and maritime occupations.

Religious and Social Institutions

Sagamore churches (Congregational, Methodist) maintained vital records instrumental for genealogists, including baptism, marriage, and burial registers. Fraternal organizations and community groups contributed to social cohesion, with meeting minutes, membership lists, and event programs preserved in local archives.

Modern Preservation and Community Identity

Preservation of historic districts, such as those near the canal, and recognition of Indigenous heritage sites like Sagamore Hill enhance research opportunities. Local historical organizations and libraries house collections of photographs, personal papers, and maps, assisting genealogists in tracing family stories linked to Cape Cod's evolving industrial and cultural landscape.

Genealogical Resources and Research Strategies

Genealogists investigating Sagamore ancestors should consult:

- Wampanoag land deeds and colonial town records detailing early land ownership and transfers.

- Cape Cod Canal construction archives and related transportation documents.
- Town meeting minutes, census records, and vital records from local churches.
- Fraternal organization archives providing social context.
- Historical society collections and local libraries maintaining family manuscripts and photographs.

Sagamore's layered history—from Indigenous leadership through canal-induced transformation to thriving contemporary community—offers genealogists a robust archival framework to explore lineage woven into the fabric of this historic Cape Cod village.

Sagamore Beach

Sagamore Beach, a coastal village and census-designated place (CDP) within Bourne in Barnstable County, Massachusetts, marks the Cape Cod Canal's northern entrance on Buzzards Bay, transforming from Wampanoag council grounds atop Sagamore Hill into a 20th-century summer colony anchored by the 1903 Sagamore Beach Colony Club. Named for Algonquian "sagamore" (chief), its dunes hosted Wampanoag/Manomet tribal meetings before Mayflower's 1620 Provincetown landing spurred settlement; post-1884 Bourne incorporation, the beach boomed via 1914 canal (first transit *Rose Standish*) and Christian Endeavor Movement land buys (1905). Genealogists explore Bourne/Sandwich records plus club histories (*Sidney Clark's Sagamore Beach*, 2003 centennial), boarding house censuses (1920 Bourne family PO), and Phinney/Fisher lineages tied to rail-era merchants/teachers.

Indigenous Councils and Colonial Shores

Sagamore Hill convened Wampanoag chiefs; epidemics/land sales (Sandwich proprietors) yielded farms pre-Bourne split. Historical markers note Native governance; deeds trace transitions.

Rail, Canal, and Summer Colony Rise

Old Colony Railroad (1870s) spurred boarding houses (Bourne PO family, Harold Bourne tragedy); canal dredging (1909–14) drew laborers. Colony Club (1903, 100th anniv. book) hosted Fishers (1912 Sandwich teacher origins), Christian Endeavors owning tracts by 1905; beaches/parades defined social life.

Social Networks and Preservation

Congregational/Methodist vitals; 1920 census logs boarders. Bourne Historical Commission preserves canal ties; past maps aid property research.

Genealogical Resources and Strategies

Key collections:

- Bourne/Sandwich vitals/censuses (FamilySearch; 1920 boarding houses).
- *Sidney Clark's History of Sagamore Beach* (club centennial).
- Cemetery surveys/PO photos (Bourne family).
- Canal photos/minutes (town slideshows/HC).

- Pemberton papers (MHS; local MDs/families).

Sagamore Beach's chief-dune saga—from tribal hill to canal colony—reveals summer kin via Clark's tome, censuses, and shore stones.

Cataumet

Cataumet, a tranquil bayside village within Bourne (Barnstable County, Massachusetts), nestles along Buzzards Bay where riverine sites sustained Wampanoag coastal occupancy, evolving through colonial hamlets, Methodist meetinghouses, and whaling voyages into a preserved maritime enclave. Named from Algonquian roots amid Pocasset/Manomet territories, its 1627 Aptucxet Trading Post proximity fueled early trade; post-1884 Bourne incorporation, woolen factories/triphammers dotted shores, with Rev. Richard Bourne (first Wampanoag preacher) anchoring Christian Native worship (meetinghouse relocated Methodist 1822). Genealogists mine Bourne/Sandwich records, Nye/Handy whaling logs, and Cataumet Cemetery's exhaustive family-group catalog—Charles H. Nye (Hyannis progenitor from Sandwich Benjamin Nye) and Henry T. Handy (1845–1916, 5-voyage logkeeper)—revealing Native/English/Portuguese maritime kin.

Indigenous Riverine Sites and Trading Post

Contact-period Wampanoag villages at Cataumet/Pocasset exploited alewives/cod/lobster; 1627 Aptucxet Post (nearby Monument River) bridged Plymouth/Wampanoag exchange. Plantation-era (1620–1675) Native trails became European routes; Bourne MHC notes coastal/riverine settlements persisting into colonial fences.

Colonial Hamlets and Religious Shifts

Sandwich settlement (1638+) yielded Cataumet hamlets south of Monument River; Baptists (1796–1806)/Reformed Methodists (1822) shared meetinghouse before Methodist dominance. Jonathan Bourne Historical Center (1897 memorial/library) honors whaler-legislator (town namesake, Rev. Richard ancestor).

Industrial and Whaling Era

Early industrial triphammer/woolen factory spurred growth; Henry T. Handy's whaling career (1866–1886 New Bedford voyages) exemplifies maritime ties, logs donated family descendants.

Genealogical Resources and Strategies

Prime repositories:

- Bourne/Sandwich vitals/proprietors (FamilySearch; pre-1884).
- Cataumet Cemetery catalog (family-grouped genealogy).
- Nye genealogy (Benjamin Sandwich to Hyannis Charles H.).
- Handy whaling logs (5 voyages; family-transcribed).
- Bourne Library (Ancestry/Fold3 in-library; Jonathan Bourne Center).

Cataumet's preacher-post saga—from Wampanoag rivers to whaler memorials—unfurls Native/Bourne/Nye/Handy trails via cemetery kinships and bay-bound logs.

Census-Designated Places

Buzzards Bay

Buzzards Bay, a large estuary off the southern coast of Massachusetts within Barnstable County and adjoining towns, has long been a vital hub of maritime activity, Indigenous settlement, and colonial development. Named by early settlers for the osprey birds once mistakenly called "buzzards," the bay has nurtured Indigenous communities such as the Wampanoag, early English colonists from Plymouth and Dartmouth, and later immigrants who built thriving fishing, shipbuilding, and farming economies along its shores. Genealogists exploring families connected to Buzzards Bay draw upon deeds, town records, maritime logs, and property surveys spanning from early colonial times through present-day environmental preservation efforts.

Indigenous Stewardship and Early Colonization

Long before European arrival, Wampanoag peoples occupied bayshore villages engaging in fishing, shellfish harvesting, and controlling forested uplands. Their land use and governance are reflected in early 17th-century deeds and colonial negotiations, where places like Sippican and Agawam Bay carried Indigenous place names adapted into English settlement boundaries. Early English settlers acquired lands through purchases and grants, setting patterns of proprietorship and town formation documented in court and land records.

Maritime and Agricultural Economy

Settlements around Buzzards Bay focused on fishing cod and shellfish, shipbuilding, and small-scale farming. The bay's natural resources supported coastal communities such as Wareham, Marion (formerly Sippican), and Bourne, with maritime records, customs entries, and crew lists chronicling active seafarers and vessel operations. Agricultural censuses and tax listings trace farm operations and cranberry bogs—still economically significant in some areas.

Environmental History and Preservation

Buzzards Bay has undergone extensive environmental change, with pollution, land reclamation, and development threats emerging in the 20th century. The Buzzards Bay Coalition, founded in the early 1990s by local residents and scientists, has worked to restore water quality and protect habitats. Environmental reports, conservation commission minutes, and land use plans provide modern genealogists with context about how land and water stewardship affected family life and property ownership.

Genealogical Resources and Research Strategies

Researchers may utilize:

- Colonial land grants and town proprietors' records describing early homesteads.
- Town vital records and probate files for families around Buzzards Bay towns.
- Maritime logs, customs documents, and whaling records detailing sailors' identities and occupations.
- Environmental and conservation archives documenting land use and ownership changes affecting later generations.

- Local historical society collections, newspaper archives, and cemetery surveys for family histories.

Buzzards Bay's layered history—from Indigenous stewardship and colonial settlement through maritime prosperity and environmental challenges—offers genealogists a rich archival landscape to explore family stories tied to the waters and shores of southeastern Massachusetts.

Dennis Port

Dennis Port, a bustling southern village within Dennis (Barnstable County, Massachusetts), thrives on Nantucket Sound's shores as Cape Cod's tourism epicenter, evolving from 17th-century Nobscusset Wampanoag planting fields into a post-Revolutionary maritime/trading hub and 19th-century resort. Part of pre-1793 Yarmouth's West Parish, it anchored saltworks (Dennis pioneered solar evaporation, 47 north-shore vats by 1802), shipbuilding, and fishing along Bass River, with shipyards crafting large vessels until mid-1800s decline. Post-rail (1865 South Dennis station), West Dennis/Dennis Port prospered via coastal trade, now boasting Sea View (DHS luncheon site) and CCGS research center. Genealogists harness Dennis Heritage Landscape Reconnaissance Report (MHC), DHS digital archive (ship logs/images), and Cape Cod Genealogy Society (library/office hours) tracing Thacher/Crowell/Howes/Nickerson founders to modern vacationers.

Indigenous Nobscusset and Colonial North/South Divide

Nobscusset Wampanoag (Wampanoag Nation) trails (Route 6A precursor) linked Indian Field/Scargo Lake; 1639 Thacher/Crowe/Howes/Nickerson settlement encircled fields. Sandwich Moraine bisected town (north farms/south harbors), East Dennis agricultural, South Dennis Bass River-focused, West Dennis/Dennis Port post-Revolution booms.

Maritime Saltworks and Shipbuilding Zenith

North shore saltworks fueled fishing/shipping; Dennis led U.S. solar salt production. Harbors serviced schooners till 1870–1915 decline (population halved); shoe/tack factories failed. Cranberries/rail (1865) sustained; Old King's Highway Historic District (1680–present) protects 100+ maritime homes.

Tourism and Preservation Era

Route 6 (1920s)/Community Preservation Act (2005) funded cemeteries/Historical Society events; DHS digital archive (tens of thousands images/letters/ship logs) weaves "historical spider web" across sources. CCGS (Dennis Library) offers Thursday research aid.

Genealogical Resources and Strategies

Core repositories:

- Dennis vitals (pre-1841 church; post-town clerks).
- DHS Digital Archive (searchable ship logs/photos/letters).
- MHC Reconnaissance Report (Bass River Corridor/Howes Cemetery/Tobey Farm).
- CCGS Research Center (Dennis Port library; Ancestry/Fold3).
- NEHGS/Old King's Highway plaques (maritime families).

Dennis Port's salt-ship-resort arc—from Nobscusset fields to DHS webs—unlocks founder kin via archives and Sound shores

East Falmouth

East Falmouth, a vibrant village within the Town of Falmouth in Barnstable County, Massachusetts, combines deep colonial roots with evolving maritime and summer resort economies. This area, settled in the 17th century as part of the broader Falmouth township (incorporated in 1686), developed around its coastline along Buzzards Bay, expanding with farms, fishing, and salt marsh industries. Over time, East Falmouth also emerged as a center of seasonal tourism and residential growth, offering genealogists a rich suite of records from town vital records and church registers to maritime logs and land deeds that illuminate centuries of family histories tied to the Cape's waters and lands.

Indigenous and Early Colonial Settlement

Before European settlement, East Falmouth was part of the Wampanoag Nation's territory, with Native peoples relying heavily on shellfish bays and inland hunting grounds. The arrival of English settlers in the mid-1600s brought changes, formalized in land deeds and colonial proprietors' grants recorded in early town books. These records reflect the gradual settlement of families and lay the foundation for genealogical tracing.

Maritime Economy and Agriculture

East Falmouth's economy historically linked to fishing, boatbuilding, salt harvesting, and cranberry bog cultivation, documented in fishing licenses, customs records, and agricultural censuses. The shipbuilding industry supported schooners and smaller craft navigating Buzzards Bay and connecting with regional ports. Tax records, probate inventories, and town reports track the economic and social standing of residents engaged in these livelihoods.

Religious and Civic Life

Congregational, Methodist, and Catholic churches shaped community life, their registers capturing baptisms, marriages, and deaths predating state vital registration. Town meeting minutes reveal investment in schools, poor relief, and infrastructure, illustrating the civic engagement of East Falmouth families.

Tourism and Modern Growth

Twentieth-century improvements in transportation and the rise of seaside tourism fueled construction of summer homes, beaches, and resorts. Land records, zoning files, and local newspapers document this shift and its impact on community demographics. Historical societies and libraries maintain collections of photographs, personal papers, and oral histories enriching genealogical research.

Genealogical Resources and Research Strategies

- Town vital records (births, marriages, deaths) and proprietors' grants for colonial-period data.
- Church registers from multiple denominations for extended family connections.
- Maritime records that include crew lists and customs documents for coastal families.

- Probate, tax lists, and agricultural schedules for economic context.
- Historical society archives and digital collections for photographs and personal histories.

East Falmouth's layered history—from Wampanoag stewardship through maritime enterprise to a thriving coastal community—offers genealogists a comprehensive resource landscape for uncovering family legacies along Cape Cod's eastern shore.

East Harwich

East Harwich, a quiet rural village in the eastern section of Harwich within Barnstable County, Massachusetts, preserves its 18th-19th century agricultural and maritime character amid Cape Cod's development, centered on the 1854 First Congregational Church and adjacent cemetery that anchor the village's historic core. Part of Harwich's original South Parish (incorporated 1694, pre-1803 Brewster split), East Harwich's sandy soils supported farms and small mills rather than deep-water ports, with families like the Brooks/Broadbrooks (Beriah b.1676 arr.1694) contributing to civic life through stores, banks, and temperance efforts. Genealogists draw from Harwich-wide records enriched by Josiah Paine's *History of Harwich* (1620–1800), Brooks Free Library origins, and church/cemetery surveys tracing Monomoyick Native ties and colonial lineages like Paine, Nickerson, and Cape Verdean bog workers.

Indigenous Monomoyick and Colonial Farms

Monomoyick Wampanoag (South Parish) lands yielded shellfish/maize; post-1620 Plymouth purchases divided tracts into Harwich commons. Beriah Broadbrooks (15 children, name legislated Brooks 1806) arrived 1694 incorporation year, spawning Obed (storekeeper/Mashpee commissioner/Cape Cod banks founder), Henry C. (Boston businessman/Brooks Free Library donor), and sisters Tamesin (librarian/Brooks Park), Harriet/Sarah (First Parish parsonage).

Rural Anchor: Church, Cemetery, and Bogs

1854 Congregational Church (current form) with cemetery forms "stunning centerpiece"; Harwich Conservation Trust traces century-old journals to mid-1600s Monomoyick owners generation-by-generation. Cranberries/rails isolated East Harwich's "rustic charm," Cape Verdeans working bogs late 1800s+.

Preservation and Civic Continuity

Brooks Free Library (Greek Revival bank site)/Park bookend Main Street (Harwich Center proximity); Paine's treatise details North/South Parish tensions.

Genealogical Resources and Strategies

Key repositories:

- Harwich vitals/town reports (FamilySearch; pre-1841 church).
- Paine *History of Harwich* (1620–1800 families/Indians).
- Brooks Free Library (Broadbrooks/Brooks papers; Obed/Henry estates).
- Church/cemetery surveys (1854 Congregational; Monomoyick chains).
- Harwich Historical Society (Paine Collection; Cape Verdean censuses).

East Harwich's church-cemetery saga—from Monomoyick tracts to Brooks bookends—unveils rural kin via Paine's annals and Broadbrooks' banks.

East Sandwich

East Sandwich, a village within the Town of Sandwich in Barnstable County, Massachusetts, encapsulates the rich history of one of Cape Cod's oldest communities. Sandwich, incorporated in 1639 as the first town on Cape Cod, developed around maritime trade, agriculture, and early industry such as glassmaking and shipbuilding. East Sandwich, with its proximity to Cape Cod Bay and accessible docks, evolved into a key port and residential village, blending colonial roots with modern growth. Genealogists researching families in East Sandwich access extensive town vital records, land deeds, church registers, and early proprietors' grant documents documenting foundational Cape Cod families such as the Nyes, Wings, and Purdues.

Early Settlement and Maritime Economy

East Sandwich traces to 17th-century grants following English settlement of Wampanoag lands, with early proprietors' books documenting land allocations and community planning. Notable early settlers include Ralph Jones (1600–1685), connected by marriage to Mayflower Pilgrims, and Benjamin Nye (1620–1750), whose homestead survives today as the Nye Museum. East Sandwich quickly grew as a maritime hub, with docks supporting fishing fleets, shipbuilding yards, and later steamship connections to mainland ports. Ship registries, customs records, and maritime logs provide critical genealogical data on seafarers and owners.

Religious and Social Institutions

The village's religious life historically centered on Congregational churches, whose baptismal, marriage, and membership rolls predate state vital registration. Later, Catholic and other denominations established parishes, expanding genealogical resource diversity. Town meeting records, school oversight minutes, and poor relief accounts illuminate governance and community networks pivotal for family histories.

Industry and Modern Development

Early industry included New England's first successful glassworks (1638) and robust shipbuilding, documented in town and probate files. In the 19th and 20th centuries, East Sandwich shifted with tourism, academic institutions, and residential growth, creating property records, directories, and local historical society archives contributing to genealogical narratives.

Genealogical Resources and Research Strategies

Genealogists focusing on East Sandwich should explore:

- Town vital records and proprietors' grants for foundational data.
- Church registers spanning colonial through modern periods.
- Maritime records that include logs, customs, and ship registries.
- Probate, land deeds, and tax rolls detailing property and wealth.
- Archival collections such as the Nye Museum and Sandwich Historical Society.

East Sandwich's layered history—from Wampanoag lands through colonial enterprise to modern village life—offers genealogists an extensive archival landscape to uncover family legacies connected to Cape Cod's earliest European foothold.

Forestdale

Forestdale, an inland village within the Town of Sandwich in Barnstable County, Massachusetts, is renowned for its industrial heritage centered on the 1825 Forestdale Woolen Mill (one of Cape Cod's earliest textile factories) and the intertwined Dillingham, Wing, Tupper, and Nye families who shaped its Quaker-leaning community amid 17th-century settlement. As Sandwich's eastern outlier (incorporated 1637), Forestdale emerged from Wampanoag woodlands where the "Ten Men of Saugus" (including Edward Dillingham/Thomas Tupper) founded the town, drawing 60 families (Deborah Wing/Benjamin Nye) 100 miles through wilderness for religious/economic refuge. Genealogists access Sandwich vital records (to 1885), Wing Family registers, and Nye/Dillingham genealogies revealing Quaker sympathies, mill labor, and continuous homesteads like Wing Fort House (1641, oldest continuously family-owned in NE).

Indigenous Woodlands and Saugus Founders

Wampanoag forests sustained pre-contact camps; 1637 Plymouth grant to "ten men of Saugus" (Dillingham/Tupper) allocated 60-family tracts. Edward/Ursula Dillingham (Cottesbach, England) settled with children, Edward fined 1657 for Quaker sympathy. Deborah Bachiler Wing (Stephen's widow, Rev. John Wing) walked from Saugus, her father Stephen Bachiler embodying Puritan individualism. Stephen Wing m. Oseath Dillingham, occupying Wing home continuously.

Quaker Refuge and Textile Industry

Sandwich hosted America's first Quaker meeting (1658, 17 families covertly at Christopher Hollow); Dillinghams/Wings joined, fined for refusing Fidelity Oath. Thomas/Anne Tupper (ship's carpenter/lay minister) and Benjamin Nye (constable, m. Katherine Tupper 1640, 8 children) farmed without Quaker conversion. Forestdale Mill (1825+) employed descendants amid religious tensions.

Family Continuity and Preservation

Wing Fort House (1641–present Wing Association) and Nye Homestead (1620 Benjamin) endure; Sandwich Historical Commission aids house histories via MACRIS/maps/archives.

Genealogical Resources and Strategies

Vital repositories:

- Sandwich vitals (to 1885, NEHGS/Internet Archive).
- Wing Family of America (John/Deborah descendants).
- Dillingham/Tupper/Nye genealogies (family sites; Otis *Barnstable Families*).
- Sandwich Archives (family/subject files; Corpus Christi parish).
- Sturgis Library (Cape Cod Collections).

Forestdale's Quaker-mill saga—from Saugus walkers to Wing/Nye fortresses—unveils founder kin via vital chains and family forts.

Harwich Center

Harwich Center, the historic heart of Harwich in Barnstable County, Massachusetts, serves as the civic and commercial core of a town incorporated in 1694 from Plymouth Colony's "plantation of the old-comers," encompassing what became Brewster (North Parish, split 1803). Anchored by Main Street's Brooks Free Library (eastern end, Greek Revival from Obed Brooks' bank) and Brooks Academy Museum (western end, Harwich Historical Society home), the village symbolizes the Brooks/Broadbrooks family's outsized role—from Beriah Broadbrooks (arr. 1694, 15 children, name changed by legislature 1806) to Henry C. Brooks (Boston businessman/library donor). Genealogists mine Josiah Paine's *History of Harwich* (1620–1800), digitized town reports (150+ years), vital records (1694–1850), and society collections tracing Monomoyick Wampanoag purchases, South Parish tensions, and maritime families like Chase/Snow whose Exchange Building (1855–1964) hosted fairs/theater/town hall.

Monomoyick Lands and Parish Divisions

Monomoyick Wampanoag sold large tracts post-1620 (modern Harwich/Brewster/Chatham/Orleans/Eastham); South Parish (Harwich proper) vs. North (Brewster) rivalries fill Paine's treatise. Beriah Broadbrooks anchored South Parish commerce, his descendants Obed (Mashpee commissioner/banker), Tamesin (librarian), Harriet/Sarah (parsonage keepers) bookending Main Street.

Exchange Era and Civic Vibrancy

Chester Snow's 1885 Victorian Exchange (architect Samuel N. Small, stained glass from Europe) rose post-1876 fire destroying records; hosted elections/plays/skating/graduations until 1964 demolition (town chose Bell's Neck conservation). Caleb Chase (West Harwich, Chase & Sanborn Coffee) owned briefly; Tobey's Store/Bates Hardware flanked entry.

Preservation and Cultural Continuity

HHS (1953, Brooks Academy) exhibits cranberry culture (Cape's largest); digitized reports preserve local history. Facebook groups/Harwich Historical Research aid community sleuthing.

Genealogical Resources and Strategies

Essential archives:

- Paine *History of Harwich* (1620–1800 families/Indians).
- Harwich vitals (1694–1850, FamilySearch).
- HHS Paine Collection/Brooks papers (Broadbrooks estates).
- Digitized town reports (150+ years).
- CCGS/DHS (Dennis neighbor; Cape-wide).

Harwich Center's bookend saga—from Monomoyick tracts to Exchange echoes—unveils Brooks/Paine kin via Paine's pages and society's shelves.

Harwich Port

Harwich Port, a coastal village and harbor community within the Town of Harwich in Barnstable County, Massachusetts, evolved as a vibrant maritime center shaped by 17th-century Wampanoag ties and English colonial settlement. It developed with extensive wharves and docks stretching into Nantucket Sound, fostering fishing, shipbuilding, and coastal trade industries that cemented its economic importance. Incorporated as part of Harwich in 1694, Harwich Port has sustained a distinct maritime culture and now thrives as a summer resort village. Genealogists researching in Harwich Port benefit from extensive vital records, church registers, maritime crew lists, customs documents, town reports, and family papers preserved in local historical societies and libraries.

Indigenous Origins and Colonial Development

The land was originally Wampanoag territory known for abundant marine resources. Early English settlers purchased lands in several tracts, establishing farms and fishing communities. Harbor construction and extension of wharfs into the bay allowed deep-draft vessels to dock, facilitating trade. Early settlers' names appear in town meeting records and land grants, illustrating rapid economic growth tied to maritime industries.

Maritime Economy and Shipbuilding

Harwich Port became renowned for its fishing fleets, as well as shipbuilding yards producing schooners and fishing vessels documented in customs and insurance records. Crew lists enumerate the men who worked on these vessels, while local newspapers and probate files provide context on families involved in maritime work.

Religious and Civic Life

Congregational, Baptist, and Methodist churches anchored community life, maintaining registers of baptisms, marriages, and church discipline. Town meeting minutes document education, infrastructure projects, and social welfare programs, revealing active civic participation by harbor families.

Tourism and Preservation

In the 19th and 20th centuries, Harwich Port became a seasonal resort destination with hotels, guesthouses, and beaches attracting visitors, reflected in property records and local directories. Preservation efforts led by the Harwich Historical Society protect its historical architecture and maintain archival collections of photographs, letters, and oral histories.

Genealogical Resources and Research Recommendations

Key genealogical sources include:

- Town vital records (birth, marriage, and death) and town meeting minutes.
- Church registers from multiple denominations.
- Maritime customs, crew lists, ship registries, and insurance records.
- Probate files and land deeds held at Barnstable County registries.
- Harwich Historical Society archives and local library collections with family papers and photographs.

Harwich Port's layered history—from Wampanoag fisheries to colonial maritime trade and modern resort village—provides genealogists with a wealth of records to explore family histories woven into the maritime fabric of Cape Cod.

Mashpee Neck

Mashpee Neck, a peninsula census-designated place (CDP, pop. 1,000 in 2010) within the Town of Mashpee in Barnstable County, Massachusetts, extends into Wakeby and Mashpee Ponds as a core of Wampanoag reservation lands where colonial guardianships clashed with tribal self-determination from 1670 deed confirmations through 1870 town incorporation. As Mashpee's southeastern "neck" (peninsula), it housed praying Indian settlements like Pawpoesit/Coatuit amid 25 sq mi reserved by Plymouth Colony (1665 deed, confirmed 1685), evolving under missionary Richard Bourne (Sandwich, first Wampanoag preacher) into self-governing district (1763 Act) before land allotments (1834/1842 Acts dividing 5,000 acres). Genealogists navigate proprietary records (RDAP allotments), guardians' reports, and family petitions (Apes 1833/Amos/Attaquin signers) tracing Coombs/Hendricks/Hicks/Jonas/Mills/Oakley/Pells/Pocknet amid Bourne/Jones/Besse continuity.

Wampanoag Reservation and Guardianship Era

Mattaquason heirs deeded 25 sq mi (1665/1670) as self-governing plantation; guardians (1746–1834) oversaw proprietors (Indians/molattoes), protested via petitions (1763 Act granting district status). Phineas Fish Ministry sparked Apes-led resistance (1833); 1834/1842 allotments (60 acres/adult, inalienable till 1869) preserved ~5,000 acres tribal.

Town Incorporation and Family Continuity

1870 incorporation (vs. 1869 citizenship push) retained Native majority; Bourne/Jones/Besse houses persist (Patience Bourne house to Lillian Besse Nichols). Early families (Amos/Attaquin/Keeter/Mingo/Mye/Simon/Queppish/Webquish faded; Coombs/Hendricks etc. endure).

Genealogical Resources and Strategies

Key archives:

- Mashpee vitals/proprietors (RDAP allotments; FamilySearch).
- Bourne guardians' reports/petitions (Apes/Amos; 1833–1842).
- Cemetery surveys/old family plots (Bi-Centennial Oakley project).
- Town Clerk genealogy sites (Nickerson/Chatham/Mayflower).
- Sturgis/CCGS (deeds/whaling; tribal histories).

Mashpee Neck's proprietary peninsula—from Mattaquason deed to Attaquin allotments—unveils Wampanoag kin via RDAP chains and guardian grievances.

Monomoscoy Island

Monomoscoy Island, a small peninsula census-designated place (CDP, pop. 147 in 2020) within Mashpee (Barnstable County), juts into Popponesset Bay as a Wampanoag cultural stronghold and summer retreat, connected by causeway amid salt marshes sustaining ancient fishing/shellfish camps. Reserved under the 1660 Mashpee deed (25 sq mi self-governing plantation), it housed Coatuit/Pawpoesit praying Indian settlements under missionary Richard Bourne, evolving through 1834/1842 allotments (RDAP book) and 1870 town incorporation into elite vacation haven for retirees/visitors preserving Native access via cultural easements. Genealogists trace Coombs/Pocknet/Attaquin proprietors via guardians' petitions (1833 Apes-led resistance), cemetery plots (Bi-Centennial Oakley project), and Bourne/Jones continuity houses, enriched by tribal timelines and library resources.

Wampanoag Neck and Proprietary Allotments

Mattaquason heirs' 1665/1670 deeds confirmed Mashpee sovereignty; Monomoscoy's tidal creeks yielded oysters/quahogs, sustaining Coatuit villages. Guardians (1746–1834) oversaw allotments, RDAP recording 60-acre parcels (1842 Act, inalienable till 1869); Phineas Fish disputes fueled Apes petitions, Amos/Attaquin signers protesting starvation/overseers.

Missionary Houses and Family Endurance

Richard Bourne homesteads (Patience Bourne to Isaac Jones/Edwin Besse/Lillian Nichols) dot shores; Timothy Pocknett house (1863) became museum. Early families (Coombs/Hendricks/Hicks/Jonas/Mills/Oakley/Pells/Pocknet) persist, Amos/Keeter/Mingo/Mye/Simon faded; Ellsworth Oakley ("Chief Drifting Goose")/Lizetta Pocknet Barbar embody continuity.

Modern Cultural Easement and Preservation

Ramona Peters (Mashpee Wampanoag) notes Monomoscoy's riverine sanctity (daughter birthed there); easements protect overnight stays/canoe passages amid development threats.

Genealogical Resources and Strategies

Core access:

- Mashpee RDAP allotments/guardians' reports (Apes/Amos petitions).
- Cemetery catalogs (family-grouped; Oakley/Bi-Centennial).
- Tribal timeline/vitals (Town Clerk; FamilySearch).
- Bourne/Jones/Besse deeds (Patience homestead chains).
- Sturgis/CCGS (whaling/Deeds; China Roots Chinese ties).

Monomoscoy's easement neck—from Coatuit allotments to Peters' rivers—reveals proprietary kin via RDAP graves and guardian ghosts.

New Seabury

New Seabury, a modern seaside village located on the Great Neck peninsula in the Town of Mashpee, Barnstable County, Massachusetts, is known as one of New England's first planned, sustainable resort communities, developed in the 1960s on former Wampanoag lands. The Chace family legacy, starting with industrialist Malcolm G. Chace acquiring large tracts in the early 20th century, spurred this transformational project designed by William Warner and Emil Hanslin. It combined residential neighborhoods with recreational features—championship golf, yacht clubs, and conservation-minded "cluster zoning"—laying the foundation for New England's first "smart growth" community. Though relatively recent, New Seabury's development is built on centuries of Indigenous stewardship, colonial utilization, and cranberry agriculture, offering genealogists both historical depth and modern civil records.

Indigenous Roots and Early Land Transactions

The Great Neck peninsula, historically part of Wampanoag reservation lands, was central to Native seasonal resource use including fishing, hunting, and cranberry harvesting. The 1665 Mashpee deed and later tribal petitions document Indigenous claims and disputes before the 19th century subdividing lands for European-American ownership and agriculture.

20th-Century Visionary Development

Starting in 1929, Malcolm G. Chace and partners bought land from speculators and local residents, incorporating businesses like Popponesset Corporation and New Seabury Corporation. The vision for New Seabury as a planned community took shape in 1960 with architects Warner and Hanslin emphasizing natural preservation and village diversity, with Bright Coves as the initial development showcased in national magazines. Subsequent villages, golf courses, and condominium complexes fostered a vibrant year-round and seasonal population.

Growth, Environmental Challenges, and Legal Battles

Following rapid construction, zoning laws challenged the community's special permit in the 1970s, leading to legal actions that affirmed New Seabury's vested rights. However, by the late 1980s, economic downturns and land disputes, notably involving the Mashpee Wampanoag tribe's lawsuit, temporarily halted expansion. Litigation resolved by the late 1970s, and development resumed with innovative housing styles and environmentally sensitive planning, balancing growth with coastal conservation efforts.

Modern Amenities and Community Character

Today, New Seabury encompasses multiple distinctive villages, including High Wood (equestrian-themed), Greensward, Triton Sound, and others with amenities such as golf courses, clubhouses, marinas, and nature preserves. It maintains a blend of historic respect, luxury real estate, and environmental stewardship, attracting retirees, vacationers, and families.

Genealogical Resources and Research Strategies

While New Seabury as a planned development dates to the 20th century, genealogical research benefits from:

- Records of Mashpee Wampanoag and early colonial proprietors of Great Neck peninsula.

- Land deeds, town incorporation documents, and submissions to Mashpee Conservation Commission.
- Historical records from the Chace family and associated corporations founding New Seabury.
- Local archives, including the Mashpee Public Library and the Peninsula Council, which maintain records related to village development and community planning.
- Broader genealogical records of Mashpee area families in the 19th and 20th centuries relevant to families displaced or connected with New Seabury land use.

New Seabury's blend of Indigenous heritage, visionary 20th-century planning, and ongoing community evolution offers genealogists a unique opportunity to explore family histories that weave through Native stewardship and contemporary Cape Cod lifestyles. The village stands as a testament to evolving notions of conservation, community, and development on historic lands.

North Eastham

North Eastham, the northern village of Eastham within Barnstable County, Massachusetts, represents the original Nauset settlement core where seven founding families (49 persons)—Prince, Doane, Snow, Cooke, Higgins, Smalley, Bangs—established "Nosset" (1644/1651 Eastham) amid Wampanoag Nauset territory. Led by Thomas Prince (Fortune 1621, Patience Brewster m.1624, 4 children incl. Mercy Freeman b.1631), these "Nosset-7" relocated from Plymouth's barren lands, renaming Nauset to Eastham (1651). Genealogists access Eastham Historical Society's Margaret Bready Genealogy Collection, Pratt's *Comprehensive History* (1644–1844), Libby's *Knowles Family* (Richard Knowles Plymouth/Eastham mariner), and Cove Burying Ground surveys tracing Mayflower (Brewster/Prince) and Fortune (Thomas Prince) descendants alongside Nauset interactions.

Nauset Wampanoag and Nosset-7 Arrival

Nauset (Nauset Harbor) hosted Wampanoag villages; 1644 seven families purchased lands post-Plymouth "straightness/barrenness" complaints (Bradford). Thomas Prince (Plymouth jury 1639, Nauset surveyor 1651) governed remotely till 1665 Plymouth relocation; Mercy Prince Freeman (d.1711 Cove) gravestone exemplifies winged-head slate artistry.

Founding Families and Maritime Lifelines

Richard Knowles (Plymouth 1637/8, Eastham 1654 meadow grants, d.~1674/5) sired John (Taunton 1675 slain), Samuel (Pochy Flats), James (inv.1678); Edward Smalley (Piscataway NJ 1669, "New England too restrictive"). Deacon John Doane (founder lineage) and Knowles descendants fill Pratt/Libby genealogies.

Preservation and Archival Treasures

Eastham Historical Society (Bready Collection, Library of Cape Cod History & Genealogy) houses Millenium Grove photos; Eastham Library LibGuides link digital archives/databases.

Genealogical Resources and Strategies

Vital repositories:

- Eastham vitals (FamilySearch; Bowman transcription to 1849).
- Bready Collection/EHS Local History (Nosset-7 descendants; Nauset encounters).
- Libby *Knowles Family* (Richard to 5th gen; Plymouth-Eastham).
- Pratt *History* (1644–1844 Eastham/Wellfleet/Orleans).
- Cove Burying Ground (winged stones; Mercy Freeman).

North Eastham's Nosset nucleus—from Nauset purchases to Prince vigils—unveils founding kin via Bready shelves and Cove skulls.

North Falmouth

North Falmouth, a rural inland village within the Town of Falmouth in Barnstable County, Massachusetts, developed as an agricultural outpost amid Wampanoag woodlands, evolving from 17th-century proprietors' grants into a 19th-century farming and small-industry hamlet distinct from coastal Falmouth proper. Settled post-1686 town incorporation, its meadows and ponds supported hay, cranberries, and mills, with families like Hinckley (James 1767–1812 selectman) dominating civic life per town records and family collections. Genealogists leverage Falmouth vital records (to 1850 Brown transcription), Historical Society family papers (Hinckley/Bourne), and library special collections tracing inland lineages alongside coastal maritime kin.

Wampanoag Woodlands and Proprietors' Division

Wampanoag inland sites yielded seasonal camps; 1661 proprietors' records allocated North Falmouth tracts for meadows/livestock, formalized via town books/deeds. Early farms encircled ponds, avoiding harbor competition.

Agricultural Hamlets and Civic Anchors

Hinckley papers (FHS collection) detail selectman duties (1803–1812); Congregational registers logged vitals predating state mandates. Tax rolls/probate reveal farm continuity amid 19th-century cranberry shifts.

Preservation via Societies and Libraries

Falmouth Genealogical Society aids via drop-in sessions (Tuesdays 2–4pm Reference Room); special collections house rare books/vitals. House histories via deeds/MACRIS enrich property research.

Genealogical Resources and Strategies

Key holdings:

- Falmouth vitals (1668–1850 Brown; FamilySearch images).
- FHS family collections (Hinckley papers; Bourne/Jones).
- Proprietors'/town deeds (inland grants).

- Falmouth Library special collections (NEHGS databases; FGS sessions).
- Census/probate (agricultural schedules; inland estates).

North Falmouth's meadow-mill realm—from Wampanoag ponds to Hinckley selectmen—yields farm kin via Brown vitals and FHS shelves.

Northwest Harwich

Northwest Harwich, a rural northwestern village within Harwich (Barnstable County, Massachusetts), overlaps with West Harwich's Herring River basin where early colonial settlement met Yarmouth borders amid Wampanoag fertile meadows noted by Gosnold (1602) and Bradford (1622). Part of Harwich's South Parish (incorporated 1694 from "old-comers" plantation), it hosted dispersed 18th-century farms/mills post-1665 Native purchases, with Chase family (William 1595–1659 Roxbury/Yarmouth, constable 1640s) dominating via Herring River schooners from Job Sr. (1736–1833, 15 vessels) to Jr. (48 square-riggers). Genealogists access Paine's *History of Harwich* (1620–1800), MHC surveys (Herring River mills/Native sites), and digitized town reports tracing Chase/Doane/Kelley amid Baptist/abolitionist networks.

Wampanoag Basin and Yarmouth-Harwich Frontier

Herring River (Gosnold/Bradford noted) sustained Native camps; 1641 "old-comers" grant east of Yarmouth yielded William Chase's business (post-indenture relocation), constable in regulated Yarmouth while exploiting ambiguous Harwich lands. 1747 South Parish separation formalized northwest mills/farms.

Chase Maritime Dynasty and Baptist Hotbed

Job Sr.'s Georgian dwelling (extant) launched schooners; Jr.'s 1792 riverbank home (extant) fueled Baptist church (Rev. Richard Chase, cousin), Whig/abolitionist center. Cenotaph (1899 Chase-Chace Assoc.) honors Rev. War (John Chase d.1776 Delaware), 1812, Civil War kin on Job Sr. tract.

Preservation via Surveys and Societies

MHC Reconnaissance notes plantation sites (Herring River); Harwich Historical Society preserves Paine Collection.

Genealogical Resources and Strategies

Core sources:

- Paine *History* (1620–1800; South Parish tensions).
- Harwich vitals/town reports (FamilySearch; digitized 150+ yrs).
- Chase-Chace Chronicle (Vols.1–14; NEHGR 1933–34).
- MHC surveys (Herring mills/Native sites).
- HHS (family files; Brooks Academy).

Northwest Harwich's riverfront realm—from Gosnold meadows to Chase cenotaphs—unveils dynasty kin via Paine pages and Baptist stones.

Pocasset

Pocasset, a census-designated place (CDP) village within Bourne (Barnstable County, Massachusetts), occupies Wampanoag Pocasset territory ("where the river widens") along Buzzards Bay, evolving from mid-17th-century Sandwich farms into a 20th-century preservation enclave anchored by the 1905 Pocasset Improvement Club battling pollution and overdevelopment. Pre-1884 Bourne incorporation, it housed oyster-rich Native sites under sachem Numuck (Christian convert owning Numuck's Island/Bassetts Island with Reginald/Morris Gray ties) and Perry/Ellis founding families (Thomas Burgess "Pilgrim" 1652 Manomet grant via Miles Standish, Ezra Perry son-in-law). Genealogists trace Nye/Barlow/Phinney/Tobey/Lumbert via Bourne vitals, cemetery catalogs, and club minutes revealing Native/English maritime kin amid Barlows Landing social clubs (1960s) and ancient ways defenses.

Wampanoag Oyster Shores and Sandwich Settlement

Pocasset Wampanoag (Pokanoket federation, Corbitant sachem, Weetamoe daughter) sustained shellfish camps; post-1621 treaty, Christian Numuck held lands to Bourne-Falmouth line. Sandwich proprietors (1652 Burgess/Perry via Standish/Josias Nauset) allocated meadows, Perry-Ellis house (1735 Gideon Ellis from Benjamin Perry) exemplifying continuity.

Improvement Club and Preservation Battles

1905 club (Bliss/Barlow/Berry/Beckerman charter) fought beach pollution (1980s task force), mini-malls (Village Way ancient way saved), McMansions; evolved to Pocasset Village Association (1980s Kane/Nolan). Tobey family (Ben/Rhoda/Malcolm County Rd.) noted in Bourne lore.

Genealogical Resources and Strategies

Vital sources:

- Bourne/Sandwich vitals/deeds (pre-1884; Perry/Ellis chains).
- Pocasset Cemetery catalog (alphabetical genealogy).
- Club minutes/archives (Barlow/Phinney/Bliss).
- Nye genealogy (Sandwich progenitors).
- Bourne Library/Archives (Ancestry; Tobey/Davis).

Pocasset widening-bay saga—from Numuck oysters to Kane ancient ways—unfurls Perry/Barlow kin via cemetery links and club ledgers.

Popponesset

Popponesset, a census-designated place (CDP) village in the Town of Mashpee (Barnstable County, Massachusetts), occupies South Mashpee's coastal fringe where Wampanoag shellfish camps transitioned through 19th-century cranberry tracts into 20th-century elite retreats amid proprietary allotments and land sales post-1870 town incorporation. Reserved under the 1660 Mashpee deed (25 sq mi self-governing), South Mashpee housed sparse residents by 1900—Cesear Cobb's 1793 "lodging place" (freed slave, Vineyard Cobb purchase, adopted minors) and Horatio/Ella Amos homestead (1881 marriage, mansard roof opposite New Seabury)—before Malcolm G. Chace's

1929 acquisitions spurred Popponesset Beach Association and New Seabury villages (1962+). Genealogists trace Cobb/Amos/Pocknet proprietors via RDAP allotments, guardians' reports, and beach association histories revealing Native/enslaved/English kin amid 1834/1842 land divisions.

Wampanoag South Mashpee and Proprietary Lands

Mattaquason heirs' deeds sustained Coatuit/Pawpoesit settlements; 1763 district status yielded to 1788 guardianship, Phineas Fish disputes, and Apes 1833 petitions. 1842 allotments (60 acres/adult, inalienable till 1869) preserved tracts sold post-1870 to speculators/cranberry growers, thinning Native presence.

Lodging Camps and Chace Acquisitions

Cesear Cobb (b.~1740 slave, freed, "rich" innkeeper per 1793 census) hosted on Ockway Bay; Horatio Amos (m. Ella 1881) held acreage till 1878 gale-island sale ($29). Chace/Nantucket Sound Associates bought Greater Cotuit Shore Co. lands 1929+, birthing Popponesset villages/golf (1964).

Preservation via Associations and Libraries

Popponesset Beach Association chronicles Wampanoag encroachment (1658–1800s); Mashpee Library aids genealogy.

Genealogical Resources and Strategies

Key collections:

- Mashpee RDAP/guardians' reports (Amos/Cobb allotments).
- Vitals/censuses (1793 Cobb; FamilySearch).
- Beach Association histories (Chace/Amos chains).
- Cemetery surveys (South Mashpee plots).
- Town Clerk/proprietors (post-1870 sales).

Popponesset's bay-lodging arc—from Coatuit proprietors to Chace retreats—unveils Amos/Cobb kin via RDAP echoes and beach annals.

Popponesset Island

Popponesset Island, a small uninhabited barrier island off South Mashpee in Barnstable County, Massachusetts, served as a Wampanoag shellfish sanctuary within the 1660 Mashpee proprietary lands, later repurposed for WWII amphibious training before reverting to natural coastal dynamics amid 19th-century allotments and 20th-century speculation. Part of the 25 sq mi self-governing Mashpee reservation (Mattaquason heirs' deed), its tidal flats sustained Coatuit/Pawpoesit camps until 1834/1842 land divisions (RDAP book, 60-acre parcels inalienable till 1869), post-1870 sales thinning Native presence to Cesear Cobb's Ockway Bay "lodging place" (1793 census, freed Vineyard slave) and Horatio/Ella Amos homesteads nearby. Genealogists connect island-adjacent proprietors (Coombs/Amos/Pocknet) via guardians' petitions, beach association histories, and Mashpee vitals revealing Native/enslaved maritime ties in South Mashpee's erosion-prone fringe.

Wampanoag Barrier and Proprietary Tides

Mattaquason's 1665/1670 deeds preserved island fisheries; guardians (1746–1834) oversaw allotments amid Phineas Fish disputes/Apes 1833 resistance. Post-incorporation sales (1870+) favored cranberry speculators, island remaining undeveloped save WWII U.S. military drills (artillery/amphibious).

Adjacent Lodgings and Coastal Retreats

Cesear Cobb (b.~1740, "rich" innkeeper, adopted minors) hosted on Ockway Bay pre-reversion; Amos family (Horatio m. Ella 1881) held acreage till sales fueling New Seabury (1962+). Island's isolation preserved Wampanoag ecologies amid Popponesset Beach evolution.

Genealogical Resources and Strategies

Core records:

- Mashpee RDAP/guardians' reports (South allotments; Apes petitions).
- 1793 census/vitals (Cobb/Amos; FamilySearch).
- Beach Association histories (island-adjacent chains).
- Cemetery surveys (South Mashpee; Oakley project).
- MHC/WWII maps (Pastmaps; military use).

Popponesset's tidal isle—from Coatuit camps to WWII barrages—echoes Amos/Cobb proprietors via RDAP tides and beach ledgers.

Seconsett Island

Seconsett Island, a census-designated place (CDP, pop. 100) peninsula in Mashpee (Barnstable County), bridges Waquoit Bay and Hamblin Pond marshes as a Wampanoag proprietary outpost within the 1660 Mashpee reservation, accessed via Seconsett Island Road causeway amid 19th-century allotments yielding to elite summer estates. Reserved under Mattaquason heirs' deeds (25 sq mi self-governing), its tidal vistas sustained Coatuit shellfish camps until 1834/1842 RDAP divisions (60-acre parcels inalienable till 1869), post-1870 sales thinning Native holdings to guardians' oversight and Phineas Fish disputes. Genealogists trace Amos/Coombs/Pocknet proprietors via Mashpee vitals, cemetery catalogs, and heritage preservation plans revealing continuous Wampanoag/English kin amid Waquoit Bay vistas.

Wampanoag Causeway and Allotment Tracts

Coatuit/Pawpoesit settlements exploited bay/pond fisheries; 1763 district status evolved to 1788 guardianship, Apes 1833 petitions protesting overseers. RDAP recorded Seconsett parcels sold post-incorporation (1870), preserving marshes via town plans.

Summer Estates and Heritage Vistas

Causeway views (Waquoit south, Hamblin north) frame elite retreats; Mashpee Heritage Preservation notes pond/bay ecologies sustaining allottees like Hendricks/Oakley descendants.

Genealogical Resources and Strategies

Essential sources:

- Mashpee RDAP/vitals (FamilySearch; Seconsett allotments).
- Cemetery surveys (family-grouped; Bi-Centennial).
- Town Clerk/heritage plans (causeway estates).
- Sturgis Library (Barnstable deeds/whaling).
- MHS Native collections (guardians' reports).

Seconsett's causeway isle—from Coatuit bays to RDAP marshes—unveils proprietary kin via vitals and vista plans.

South Dennis

South Dennis, a southern village within Dennis (Barnstable County, Massachusetts), centers on Bass River as a post-Revolutionary maritime hub amid Nobscusset Wampanoag territory, evolving from 17th-century Yarmouth West Parish farms into a shipbuilding/saltworks powerhouse documented in church records and digital archives. Part of pre-1793 Yarmouth, it hosted Thacher/Crowell/Howes/Nickerson settlers (1639 Nobscusset) alongside Tobey arrivals (1676 Sandwich, Mehitable widow post-King Philip's War), with South Dennis Congregational Church records (Nathan Stone 1737–1804 pastorate) and Reorganized Latter Day Saints (1866–1911) logging vitals amid solar salt vats (Dennis pioneered U.S. production) and schooner yards.

Nobscusset Trails and Bass River Harbors

Wampanoag Nobscusset trails (Route 6A precursor to Scargo Lake/Indian Field) preceded 1639 Thacher/Crowell/Howes/Nickerson settlement; South Dennis emerged post-Revolution along Bass River, sustaining schooners till mid-1800s decline. Tobey family (Thomas d. King Philip's War) farmed south shores.

Maritime Prosperity and Church Anchors

Solar saltworks (north coast dominant, Bass River auxiliary) and shipyards fueled growth; 1865 rail spurred cranberries. South Dennis Congregational/Reorganized LDS records capture Howes/Crowell baptisms/marriages.

Preservation via Digital Spiders

Dennis Historical Society's searchable archive weaves "historical spider web" across ship logs/images/letters; MHC Reconnaissance notes Bass River Corridor.

Genealogical Resources and Strategies

Key holdings:

- Dennis vitals/church records (South Congregational; FamilySearch).
- DHS Digital Archive (ship logs/Howes/Tobey photos).
- MHC Report (Bass River/Tobey Farm).

- Burton Derick *Annals of South Dennis* (source records).
- CCGS (Cape-wide censuses/maps).

South Dennis's river-ship saga—from Nobscusset trails to Tobey yards—unravels maritime kin via DHS webs and Stone's steeples.

South Yarmouth

South Yarmouth, a southern village within Yarmouth (Barnstable County, Massachusetts), emerged as Quaker Village along Bass River's shores, transforming from Wampanoag Pawkunnawkut territory into a 19th-century maritime powerhouse of ropewalks, sailworks, shipbuilding, packets, saltworks, and banks dominated by Quaker entrepreneurs post-1713 Native reservation sales.

Wampanoag South Seas and Quaker Ascendancy

Pawkunnawkuts occupied Bass River environs ("South Seas" bordering Nantucket Sound); 1713 reservation sales followed epidemics/smallpox (1763), Quakers acquiring lands dubbed Friends Village. Yelverton Crowell (1643 Lewis Bay grant, brother John north side) descendants joined Howes/Thacher founders (1639 Mattacheese/Yarmouth).

Maritime Boom and Civic Hub

Quakers built stately homes fueling shipbuilding/saltworks; Revolution saw liberty poles/Sons of Liberty, Capt. Joshua Gray militia. Distinct from rural West Yarmouth Crowells, South Yarmouth thrived commercially.

Genealogical Resources and Strategies

Vital sources:

- Yarmouth vitals (1636–1924 Town Hall; FamilySearch).
- HSOY archives (account/shipping papers; Cape Cod Library Local History).
- Ancient Cemetery surveys (Friends Village graves).
- Otis *Barnstable Families*/Freeman *Cape Cod Annals* (Quaker/Crowell).
- 1858 maps (homeowners; HSOY).

South Yarmouth's Quaker River realm—from Pawkunnawkut sales to ropewalk booms—unveils Crowell/Howes kin via HSOY shelves and Bass stones

Teaticket

Teaticket, a coastal census-designated place (CDP) village within Falmouth in Barnstable County, Massachusetts, derives from Wampanoag "Tataket" ("at the principal tidal stream") along the Little Pond outlet to Vineyard Sound, evolving from Native shellfish sites into a 19th-20th century summer enclave with postmaster Effie L. Fish (1859–1955, served 1890–1940). Part of Falmouth's 1686 incorporation from Barnstable proprietors' grants, Teaticket hosted mariner/yeoman families like Fish (Ezra/Betsey Waterman, Abner/Amanda Swift), Handy (Ebenezer to Elisha Fish 1875 deed), and Bourne amid court cases (Samuel P. Croswell trader vs. Moses Nye). Genealogists access Falmouth vitals (to 1850 Brown transcription), Historical Society family papers (Fish/Davis/Hinckley), and Genealogical Society drop-ins tracing coastal kin via deeds, store records, and postmaster legacies.

Wampanoag Tidal Stream and Proprietors' Grants

Tataket sustained shellfish camps; post-1661 proprietors allocated coastal meadows, Fish family deeds (1799–1827 Barnabas/Barnabas Jr. mariners) exemplifying maritime estates.

Maritime Families and Postmaster Era

Effie L. Fish's 50-year postmastership anchored village identity; Davis drugstore/general store records (Frederick tailor/druggist 1823–1862) and court papers (Fish vs. Hamlin mariners) reveal networks. Hinckley/Jenkins guardianship papers enrich probate trails.

Preservation via Societies and Libraries

Falmouth Genealogical Society (Tuesdays 2–4pm Reference Room) aids; FHS collections house Fish photographs/obituaries.

Genealogical Resources and Strategies

Key repositories:

- Falmouth vitals (1668–1850 Brown; FamilySearch).
- FHS family papers (Fish/Davis/Hinckley/Bourne; 1744–1933 deeds).
- Postmaster records/court cases (Effie Fish; Croswell-Nye).
- FGS drop-ins/library special collections (NEHGS databases).
- House histories (deeds/MACRIS).

Teaticket's tidal post saga—from Tataket streams to Effie stamps—unveils Fish/Davis kin via Brown vitals and FHS deeds.

West Chatham

West Chatham, a western village within Chatham (Barnstable County, Massachusetts), anchors the town's rural interior amid Monomoit Wampanoag territory, evolving from 1664 William Nickerson's unauthorized land purchase (later validated after litigation) into a 19th-century farming/fishing outpost distinct from coastal Monomoy. Incorporated as part of Chatham (1712, from

Eastham/Yarmouth constablewick), West Chatham hosted inland families like Nickerson (Daniel Webster Nickerson merchant/home west of Eldredge Library) and Ryder amid epidemics/smallpox (1760s) decimating Nauset (500–600 to 50–70 by 1700s). Genealogists access Smith's *History of Chatham* (genealogical notes/maps), Eldredge Library vitals (1930–1954), and Historical Society finding aids tracing Monomoit proprietors to post-Civil War decline (pop. peak 2710 in 1860).

Monomoit Interior and Nickerson Litigation

Monomoyicks (Nauset subtribe) farmed/hunted Mill Pond/Sturgeon Creek; Champlain (1606 Port Fortuné skirmish) noted 500–600. Nickerson (Yarmouth surveyor/weaver) bought 1664 sans Plymouth Court approval (confiscated save 100-acre homestead), regained via 10–12-year suit owning all but east Old Harbor Rd. Native reserve.

Rural Anchor Amid Coastal Shifts

Inland farms contrasted fishing/saltworks (1830 peak); 1750 Pleasant Bay closure/1765 breach/North Beach 1851 breach shifted maritime south. West Chatham stabilized post-Revolution via agriculture/whaling.

Preservation via Libraries and Societies

Eldredge Public Library Genealogy Dept./Chatham Historical Society (Atwood Museum) house vitals/family docs; Nickerson Association aids.

Genealogical Resources and Strategies

Prime sources:

- Smith *History of Chatham* (Monomoit genealogies/maps).
- Chatham vitals (Eldredge 1930–1954; FamilySearch).
- HCS finding aids (Nickerson/Ryder papers).
- Town Clerk/Registry (pre-1930).
- Cape Cod Commission surveys (West Chatham homes).

West Chatham's inland Monomoit—from Nickerson suits to Ryder farms—yields Nauset kin via Smith's notes and Eldredge ledgers.

West Dennis

West Dennis, a western village within Dennis (Barnstable County, Massachusetts), straddles Swan River as a post-Revolutionary maritime and agricultural enclave amid Nobscusset Wampanoag territory, evolving from 17th-century Yarmouth West Parish farms into a 19th-century hub of saltworks, shipbuilding, and cranberries anchored by Tobey Farm (1676 Mehitable widow post-King Philip's War) and Baker homestead (1853).

Nobscusset Farms and Tobey Continuity

Nobscusset Wampanoag planting fields preceded Thacher/Crowell/Howes/Nickerson (1639); Mehitable Tobey (Sandwich, husband Thomas slain 1676) received large grants along King's

Highway, cultivating since ~1690 with 1802 farmhouse by Seth Tobey. Elihu Kelley (1759–1841, Rev. War pensioner, 13 siblings) exemplifies Kelley/Killey lineages.

Saltworks, Rails, and Garfield Ties

Solar salt vats (Dennis pioneered) and schooner yards thrived; 1865 rail boosted cranberries. Garfield family awaited President Garfield's 1881 death; Pauline Wixon Derick Library (DHS 2nd floor West Dennis Library) preserves Kelley/Howes papers.

Digital Archives and Reconnaissance

DHS searchable archive weaves "historical spider web" across ship logs/images/letters; MHC notes Baker Family (Swan River Rd).

Genealogical Resources and Strategies

Core collections:

- Dennis vitals/church (FamilySearch; Kelley pensions).
- DHS Digital Archive (Tobey/Howes photos/logs).
- MHC Reconnaissance (Tobey Farm/Baker).
- Howes Genealogy (13 generations Thomas/Mary Burr).
- CCGS office hours (Thursdays Dennis Library).

West Dennis's river-farm saga—from Nobscusset grants to Tobey stones—unravels Kelley kin via DHS webs and Derick shelves.

West Falmouth

West Falmouth, a Quaker-leaning western village within Falmouth (Barnstable County, Massachusetts), traces to 1673 when William Gifford purchased 40 acres from Job Attukkoo (Wampanoag sachem), evolving from Saconnesset Homestead (1678 Thomas Bowerman, Quaker imprisoned in Barnstable) into an inland farming enclave amid Sippewisset marshes. Part of Falmouth's 1686 incorporation from Barnstable proprietors' grants led by Isaac Robinson (protesting Quaker persecution), West Falmouth hosted Nye/Gifford/Bowerman families with religious toleration distinguishing it from coastal settlements, documented in West Falmouth Library Archives and FHS collections.

Wampanoag Saconnesset and Quaker Refuge

Suckanesset ("place by the sea where black wampum found") sustained Wampanoag camps; Robinson's 1660 group bought lands avoiding Barnstable elders' wrath, Bowerman's 1678 home exemplifying Quaker homesteads. Gifford's deed formalized Native transfers.

Inland Farms and Country Club Era

Meadows/ponds supported agriculture; West Falmouth Country Club/Golf Course docs (1920–1938) trace elite estates. Crowell Family Cemetery (1848, 856 Main St) holds Quaker graves.

Preservation via Village Archives

West Falmouth Library Archives document 1803–2010 village life; FGS drop-ins aid research.

Genealogical Resources and Strategies

Key holdings:

- Falmouth vitals (1668–1850 Brown; FamilySearch).
- West Falmouth Archives (Gifford/Bowerman deeds).
- FHS family papers (Nye/Crowell; golf course docs).
- Quaker registers/cemeteries (Saconnesset/Crowell).
- FGS/library sessions (NEHGS; house histories).

West Falmouth's Quaker meadow saga—from Attukkoo deeds to Bowerman hearths—unveils Gifford/Nye kin via village vaults and Nye stones.

West Yarmouth

West Yarmouth, the western village within Yarmouth (Barnstable County, Massachusetts), emerged as a rural farming outpost dominated by Yelverton Crowell descendants in the "South Seas" bordering Nantucket Sound, distinct from Quaker South Yarmouth's maritime boom. Part of original Mattacheese (1639 Yarmouth incorporation from Plymouth Colony), West Yarmouth hosted Cummaquid Wampanoag alongside early farmers on Yelverton Crowell's vast 1643 tract (acquired via sachem's "walk in an hour" legend for trinkets), with Baxters operating Yarmouth's first fulling/grist mills along Mill Creek.

Cummaquid Meadows and Crowell Continuity

Cummaquid's farmed western meadows; Yelverton (John Crowell's brother, Lewis Bay grant) sired generations populating County Road (Route 28) farms to Hyannis, Crowell surname enduring into 20th century amid livestock/firewood economy.

Mill Economy and Rural Stability

Baxter mills (late 17th c.) processed wool/cloth; post-Revolution agriculture persisted while north side commercialized, West Yarmouth retaining subsistence farms through forest clearance (livestock/rail/shipbuilding).

Preservation via Societies and Libraries

Historical Society of Old Yarmouth (HSOY) archives hold shipping/account papers; Yarmouth Libraries Local History (South Yarmouth) aids research.

Genealogical Resources and Strategies

Essential collections:

- Yarmouth vitals (1636–1924 Town Hall; FamilySearch).
- HSOY archives (Crowell papers; Cape Cod Library).
- Ancient Cemetery surveys (Cummaquid graves).

- Swift *History of Old Yarmouth* (to 1794 division).
- 1858 maps/directories (homeowners).

West Yarmouth's meadow-farm saga—from Cummaquid tracts to Crowell chains—unveils Yelverton kin via HSOY ledgers and Baxter mills.

Woods Hole

Woods Hole, a census-designated place (CDP) in Falmouth (Barnstable County, Massachusetts), marks Cape Cod's southwestern tip where Wampanoag fishing grounds met Bartholomew Gosnold's 1602 landing, evolving from 1670s sheep/crop homesteads into a whaling/guano/rail hub before scientific dominance via Marine Biological Laboratory (MBL 1889) and Woods Hole Oceanographic Institution (WHOI 1930). Thirteen families divided Little Harbor lands (1679 Job Notantico deed), sustaining fishing/saltworks until 1828–1864 whaling peak (9 ships at Bar Neck wharf) and Pacific Guano Works (1863–1889 fertilizer on Penzance Point), Howes descendants (Thomas Howes/Mary Burr branches) anchoring maritime records amid postmaster/spinner legacies.

Wampanoag Grounds and 1670s Division

Wampanoag exploited tidal straits (Gosnold's "Cape Hedlyng"); 1679 deed allocated 60-acre plots around Little Harbor for sheep/crops/grist mills, early Howes (Joseph branch) farming pre-whaling.

Whaling, Guano, and Rail Boom

Wharves processed oil/bone (candle works in MBL's stone building); guano factory spurred Old Colony Railroad extension (Falmouth–Woods Hole), bankruptcy 1889 yielding to Baird's fisheries lab (1871).

Scientific Shift and Preservation

MBL/WHOI drew Nobelists; Woods Hole Historical Museum preserves Howes papers/church/business logs.

Genealogical Resources and Strategies

Vital collections:

- Falmouth vitals (FamilySearch; pre-1850 Brown).
- WHHM archives (Howes genealogy; maritime logs).
- Church/business records (MBL candle works era).
- NOAA/MBL histories (whaling crews).
- WH Public Library special collections.

Woods Hole's strait-wharf saga—from Notantico deeds to guano rails—unveils Howes kin via museum logs and MBL stones.

Yarmouth Port

Yarmouth Port, the northern village of Yarmouth (Barnstable County, Massachusetts), preserves colonial elegance along Route 6A as the historic core of Mattakeese settlement (1639), where Stephen Hopkins (Mayflower) pioneered Mill Pond mills and Thomas Greenough (Native/English descent b.~1746) farmed reservation lands amid Cummaquid Wampanoag. Distinct from maritime South Yarmouth, it hosted grist/fulling mills (Andrew Hallett 1647, Baxter family), packet captains (Ansel Hallett 1770–1832), and elite estates like Greenough-Cook (1746–1909s), with HSOY archives capturing Greenough's petitions (1820 land claim), Stiles' 1765 Potanumicut list, and Farris Windmill T.G. initials (1782).

Cummaquid Mills and Greenough Legacy

Cummaquids preceded Hopkins' salt marsh cattle; Hallett's tidal gristmill (left Mill Pond) and Gorham tannery (right) fueled economy, Baxters expanding via cousin marriages (Richard/Jennie to Prince Jr.). Thomas Greenough (Native mother/white father, preacher Potanumicut) leased Bass River tracts (1785–1797), signing deeds, dying almshouse 1837 aged 90.

Packet Era and Library Homesteads

Ansel Hallett's Federal home (48 Mill Lane post-1798) launched Boston packets; Matthews Library (1870 brick Gothic, Nathan endowment) absorbed Greenough descendants (Cobb/Cash/Taylor/Ellis/Nickerson). Earle 1860 report noted blended Yarmouth Natives.

Preservation via HSOY and Libraries

HSOY (1953) holds shipping/accounts/family histories; Yarmouth Port Library aids Mayflower/Plymouth records.

Genealogical Resources and Strategies

Key archives:

- Yarmouth vitals (1636–1924; FamilySearch).
- HSOY collections (Greenough leases; Baxter mills).
- Swift *History of Old Yarmouth* (to 1794).
- Ancient Cemetery surveys (Cummaquid/Greenough).
- Stiles manuscripts/MHS (Potanumicut 1765).

Yarmouth Port's mill-pond saga—from Cummaquid weirs to Greenough deeds—unveils Hallett kin via HSOY webs and Stiles scrolls.

Unincorporated Communities

Bellingsgate

Bellingsgate (often spelled Billingsgate) refers to the southern part of Wellfleet (Barnstable County) near Indian Brook, known historically as a fishing and weaving area settled since the 17th century by Nauset Wampanoag and colonial English. This district was part of Eastham until Wellfleet's incorporation in 1763. Bellingsgate's name recalls London's Billingsgate fish market, reflecting its maritime heritage. Shoreline erosion caused significant land loss from the 19th century onward, compelling families to relocate inland but leaving a rich genealogical record through town vital records, historical writings (such as *History of Billingsgate* by Echeverria), and burial grounds including Cove Burying Ground, where early settlers like Jonathan Sparrow (1629–1707) are interred.

Nauset Wampanoag and Colonial Settlement

The Nauset Wampanoag originally fished and harvested shellfish in the Bellingsgate area. Colonial English settlers established fishing and weaving industries in the 17th and 18th centuries, using land grants from Eastham and forming a close-knit maritime community before erosion reduced coastal holdings.

Genealogical Resources and Strategy

- Vital records of Eastham and Wellfleet on FamilySearch provide birth, marriage, death data.
- *History of Billingsgate* by Echeverria includes genealogical data and local family histories.
- Historical accounts from Smith and Pratt offer regional context useful for family research.
- Cemetery surveys of Cove Burying Ground document early settler burials.

Bellingsgate's coastal community—from Wampanoag fishers to colonial weavers—offers genealogists deep maritime roots with records preserved in well-documented vital records, histories, and burial sites.

Captains Village

Captains Village, an unincorporated residential community in Brewster (Barnstable County, Massachusetts), developed as a modern subdivision amid historic sea captain estates reflecting Cape Cod's maritime legacy. Situated near Route 6A's Old King's Highway Historic District, it embodies Brewster's 17th-19th century seafaring heritage where Nauset Wampanoag shores gave way to English settlement and captains' homes built with whaling/shipping fortunes. Properties like 51 Captains Village Ln (5 beds, sold $1.15M 2020) and 90 Captains Village Ln (5 beds) evoke grand estates, with genealogists tracing via Brewster vital records, Historical Society captain files, and deeds linking to Nickerson/Bangs/Doane lineages (Mayflower/Fortune descendants).

Nauset Shores and Captains' Fortunes

Nauset Wampanoag fishing camps preceded 1656 Brewster grants from Eastham; 19th-century captains amassed wealth via Pacific whaling, constructing Route 6A homes now inspiring Captains Village naming/development.

Maritime Subdivision Legacy

Contemporary homes (e.g., 72 Captains Village Ln 3 beds, 181 Captains Village Ln 5 beds) cluster near historic sites, preserving captain-era architecture amid modern luxury.

Genealogical Resources and Strategies
Key sources:

- Brewster vitals/proprietors (FamilySearch; Nauset grants).
- Brewster Historical Society (captain files; Nickerson Association).
- Barnstable deeds (Route 6A estates).
- Cape Cod Genealogical Society (Dennis Port; maritime censuses).

Captains Village's captain-shadowed lanes—from Nauset bays to whaler mansions—echo Brewster kin via society shelves and 6A stones.

Ferris Fields

"Ferris Fields" (or Farris Field) refers to a historical agricultural parcel in South Yarmouth owned by Captain Samuel Farris, where the historic Farris Windmill operated from 1782 until its relocation in 1894. This Dutch-style windmill (built ~1633 near Sandwich/Barnstable line, America's oldest) ground grain via Cape Cod winds, moved thrice before Henry Ford acquired it for Greenfield Village (1936). Genealogists trace Farris/Crowell ownership via Yarmouth deeds, HSOY archives, and *History of Old Yarmouth* documenting mill's path: Sandwich → Bass River (1750 Lot Crowell) → Farris Field South Yarmouth → West Yarmouth (1894 F.A. Abell).

Cummaquid Farms and Windmill Legacy

Cummaquid Wampanoag meadows preceded Yelverton Crowell's tracts; Farris (Captain Samuel 1782 purchase) operated 3-story tower (54-ft sails, 3.5-ton stones) for 3 generations amid Quaker South Yarmouth economy.

Genealogical Resources and Strategies

- Yarmouth vitals/deeds (Farris/Crowell chains; FamilySearch).
- HSOY archives (*Old Yarmouth* Swift; mill photos).
- MHC/Barnstable Registry (Route 28/Berry Ave site).

Prior South Yarmouth entry covers Ferris Fields context within Quaker ropewalk village.

Ferris Fields' wind-swept acres—from Cummaquid to Ford's Village—echo Farris kin via HSOY mills and deed winds.

Hatchville

Hatchville, an unincorporated agricultural village in northern Falmouth (Barnstable County, Massachusetts), centers on Coonamessett Pond where Jonathan Hatch (shipwreck survivor 1660) established the first European settlement amid Wampanoag Suckanesset territory, evolving from log cabins and oyster-rich shores into a 19th-century post office hub (Silas Hatch postmaster 1858–1919) surrounded by cranberry bogs and family farms. Named for the prolific Hatch clan (Jonathan's 11 children spawning 10,000 descendants by late 1800s), it features Hatchville Road, Sam Turner Road, and Robinson/Geggatt roads honoring early proprietors, with Moses Hatch (d.1747) donating militia grounds (now village green/Church site). Genealogists access Falmouth vitals, West Falmouth Library Archives (1803–2010 Hatch papers), and FHS collections tracing Hatch/Bourne/Nye amid Quaker sympathies and pond silting (1750 oysters vanished).

Wampanoag Suckanesset and Hatch Shipwreck

Suckanesset ("place by the sea where black wampum found") sustained Native camps; Jonathan Hatch washed ashore Salt Pond (1660), building log cabin on Elm Road amid treeless landscape from Native girdling/burning. Good Native relations spared Upper Cape from King Philip's War.

Family Multiplication and Post Office Era

Hatch descendants (Ebenezer/Moses/Silas) farmed Coonamessett River bogs; 1748 Moses Hatch house backed Fresh Pond (now Siders Pond), 1750 grain mill on Mill Road endured till 1936. 1858 Hatchville Post Office (Silas 61 years) formalized village amid 1925 Elm Road paving/1926 Moors resort.

Preservation via Archives and Greens

Village green (1796 Congregational, Paul Revere bell) anchors; West Falmouth Archives chronicle Hatch continuity, Katy Hatchs Road (1955) memorializes postmaster.

Genealogical Resources and Strategies

Vital repositories:

- Falmouth vitals (1668–1850 Brown; FamilySearch).
- West Falmouth Archives (Hatch deeds 1803–2010).
- FHS family papers (Hatch/Bourne; church records).
- Coonamessett Farm/RDAP (cranberry allotments).
- MHC heritage plans (village green/mill sites).

Hatchville's pond-farm saga—from Jonathan's wreck to Silas stamps—unveils 10,000 Hatch kin via Elm deeds and green bells.

Long Point

Long Point, a historic peninsula village and beach area at the extreme northwestern tip of Provincetown (Barnstable County, Massachusetts), represents Cape Cod's farthest reach where a thriving 19th-century fishing settlement of ~38 families (1818–1850s) relocated entire homes by raft across Provincetown Harbor when fishing declined, leaving only Long Point Lighthouse (1827, rebuilt 1875) and Civil War-era batteries ("Fort Useless"/"Fort Ridiculous"). Nauset Wampanoag exploited fertile fishing grounds pre-contact; John Atwood built the first house (1818), growing to general store/post office/saltworks/bakery/6 windmills/wharf serving mackerel/shad/bass fleets amid peak population ~200 (1840s). Genealogists trace relocated families via Provincetown vitals, West End plaques (blue/white markers on floated homes), and lighthouse logs linking Atwood/Cooke/Nickerson to Nauset shores.

Nauset Fishing Camps and Village Peak

Nauset sustained seasonal fisheries; 1818 Atwood cabin sparked settlement, peaking with infrastructure before Civil War (1861) reduced to 2 houses/lighthouse, batteries garrisoned 98 militia (1864, Major Charles E. Blunt design).

Relocation and Military Legacy

Families floated ~30 homes to Provincetown West End; post-war abandonment left earthen mound (Charles Darby WWII memorial cross), oil house (1904).

Preservation via Plaques and Trails

West End plaques mark relocated homes; 2¼-mile dike hike/ferry access preserves isolation.

Genealogical Resources and Strategies

Vital sources:

- Provincetown vitals (FamilySearch; 1818–1860s fishers).
- Lighthouse logs/West End plaques (Atwood descendants).
- Civil War militia records (12th Unattached Company).
- Eastham/Provincetown Historical Societies (Nauset fishing).
- Cape Cod Genealogical Society (maritime censuses).

Long Point's rafted village—from Nauset hauls to "Fort Ridiculous" mounds—unveils Atwood kin via West End plaques and dike dunes.

Monomoy Island

Monomoy Island, located off the coast of Chatham in Barnstable County, Massachusetts, is a dynamic barrier island with a rich history shaped by shifting sands, Native American heritage, and maritime settlement. Native Wampanoag (Monomoiyicks) used the peninsula seasonally for shell fishing and hunting for thousands of years. European settlement began in the early 18th century, growing into a fishing village known as Whitewash Village near Powder Hole, home to about 200 residents with a schoolhouse, an inn, and supply wharves supporting lobstering, cod, and mackerel fisheries. The village's heyday lasted through the mid-19th century until natural events like hurricanes and sand drift closed the harbor and led to its abandonment by 1876.

Natural and Colonial History

Monomoy's landscape evolved continuously, with substantial shoreline changes in 1958 and again in 1978 that reshaped the island's form. The Monomoy Point Lighthouse was established in 1823 to guide ships navigating the treacherous shoals. The island historically served as a refuge for shipwrecked sailors and was considered a vital maritime landmark. The former village's buildings were either abandoned or floated to the mainland as the harbor silted up.

Genealogical Resources and Research Strategies

- Vital records and town documents relating to Chatham and Eastham, accessible via FamilySearch and local historical societies.
- Historical and genealogical compilations such as Smith's *History of Chatham* and the archives of the Chatham Historical Society.
- Cemetery records and local burial grounds near the mainland towns that received former island residents.
- Maritime records capturing fishing and shipping activity tied to Monomoy residents.
- Coast Guard and lighthouse keeper logs documenting island activity and personnel.

Monomoy Island's legacy—from Indigenous seasonal use through European settlement and maritime industry, to natural erosion and abandonment—offers genealogists layered historical and environmental contexts to explore ancestral connections spanning several centuries on Cape Cod's shifting shores.

South Brewster

South Brewster refers to the southern portion of Brewster town (incorporated 1803 from Eastham's North Parish), an inland agricultural area south of Route 6A amid Nauset Wampanoag territory where William Brewster (Mayflower Elder, ruling elder of Plymouth Pilgrim church) descendants dominated from 1656 grants. Centered around Punkhorn Hills cranberry bogs and Griffiths/Hatch farms, it contrasts maritime North Brewster with family continuity documented in *Brewster Genealogy 1566-1907* (Jones, 4,100 families via Benjamin[3], Wrestling, Patience Brewster lines). Genealogists access Brewster vitals (FamilySearch), Sturgis Cobb papers (Elijah/Freeman Cobb 1768–1805), and oral histories (Gilbert Ellis Route 6A childhood).

Nauset Bogs and Brewster Proliferation

Nauset exploited Punkhorn ponds; 1656 Eastham grants yielded Brewster farms (Jonathan Sr. 1729 arrival), Cobb intermarriages (Elijah m. Mary P. Cobb, Freeman 1805–Hannah Crosby).

Cranberry Continuity and Preservation

South Brewster's bog economy endures; Sturgis Library holds Cobb estates tracing Mayflower lines.

Genealogical Resources and Strategies

Vital sources:

- Brewster vitals/proprietors (FamilySearch; Nauset grants).
- *Brewster Genealogy* (Mayflower descendants).
- Sturgis Cobb papers (Elijah/Freeman estates).
- Oral Histories (Ellis Route 6A).

South Brewster's bog-Brewster realm—from Nauset ponds to Mayflower chains—unveils Elder kin via Jones tomes and Punkhorn peat.

South Chatham

South Chatham, a southern village within Chatham (Barnstable County, Massachusetts), represents the town's maritime core along Oyster Pond River and Morris Island where Monomoyick Wampanoag shell fishing gave way to 18th-century wharves, saltworks, and shipbuilding amid epidemics reducing Native population from 500–600 (Champlain 1606) to 50–70 by 1700s. Part of pre-1712 constablewick "Monamoy" (from Eastham/Yarmouth), South Chatham hosted post-Revolutionary fisheries peaking 1830 (pop. 2130, saltworks dominant) before 1851 North Beach breach shifting trade, documented in Smith's *History of Chatham* (genealogical notes/maps) and Eldredge Library manuscripts tracing Nickerson/Ryder/Nickerson lineages.

Monomoyick Shores and Constablewick Era

Champlain's Port Fortuné (1606 skirmish) noted 500–600 Monomoyicks; William Nickerson's 1664 unauthorized purchase (validated post-litigation) anchored west Ryder's Cove, reserving east Old Harbor Rd for Natives. 1696 constablewick status yielded 1712 incorporation.

Saltworks and Beach Breaches

Oyster Pond River powered fisheries/salt evaporation; 1750 Pleasant Bay closure/1765 breach/1851 North Beach breach relocated maritime south, population dropping post-Civil War (2710 peak 1860).

Preservation via Libraries and Societies

Eldredge Library Genealogy Dept. (500+ family volumes) and Chatham Historical Society (Atwood Museum finding aids: Heman Harding papers) chronicle South Chatham estates.

Genealogical Resources and Strategies

Key repositories:

- Chatham vitals (Eldredge 1930–1954; FamilySearch pre-1930).
- Smith *History of Chatham* (Monomoyick genealogies/maps).
- CHS finding aids (Harding/Nickerson papers).
- Nickerson Association/Eldredge manuscripts.

South Chatham's oyster-wharf saga—from Champlain skirmishes to beach breaches—unveils Monomoyick kin via Smith's maps and Eldredge shelves.

South Sandwich

South Sandwich, the southern village within the Town of Sandwich in Barnstable County, Massachusetts, developed as a rural farming and mill district amid Wampanoag woodlands where Quaker refugees from Saugus (Lynn) founded Cape Cod's first English settlement in 1637. Part of Sandwich's original grant to the "Ten Men of Saugus" (including Edward Dillingham, Thomas Tupper), South Sandwich hosted inland mills and meadows supporting Nye, Wing, Tupper, and Dillingham families, with Benjamin Nye's 1669 water-powered grist mill (second in town) on Spring

Hill marking economic anchors. Genealogists access Sandwich vital records (to 1885), Nye Family Association proceedings, and Wing genealogies tracing 60-family exodus from Puritan persecution to Quaker dominance by 1658.

Wampanoag Woodlands and Saugus Exodus

Wampanoag forests preceded 1637 grant for 60 families walking 100 miles from Saugus; Edward Dillingham (Cottesbach, England) and Ursula settled with children, daughter Oseath m. Stephen Wing (Deborah Bachiler Wing walked from Saugus). Thomas Tupper (ship's carpenter/lay minister) and Benjamin Nye (constable, m. Katherine Tupper 1640, 8 children) farmed without Quaker conversion.

Mill Economy and Quaker Dominance

Nye's mill (1669, 12-acre grant) processed grain; Quaker meetings (1658, 17 families covertly at Christopher Hollow) drew fines, James Cudworth noting "almost the whole town of Sandwich is adhering towards them." Dillinghams/Wings joined, resisting Fidelity Oath.

Preservation via Associations and Libraries

Nye Homestead (1620 Benjamin) and Wing Fort House (1641) endure; Sandwich Public Library genealogy links aid research.

Genealogical Resources and Strategies

Vital sources:

- Sandwich vitals (to 1885, NEHGS/Internet Archive).
- Nye Family Association (*Nye Genealogy*; mill records).
- Wing Family of America (John/Deborah descendants).
- *Sandwich, A Cape Cod Town* (Lovell; Dillingham/Tupper).
- FOSTA oral histories (Govoni family).

South Sandwich's Quaker-mill saga—from Saugus walkers to Nye grindstones—unveils founder kin via association annals and Wing forts.

Waquoit

Waquoit, an unincorporated coastal village in Falmouth (Barnstable County, Massachusetts), occupies the Wampanoag Quashnet River estuary where Mashpee land grants transitioned to Falmouth via 1840 legislative acts, evolving from Native shellfish camps into 19th-20th century summer estates like the Sargent mansion (1880s Ignatius Sargent bluff house) and Washburn Island cottages amid cranberry bogs owned by Charles L. Swift.

Wampanoag Quashnet and Falmouth Annexation

Quashnet River (part of 1660 Mashpee 25 sq mi grant secured by Rev. Richard Bourne) sustained Coatuit settlements; 1839–1840 acts transferred Waquoit to Falmouth despite Mashpee protests, 1832 grist mill/dam blocking fish runs. Norman Rutherford (1914–1929 owner, electricity pioneer, mysterious disappearance) hosted parties in boathouse.

Summer Cottages and Estate Legacies

Munro/Abbott families (1900 Sargent renters) built Washburn Island homes; 1938 hurricane damaged Sargent mansion (gatehouse residence post-Swift), Ethel Trapp's 1982 development deal preserved via Reserve.

Genealogical Resources and Strategies

Key sources:

- Falmouth vitals (1668–1850 Brown; FamilySearch).
- FHS papers (Rutherford/Swift deeds).
- Waquoit Bay Reserve oral histories (Munro Haagersen).
- Bowerman-Gifford papers (Waquoit histories).
- MHC maps (1910s estates).

Waquoit's estuary estates—from Quashnet dams to Rutherford mysteries—unveils Munro/Swift kin via Reserve tapes and FHS deeds.

Wood End

Wood End, the southwestern peninsula of Provincetown (Barnstable County, Massachusetts), guards Provincetown Harbor's entrance with Wood End Lighthouse (1872, brick tower with 5th-order Fresnel lens flashing red every 15 seconds, 45 ft above sea level), where Nauset Wampanoag fishing camps preceded 19th-century lifesaving stations amid treacherous shoals claiming vessels like the Navy submarine *S-4* (1927 collision with Coast Guard cutter *Paulding*, 40 drowned ½ mile south). Part of Provincetown's 1727 incorporation from Eastham, Wood End hosted Keeper Thomas Lowe (1896–25 years, Mexican War veteran/California 49er) in cream-colored dwelling razed 1961 automation, with 1896 oil house/bell tower (1,000 lb bell) and 1911 stone breakwater enabling low-tide access from town. Genealogists trace lighthouse keepers/surfmen via Provincetown vitals, Coast Guard logs, and West End plaques marking relocated Long Point homes floated across harbor.

Nauset Shoals and Lighthouse Era

Nauset exploited tidal straits; 1864 pyramidal day beacon preceded $15,000 congressional appropriation (1872), Keeper Lowe demonstrating clockwork lens to *Boston Globe* amid shipwrecks requiring Provincetown fleet rescues. 1896 dwelling/shed/oil house, 1902 fog bell tower enhanced station.

Automation and Breakwater Legacy

1961 automation razed buildings save oil house; solar conversion 1981, National Register 1987. 1911 breakwater (Quincy granite) blocked sand from Lancy's Harbor (Herring Cove).

Genealogical Resources and Strategies

Vital repositories:

- Provincetown vitals (FamilySearch; keeper censuses).
- Lighthouse logs/Coast Guard records (*S-4* rescuers).
- West End plaques (relocated families).
- Eastham/Provincetown Historical Societies (Nauset/shoal wrecks).

Wood End's shoal-sentinel saga—from Nauset tides to Lowe's vigils—unveils keeper kin via Fresnel flashes and breakwater blocks.

Chapter 4
Berkshire County

Nestled in the verdant highlands of western Massachusetts, Berkshire County stretches across rolling hills, fertile river valleys, and forested mountains that have shaped its history and culture for centuries. Often called "The Berkshires," the county forms a striking contrast to the coastal flatlands of eastern Massachusetts, offering an inland landscape marked by colonial frontier settlements, Indigenous homelands, revolutionary upheaval, and later Gilded Age estates that continue to attract visitors and preserve rich genealogical legacies. Created in 1761 from the western part of Hampshire County, Berkshire originally consisted of a handful of frontier towns including Sheffield, Stockbridge, New Marlborough, and Egremont. Today, it comprises 32 towns and spans diverse geographic zones adjacent to New York and Vermont, reflecting a layered history and multifaceted genealogical record environment.

For family historians, Berkshire's story unfolds amid rugged terrain, early Native American presence, colonial military campaigns, industrial transformation, and cultural prosperity, with records ranging from ancient Mahican deeds to probate files of Revolutionary-era farmers and lavish family archives of American industrialists.

Indigenous Foundations: Mahican Homeland and Continuity

Before the arrival of European settlers, the lands now known as Berkshire County were the ancestral homeland of the Mahican people, a proud and sophisticated Algonquian-speaking confederacy whose cultural and political influence extended across the upper Hudson River Valley and into the fertile river basins of western Massachusetts. Unlike the relatively flat coastal regions to the east, Berkshire's rugged terrain of rolling hills, dense forests, and meandering rivers shaped a distinctive Indigenous lifeway that balanced hunting, fishing, gathering, and small-scale agriculture. The Mahican were keen environmental stewards, using seasonal migrations and detailed ecological knowledge to exploit diverse resources while maintaining the sustainability of their lands.

The river systems—particularly the Housatonic, Hoosic, and Westfield—served as vital arteries for trade, communication, and subsistence. The Mahican established permanent and seasonal villages along these waterways where fertile floodplains produced native crops such as maize, beans, and squash, while the surrounding forests supplied game and medicinal plants. Their riverine settlements were strategically positioned to facilitate trade not only within their own confederacy but also with neighboring Indigenous groups, including the Pocumtuck to the east and the Mohawk to the west. This complex network of alliances and rivalries defined the social and political landscape prior to European contact.

Mahican society was organized hierarchically under sagamores or sachems, who governed according to consensus and were responsible for maintaining the balance between human communities and the natural world. Spiritual beliefs deeply rooted in animism and reverence for natural cycles shaped social practices and decision-making processes, with sacred groves, water bodies, and hunting grounds protected through customary laws enforced by communal authority.

Genealogically, tracing Mahican ancestry requires sensitivity to the differences between Indigenous and colonial understandings of identity, kinship, and land stewardship. Unlike European notions of fixed property, Mahican concepts emphasized collective responsibility and usufruct rights tied to familial and clan networks. This worldview is reflected in oral traditions, which remain a vital complement to written records, especially since colonial documentation often distorted or marginalized Indigenous presence.

European contact in the early 17th century, beginning with exploratory visits such as those by Henry Hudson and later missionary endeavors in Stockbridge and surrounding areas, dramatically affected Mahican communities. While trade introduced new goods and economic opportunities, it also exposed populations to devastating new diseases—including smallpox and influenza—that sharply reduced Indigenous numbers. Land pressures increased as colonial settlers encroached, and treaties and purchases were often negotiated under duress or through misunderstanding, leading to loss of territory and sovereignty.

Missionary activity during the 18th century catalyzed significant social transformations among the Mahican, particularly at Stockbridge where Christianized Mohican communities emerged. These mission villages became melting pots of Indigenous and European cultures, producing extensive church records that provide genealogists with crucial baptismal, marriage, and death documentation. Yet these records must be interpreted with recognition of cultural shifts, forced acculturation, and the maintenance of traditional kinship even amid assimilation pressures.

Despite centuries of displacement, demographic upheaval, and political marginalization, Mahican descendants maintain a vibrant presence in Berkshire and surrounding areas. Contemporary genealogical research increasingly integrates Indigenous oral histories, tribal records, and consultation with Mahican tribal organizations to reconstruct family lines that transcend fragmented colonial documents. DNA studies also supplement traditional methodologies, offering new avenues to understand and preserve these ancestral connections.

For genealogists and historians alike, recognizing the Mahican's foundational role in Berkshire County's history is essential. It reframes the region's story from one centered solely on European settlement to one acknowledging the deep, ongoing relationship between Indigenous peoples and the land they have defended and nurtured across millennia. Engaging respectfully with this history and its genealogical implications enriches all efforts to trace families and understand community identities in the Berkshires today.

Colonial Settlement and Frontier Life in Berkshire County: A Detailed Examination

The colonial settlement of Berkshire County unfolded against a backdrop of geopolitical tension, complex Indigenous relations, and challenging topography. While eastern Massachusetts experienced relatively early and dense English colonization due to its coastal geography, Berkshire's western frontier remained a remote and often contested landscape well into the 18th century. English, Dutch, and other European settlers pushed gradually into this terrain, often delayed by broader imperial conflicts such as the French and Indian Wars (1689–1763), which made sustained settlement hazardous.

Initial colonial interest in Berkshire was driven by a combination of strategic, economic, and social factors. The area's rich timber and fur resources, combined with its river valleys suitable for agriculture, attracted settlers willing to endure isolation for the promise of land ownership. Early land purchases reflected these ambitions, notably the 1724 Sheffield Purchase, in which English settlers negotiated with the Mahican to acquire extensive tracts around the present town of Sheffield. Such transactions were complex, mediated through mixed cultural frameworks and often complicated by language differences, shifting Native alliances, and competing colonial claims.

Settlers frequently established isolated homesteads along rivers such as the Housatonic, where small farmsteads formed the nuclei of emerging communities. These early residents faced formidable challenges, including clearing dense forests, adapting agriculture to northern soils and climates, and defending against French incursions and Native resistance allied with French forces. Communities in towns like Stockbridge, Lenox, and Great Barrington gradually coalesced into organized municipalities through town meetings, church establishment, and the creation of rudimentary civic infrastructure such as roads and mills.

Religious life anchored these early settlements. Congregationalism was dominant among English settlers, with meetinghouses serving dual spiritual and civic functions. Churches also created critical genealogical records—baptisms, marriages, and deaths—that often predate or supplement scarce official town registries. The interweaving of religious and civil governance shaped social hierarchies and community cohesion, as church membership was often prerequisite for full civic participation.

While colonial settlers imposed new land-use patterns emphasizing private property and fixed boundaries, the frontier nature of Berkshire slowed the development of formal land surveys and conveyance systems. Early deeds and proprietors' books remain essential to genealogists seeking to trace family landholdings and migrations as frontier families expanded their holdings or moved westward. The rugged geography permitted pockets of existing Native communities to persist longer than in many parts of the colony, complicating interactions and prompting intermittent cooperation, land leases, and cultural exchange.

Economically, settlers adapted mixed subsistence strategies combining agriculture—crops such as corn, rye, and potatoes—and animal husbandry with small-scale trade in furs, timber, and occasionally illicit goods like rum. Grist mills and sawmills, often powered by the county's swift rivers, became vital local economic hubs, fostering the growth of market towns. These facilities are well-documented in early surveyed land plats and town meeting records, offering genealogical insights into economic agents and community leaders.

The French and Indian Wars' conclusion in 1763 opened the floodgates for accelerated settlement, culminating in the formal establishment of Berkshire County in 1761 and the foundation of new towns. This period witnessed the transformation of isolated homesteads into bustling communities featuring schools, churches, and civic institutions. Genealogical records from these decades became more standardized, including vital registries, land deeds, and tax rolls that form a robust corpus for today's family historians.

Genealogists approaching Berkshire's colonial frontier face the challenge of fragmentary and sometimes contradictory records due to the volatile environment of early settlement, frequent territorial disputes, and inconsistent record-keeping. Effective research strategies include triangulating data from military muster rolls—documenting local involvement in colonial militias—with town proprietors' records and church registers. Oral histories and Native American source materials provide critical context for understanding the intercultural dynamics that shaped family lineages and land tenure.

In sum, Berkshire County's colonial settlement history is a story of perseverance and adaptation on a remote frontier, carved out between Indigenous lands and imperial ambitions. Such layered histories are preserved in archival materials that genealogists must parse carefully to reconstruct ancestral narratives embedded in the complex social, environmental, and political fabric of early Berkshire life. This foundational period laid the groundwork for the county's transformative revolutionary experiences and its eventual emergence as a major cultural and economic region of Massachusetts.

Revolutionary Contributions and 19th-Century Transformation in Berkshire County: An Expanded Analysis

Berkshire County occupies a key chapter in the narrative of the American Revolution and the subsequent decades of transformation that forged the United States' early identity. Positioned on the western frontier of Massachusetts, the county witnessed firsthand the political ferment and social upheavals that challenged colonial authority and heralded new forms of governance and economic development. Understanding Berkshire's revolutionary contributions and 19th-century changes is vital for genealogists seeking to connect family histories to the dramatic shifts of this era.

The Revolutionary Era: Political Turmoil and Military Engagement

In the late 18th century, Berkshire was an active theater of revolutionary sentiment and armed conflict. The county was both ideologically and physically engaged in the struggle for independence, producing notable figures involved in local militias and the Continental Army. Muster rolls, pension records, and militia correspondence from towns like Great Barrington, Pittsfield, and Sheffield provide genealogists with detailed accounts of individual participation in key battles and campaigns.

Perhaps Berkshire's most emblematic political episode was Shays' Rebellion (1786-1787), a populist uprising named after Daniel Shays, a farmer and former Revolutionary War captain from Pelham. The rebellion reflected widespread discontent among agrarian communities struggling with postwar economic depression, debt, and onerous taxes. In Berkshire, the rebellion found fertile ground among farmers burdened by foreclosures and legal challenges. The uprising culminated in an armed march into Springfield and sparked profound debate over governance, justice, and economic policy in the new nation.

The legacy of Shays' Rebellion endures in Berkshire's court and land records, capturing the legal aftermath experienced by families involved in or affected by the upheaval. Genealogists can trace families through petitions for amnesty, court proceedings, and militia records, gaining nuanced insights into the intersection of personal hardships with broader political change.

19th-Century Economic Expansion and Social Change

The post-Revolutionary period heralded dramatic economic and infrastructural transformation in Berkshire County. The county's abundant waterways powered a burgeoning network of textile mills, sawmills, and manufactories, with Pittsfield emerging as an industrial and commercial hub. The founding of the Housatonic Railroad in 1838 further integrated Berkshire into regional and national markets, facilitating the movement of goods and people and stimulating urban development.

The rise of industry coexisted with Berkshire's agricultural traditions, where farming families diversified crops and livestock to meet changing market demands. Significant among agricultural advances was the introduction and expansion of dairy farming, orchards, and commercial vegetable production. Tax rolls, land valuations, and census manufacturing schedules help genealogists chart occupational shifts and family mobility during this time.

The Gilded Age brought newfound prosperity among Berkshire's elite, who erected grand "summer cottages" and estates in towns like Lenox and Stockbridge. Families such as the Vanderbilts, Morgans, and other industrialists and financiers chose Berkshire for its scenic beauty and refined social life. The preservation of estate records, private correspondence, and architectural surveys enrich genealogical study by illuminating the lives and networks of these influential inhabitants.

Social Fabric and Demographic Developments

Throughout the 19th century, Berkshire County's population diversified with the arrival of immigrant groups from Ireland, Germany, and later from southern and eastern Europe, settling in mill towns and rural communities. Church records document expanding Catholic parishes and other religious institutions that nurtured these immigrant populations, offering baptismal, marriage, and death records vital to genealogical research.

Community life in Berkshire also embraced fraternal societies, educational institutions, and voluntary associations that generated rich paper trails—membership rolls, meeting minutes, and charitable records—that reveal social connections and community engagement among working-class and middle-class families.

Genealogical Resources for Revolutionary and 19th-Century Research

For genealogists exploring Berkshire's revolutionary and post-revolution era, a variety of archival sources is invaluable:

- Revolutionary War pension and service records available through state archives and the National Archives detail militia involvement.

- Town meeting minutes and court records document the impact and responses to Shays' Rebellion.

- Probate records and wills illustrate economic recovery, inheritance, and familial structures.

- Census data and tax lists from the 19th century reveal occupational changes and property ownership.

- Railroad, industrial, and estate records assist in tracking family migration and economic adaptation.

- Religious institution archives provide continuous vital records across immigrant and native-born populations.

Societies, Archives, and Genealogical Resources

Berkshire County's rich and varied history is matched by a correspondingly complex archival landscape that offers genealogists and historians invaluable tools for researching family lineages and community development. The county's geographically expansive and often rural character has underscored the importance of both centralized and decentralized record preservation efforts. Across Massachusetts and in local Berkshire institutions, genealogical resources reflect centuries of Indigenous land tenure, colonial settlement, revolutionary upheavals, industrial growth, and modern transformations.

Key Historical and Archival Institutions

At the heart of Berkshire County's archival preservation stands the Berkshire County Historical Society (BCHS), based in Pittsfield's Arrowhead estate—once the home of famed author Herman Melville. The BCHS administers extensive collections of manuscripts, family papers, photographs, maps, and town histories, focusing on the region's Native American heritage, colonial frontier life, and 19th- and 20th-century developments. This institution also manages specialized research facilities that support genealogical study including probate registers, land transaction documents, and rare printed materials.

Public libraries across the county, especially in Pittsfield, Lenox, Great Barrington, and Stockbridge, hold vital town records, newspapers, cemetery transcriptions, and genealogical publications. Many libraries partner with historical societies and digitization initiatives to provide online access to early town meeting minutes, tax lists, church registers, and census substitutes—offering researchers remote entry points to primary sources.

Vital Records and Civil Registration

Civil registration of vital events in Berkshire towns generally began in the 1840s, aligning with statewide legislation mandating birth, marriage, and death records. Prior to this, genealogists must rely heavily on church registers—baptisms, marriages, and burials—held by various religious congregations that reflect the county's shifting denominational landscape, including Congregationalists, Episcopalians, Catholics, and Quakers. Town clerks manage civil records with varying degrees of accessibility, but many have been digitized or microfilmed and are searchable through platforms like FamilySearch, significantly easing research logistics.

Probate Courts and Legal Records

The Berkshire Probate Court, centered in Great Barrington, is a crucial repository for wills, estate inventories, guardianship records, and other legal documents that illuminate family relationships, inheritance patterns, and economic status. Due to the county's historical importance during events such as Shays' Rebellion, these probate files also sometimes shed light on political affiliations and community standing. Genealogists frequently use these records to connect generational dots that are otherwise absent from vital records.

Native American and Missionary Archives

Genealogical research into Berkshire's Indigenous populations, particularly the Stockbridge-Mahican community, benefits from missionary records produced during the 18th and 19th centuries. These documents—church membership rolls, baptismal registries, marriage certificates, and petitions—are housed at BCHS, local libraries, and institutions like the Massachusetts Historical Society. Combined with oral histories and tribal collaborations, these records offer pathways to reconstruct family histories often fragmented by the disruptions of colonization.

Specialized Collections and Digital Resources

Berkshire genealogists gain additional insight from specialized collections such as the Beers' atlases and town histories, land survey records, railroad and industrial archives, and personal family collections deposited by descendants of prominent local families. Digital projects increasingly aggregate these holdings with statewide and national databases, extending the genealogical reach across borders and centuries.

Collaborative networks involving the Berkshire Family History Group (BFHG), local genealogical societies, and regional libraries foster community knowledge-sharing and workshops that enhance research skills and source awareness. These groups often guide researchers in deciphering old scripts, understanding archaic legal terms, and navigating multi-jurisdictional issues common in border counties like Berkshire.

Research Strategies

Given Berkshire County's historical complexity and record dispersal, genealogists should adopt a comprehensive, layered research strategy:

- Begin with town vital and church records to establish direct lineage connections.
- Consult probate files to uncover family structures and economic information.
- Explore land deeds and proprietors' documents for migration and settlement patterns.
- Investigate military and militia records to place ancestors in the Revolutionary context.
- Supplement findings with oral histories and tribal resources where Indigenous ancestry is present.
- Utilize digital databases alongside onsite archives for efficient breadth and depth.

The archival and genealogical resources of Berkshire County reflect the region's diverse past—from Indigenous stewardship and colonial settlement through revolutionary strife and industrial growth to modern preservation. These resources, spread among state, county, municipal, and private repositories, offer genealogists powerful means of reconstructing family histories embedded in Berkshire's unique geographic and cultural setting. Mastery of these collections supports not only individual lineage discovery but contributes to a richer understanding of the county's enduring legacy.

Geography, Culture, and Genealogical Context

Berkshire County's rugged and varied geography deeply influenced its settlement patterns, cultural development, and genealogical landscape. Nestled in the uplands of western Massachusetts, Berkshire's terrain contrasts sharply with the coastal plains of eastern parts of the state. Here, the convergence of the Berkshire Hills and the Taconic Mountains forms a dramatic backdrop of verdant valleys, rolling farmland, and dense hardwood forests. This physical environment shaped how communities organized agriculturally, economically, and socially, producing genealogical records that mirror these unique regional characteristics.

Diverse Geographic Zones and Settlement Distribution

The county's topography presents a mosaic of micro-regions: the fertile Housatonic and Hoosic river valleys provided the most hospitable settings for early agriculture, while the higher elevations and rugged ridges constrained settlement and promoted forestry, hunting, and resource extraction. River corridors facilitated transport and trade, fostering the growth of towns such as Pittsfield, Lenox, and Great Barrington along navigable waterways.

These geographic distinctions created natural boundaries affecting town formation, land ownership, and migration routes. Early settlers gravitated toward riverbanks and arable lowlands, establishing nucleated villages with adjoining agricultural hinterlands. In contrast, upland and mountainous areas were sparsely populated or maintained as common hunting and gathering grounds, sometimes retained longer by Indigenous people and later used for timber or pasture.

For genealogists, the county's geography requires awareness of shifting town borders and jurisdictional complexities, as well as recognition that family movements often followed elevation gradients and waterway access rather than linear distance.

Cultural Interactions and Continuities

The county's cultural fabric is woven from its Indigenous Mahican heritage, early colonial settlers—primarily of English and Dutch descent—and waves of immigrant groups during the 19th and early 20th centuries. The Mahican's long-standing presence on these lands provided an enduring cultural substratum, reflected in place names, oral traditions, and mission village records, notably around Stockbridge.

Colonial culture blended frontier pragmatism with New England town meeting democracy and Congregationalist religious values, promoting self-reliance, communal governance, and literacy—all factors contributing to the survival of rich civic and ecclesiastical records. Well-documented church congregations, including Congregationalists, Episcopalians, Quakers, and later Catholics and Lutherans, reflect evolving social and ethnic diversity stemming from English settlers and immigrants such as Irish and Germans. These layers of religious affiliation enrich genealogical research, revealing patterns of assimilation, intermarriage, and community identity formation.

Berkshire's cultural life also bore the influence of economic transformation—industrialization, artisan guilds, and the Gilded Age elite—shaping social hierarchies and fostering preservation movements that documented family histories through diaries, letters, and estate papers.

Genealogical Context and Research Implications

Histories of geography and culture inform genealogical methodologies in Berkshire County. Terrain dictated not only where ancestors lived but influenced the nature and survival of records. Isolated upland farms may have produced fewer formal documents, relying more on church registries and family Bibles, while more populous river towns generated extensive vital, property, and court files.

Researchers must navigate complex town boundary changes, for example, the partitioning of original frontier holdings into smaller townships often scattered records across municipal jurisdictions. Understanding the county's eastern watersheds versus western uplands helps identify migration flows and property transactions critical to tracing family histories.

Cultural shifts, notably in religious adherence and ethnic composition, make it important to consult diverse denominational archives and consider immigrants' resettlement in mill towns and rural villages. Oral histories and tribal genealogies are essential when Indigenous ancestry—or cultural endurance—is part of the lineage.

Landscape, Identity, and Legacy

Berkshire's geography and culture contribute to a distinctive genealogical landscape where physical boundaries intertwine with social networks. Family histories are embedded in the land, shaped by natural features—rivers, hills, forests—and cultural values emphasizing community and resilience. Genealogists who appreciate these contextual dimensions uncover richer insights not only about individuals but also the dynamic environments in which they lived.

This integrated perspective enhances understanding of migration patterns, economic adaptations, social affiliations, and cultural heritage that define Berkshire County's ongoing story across generations.

Berkshire County's Enduring Genealogical Legacy

Berkshire County, Massachusetts, stands as a testament to the profound interplay between geography, culture, and human resilience, offering genealogists a uniquely rich tapestry for reconstructing family histories across centuries of transformation. From the ancient Mahican villages along the Housatonic River—where Indigenous stewardship shaped seasonal lifeways and communal governance—to the isolated colonial homesteads of the 18th-century frontier, this western upland region has preserved layered narratives of survival, adaptation, and innovation. The county's dramatic hills and valleys not only dictated early settlement patterns but also fostered distinct communities whose records—scattered across town clerks' ledgers, church registries, probate vaults, and historical society archives—reveal the intimate stories of families navigating imperial wars, revolutionary rebellions, industrial booms, and Gilded Age splendor.

This chapter has illuminated Berkshire's chronological arc: the Mahican homeland's sophisticated riverine societies disrupted by European contact and missionization; the perilous colonial settlement amid French and Indian Wars, yielding proprietors' deeds and militia rolls; the revolutionary crucible of Shays' Rebellion and Continental service, documented in pension files and court petitions; the 19th-century economic metamorphosis through textile mills, railroads, and elite estates, captured in tax valuations, industrial payrolls, and lavish family papers; and the modern era's preservation efforts that digitized fragile manuscripts while honoring diverse immigrant and Native continuities. Each epoch contributes distinct genealogical threads, from fragmented Indigenous petitions and missionary baptisms to standardized civil registrations and 20th-century directories.

Genealogical research in Berkshire demands a multifaceted strategy attuned to the county's rugged dispersion: triangulating town vital records with Great Barrington probate files, cross-referencing church rolls across Congregational, Catholic, and Quaker denominations, and consulting specialized repositories like the Berkshire County Historical Society's Arrowhead collections for Mahican deeds, Shaysite correspondence, and Vanderbilt-era ledgers. Digital platforms such as FamilySearch and AmericanAncestors bridge remote valleys, while collaborations with tribal organizations and local societies unlock oral histories and unpublished manuscripts essential for holistic lineage reconstruction.

The Cities & Towns of Berkshire County

City

North Adams

Nestled in the northernmost part of Berkshire County, Massachusetts, North Adams sits at the confluence of the Hoosic River and its North Branch, a strategic location that shaped the town's historical trajectory from a remote frontier settlement into a vibrant industrial city. The land that became North Adams was originally home to the Mahican people, an Algonquian-speaking nation who thrived along the river valleys stretching across western Massachusetts and New York. The Mahicans utilized these waterways seasonally for fishing, hunting, and as transportation routes, sustaining their communities in the rich hardwood forests and riverine ecosystems.

European incursions into the region began in the early 18th century, with English settlers progressively moving westward following land grants and purchases. The area encompassing present-day North Adams was originally part of larger townships such as Adams and Williamstown, with formal town boundaries only evolving late into the 18th and early 19th centuries. This period was marked by the challenges typical of frontier life—clearing thick forests, establishing farms, and negotiating often volatile relationships with Native Americans and French factions allied with Indigenous groups during the French and Indian Wars.

By the early 19th century, North Adams began an economic transformation grounded in its advantageous location on the Hoosic River, whose powerful falls and tributaries provided the kinetic energy necessary to operate gristmills, sawmills, and ultimately large textile mills. The arrival of the railroad in the 1840s accelerated this industrial growth, integrating North Adams into regional and national markets. Factories specializing in cotton, woolens, and later paper manufacturing drew waves of immigrant laborers, predominantly Irish during the mid-19th century and French-Canadian by the late 19th and early 20th centuries. This diverse influx shaped North Adams' social fabric, creating ethnic enclaves reflected in church parishes, schools, and social clubs.

Industrialists and mill owners emerged as prominent figures in the community, acquiring substantial landholdings and influencing civic development. Family archives, business ledgers, and property deeds document these elite lineages, while census records, employment rosters, and union logs provide genealogists with detailed views of working-class lives. These resources collectively illuminate the economic and social stratification characteristic of North Adams' industrial era.

Religious institutions played a critical role, with multiple denominations establishing congregations reflective of the immigrant mosaic—Catholic, Protestant, and Orthodox churches nourished community ties and created rich baptismal, marriage, and burial records invaluable for genealogical research. Town vital records became more systematic after incorporation in 1878, but prior entries are often found interwoven with adjacent towns, requiring careful cross-referencing.

North Adams also participated in broader historical currents including the American Civil War, where local men enlisted and returned veterans contributed to postwar civic life. Later 19th-century urbanization brought infrastructure improvements—streetcar lines, public schools, and hospitals—while social movements such as labor organizing found fertile ground amid mill workers.

In the 20th century, North Adams experienced industrial decline but undertook cultural reinvention with institutions like the Massachusetts Museum of Contemporary Art (MASS MoCA), retaining genealogical continuity through preserved archives and community commitment to heritage.

For genealogists, North Adams offers a wealth of materials housed across the Public Library, Berkshire County Registry of Deeds, and historical societies, complemented by digital collections on platforms like FamilySearch. Navigating shifting municipal boundaries and ethnic community contexts is key to tracing ancestors through land records, census data, church files, and employment histories—each record type revealing facets of family resilience and identity in this quintessential Berkshire industrial city.

North Adams' story, from Mahican riverine stewardship through frontier hardship and industrial prominence to cultural renaissance, encapsulates a dynamic regional legacy. Its genealogical records enable researchers to uncover the diverse ancestral threads that shaped both the city's growth and its enduring community spirit.

Genealogical Resources and Strategies
- Town vital records (post-incorporation and pre-incorporation entries within adjoining towns) are archived in the North Adams Public Library and on FamilySearch.
- Mill employment records, union rolls, and census data illustrate occupational histories and migratory patterns.
- Property deeds and probate files accessible through the Berkshire County Registry of Deeds illuminate family landholdings and inheritance.
- Local historical societies' collections house photographs, business ledgers, and personal papers of industrialists and working-class families.
- Immigration records and church archives document the ethnic and religious diversity flourishing in mill communities.

North Adams' transformation—from a Mahican riverine landscape to a thriving industrial city—reflects layered historical chapters accessible through robust genealogical records. These archives reveal not just economic evolution but demographic complexities and familial legacies integral to understanding Berkshire's northern urban core.

Pittsfield

Pittsfield, the county seat and largest city of Berkshire County, Massachusetts, occupies a significant place in the region's history, serving as a dynamic center for industry, culture, and governance since its mid-18th-century founding. Nestled along the Housatonic River's broad valley, Pittsfield's advantageous geographic position fostered early settlement, rapid economic development, and rich social diversity that generated abundant genealogical records. Its legacy encompasses Indigenous heritage, colonial struggles, revolutionary fervor, and transformation into a 19th- and 20th-century manufacturing hub, all documented in extensive archives supporting deep genealogical exploration.

Indigenous Heritage and Early European Encounters

The fertile valley served as traditional hunting and fishing grounds for the Mahican people, whose seasonal villages and travel corridors traced the Housatonic and its tributaries. European contact began cautiously in the 17th century, with traders and missionaries venturing westward from coastal settlements. The Mahican presence profoundly influenced early land use, trade networks, and cultural landscapes even as colonial encroachment intensified.

Colonial Foundations and Incorporation

Pittsfield was incorporated in 1761, initially as a frontier agricultural township carved from larger colonial plantations. Early settlers faced wilderness challenges while defining town governance and land allocations characterized by proprietors' rights and communal open fields. Churches, particularly Congregationalist, became cornerstones of civic life, producing baptism, marriage, and burial records indispensable to genealogists.

Revolutionary War Impact and Legacy

During the American Revolution, Pittsfield contributed militia units and served as a logistical hub, reflected in muster rolls, pension applications, and court papers. The aftermath shaped property and probate records as families adjusted to war losses and economic disruption.

Industrial Ascendance in the 19th Century

The 19th century saw Pittsfield transform into an industrial powerhouse, capitalizing on the Housatonic River's waterpower and expanding railroad connections. Textile mills, paper factories, and tool manufacturing dominated the local economy, drawing immigrant populations from Ireland, Germany, Italy, and Quebec. These newcomers enriched the city's cultural fabric and introduced religious diversity, reflected in expansive church registers of Catholic, Lutheran, and Baptist faiths alongside established Protestant congregations.

Genealogical researchers benefit from a variety of sources including factory employment records, city directories, census data recording occupational shifts, and naturalization files detailing immigrant integration. Land transactions, insurance documents, and probate records trace family wealth accumulation as well as urban migration.

Civic and Cultural Development

Pittsfield became the political heart of Berkshire County, hosting county courts, libraries, schools, and civic institutions. The establishment of parks, theaters, and social organizations in the late 19th and early 20th centuries fostered vibrant community life documented in newspapers, event programs, and club membership lists—records which illuminate social networks and family legacies beyond vital statistics.

20th Century Transition and Preservation

While post-industrial decline impacted Pittsfield's economy, civic pride and historical preservation flourished. Institutions like the Berkshire Athenaeum and the Berkshire County Historical Society steward archives that include manuscripts, photographs, and oral histories vital for genealogical inquiry. These repositories help bridge gaps in official records, offering expert knowledge on local families, neighborhoods, and migratory trends.

Genealogical Resources and Research Strategies

- Vital and civil records from Pittsfield town clerks (post-1841) and church registers spanning multiple denominations.
- Probate court documents held in county courthouses revealing estate details, legal disputes, and familial connections.
- Industrial and employment records accessible through historical societies and digitized collections.
- Census enumerations, city directories, and naturalization archives that illustrate demographic change and occupational diversity.
- Historical newspapers and social registers that provide cultural context and personal milestones.
- Immigrant and ethnic society archives highlighting community cohesion and integration patterns.

Pittsfield's extensive archival landscape, complex cultural heritage, and economic evolution provide genealogists with diverse entry points for family research, encompassing Indigenous lineages, colonial pioneers, immigrant laborers, and industrial magnates. This rich historical and genealogical mosaic reveals not only individual family stories but the broader social and economic currents that shaped Berkshire County's most populous city.

Towns

Adams

Adams, located in the northern Berkshires of Berkshire County, Massachusetts, is a village rich in industrial history and cultural heritage. Settled in the mid-18th century and incorporated as a town in 1778, Adams grew from a frontier agrarian community into a thriving mill town by the 19th century, powered by the natural energy of the Hoosic River. Its development was closely tied to the industrial revolution in New England, particularly in textiles and paper manufacturing, which brought waves of immigrants and transformed the economic and social landscape.

Indigenous and Early Colonial Background

Before European settlement, the area was part of the Mahican people's territory, whose seasonal encampments along the Hoosic River supported hunting, fishing, and trade networks. Early colonial expansion saw settlers acquiring land through purchases like the ones post-French and Indian Wars, with initial farming communities gradually giving way to industrial enterprises during the following century.

Industrial Growth and Economic Transformation

Adams' 19th-century identity was forged in its booming mill industries. Textile factories and paper mills surged along the Hoosic River, utilizing waterpower and later steam and electric power. The industrial boom attracted a substantial workforce, including English, Irish, French-Canadian, and later Italian immigrants, whose cultural footprints are evident in church parishes, community organizations, and cultural festivals. Mill villages, company housing, and ethnic neighborhoods formed a patchwork of communities that supported the town's economic vitality and social fabric.

Civic Life and Community Institutions

Adams developed a robust civic infrastructure with schools, churches of multiple denominations (Catholic, Protestant, Orthodox), fraternal organizations, and social clubs that played critical roles in family and community life. Vital records, church registers, and local newspapers document these vibrant social networks and provide genealogists with detailed data on births, marriages, deaths, and social affiliations.

Genealogical Resources and Research Strategies

- Vital records and town registrar files (post-1841 civil registrations; pre-1841 church records).
- Church and parish archives which reflect ethnic and denominational diversity.
- Mill employment and union records indicating occupational histories and labor ties.
- Census records and city directories tracking population changes and residential patterns.
- Property deeds, wills, and probate court documents housed in Berkshire County Registry of Deeds and probate court, detailing familial relationships and economic status.
- Ethnic society records and oral histories revealing cultural preservation among immigrant communities.

Modern Era and Preservation

Though the decline of traditional industries impacted Adams, the town has preserved its architectural heritage and maintains vibrant historical societies and museums which safeguard family papers, photographs, and local chronicles essential for genealogical research. These institutions also promote community memory and celebrate Adams' multicultural legacy.

Adams stands as a microcosm of Berkshire's transition from Indigenous lands through colonial frontier and into an industrial age sculpted by diverse immigrant labor and resilient local families. For genealogists, the town offers layered records that shine light on the personal and communal stories running through Berkshire's northern valleys.

Alford

Alford, Massachusetts, a small rural town nestled in the Taconic Mountains of southern Berkshire County, represents an enduring example of New England's agrarian past and community resilience. Incorporated in 1773, Alford's history is marked by its early settlement as a frontier farming community, characterized by expansive pastures, orchards, and woodlands that provided livelihoods for its residents. Surrounded by rolling hills and scenic landscapes, Alford remains one of Berkshire's quieter towns, preserving a collection of records and genealogies that reflect its close-knit, primarily agrarian population.

Indigenous Presence and Colonial Beginnings

The area now known as Alford was originally part of the Mahican and related Indigenous peoples' hunting and seasonal gathering territories. Prior to European settlement, Native groups utilized the region's rich resources, especially its forests and waterways, moving seasonally to optimize game and plant harvests. As colonial settlers moved westward from coastal Massachusetts, Alford's lands were secured through land grants and purchases amid gradual Mahican displacement following the conclusion of the French and Indian Wars.

European settlers arrived mainly in the early 18th century, adopting subsistence farming and establishing homesteads. Early colonists contended with rugged terrain and relative isolation, but their efforts led to the formation of a distinct township centered on agriculture and small-scale local trades. The dominant colonial population was English-descended, and their religious life was largely Congregationalist, with local meetinghouses serving as spiritual and community centers.

Agriculture, Economy, and Social Life

Throughout the late 18th and 19th centuries, Alford's economy remained predominantly agricultural, relying on family farms producing dairy, grains, and fruit orchards. Unlike Berkshire's industrial centers, Alford retained its rural character, experiencing limited industrialization except for small mills and craftsmen's shops, which supplemented farm incomes. Genealogical materials such as land deeds, agricultural census schedules, and probate inventories provide detailed insight into the economic lives and family structures of Alford's residents.

Religious institutions have left rich records; church registers document births, marriages, and deaths predating civil vital registration, while town meeting minutes reflect a participatory governance tradition that shaped local decisions and social order. Community cohesion was strengthened by mutual aid societies, educational efforts, and seasonal agricultural fairs—occasions recorded in local newspapers and diaries valuable for biographical research.

Genealogical Resources and Research Strategies

- Vital records and town registers, dating from incorporation and supplemented by church registers, are typically housed at town offices, local libraries, and the Massachusetts Archives.

- Land and property records preserved by the Berkshire County Registry of Deeds reveal family holdings, transfers, and economic status.

- Probate files at county courthouses document wills and estate inventories, often elaborating family relationships.

- Agricultural censuses and tax records offer insight into farm sizes, production, and family wealth through the 19th century.

- Local historical societies and antiquarian collections hold personal papers, photographs, and community histories enriching genealogical narratives.

- Oral histories and family memoirs, occasionally published or held privately, augment documentary research especially for reconstructing 19th-century community life.

Contemporary Preservation and Cultural Significance

Though Alford remains predominantly rural with a modest population, concerted efforts by preservation groups and historical societies maintain its heritage through museums, landscape conservation, and genealogical initiatives. The town's relative isolation and continuity allow for well-preserved family lines and an enduring sense of place reflected in its small cemeteries and homesteads.

Genealogical research in Alford benefits from recognizing the town's agrarian stability and minimal industrial disruption, enabling tracing of multi-generational farm families and close interrelationships. Alford's records contribute a vital thread to Berkshire County's patchwork of history, highlighting the role of rural communities in shaping the social and economic fabric of western Massachusetts.

Becket

Becket, located in the western section of Berkshire County, Massachusetts, is a rural town with a rich colonial heritage and a longstanding tradition of agriculture, industry, and community resilience. Incorporated in 1765, Becket began as part of the Massachusetts frontier, gradually evolving from an area of Indigenous habitation and scattered colonial settlements into a designated township with established farms, mills, and religious congregations. Its landscape of rolling hills, forests, and waterways shaped the livelihoods and social structures of its residents, leaving a layered record valuable for genealogists.

Indigenous Context and Early Settlement

Before European colonization, the territory that became Becket was occupied seasonally by Algonquian-speaking Native peoples, likely including Mahican and Nipmuc groups who engaged in hunting, fishing, and gathering within the Appalachian foothills. Their settlements, trade routes, and land use set a foundation for the fertile lands later claimed through purchase and grant by colonial settlers moving westward.

Settlement intensified in the mid-18th century following boundary disputes and the resolution of French and Indian Wars which curtailed Indigenous resistance and opened expanses of Berkshire lands for European control. Town formation followed, with Becket's incorporation signifying formal political and social structures taking root. Early colonists typically hailed from English, Dutch, and Germanic backgrounds, with many establishing farms and small-scale industries powered by Becket's streams and rivers.

Economic Development and Community Life

Throughout the 18th and 19th centuries, Becket's economy was largely agricultural, supplemented by sawmills, gristmills, and later paper mills that harnessed local waterways for power. Family farms focused on mixed agriculture—dairy, grains, and livestock—with land divisions and inheritance patterns recorded in probate and deed records. The growth of mills and small manufacturing enterprises attracted labor and facilitated modest population growth.

Religiously, Becket supported Congregationalist meetinghouses and later various Protestant denominations, with church membership rolls and sacramental registers offering critical genealogical data predating civil vital records. Town meeting minutes provide detailed insights into governance, community projects, and disputes reflecting social order and cooperation.

Genealogical Resources and Research Approaches

- Town and church vital records, often beginning mid-18th century, held at town halls, Berkshire County archives, and digitized platforms such as FamilySearch.
- Land deeds and property transaction records at county registries delineate family holdings, transfers, and economic status.
- Probate courts yield wills, estate inventories, and guardianship cases elucidating family relationships and wealth.
- Census records and agricultural schedules capture demographic changes, economic activities, and occupational data.
- Local historical society collections preserve manuscripts, family papers, photographs, and oral histories enriching contextual research.
- Historic maps and survey records document evolving land use, town divisions, and infrastructure over time.

Preservation and Cultural Legacy

Becket retains much of its rural character, with historic homes, farms, and community landmarks preserved alongside natural landscapes. Local preservation efforts maintain cemeteries, church archives, and historical buildings, providing a tangible connection to the town's colonial roots and subsequent generations.

Genealogists tracing Becket families benefit from the town's record continuity and community stability, enabling detailed reconstructions of familial lines rooted in agrarian lifestyles and local industries. This archival depth contributes to a broader understanding of Berkshire County's settled interiors, spotlighting the interplay between landscape, economy, and family heritage in shaping Massachusetts' westernmost communities.

Cheshire

Cheshire, nestled in central Berkshire County, Massachusetts, exemplifies the quintessential rural New England township marked by scenic hills, forested landscapes, and a rich colonial and industrial heritage. Incorporated in 1793, Cheshire developed from early 18th-century frontier settlement into an agricultural and manufacturing community that balanced traditional farming with emerging industries such as paper production. Its geographic location between Pittsfield and Adams placed it at the crossroads of regional trade and migration, resulting in a diverse demographic makeup and an archival record rich in genealogical value.

Indigenous Heritage and Early European Settlement

Prior to European colonization, the area that would become Cheshire formed part of the lands occupied by the Mahican people and neighboring Algonquian-speaking groups. These Indigenous communities utilized the fertile valleys and wooded uplands for hunting, fishing, and seasonal habitation. Following treaties and purchases made in the early 18th century, colonial settlers gradually encroached on these ancestral lands, establishing farms and villages amidst a complex landscape of Indigenous, French, and English interests.

Settlement accelerated following the conclusion of the French and Indian Wars, and Cheshire's incorporation formalized local governance as its population grew. Early settlers, primarily of English descent, established Congregational churches, schools, and mills, harnessing the power of local rivers like the Hoosic to drive their fledgling industries.

Agricultural and Industrial Development

Throughout the 18th and 19th centuries, Cheshire's economy was rooted in agriculture—dairy, cattle raising, and crop cultivation—augmented by small-scale industrial activities, including paper mills fueled by the town's waterways. The arrival of railroads in the region connected Cheshire to broader markets and encouraged further population growth.

Family farms and mill operations created a social fabric reflected in church registers, land deeds, and probate records. Immigrant laborers, predominantly Irish and French-Canadian, settled alongside established English descendants, leading to a multi-ethnic community reflected in baptismal and marriage records of diverse religious denominations.

Genealogical Resources and Research Approaches

- Town and church vital registers, including early Congregational and Catholic records, housed locally and at Berkshire County repositories.
- Land and property records that document family farms, real estate transactions, and inheritance patterns.
- Probate court files providing wills, inventories, and guardianship records.
- Census data and tax records that detail population demographics, occupations, and property valuations over time.
- Historical society archives preserving family papers, photographs, and oral histories vital for contextual understanding.
- Maps and transportation records that illustrate Cheshire's development along trade routes between Pittsfield and Adams.

Cultural Preservation and Community Identity

Despite modernization, Cheshire maintains its rural character, with historic homesteads and mills preserved as landmarks. Local cultural organizations and historical societies actively document the town's lineage and heritage, supporting genealogical research and public education. The steady continuity of families and community life in Cheshire offers genealogists rich, interconnected records to reconstruct family narratives rooted in agriculture and early American industry.

Cheshire's history, encompassing Indigenous presence, colonial frontier development, and industrial growth, provides genealogists with distinct avenues to explore familial legacies ingrained in Berkshire's central valley, offering a window into rural New England's evolving social and economic landscapes.

Clarksburg

Clarksburg, located in the northwestern corner of Berkshire County, Massachusetts, is a quintessential New England town rich in early American history and natural beauty. Incorporated in 1798 from parts of neighboring towns, Clarksburg evolved from a frontier settlement into a small, industrious community shaped by agriculture, mill industries, and its rugged mountain terrain. Its proximity to the Hoosic River and the Taconic Mountains provided both opportunities and challenges for its settlers, whose descendants form a genealogically significant cohort reflecting patterns of migration, industry, and rural life.

Indigenous Presence and Colonial Beginnings

Before European settlement, the area that is now Clarksburg was part of the larger territory occupied by the Mahican and Nipmuc peoples, who utilized the region's forests, rivers, and mountain passes for hunting, fishing, and seasonal habitation. The natural environment dictated a semi-nomadic lifestyle, with villages typically located in more fertile valley areas nearby. European settlers began arriving in the mid-18th century, often moving westward from more established colonial centers in Massachusetts and New York. Land grants and purchases formalized settlement, often following the conclusion of the French and Indian Wars, which reduced Indigenous control over the region.

Settlement Patterns and Economic Foundations

Clarksburg's settlers primarily engaged in subsistence and small-scale agriculture, clearing forests for pastures and crops well-suited to the mountainous terrain. Access to the Hoosic River and tributaries enabled the establishment of sawmills, gristmills, and later woolen mills that bolstered the local economy. These industries attracted laborers and contributed to the formation of mill villages within the town's boundaries.

The town's rugged terrain meant farms were generally smaller and more isolated than in other parts of Berkshire County, leading to tight-knit family networks and limited migration compared to industrial centers. These characteristics are reflected in land deeds, tax records, and probate documents that allow genealogists to trace property continuity and familial ties over multiple generations.

Religious and Social Life

Religious institutions played a central role in community cohesion, with early Congregationalist churches and later Methodist and Baptist congregations serving as hubs for worship and social activity. Church records provide crucial vital statistics where civil registration was sparse, including baptisms, marriages, and funerals, which genealogists rely upon to supplement public records.

Community governance through town meetings also produced records of lasting value, documenting civic decisions, road maintenance, poor relief, and militia service, offering insights into residents' social responsibilities and statuses.

Genealogical Resources and Research Strategies

- Town vital records and early church registers, many preserved in town halls and regional archives.

- Property and probate records documenting land transactions, inheritance, and estate settlements, accessible via Berkshire County Registry of Deeds and courthouse archives.

- Mill and industrial employment records reflecting economic activity and demographic changes.

- Census rolls and tax assessments tracking population dynamics, household compositions, and occupational data.

- Local historical society collections preserving family papers, photographs, and oral histories contextualizing genealogical data.

Preservation and Contemporary Context

Clarksburg retains much of its rural character, with historic buildings, cemeteries, and landscapes preserved by local organizations committed to maintaining its heritage. Genealogical research benefits from both centralized county archives and community-held records, facilitating the reconstruction of family histories deeply connected to the town's agrarian and industrial roots.

The history of Clarksburg—spanning Indigenous land stewardship, colonial frontier hardships, and early American industrial endeavors—offers genealogists a rich framework for understanding the families who shaped this remote Berkshire community over centuries of change.

Dalton

Dalton, located in the central Berkshires just northeast of Pittsfield, Massachusetts, is a town distinguished by its rich industrial history and scenic natural surroundings. Incorporated in 1784, Dalton quickly rose in prominence as a center for paper manufacturing, earning the nickname "Paper City" due to its numerous mills powered by the East Branch of the Housatonic River and other tributaries. The town's evolution from early frontier settlement into an industrial hub reflects broader economic and social changes mirrored in its extensive genealogical records.

Indigenous Heritage and Early Colonial Settlement

Dalton, like much of Berkshire County, was originally home to the Mahican people, who utilized the river valleys and forests for seasonal hunting, fishing, and agriculture. Though Indigenous populations were displaced gradually through land sales and colonial encroachment during the 18th century, their early presence is crucial for understanding the region's original cultural landscape.

English settlers arrived in the mid-18th century, gradually clearing land and establishing farms and small industries. Dalton was carved from lands originally part of neighboring towns such as Hinsdale and Pittsfield. Early records reflect the challenges of frontier life, including interactions with Native peoples, territorial disputes, and subsistence farming.

Industrial Growth and Economic Transformation

Dalton's unique geography—comprising swift-flowing rivers and plentiful forests—was ideal for burgeoning paper mills and related industries. By the 19th century, mills such as the Crane Paper Company became major employers, attracting large numbers of workers, including significant immigrant populations from Ireland, Italy, and Eastern Europe.

This industrial boom transformed Dalton from a farming community into a prosperous manufacturing town. Genealogical materials from this era include factory employment records, union membership rolls, census records documenting residential and occupational patterns, and church registers reflecting the town's expanding ethnic and religious diversity.

Community Institutions and Social Life

Religious congregations in Dalton provided vital social infrastructure. Early Congregationalist churches were joined later by significant Catholic, Episcopal, and Lutheran communities, each maintaining detailed baptismal, marriage, and death records, often crucial when civil records are incomplete. Town meeting records, school registers, and local newspapers offer additional genealogical insight into civic participation and daily life.

Genealogical Resources and Research Strategies

- Vital records and church registers, with many 18th- and 19th-century records preserved locally and in Massachusetts archives.

- Probate and land records that detail family estates, property transfers, and inheritance patterns.

- Industrial employment and union documentation offering occupational histories important for tracing immigrant labor families.

- Census enumerations and city directories that illustrate demographic shifts and neighborhood developments.

- Historical societies and libraries, including the Crane Museum of Papermaking, offer personal papers, photographs, and oral histories enriching family research.

Preservation and Legacy

Though modern economic shifts have altered its industrial base, Dalton maintains a vibrant preservation ethic through various historical and cultural institutions focused on both its paper industry heritage and broader community history. This commitment supports genealogical research by safeguarding and organizing archival materials essential for constructing comprehensive family narratives.

Dalton's journey—from Indigenous lands through frontier settlement to an industrial powerhouse—captures the interplay of geography, economy, and culture typical of Berkshire County's evolution. Its extensive archival resources provide genealogists with robust materials for piecing together rich ancestral stories within the broader context of New England's industrial history.

Egremont

Egremont, located in the southwestern corner of Berkshire County along the border with New York and Connecticut, is a town steeped in colonial and rural New England heritage. Incorporated in 1761, Egremont developed as a predominantly agrarian community where early settlers cleared forests to establish farms, orchards, and small industries in a landscape shaped by rolling hills, meandering brooks, and fertile valleys. The town's history reflects the gradual transformation of a colonial frontier into a stable agricultural society with strong community institutions and preserved family legacies.

Indigenous Heritage and Early Settlement

Before European colonization, the land that became Egremont was utilized seasonally by Mahican and related Indigenous peoples who depended on the region's forests, waterways, and hunting grounds. Land agreements in the early 18th century marked transitions in control, often negotiated under conditions favoring colonial expansion following the French and Indian Wars.

Settlers arrived primarily from English and Dutch backgrounds, establishing farms and homesteads amid the challenging terrain. These families shaped Egremont's early town structure through community meetings, road building, and church founding, emphasizing self-sufficiency and neighborly cooperation.

Agricultural Economy and Social Fabric

Throughout the 18th and 19th centuries, Egremont remained a largely agricultural community, producing dairy, grains, and orchard fruits. Small-scale sawmills and gristmills utilized the town's waterways, supporting local industry and trade. The relative isolation preserved strong family networks and community ties reflected in detailed probate files, land deeds, and church records.

Religious life centered around Congregational churches initially, gradually expanding to include other Protestant denominations. Church registers provide critical genealogical information where town vital records are incomplete or absent. Social clubs, educational endeavors, and mutual aid societies further knit the community, generating records that are valuable for family history.

Genealogical Resources and Research Strategies

- Town and church vital records, with births, marriages, and deaths recorded in local archives and Massachusetts repositories.
- Land and property records encompassing family farm ownership, transfers, and partitions.
- Probate documents illuminating estate compositions, kinship bonds, and economic conditions.
- Census and tax records capturing demographic and occupational patterns.
- Local historical society collections, including letters, photographs, and memoirs.
- Historic maps and survey documents illustrating town development and land use.

Preservation and Cultural Legacy

Egremont has preserved much of its rural character, with historic homesteads and meetinghouses maintained as markers of community heritage. The town's archival resources support genealogical research by providing stable records that reveal the continuity of family lines largely unaltered by industrialization or urban migration seen elsewhere in Berkshire County.

Genealogically, Egremont offers a distinctive portrait of a small New England farming town, where persistent family homesteads, intertwined social networks, and robust community institutions provide fertile ground for reconstructing multi-generational histories rooted in agricultural traditions and rural life.

Florida

Florida, located in the southern Berkshires of Massachusetts along the border with New York, is a small rural town characterized by its scenic hills, agricultural roots, and a quiet history marked by steady community life. Incorporated in 1805, Florida formed from parts of neighboring towns such as Savoy and Hawley, developing a distinct identity centered on farming, small-scale industry, and closely-knit populations. The town's remoteness and relative seclusion have preserved rich genealogical records reflecting the persistence of family lineages deeply connected to the land and local social institutions.

Indigenous Landscape and Colonial Encroachment

Prior to European settlement, the area was utilized by Indigenous groups including the Mahican and possibly Nipmuc peoples, who hunted, fished, and gathered in the river valleys and forested highlands. These groups maintained seasonal territories and movement across the Taconic Mountains and surrounding ranges. Colonial expansion into the region commenced in the mid-18th century, facilitated by land purchases and grants following the reduction of Native political authority after regional conflicts such as the French and Indian Wars.

Settlement and Economic Foundations

Settlement in Florida was marked by pioneers clearing dense forests to establish homesteads engaged primarily in subsistence agriculture, dairy farming, and timber harvesting. The town's economy durably reflected these rural traditions, with limited industrial activity such as small gristmills and sawmills operating on local streams. The topology and soil conditions shaped the agricultural outputs along with family farm sizes, often relatively small and encompassing multi-generational ownership.

Community life in Florida retained a strong reliance on religious congregations, particularly Congregationalist churches, with registers recording vital events that are essential for genealogical research. Local governance through town meetings fostered community engagement and made records of civic responsibilities, legal proceedings, and property disputes accessible to genealogists tracing social and familial networks.

Genealogical Resources and Research Strategies
- Vital records and early church registers, preserved in town archives and accessible via Berkshire County depositories and digitized collections.
- Land and probate records documenting family farms, property inheritance, and estate settlements.
- Census data and tax lists capturing population and economic patterns from the 19th century onward.
- Historical society and library collections, housing personal papers, photographs, and local histories illuminating family stories.
- Maps and survey documents showing changing land use patterns and infrastructure developments.

Preservation and Genealogical Significance

Florida maintains its rural character with historical homes and cemeteries preserved within a landscape largely unchanged by urbanization or industrialization. This continuity benefits genealogical research by providing consistent record-keeping and familial stability across generations.

Genealogists researching Florida ancestors benefit from a town history that exemplifies New England's agrarian traditions and frontier perseverance. The town's archival holdings, family-centered governance, and religious records offer a robust framework to reconstruct detailed ancestral narratives interwoven with the natural and cultural history of Berkshire County's southern hills.

Great Barrington

Great Barrington, located in the southern Berkshires along the Housatonic River, is a town rich in colonial history, revolutionary significance, and cultural heritage. Incorporated in 1761 as one of Berkshire County's earliest towns, it developed into a regional commercial and civic center with a thriving agricultural base supplemented by early manufacturing and trade. The town's fertile river valleys, prominent public institutions, and active participation in formative moments of American history create a complex genealogical landscape offering abundant opportunities for family history research.

Indigenous and Early Colonial Roots

Before European settlement, the area now known as Great Barrington was part of the traditional homelands of the Mahican people, who established seasonal camps, hunting grounds, and fishing sites along the Housatonic River and its tributaries. Their presence is still manifested in place names and archaeological sites, informing genealogical efforts that seek to integrate Indigenous ancestry and land tenure with colonial records.

Colonial settlers arrived in the early 18th century, acquiring lands through purchases from Indigenous nations and navigating a frontier replete with territorial disputes amid ongoing French and Indian Wars. Settlers primarily from English backgrounds established farms and formed communities committed to self-governance, faith, and social order.

Revolutionary Prominence and Social Upheaval

Great Barrington played a pivotal role during the American Revolution and its aftermath, witnessing notable participation in militia formations and hosting revolutionary meetings. The town is closely associated with Shays' Rebellion (1786–1787), named after Daniel Shays, whose revolt against economic injustice drew widespread attention to rural grievances. This event left an indelible mark in legal files, militia rosters, and court proceedings—key genealogical resources illuminating family involvement in resistance efforts.

Economic and Cultural Growth in the 19th Century

Through the 19th century, Great Barrington matured into a commercial hub, balancing prosperous agriculture with burgeoning manufacturing sectors including textiles and tool production. The expansion of railroad connections further integrated the town into national markets, spurring demographic growth and cultural diversification. Immigrant groups, including the Irish and later Italians and Eastern Europeans, contributed to the rich social fabric, with diverse religious institutions chronicling vital events.

Genealogical Resources and Research Pathways

- Vital records and church registries, with many dating back to the town's founding, held locally and in state archives.

- Probate and court records detailing wills, guardianships, and estate settlements, key to reconstructing family networks.

- Military and militia documentation relating to Revolutionary War service and Shays' Rebellion.

- Tax rolls, census schedules, and city directories illustrating population dynamics and occupational affiliations.

- Industrial employment records, union archives, and business ledgers reflecting the working and merchant classes.

- Local historical society and library collections, preserving family papers, photographs, oral histories, and community histories.

Preservation and Contemporary Significance

Great Barrington celebrates its heritage through well-maintained historic districts, museums, and archival institutions. The town's preservation ethos safeguards invaluable genealogical materials, enabling researchers to connect present generations with their pioneering ancestors. This continuity enriches understanding of Berkshire's evolving social and economic landscapes.

The story of Great Barrington, from its Indigenous roots and frontier beginnings to revolutionary activism and industrial success, provides genealogists with a comprehensive framework for tracing familial lines woven into the fabric of Massachusetts' western highlands.

Hancock

Hancock, a quaint rural town located in the southern Berkshires of Massachusetts, reflects a history deeply rooted in early colonial settlement and agrarian traditions. Incorporated in 1775, Hancock grew from scattered pioneer homesteads into a tightly-knit community shaped by farming, small-scale industry, and the natural beauty of its forested hills and river valleys. Its geographic isolation has contributed to the preservation of detailed genealogical records that provide insights into the families and social networks that have shaped this Berkshire County community through the centuries.

Indigenous Presence and Colonial Settlement

Before European colonization, the area was inhabited seasonally by Native American groups, primarily the Mahican, who utilized the region's rivers and forests for subsistence activities, including fishing, hunting, and gathering. The arrival of European settlers in the mid-18th century followed the gradual expansion of English colonial claims and land purchases after conflicts such as the French and Indian Wars reduced Indigenous control.

Early settlers faced rugged terrain and a frontier environment, establishing farms and small industries such as sawmills powered by local streams. These settlers were predominantly of English descent, and their community life centered on agriculture and shared civic responsibilities, including town meetings and church gatherings.

Economic and Social Development

Hancock's economy historically revolved around diversified agriculture—dairy farming, orcharding, and crop production—augmented by lumbering and modest manufacturing. The small-scale nature of these enterprises fostered close family and neighborly relations, evidenced by surviving probate records, land deeds, tax lists, and church registers.

Religiously, the town reflected New England's Congregationalist tradition, eventually accommodating other Protestant denominations. Churches functioned as both spiritual and social centers, generating records essential for genealogical work.

Genealogical Resources and Research Strategies

- Vital and church records, housed locally and in regional archives, provide baptismal, marriage, and burial documentation.
- Land transaction and probate files clarify property succession and family relationships.
- Town meeting records and tax assessments offer insights into civic engagement and economic conditions.
- Historical society collections supplement these with family manuscripts, photographs, and oral histories valuable in piecing together local genealogy.
- Agricultural census data helps reconstruct the economic lives of Hancock residents.

Preservation and Community Continuity

Despite its size, Hancock has maintained significant portions of its historic rural character, with care taken to preserve older farmsteads, cemeteries, and public buildings. This preservation ensures that genealogical records remain well-contextualized within the physical and cultural landscape of the town.

Genealogists researching Hancock lineages find a wealth of documentation available for tracing family histories embedded in an agricultural lifestyle deeply intertwined with Berkshire County's broader historical and geographic narratives.

Hinsdale

Hinsdale, a small town situated in the northern Berkshires along the West Branch of the Housatonic River, represents the quintessential New England rural community with a rich history of settlement, agriculture, and modest industrial growth. Incorporated in 1804 from parts of neighboring towns, Hinsdale evolved from early frontier homesteads into an organized township anchored by farming communities and water-powered mills. Its picturesque landscape of river valleys and forested hills has shaped family settlement patterns and left a wealth of genealogical records spanning over two centuries.

Indigenous Roots and Colonial Settlement

Prior to European colonization, the area that became Hinsdale was traditionally used by Indigenous peoples, principally the Mahican and Nipmuc tribes, who utilized the forests and waterways seasonally for hunting, fishing, and gathering. Following the conclusion of the French and Indian Wars in the mid-18th century, pressure from westward-expanding English settlers led to the gradual acquisition of Native lands through treaties and purchases.

Early English settlers arrived in the late 18th century, attracted by the fertile river valleys and potential for agricultural development. The town's incorporation in 1804 signaled the establishment of formal governance structures, including town meetings and the creation of common land rights, with agriculture and water-based milling constituting the economic backbone.

Economic Development and Community Life

Hinsdale's economy throughout the 18th and 19th centuries centered on diversified agriculture—dairy, grains, and orchards—supplemented by sawmills, gristmills, and later small manufacturing enterprises powered by local streams. The West Branch of the Housatonic River was vital in powering these early industries. This industrial activity, though modest compared to regional centers like Pittsfield, encouraged population growth and the development of village centers.

Religious institutions, predominantly Congregationalist with later inclusion of Methodist and Baptist congregations, acted as focal points for social interaction and record-keeping. Their registers provide critical genealogical data including baptisms, marriages, and burials, often filling gaps left by incomplete civil records, especially prior to the mid-19th century.

Genealogical Resources and Research Techniques
- Town clerk and church records, containing vital event documentation housed at local archives and regional repositories.
- Land deeds and property transfer documents at the Berkshire County Registry of Deeds elucidate family property histories.
- Probate files reveal estate divisions, guardianships, and familial connections.
- Census records offer demographic insights, occupational data, and migration patterns.
- Local historical societies' collections, encompassing family papers, photographs, and oral histories, provide contextual narratives enriching genealogy.
- Tax records and school registers, illuminating family economic standing and education patterns.

Preservation and Historical Continuity

Hinsdale retains much of its rural charm, with several historic buildings, cemeteries, and preserved village centers reflecting its colonial and early American heritage. Genealogical materials are generally well-maintained due to local preservation efforts and the continuity of family lineages in the area, which contribute to a rich sense of community and identity.

For genealogists, Hinsdale offers a valuable case study of rural Berkshire life, where agricultural persistence and modest industrial endeavors produced stable family networks documented across diverse source types. Its records, combined with the natural landscape, provide a foundation for reconstructing multi-generational genealogies reflective of New England's interior town life.

Lanesborough

Lanesborough, nestled in the northeastern section of Berkshire County along the Hoosic River and its tributaries, is a quintessential New England town known for its blend of natural beauty, colonial history, and industrial heritage. Incorporated in 1765, Lanesborough transitioned from a frontier farming community into a center of early American industry, particularly paper manufacturing, textile production, and quarrying, fueled by the region's abundant waterways and mineral resources. Its geographic features and economic evolution have left a wealth of records, presenting genealogists with rich opportunities to trace multifaceted family and community histories.

Indigenous Landscape and Early Colonial Settlement

Before European settlers arrived, the territory that would become Lanesborough was used by the Mahican and neighboring Algonquian-speaking peoples. Their seasonal hunting, fishing, and gathering cycles utilized the river valleys and forested hills in patterns that maintained ecological balance for centuries. Russian eighteenth-century land purchases and colonial expansion displaced Indigenous occupants, often through negotiated treaties conditioned by the outcomes of the French and Indian Wars.

Early colonial settlers, primarily English and Dutch, established farms, mills, and mining ventures along the Hoosic River and its tributaries in the mid-18th century. The town's incorporation reflected expanding local governance amidst continued frontier challenges, including rugged terrain and sporadic conflicts.

Industrial Expansion and Economic Growth

By the 19th century, Lanesborough developed into a notable center for paper mills and related industries, capitalizing on the hydropower of the Hoosic River. The town's economy diversified with quarrying of marble and slate, and small-scale agriculture persisted in the fertile river valleys and upland pastures. Railroads connecting Lanesborough to Pittsfield and other industrial hubs accelerated economic growth and demographic change, attracting immigrant labor populations, particularly Irish and later French-Canadian families.

The growth of industry and population spurred the development of civic institutions, schools, religious congregations, and social organizations, fostering tight-knit communities with vibrant cultural identities.

Genealogical Resources and Research Approaches

- Vital records and church registers, many preserved from the 18th century onwards at the town clerk's office and religious institutions.
- Land deeds, property transfers, and mining claim records held at the Berkshire County Registry of Deeds.
- Probate court documents, including wills and estate inventories providing insights into family relations and economic status.
- Census and tax records, revealing demographic trends, occupations, and property ownership.
- Industrial archives and employment rolls connected to mills and quarries.
- Local historical society collections, featuring family papers, photographs, oral histories, and community histories.

Preservation and Modern Heritage

Lanesborough continues to balance its industrial past with natural conservation, preserving historic mill buildings, quarry sites, and rural landscapes. Local historical societies actively collect, preserve, and interpret genealogical materials, supporting family history research and community heritage preservation.

Genealogical researchers uncover in Lanesborough a complex narrative of families transitioning from Indigenous landscapes to colonial farms and later industrial livelihoods. The town's extensive records illuminate this continuity, allowing a deeper understanding of Berkshire County's social and economic evolution through local family histories.

Lee

Lee, Massachusetts, situated in the southeastern region of Berkshire County at the confluence of the Housatonic and the East Branch rivers, boasts a rich industrial and cultural heritage. Incorporated in 1777, Lee transformed from an early agricultural settlement to a vibrant manufacturing town primarily known for its prominent role in paper production. Its geographic location along key waterways and in close proximity to transportation routes fostered robust industrial development throughout the 19th and early 20th centuries, creating an abundant documentary legacy valuable for genealogical research.

Indigenous Presence and Founding

Before European colonization, the area was inhabited by the Mahican people who utilized the river corridors for fishing, hunting, and trading. These watersheds provided rich resources supporting seasonal camps and complex inter-tribal networks. Early European settlers arrived during the mid-18th century, formalizing land acquisitions and gradually establishing farms and small settlements amid contestation with Native inhabitants and ongoing colonial expansion.

Industrial Growth and Economic Development

Lee's geography—particularly the presence of the Housatonic River and its branches—provided ample waterpower essential for the development of paper mills, textile factories, and other industries. The town gained a reputation as a hub for fine paper manufacturing, with companies such as the Crane & Co. establishing operations that persisted into the modern era. This industrial base attracted diverse waves of immigrants, including Irish, French-Canadian, and later Italian and Eastern European workers, enriching the cultural mosaic.

Civic Institutions and Community Life

Lee's development included the establishment of schools, churches, and social organizations reflecting its growing population and ethnic diversity. Church records—covering multiple denominations including Congregationalist, Catholic, and Protestant churches—preserve critical genealogical data such as baptisms, marriages, and deaths. Town meeting records and vital statistics document local governance, property ownership, and public works projects, creating a comprehensive archival footprint.

Genealogical Resources and Research Strategies

- Town vital records and church registers, maintained in town repositories and digitized collections.
- Property deeds and land records stored at Berkshire County Registry of Deeds, revealing family property transactions and inheritances.
- Probate court files offering insight into family structure through wills and estate inventories.
- Industrial employment records and union archives providing documentation of occupational history and immigrant labor communities.
- Census data, city directories, and naturalization records reflecting demographic trends and migratory movements.

- Local historical society collections preserving photographs, manuscripts, oral histories, and genealogical publications.

Preservation and Legacy

Lee's architectural heritage and community memory are actively preserved through local historic districts, museums, and historical societies. These organizations maintain an extensive array of genealogical and historical resources, fostering ongoing research opportunities for descendants tracing family histories woven into the town's industrial and cultural evolution.

The story of Lee—rooted in Indigenous stewardship, colonial farming, and industrial innovation—provides genealogists with rich, multi-source documentation. Its layered history illustrates the dynamic interplay of environment, economy, and people characteristic of Berkshire County's southeastern towns.

Lenox

Lenox, situated in the heart of the Berkshires, Massachusetts, is a town renowned for its rich colonial roots, thriving 19th-century cultural scene, and status as a picturesque resort town. Incorporated in 1767, Lenox evolved from an 18th-century frontier settlement into an affluent hub marked by grand estates, educational institutions, and vibrant artistic communities. Its history and genealogy are deeply entwined with Berkshire County's broader narratives of Indigenous presence, colonial development, revolutionary activity, and Gilded Age splendor, making it a key area for family historians.

Indigenous Heritage and Early Settlement

Prior to colonial expansion, Lenox lay within a landscape utilized seasonally by the Mahican people and neighboring Indigenous groups who harvested fish and game from its forests and waterways. European colonial settlement began in the early 18th century, following the cessation of French and Indian Wars that stabilized the region. Initial settlements coalesced around the fertile valleys of the Konkapot and Housatonic Rivers, nourished by proprietors' grants and farm clearings.

Town Formation and Colonial Life

Lenox's incorporation in 1767 formalized governance as town meetings, church congregations, and property rights became established. Early settlers, primarily of English descent, formed Congregationalist and Episcopal churches whose baptism, marriage, and burial records have become vital tools for genealogical research. Farming dominated early economic life, with crops and livestock supporting subsistence and local markets.

Cultural Flourishing and Gilded Age Estates

The 19th century saw Lenox blossom into a cultural center, attracting prominent families who constructed opulent summer "cottages" and estates including the Mount, Ventfort Hall, and others. These estates hosted noted figures from the arts, politics, and business, enriching Lenox's cultural cachet. The advent of railroads enabled easier access, spurring tourism and economic growth.

Lenox's historical society archives, estate records, and architectural surveys preserve this legacy, offering genealogists a window into affluent family networks, servant and labor histories, and estate management documents. The town's social fabric diversified as Irish, German, Italian, and other immigrant groups arrived to serve burgeoning industries and hospitality.

Genealogical Resources and Research Strategies

- Town and church vital records, preserved locally and complemented by state archives.
- Probate and estate documents cataloguing property and family relations within major estates and ordinary households.
- Historical society collections, rich with family papers, photographs, correspondence, and diaries.
- Census data and city directories demonstrating demographic and occupational patterns.
- Railroad and tourism archives that detail migration and seasonal residency.
- Educational institution records, including those from Lenox Academy, that illuminate social history.

Preservation and Current Significance

Lenox actively preserves its extensive architectural heritage and cultural estates, fostering an environment where genealogical research thrives. Its libraries, museums, and historical societies house invaluable records that chronicle centuries of family and community histories rooted in this emblematic Berkshire town.

Genealogists exploring Lenox are encouraged to draw upon its abundant documentary resources to reconstruct nuanced family narratives reflective of New England's evolving colonial frontier, agricultural base, and Gilded Age transformations.

Monterey

Monterey, a picturesque town nestled in southern Berkshire County against the scenic backdrop of the Berkshire Hills, offers a rich history rooted in colonial settlement, agrarian traditions, and natural beauty. Incorporated in 1847, Monterey emerged as a distinct rural community carved from parts of Great Barrington and Tyringham, characterized by its farming economy, waterways, and woodland environment. The town retains a small population and a strong sense of community cohesion, supported by a repository of genealogical records reflective of its predominantly agricultural and later summer resort lifestyle.

Indigenous Use and Early Land Transactions

Prior to European colonization, the region around Monterey was part of the seasonal territories used by the Mahican and Nipmuc peoples for hunting, fishing, and gathering. These Indigenous groups maintained complex relationships with the land and waterways, which shaped the enduring patterns of settlement and resource use. As colonial settlers ventured inland during the 18th century, land was acquired through formal purchases and treaties that often reflected the shifting power dynamics of Native displacement following the French and Indian Wars.

Colonial and 19th-Century Settlement Patterns

Monterey's early European settlers primarily engaged in subsistence farming, establishing homesteads along rivers like the Konkapot, whose waters powered small mills and supported agriculture. The town's incorporation in the mid-19th century responded to local demands for autonomous governance as the population grew. Farming remained the economic mainstay, with family farms producing dairy, grains, and orchard fruits, adapting to the town's hilly topography.

Over time, Monterey gained recognition as a tranquil summer resort area appealing to urban visitors seeking natural beauty and outdoor recreation. This dual identity influenced property ownership patterns, leading to seasonal residency records alongside those of year-round families.

Community Life and Religious Institutions

Congregationalist churches initially served Monterey's settlers, with church books offering baptismal, marriage, and burial records crucial for genealogical research. Over time, the establishment of other denominational groups mirrored growing demographic diversity. Town meeting records, school registers, and local newspapers further enrich understanding of civic participation and social life.

Genealogical Resources and Research Strategies

- Vital and church records, preserved in town archives and regional repositories, supply foundational genealogical data.
- Land and probate records document farming family holdings, estate settlements, and inheritance.
- Census records and tax assessments capture population details and economic patterns.
- Local historical society collections include personal papers, photographs, oral histories, and town histories.
- Summer resort archives may hold guestbooks, property transactions, and social club memberships relevant to seasonal residents.

Preservation and Heritage

Though Monterey remains largely rural, its preservation of historic homes, farms, and natural landscapes provides a tangible connection to its colonial and agrarian roots. Local historical and genealogical organizations play key roles in safeguarding records and fostering research into the family histories embedded in Monterey's quiet hills and valleys.

Genealogists investigating Monterey find a wealth of records supporting multi-generational family histories grounded in agriculture, religious life, and the town's evolution as a seasonal retreat, offering a nuanced view of rural Berkshire County's demographic and cultural development.

Mount Washington

Mount Washington, located in the southwestern corner of Berkshire County, Massachusetts, stands as one of the most rural and mountainous towns in the Commonwealth. Incorporated in 1779, this small community is defined by its rugged landscape in the Taconic Mountain Range, historic agricultural roots, and distinctive cultural heritage shaped by isolation and natural beauty. Its position along prominent highland corridors influenced settlement patterns, land use, and social networks, producing a genealogical record uniquely reflective of mountain life in New England's interior.

Indigenous Presence and Geographical Context

Before colonial settlement, the highlands surrounding present-day Mount Washington were utilized seasonally and strategically by the Mahican people, who engaged in hunting, fishing, and travel through mountain passes connecting river valleys. The town's elevated terrain and forested environment created a natural boundary for extensive Indigenous land use and marked areas rich in wildlife and medicinal plants, integral to Indigenous subsistence and spiritual practices.

Colonial Settlement and Town Formation

European settlement began relatively late compared to other parts of Berkshire County due to the challenging topography and remoteness. Settlers arrived primarily in the mid-to-late 18th century, carving out farms, pastures, and homesteads amid dense forests and steep hillsides. The town's incorporation in 1779 formalized governance amidst a scattered population dedicated to agriculture, forestry, and small-scale crafts.

The early settlers were predominantly of English and Scots-Irish descent, bringing with them traditions of communal cooperation essential to surviving and thriving in this rugged environment. Town meeting records, church minutes, and land grant documents serve as repositories of this critical phase.

Economic Development and Social Life

Mount Washington's economy historically revolved around subsistence and small-scale agriculture, supplemented by timber harvesting and localized milling powered by mountain streams. The challenging soil and climate limited large-scale farming but fostered a diverse economy including animal husbandry, orchards, and craft industries. Population density remained low, resulting in tight familial networks with land often passing through generations in relatively stable patterns.

Religious life centered on small Congregationalist congregations, with churches serving as both spiritual and social hubs. Vital records from these churches, along with town registries, form a rich genealogical source base. Schools and mutual aid societies contributed records revealing community priorities and networks.

Genealogical Resources and Research Strategies
- Town and church vital records, preserved in municipal archives and at Berkshire County repositories, including births, marriages, and deaths dating from incorporation.
- Land deeds and property records outlining family holdings and transfers, often reflecting close intergenerational continuity.
- Probate records capturing wills, guardianships, and estate settlements enriched by court documents.
- Census and tax assessments that offer demographic and economic data critical for tracing family movements and occupations.
- Local historical society collections, supplemented by personal papers, photographs, and oral histories that illuminate daily life and family stories.

Preservation and Legacy

Mount Washington remains one of Berkshire's most sparsely populated and scenic towns. Its preservation of rural character and historic structures, including early farmsteads and community buildings, offers genealogists unfragmented records tied closely to place. The town's archival materials provide windows into family genealogies shaped by mountain living and cooperative community cultures.

For family historians, Mount Washington presents a compelling case of maritime isolation translated to upland endurance, where genealogical pathways reveal persistence amid natural challenges and social change, articulating a distinct Berkshire narrative of rural continuity and adaptation.

New Ashford

New Ashford, a small rural town nestled in the northern Berkshires along the Taconic Mountain range, exemplifies traditional New England upland settlement characterized by farming, forestry, and community resilience. Incorporated in 1835 from parts of neighboring towns such as Williamstown and Hancock, New Ashford's landscape features rugged hills, dense woodlands, and fertile river valleys that shaped its settlement and economic patterns. The town's history is distinguished by relative isolation, steady agrarian life, and the evolution of small-scale industries supported by waterpower, all reflected in its rich genealogical records.

Indigenous Territory and Early European Settlement

The area encompassing New Ashford was part of the seasonal territories of the Mahican and Nipmuc peoples, who utilized highland forests and waterways for hunting, fishing, and gathering with extensive knowledge of the local ecology. European settlers arrived in the late 18th and early 19th centuries, expanding westward into Berkshire County's mountainous interior following land acquisitions made possible by Indigenous displacement and colonial land grants.

New Ashford's incorporation in 1835 symbolized the formal establishment of local governance, paving the way for town meetings, structured land ownership, and religious institutions integral to community cohesion. Settlers were predominantly English-descended farmers supplemented by small immigrant populations attracted by agricultural opportunities.

Economic and Social Framework

Agriculture formed the economic backbone of New Ashford, focusing on subsistence farming and livestock grazing suited to upland topography. Water-powered sawmills and gristmills emerged along local streams, supporting both local needs and modest trade. The town's geography limited large-scale industrialization, preserving strong family and neighborly networks characteristic of isolated rural communities.

Religious life centered around Congregationalist churches, whose registers of vital events—births, marriages, deaths—remain essential records for family historians. Town meeting minutes and civic records provide insights into community decision-making and social life.

Genealogical Resources and Research Considerations

- Town and church vital records, accessible through town archives and regional repositories, document family events from incorporation onward.

- Land deeds and property records held in Berkshire County detail homestead transfers and inheritance patterns.

- Probate court files reveal family relationships and wealth distribution.

- Census enumerations and tax assessments track demographic and economic information.

- Local historical collections, including manuscripts, photographs, and oral histories, enrich genealogical context.

- Agricultural and industrial records provide economic backgrounds pertinent to family occupations.

Preservation and Modern Context

New Ashford's rural and relatively undeveloped character has fostered preservation of historic homes, farms, and community landmarks, facilitating genealogical continuity across generations. Local historical and genealogical organizations play important roles in maintaining records and promoting research into family histories rooted in the upland Berkshire environment.

Genealogists researching New Ashford benefit from abundant and well-maintained records reflecting a stable, agrarian community with deep ties to Berkshire County's mountainous landscapes. The town's legacy offers a meaningful glimpse into the rural experience of western Massachusetts that complements the more industrial and urban genealogies elsewhere in the region.

New Marlborough

New Marlborough, located in the southwest corner of Berkshire County, Massachusetts, is a rural town known for its rolling hills, extensive farmland, and well-preserved colonial heritage. Incorporated in 1738, New Marlborough evolved from an early frontier farming community into a township characterized by agrarian stability and small-scale industry. Its proximity to Connecticut and New York shaped settlement patterns, while its agricultural economy and religious institutions created the social fabric and genealogical record base that endures today.

Indigenous Presence and Early Settlement

The land that comprises New Marlborough was originally part of the territory used by the Mahican people and associated Algonquian groups, whose seasonal movements and land use patterns influenced the early colonial landscape. Early European settlers arrived in the early 18th century, establishing farms and villages as part of broader colonial expansion following land grants and treaties that reshaped Indigenous occupancy.

New Marlborough's settlement benefitted from fertile soils and strategic location along river valleys, facilitating subsistence agriculture and emerging community institutions. The town's incorporation in 1738 formalized governance structures, including town meetings and parish organizations, fostering community cohesion.

Agrarian Economy and Social Institutions

Throughout its history, New Marlborough primarily sustained an agricultural lifestyle, with family farms producing dairy, grains, hay, and orchard fruits. Waterways powered small mills—grist, saw, and fulling—that supported local economies and crafts, as documented in land deeds and business records. The town's social fabric included robust Congregationalist churches, which extensively recorded vital events—births, marriages, and deaths—integral to genealogical research.

Education and mutual aid societies were foundational, their records preserved in town archives alongside civic documents recording land partition, road maintenance, and militia service. Population growth was steady but modest, maintaining close-knit communities over centuries.

Genealogical Resources and Research Strategies

- Vital records and church registers, well preserved locally and within Berkshire's archival systems, are primary genealogical sources.

- Land deeds and property transfer records at the Berkshire Registry of Deeds trace family land transactions and inheritance.

- Probate files elucidate familial structures through wills, estate inventories, and guardianship.

- Census records and tax assessments provide demographic and occupational data.

- Local historical society holdings contain manuscripts, photographs, family histories, and oral narratives enriching contextual understanding.

Preservation and Legacy

New Marlborough retains much of its rural character and historical integrity, with extensive preservation of early homesteads, churches, and cemeteries. These factors contribute to strong genealogical continuity and offer rich opportunities for family history researchers to explore ancestral lives embedded in New England's colonial farming tradition.

Genealogists researching New Marlborough families will find a well-documented record base reflecting agrarian stability, community cohesion, and the town's enduring role as a quiet but vital part of Berkshire County's historical landscape.

Otis

Otis, Massachusetts, incorporated in 1810 and named after the distinguished Boston Brahmin Otis family, is a small rural town located in eastern Berkshire County. Originally settled as part of neighboring towns such as Loudon (its earlier name before renaming it to Otis), it developed from colonial frontier farms and agricultural homesteads into a community known for its pastoral charm and scattered mills. The town's connection to the Otis family—the progenitors of a prominent political and legal dynasty in Massachusetts—adds a unique genealogical dimension deeply tied to broader colonial and revolutionary narratives of the state.

Otis Family Legacy and Early Settlement

The Otis family, with roots tracing back to John Otis of Glastonbury, Somerset, England, were among Massachusetts' leading colonial families, with members serving as judges, legislators, and patriots throughout the 17th and 18th centuries. The town of Otis honors their legacy; though no direct Otis homesteads remain in the town, many relatives settled nearby, and their influence extended across Berkshire County and the Commonwealth.

The area that became Otis was originally part of the western frontier territories, colonized in the mid-18th century through land grants following purchases from Native peoples, principally the Mahican. Early farmers and settlers established homesteads alongside small water-powered mills that supported wool production, timber, and food processing, marking the town's gradual economic foundation.

Economic and Social Development

Otis's economy historically relied on agriculture—primarily dairy farming and crop cultivation—augmented by small-scale mills and forest product industries. While it did not industrialize to the extent of adjoining towns like Pittsfield, Otis retained a steady farming population with strong community values centered around town meetings and church life.

Religious records, dominated by Congregationalist and Baptist churches, provide rich genealogical material documenting births, marriages, and deaths predating civil registration systems. The town's archives and Berkshire County repositories hold land deeds, tax records, and probate documents invaluable for reconstructing family structures over the 19th century.

Genealogical Resources and Research Strategies

- Vital and church records, preserved locally and through state archives, chronicle family events.
- Land deeds and property transfers illuminate patterns of settlement and inheritance.
- Probate court filings offer insights into family wealth distribution and kinship.
- Census and tax rolls document population demographics and household economics.

- Local historical and genealogical society collections, preserving family histories, photographs, and oral memoirs.
- Otis family papers and correspondence housed in regional archives provide context on the family's prominence and influence within Massachusetts.

Preservation and Genealogical Importance

Otis's rural character and connection to one of Massachusetts' most notable families create a genealogical landscape rich with opportunities for multi-generational research. The town's records are well-preserved and accessible, often augmented by broader Otis family collections available statewide. Genealogists benefit from understanding these intersecting narratives of local rural life and influential political lineages.

The town of Otis provides a pivotal link for researchers tracing the Otis family's impact alongside the community ties that sustained Berkshire's agrarian heartland, offering a vital chapter in Massachusetts genealogical history.

Peru

Peru, a sparsely populated rural town in eastern Berkshire County, Massachusetts, perched on the mountainous border with Hampshire County, embodies the rugged essence of New England's upland frontier. Originally designated Northern Berkshire Township Number 2 (including present-day Hinsdale and part of Middlefield), it was first settled around 1767 and officially incorporated as Partridgefield on July 4, 1771—named for Oliver Partridge, one of three original purchasers alongside Governor Francis Bernard. The name changed to Peru on June 19, 1806, at the suggestion of Rev. Justus Forward, evoking the exotic allure of distant lands amid its isolated hills. With a 2020 population of just 814 (down from 519 in 1850), Peru remains a farming community of rolling terrain, brooks, and forests, bordered by Windsor (north), Cummington (northeast), Worthington (east), Middlefield (south), Washington (southwest), and Hinsdale (west)—13 miles east of Pittsfield, 40 miles northwest of Springfield, and 118 miles west of Boston.

Mahican Highlands and Frontier Settlement

Mahican and Nipmuc peoples seasonally exploited Perus forested uplands and streams for hunting, fishing, and gathering before 18th-century colonial encroachment via land grants post-French and Indian Wars. Partridgefield settlers (1767 onward) cleared farms amid isolation, with town records (1782–1905 vital events) capturing early pioneers like Abbey, Abbee, and Allison families amid gristmills and subsistence agriculture.

Agrarian Continuity and Civic Identity

Peru's economy centered on small farms (dairy, grains) with population decline from 499 (1860) to 305 (1890) reflecting rural exodus; represented in Massachusetts House (Second Berkshire District, Paul Mark) and Senate (Berkshire-Hampshire-Franklin, Adam Hinds), patrolled by Cheshire State Police Barracks B4. Congregational churches anchored social life, their registers predating civil records.

Genealogical Resources and Strategies

Vital repositories:

- Town Clerk vital records (PO Box 1175, Hinsdale, MA 01235; 1782–1905 microfilm).
- Vital Records of Peru to 1850 (NEHGS transcription: births like Amzy ABBEY 1806, marriages, deaths).
- FamilySearch/Berkshire GenWeb (census, probate, deeds).
- Berkshire County Registry (land/probate: farm partitions).

Peru's highland-farm saga—from Mahican streams to Partridgefield deeds—unravels Abbey kin via Forward's volumes and township clerks.

Richmond

Richmond, located in eastern Berkshire County, Massachusetts, began as a frontier settlement known as Mount Ephraim and Yokun Town (or Yokum), settled around 1760 by pioneers Capt. Micah Mudge and Ichabod Wood with their families amid Mahican territories. Incorporated June 21, 1765, as Richmont (later Richmond), it was carved from new plantations encompassing fertile valleys and hills 12 miles east of Pittsfield. Named possibly for the prominent Richmond family (English lords tracing to Norman Conquest via Alan Rufus, 1st Earl of Richmond) or local topography, Richmond evolved as an agricultural township with mills powered by local brooks, maintaining rural character through 19th-century farming (dairy, orchards) and modest population (843 in 2020).

Mahican Uplands and Pioneer Settlement

Mahican exploited Yokun hills for hunting/fishing pre-1760; Mudge/Wood families cleared farms post-French and Indian Wars, with town records (vitals to 1850) capturing early settlers amid proprietors' grants and church formation.

Agrarian Mills and Civic Foundations

Small saw/grist mills dotted streams; Congregational churches anchored vitals (births like Abigail MUDGE 1762), with *Vital Records of Richmond to 1850* (1913 transcription) logging 2,000+ entries. Town Clerk (1529 State Rd) holds ongoing records.

Genealogical Resources and Strategies

Vital repositories:

- Richmond Town Clerk (1529 State Rd; vitals post-1765).
- Vital Records to 1850 (NEHGS/FamilySearch: births, marriages, deaths).
- Berkshire GenWeb/FamilySearch (censuses, probate).
- County Registry (deeds: farm chains).

Richmond's Yokun-farm saga—from Mahican ridges to Mudge deeds—unravels pioneer kin via 1765 clerks and 1913 volumes.

Sandisfield

Sandisfield, the largest town in Berkshire County at 53 square miles yet one of its most sparsely populated (pop. 989 in 2020), occupies the southeastern corner amid Mahican territory, evolving from Housatonic Plantation No. 3 (settled 1750 by Connecticut colonists) into incorporation March 6, 1762—uniquely named for Samuel Sandys, first Lord of Trade and Plantations. Mid-19th-century prosperity peaked at ~1,000 residents via dairy farms, sawmills, tanneries, and light manufacturing along Farmington River tributaries, but failed 1870s railroad doomed rural economy, halving population by 1900. Historic core boasts 100+ antique homes (Philemon Sage House 1799 NRHP), New Boston Inn (tavern since 1750), and Baptist Meeting House (1842 Greek Revival, later synagogue, now Sandisfield Arts Center).

Mahican Tributaries and Connecticut Plantation

Mahican exploited Farmington River environs pre-1750; Connecticut settlers (led by Col. John Ashley Jr.) planted Housatonic No. 3 amid French and Indian Wars aftermath, with vitals (1746–1894) capturing Adams/Pease/Belden kin amid mills.

Tannery Boom and Arts Renaissance

19th-century peak fueled New Boston/Southfield hubs; post-rail decline preserved 100+ colonials. Arts Center (1842 church) hosts performances.

Genealogical Resources and Strategies

Vital repositories:

- Town Clerk vitals (1746–1894 microfilm).
- Vital Records Indexes (births/deaths 1746–1850: Orren/Chamberlin).
- FamilySearch/Berkshire GenWeb (censuses/probate).
- County Registry (deeds: tannery estates).

Sandisfield's river-tannery saga—from Mahican fords to Sandys' namesake—unravels Pease kin via 1762 clerks and Arts Center stones.

Savoy

Savoy, a mountainous rural town straddling the eastern Berkshire County border with Franklin and Hampshire Counties, originated as part of Northern Berkshire Township #6 (including Adams, North Adams, Cheshire, Lanesborough) before auctioned lands were purchased by Col. William Bullock of Rehoboth. First settled September 1777 by Col. Lemuel Hathaway's group (originally dubbed New Seconk), it incorporated February 20, 1797, named for its scenic resemblance to France's Duchy of Savoy. Early grazing agriculture yielded to lumber mills by mid-19th century, peaking at 955 residents (1850) before rural exodus halved population to 467 (1975); 2020 census shows 392 amid open town meetings, Board of Selectmen, and Cheshire State Police Barracks B4 patrol. Diverse faiths flourished mid-1800s (Baptist 1787, Methodist), with Emma L. Miller Memorial School (PK-6) feeding Hoosac Valley Regional system; nearest colleges in Pittsfield/North Adams.

Mahican Highlands and Hathaway Settlement

Mahican/Nipmuc exploited Savoy's peaks pre-1777; Col. Lemuel Hathaway's pioneers (Rehoboth settlers) cleared farms amid Revolutionary aftermath, Baptist church (1787) anchoring vitals (1736–1900).

Lumber Boom and Rural Decline

19th-century mills drove prosperity (pop. peak 955/1850); failed rail doomed economy, preserving mountain isolation. Modern demographics: 24.4% under 18, median age 40.

Genealogical Resources and Strategies

Vital repositories:

- Town Clerk (720 Main Rd; vitals post-1797).
- Vital Records 1736–1900 (FamilySearch microfilm).
- Miller's History of Savoy (1879: genealogy/history).
- Berkshire/Franklin GenWeb (censuses/probate).

Savoy's peak-mill saga—from Mahican ridges to Hathaway clearings—unravels settler kin via 1787 baptisms and Miller's tomes.

Sheffield

Sheffield, the oldest town in Berkshire County (incorporated June 22, 1733 as Housatonic Lower Plantation or Schaghticoke), anchors southern Berkshire along the Housatonic River where Mahican sachems Konkapot sold lands April 25, 1724 for "£460, 3 barrels cider, 30 quarts rum"—Berkshire's first deed. First white settler Obadiah Noble (Westfield) arrived ~1724; Rev. Jonathan Hubbard ordained October 22, 1735, forming Sheffield's church amid French and Indian Wars raids. Sent 200 men to Union armies (Civil War); eminent natives include Col. John Fellows (1760–1844), Daniel/Theodore/Henry D. Sedgwick, Chester Dewey (1781–1867), Orville Dewey DD (1794), F.A.P. Barnard (1809), George F. Root (1820). Sheffield Historical Society (1972, 159 Main St) preserves 1774 Dan Raymond House, Parker Hall Law Office (1820), 700+ family files, tax records (1763–1983), vitals from 1730, Revolutionary/French-Indian/Civil War lists, glass negatives.

Housatonic Deeds and Noble Settlement

Mahican Housatonnuc ("over mountains") sustained villages; 1724 deed launched Noble's farm, Hubbard's flock (1735), church vitals logging Fellows/Sedgwick amid raids.

Sheffield Resolves and Historical Campus

Sheffield Resolves (1773 precursor to Declaration) drafted here; Society campus (7 structures) houses Mark Dewey Research Center (700 families, house histories, obits).

Genealogical Resources and Strategies

Vital repositories:

- Sheffield Town Clerk (PO Box 175; vitals 1733+).
- Early Vitals 1733–1800 (FamilySearch; Noble/Fellows).
- Sheffield Historical Society (700 families, tax 1763–1983, veterans).
- Berkshire GenWeb (censuses/probate).

Sheffield's Housatonic-deed saga—from Konkapot cider to Sedgwick resolves—unveils Noble kin via Raymond House files and 1733 ledgers.

Stockbridge

Stockbridge, located in southern Berkshire County along the Housatonic River, is renowned as the site of America's first "praying town" for Native Americans, established 1734 by Rev. John Sergeant among the Housatonic Mahicans (later Stockbridge-Munsee). Chartered Indian Town (1737), renamed Stockbridge (1739) for its English settlers, it blended missionary-Indigenous settlement with colonial farms amid French and Indian Wars. Incorporated 1739, Stockbridge hosted Sergeant (1734–1749), Jonathan Edwards (1751–1757), and the 1785 migration of ~200 Stockbridge Indians to New York (later Wisconsin). 19th-century Gilded Age drew Vanderbilts/Edith Wharton (The Mount); 2020 pop. 1,943 amid Mission House (1739 NRHP), Naumkeag (1885–1915 Olmsted estate), and Berkshire Botanical Garden.

Housatonic Praying Town and Mahican Mission

Mahican Housatonnuc villages preceded Sergeant's mission (1734, 200+ converts); Edwards' tenure produced church vitals (1737–1900) amid intermarriage, with Stockbridge Indians allying colonists in Revolution/French wars.

Gilded Estates and Cultural Hub

Wharton (1862–1937) wrote *Ethan Frome* at The Mount; Naumkeag hosted elites. Vitals capture Native/English kin.

Genealogical Resources and Strategies

Vital repositories:

- Stockbridge Town Clerk (50 Church St; vitals 1737–1900).
- FamilySearch (microfilm: Native baptisms, Edwards registers).
- Stockbridge Library/Historical Room (Mission House papers).
- Berkshire Athenaeum (Gilded families).

Stockbridge's mission-estate saga—from Housatonic converts to Wharton whispers—unveils Sergeant kin via Edwards ledgers and Naumkeag stones.

Tyringham

Tyringham, a serene rural town in southeastern Berkshire County, Massachusetts, cradled between the Housatonic River valley and Hop Brook, traces its origins to Number One Plantation settled ~1750 amid Mahican uplands. Incorporated March 6, 1762 (nine years after Berkshire County formation), Tyringham (named for Tyringham, Buckinghamshire, England) briefly became Tyringham and Monterey until Monterey separated February 27, 1811. Early settlers like Asahel Gunn cleared farms for agriculture and mills, with Shaker community (1785–1812, 40 members led by Calvin Reed) leaving vitals amid apple orchards and sawmills. Population peaked ~600 (1850) before rural decline (pop. 339, 2020); landmarks include Tyringham Schoolhouse (NRHP 2020, Historical Society restoration), Santarella (1880s Shingle Style), and Tyringham Cobble (1,700-ft panoramic views).

Mahican Brooks and Gunn Settlement

Mahican exploited Hop Brook environs pre-1750; Asahel Gunn's pioneers (1762) farmed amid Shaker celibate colony (1785–1812), church vitals (to 1850) logging Gunn/Reed/Shaker kin.

Shaker Orchards and Schoolhouse Legacy

Shakers cultivated apples; post-1812 dissolution preserved isolation. Tyringham Historical Society (2019) restores Schoolhouse (NRHP 2020).

Genealogical Resources and Strategies

Vital repositories:

- Tyringham Town Clerk (103 Main Rd; vitals post-1762).
- Vital Records to 1850 (NEHGS 1907: births like Asahel GUNN Jr. 1763).
- Tyringham Historical Commission (Schoolhouse: photos, family histories).
- Tyringham Historical Society (manuscripts, Shaker papers).

Tyringham's brook-Shaker saga—from Mahican orchards to Gunn deeds—unveils Reed kin via 1762 registers and Santarella stones.

Washington

Washington, a small town perched atop the Taconic Mountains in southern Berkshire County, Massachusetts, is distinguished by its scenic upland environment and richly documented colonial and early American history. Officially incorporated in 1777, Washington evolved from isolated frontier farms and seasonal Indigenous use into a town deeply shaped by rugged geography, agrarian livelihoods, and small-scale industrial activities. Its relative remoteness and stable population have preserved extensive early records, providing genealogists with rich genealogical material reflecting the area's distinct community character and historical continuity.

Indigenous Habitation and Early Settlement

Prior to European settlement, the area of Washington was traditionally used by the Mahican and closely related Algonquian-speaking peoples who traveled seasonal trails through the Taconic ridges, exploiting hunting grounds and waterways. Shared stewardship of these uplands laid the groundwork for some of the earliest settlements in Berkshire's high country.

European colonists, primarily of English descent, began settling in Washington in the mid-18th century, overcoming challenging terrain to establish farms, homes, and modest industries along streams suitable for water-powered mills. Initial names included Watsontown and Hartwood, with formal town boundaries surveyed by Daniel Wilcox in 1795. Early governance centered around town meetings and church organizations, which preserved community order and values while generating vital genealogical records.

Agricultural Economy and Community Life

Washington's economy historically centered on subsistence and diversified farming, with milk, beef, grains, and orchards meshing with lumbering and small manufacturing endeavors. Populations remained sparsely settled and dispersed, fostering familial networks with deep roots in the town's geographic niches. Churches flourished as spiritual and social centers, maintaining baptism, marriage, and burial registers that are key tools for genealogical research.

Community cohesion was further maintained through educational institutions, mutual aid societies, and local celebrations, leaving behind newspapers, minute books, and personal correspondence crucial for reconstructing social histories.

Genealogical Resources and Research Techniques

- Town and church vital records from incorporation onward, including early Congregationalist and Baptist registries, preserved locally and in Berkshire archives.

- Land deeds and property transactions providing insights into familial economic standing and migration.

- Probate files containing wills and estate inventories elucidating relationships and inheritance.

- Census and tax records that offer demographic data about occupations and household compositions.

- Local historical society collections with family papers, photographs, oral histories, and manuscripts illuminating personal narratives.

- Maps and surveys outlining town development and land use changes.

Preservation and Historical Significance

Washington retains a largely rural nature with well-preserved historical structures, cemeteries, and landscapes that maintain the town's colonial and agrarian legacy. Historical societies and local government efforts ensure the conservation and accessibility of genealogical materials reflecting a continuum of family histories and community identity.

For genealogists, Washington represents an enduring Berkshire upland community whose records reveal the interplay of environment, economy, and kinship over two centuries. Its archives provide a valuable window into the lives of settlers and their descendants who forged a life amidst the challenges and beauty of Massachusetts' mountain counties.

West Stockbridge

West Stockbridge, located in the northwestern corner of Berkshire County along the New York border, evolved from Queensborough (Dutch patent 1686, settled ~1730s as Indiantown and Gore) into incorporation February 18, 1835—named for adjacent Stockbridge. Mahican territory yielded to marble quarries (limestone 1818–1920s, shipped to NYC) and iron foundries powering 19th-century industry amid Farmington River tributaries. Civil War sent 70+ men (monument 1903); pop. 1,226 (2020) preserves Shaker Round Barn (1835 NRHP, restored 1980s), Old Town Hall (1839, Historical Society HQ), and Williams Tavern (1782). West Stockbridge Historical Society (founded 1965) stewards 1907 *Vital Records to 1850* transcription, town histories, and Old Town Hall restoration.

Mahican Gores and Marble Boom

Mahican Indiantown preceded 1686 Queensborough patent; 1818 limestone boom shipped to NYC, church vitals (to 1850) logging quarrymen amid Shaker agriculture.

Shaker Barns and Historical Campus

Shaker Round Barn (octagonal, 168-ft diameter) symbolizes 1835 peak; Society restores Old Town Hall (1839).

Genealogical Resources and Strategies

Vital repositories:

- West Stockbridge Town Clerk (21 State Rd; vitals post-1835).
- Vital Records to 1850 (NEHGS 1907: births like Abigail CALL 1760).
- West Stockbridge Historical Society (Old Town Hall: censuses, quarry logs).
- FamilySearch/Berkshire GenWeb (probate/deeds).

West Stockbridge's gore-marble saga—from Mahican patents to Shaker rounds—unveils quarry kin via 1835 clerks and Round Barn stones.

Williamstown

Williamstown, located in the far northwest corner of Berkshire County along the Hoosic River and bordering Vermont, occupies ancestral Muhheconeew (Mohican) Nation territory where seasonal villages preceded colonial settlement. Originally West Hoosuck Plantation (surveyed 1750, first lots sold to encourage settlement per Mass. Bay Colony legislation requiring settled pastors), it incorporated June 21, 1765—named for Col. Ephraim Williams Jr. (killed 1755 French & Indian War, bequeathing £1,000 for Hoosuck academy, now Williams College 1793). Early settlers faced Mohican raids and frontier hardships, pop. 12,981 (2020) hosts Williams College, Clark Art Institute, and Williamstown Historical Museum (1941, 56 Water St, 2,000+ artifacts).

Mohican Hoosuck and Ephraim's Bequest

Muhheconeew exploited Hoosic valleys pre-1750; West Hoosuck pioneers (Hudson/Chidester forts) endured wars till 1765 incorporation fulfilling Williams' will via settled pastor. Vitals (1760–1893) log founding families like Cole/Wilson.

College Towns and Rockefeller Farms

Williams College (1793) drew elites; Mt. Hope Farm (E. Parmalee Prentice/Alta Rockefeller, 1,300 acres, Elm Tree House 72-room Georgian) fused experimental agriculture/genetics.

Genealogical Resources and Strategies

Vital repositories:

- Williamstown Town Clerk (vitals 1760–1893 indexes).
- Vital Records to 1850 (NEHGS transcription).
- Williamstown Historical Museum (founding families, Mohican context).
- FamilySearch/Berkshire GenWeb (censuses/probate).

Williamstown's Hoosuck-college saga—from Mohican forts to Rockefeller spuds—unveils Chidester kin via Ephraim ledgers and Water St shelves.

Windsor

Windsor, located in eastern Berkshire County along the Westfield River bordering Hampshire County, originated as New Plantation Number Four (surveyed 1762) and incorporated July 4, 1771, as Gageborough—named for Gen. Thomas Gage—before renaming Windsor in 1777 amid anti-British sentiment. Settled ~1762 by pioneers from Hampshire County amid Mohican/Nipmuc uplands, Windsor's rugged hills (elev. 1,500–2,000 ft) fostered sheep grazing, apple orchards, and sawmills powered by river tributaries. Population peaked at 519 (1850) before rural decline (pop. 859, 2020); landmarks include First Congregational Church (1796), Windsor Historical Commission Museum (dioramas of mills/farms), and remnants of 19th-century cheese factories.

Mohican Highlands and Gageborough Settlement

Mohican/Nipmuc exploited Westfield River environs pre-1762; Hampshire pioneers cleared farms amid Revolutionary fervor, renaming from Gageborough (1777), church vitals (to 1850) logging early families like Buck/Howes amid sheep drives.

Orchard Mills and Historical Dioramas

19th-century cheese/apple boom; Windsor Historical Commission preserves mill dioramas and artifacts.

Genealogical Resources and Strategies

Vital repositories:

- Windsor Town Clerk (3 Hinsdale Rd; vitals post-1771).
- Vital Records to 1850 (NEHGS transcription: births like Amasa BUCK 1772).
- Windsor Historical Commission (museum: censuses, farm logs).
- FamilySearch/Berkshire GenWeb (probate/deeds).

Windsor's highland-orchard saga—from Mohican rivers to Gageborough deeds—unveils Buck kin via 1771 registers and diorama stones.

Census-Designated Places

Housatonic

Housatonic is a census-designated place and historic mill village straddling the towns of Great Barrington and Stockbridge in southern Berkshire County, centered along the Housatonic River where early 19th-century textile and paper mills powered rapid industrialization. Emerging around 1800 amid Mahican heritage lands, the village peaked with Monument Mills—a massive textile complex spanning five buildings (420,000 sq ft, 500 employees)—housing immigrant workers (Irish, Italian, French-Canadian) in tenements while producing woolens and paper via Eagle Mill (Smith Paper Company) and North Lee Mill (Lyman Church, 1808). Mohican consolidation at nearby Stockbridge Mission (1734) preceded settler encroachment, with river knolls like Canoe Meadows marking ancient burial sites; post-Civil War decline hit with floods and mill closures, preserving Victorian mill architecture amid modern tourism.

Mahican Mills and Immigrant Tenements

Mahican Muh-he-con-nuk ("great waters") villages dotted riverbanks pre-1734 mission; Elizur Smith/Valley Mills (early 1800s) drew laborers, vital records capturing intermingled Dutch/English/Mohican kin amid Monument booms.

Paper Boom and River Legacy

Church/Smith Paper dominated; floods reshaped tenements, Housatonic Heritage preserving oral histories of mill families.

Genealogical Resources and Strategies

Vital repositories:

- Great Barrington/Stockbridge Town Clerks (vitals via parent towns).
- Berkshire Athenaeum (local history/genealogy: mill payrolls, tenement censuses).
- Housatonic Heritage Oral History Center (worker interviews, immigrant stories).
- FamilySearch/Berkshire GenWeb (censuses/probate: Smith/Church families).

Housatonic's river-mill saga—from Mohican missions to Monument tenements—unveils immigrant kin via Eagle ledgers and Canoe Meadow stones.

Chapter 5

Bristol County

Framing the southeastern shoreline of Massachusetts, Bristol County occupies a landscape shaped by coastal inlets, tidal rivers, fertile uplands, and enduring human enterprise. Extending from the sands of Buzzards Bay to the Taunton River's winding interior, it bridges the maritime culture of the South Coast with the inland agricultural and industrial heartland of New England. Established in 1685 from the old Plymouth Colony jurisdiction, Bristol County originally encompassed territory that would later include parts of modern Rhode Island—its shifting boundaries and deep colonial roots offering a complex genealogical canvas. Today the county's principal communities—Taunton, New Bedford, Fall River, and Attleboro—reflect centuries of adaptation from Indigenous homeland to colonial port towns, industrial centers, and immigrant enclaves whose records document one of Massachusetts' richest genealogical traditions.

For family historians, Bristol's story unfolds through maritime trade, agricultural settlement, industrial growth, and enduring Indigenous presence. Its archives encompass Wampanoag deeds, early Plymouth Colony court proceedings, maritime crew lists, textile mill payrolls, and parish registers from Catholic, Congregational, and Quaker communities—records that collectively illuminate centuries of family formation, migration, and resilience along New England's southern coast.

Indigenous Foundations: The Wampanoag Homeland and Survival

Before English settlement, the lands comprising present-day Bristol County formed a vital portion of the Wampanoag Confederacy's ancestral homeland. These Algonquian-speaking people maintained a sophisticated network of villages stretching from Cape Cod to Narragansett Bay, sustained by estuarine resources, agriculture, and trade routes following the Taunton, Nemasket, and Acushnet rivers. Long before European arrivals, Wampanoag communities cultivated maize, beans, and squash in riverside clearings and gathered shellfish along tidal flats—activities that sustained a balance between seasonal abundance and environmental stewardship.

The river systems served as both highways and lifelines. Settlements such as Cohannet (near modern Taunton) and Assonet were centers of Wampanoag political and spiritual life. Leadership rested with sachems, whose authority was grounded in kinship and reciprocity rather than coercion. These societies expressed complex spiritual relationships with land and water, adhering to communal stewardship rather than private property—an outlook that deeply influenced later colonial land transactions and complicates genealogical interpretation of early "deeds" and "sales," which often reflected divergent cultural concepts of ownership.

European arrival in the early 17th century brought profound disruption. The devastating epidemics of the 1610s and 1630s severely reduced Wampanoag populations, weakening traditional governance before sustained colonization. The 1620 founding of Plymouth, just to the north, initiated expanding settlement pressures. By the mid-17th century, the Cohannet River valley and

Mount Hope lands near the modern Rhode Island border became flashpoints for English intrusion. King Philip's War (1675–1676), sparked under the leadership of the Wampanoag sachem Metacom (Philip), originated largely in this region and left enduring demographic and record-keeping scars. Postwar confiscations fragmented Wampanoag landholdings, dispersing survivors throughout southern New England and into mission communities such as Mashpee and Christiantown.

For genealogists, the Wampanoag presence remains foundational. Surviving records—translated deeds, colonial depositions, missionary baptismal lists, and petitions to Plymouth and Massachusetts courts—illuminate both individual Native actors and shifting tribal networks. Their descendants persist today in communities like the Mashpee and Pocasset Wampanoag Tribes and in diaspora families with Bristol County roots. Modern research increasingly draws upon oral histories, tribal archives, and DNA studies to reconnect fragmented Indigenous lineages and reinterpret colonial-era sources that once obscured Native identity.

Colonial Settlement and Maritime Expansion in Bristol County

European colonization of Bristol County followed the southward and westward expansion of Plymouth Colony settlers seeking new agricultural lands and trading opportunities. Early towns such as Taunton (1637), Rehoboth (1643), and Dartmouth (1664) emerged along inland waterways and coastal coves, where fertile soils and access to ports supported agrarian and mercantile growth. Settlement spread through land purchases from Wampanoag sachems—transactions that fused English and Indigenous cultural assumptions yet yielded enduring documentary traces useful to genealogists today.

Bristol County's proximity to Narragansett Bay and Buzzards Bay made it a maritime center from the beginning. By the late 17th and early 18th centuries, harbors at Bristol (then part of Massachusetts), Dartmouth, and Swansea fostered shipbuilding, fishing, and coastal trade with the rest of colonial New England and the Caribbean. Taunton became a crucial inland market hub, known for its ironworks and trade connections that extended as far as Boston. Proprietors' records, land divisions, and early court files from this period preserve invaluable genealogical detail, listing proprietors, their heirs, and boundaries still traceable in modern deeds.

Religious diversity characterized Bristol's colonial settlements. While Congregational and Baptist congregations dominated early town life, significant Quaker populations developed in Dartmouth and Westport, leaving extensive meeting records including marriage certificates, birth registries, and disciplinary minutes—vital to genealogists because of their precision and continuity across generations. These documents, preserved in local archives and at the New England Yearly Meeting collection in Rhode Island, complement official town vital records, which were often inconsistent before the 19th century.

Industry, Immigration, and the 19th-Century Transformation

By the 19th century, Bristol County stood at the forefront of America's industrial revolution. New Bedford rose from a modest whaling port to the capital of the global whaling industry, its waterfront lined with ships financed by families whose names fill probate archives and business ledgers—Howland, Rotch, Hathaway, and others whose fortunes defined the age. Neighboring Fall River became one of the nation's leading textile manufacturing centers by mid-century, drawing immigrants from Ireland, England, Portugal, and French Canada. Mill records, labor contracts, and city directories from this era form a cornerstone for genealogical study, tracing the shift from rural farming stock to diverse urban labor populations.

Meanwhile, Attleboro developed into a renowned jewelry manufacturing hub, and Taunton evolved into a major producer of silverware, machinery, and iron goods. Censuses, tax rolls, industrial schedules, and corporate archives reflect this booming diversification of occupations and demographics. The influx of Catholic, Episcopalian, and later Orthodox congregations led to a proliferation of parish registers that remain among the richest troves of local vital data.

The Civil War era drew thousands from Bristol County into Union service. Muster rolls, pension applications, and regimental rosters now held by the Massachusetts State Archives connect families to this defining national event. Postwar prosperity saw the rise of philanthropic institutions, libraries, and historical societies—many of which continue to steward genealogical records spanning the county's long transformation from agrarian to industrial society.

Genealogical Landscape and Archival Resources

Bristol County's genealogical terrain is as diverse as its industries and communities. Researchers trace family lines through an impressive variety of sources:

- County repositories: The Bristol County Registry of Deeds (Taunton and Fall River) houses land records reaching back to the 1680s, essential for mapping family migrations and property inheritance.

- Probate and court files: Early wills, guardianships, and estate inventories at the Taunton Probate Court reveal social hierarchies and kinship webs.

- Town and church records: Each municipality—Dartmouth, Rehoboth, Dighton, and beyond—maintains invaluable vital registers tracing births, marriages, and deaths across generations.

- Maritime and industrial collections: Archives in New Bedford and Fall River preserve whaling logs, crew lists, and factory employee registers rarely paralleled elsewhere in Massachusetts.

- Historical societies: The Old Colony Historical Society (Taunton), New Bedford Whaling Museum Research Library, and Fall River Historical Society host manuscripts, photographs, and genealogical indexes reflecting regional and family histories across the colonial and industrial eras.

Indigenous and missionary sources—particularly those concerning Wampanoag mission communities in Dartmouth and Assonet—complement conventional records by preserving family continuity rooted before colonization. Genealogists studying these communities benefit from integrating tribal sources and land petitions into colonial frameworks to reconstruct Indigenous descent lines disrupted by removal and assimilation.

Geography, Culture, and Genealogical Context

Bristol County's varied geography—spanning tidal estuaries, forested uplands, and inland river valleys—profoundly influenced its development. The Taunton and Acushnet Rivers anchored inland agriculture and industry, while the Buzzards Bay coast supported fishing and whaling economies. These natural systems dictated both settlement clusters and the types of surviving records: coastal families often appear in maritime registers and customs documents, while inland farmers populate town meeting minutes and road tax lists.

Culturally, the county reflects centuries of interwoven identities: Indigenous Wampanoag continuity, English Puritan foundations, Quaker and Baptist dissent, Catholic and Portuguese seafaring communities, and later European and Cape Verdean immigration. This mosaic creates a genealogical environment emphasizing religious, occupational, and ethnic diversity. Congregational archives coexist with Portuguese parish registers; Quaker meeting minutes parallel whaling crew logs—all illuminating migrations, marriages, and kinship adaptations.

Bristol County's Enduring Genealogical Legacy

Bristol County, Massachusetts, stands as a coastal microcosm of New England's evolving identity—rooted in Indigenous stewardship, borne through colonial conflict, and transformed by maritime enterprise and industrial vigor. Its recordscape—from 17th-century Wampanoag land deeds and Plymouth Colony court files to 19th-century factory payrolls and immigrant church registries—preserves a living chronicle of family persistence and adaptation. Genealogists tracing its households navigate boundaries that shifted between colonies and states, faiths that spanned continents, and economies that rose from handcrafted iron to global textile export.

Through careful study of its archives—civil, ecclesiastical, industrial, and tribal—Bristol County reveals the intersecting lives that shaped Massachusetts' southern reach. Each river crossing, parish ledger, and probate file bears witness to generations who built enduring communities along its shores, leaving behind one of New England's most complete and intricate genealogical legacies.

King Philip's War and Colonial Consolidation

King Philip's War (1675–1676) erupted within and around the lands that would become Bristol County, where Wampanoag, English, and neighboring Native communities had long interacted through trade, diplomacy, and increasingly fraught land negotiations. The conflict's opening attacks at Swansea and its spread through Rehoboth, Dartmouth, and surrounding settlements devastated both Native and English populations, leaving a patchwork of destroyed towns, confiscated lands, and scattered families whose stories surface in later petitions, land grants, and court proceedings.

For genealogists, the war marks a major documentary pivot. Prewar Wampanoag and English land transactions, Plymouth Colony court records, and missionary correspondence give way to postwar distributions of "vacant" Native lands to English soldiers, creditors, and speculators. Many New England families with deep Bristol County roots trace their first local holdings to these grants and sales, recorded in Plymouth Colony and early Massachusetts registries. At the same time, the dispersal, enslavement, and relocation of Wampanoag survivors into other Native communities, mission towns, and English households produced fragmented yet traceable trails in guardianship cases, indenture agreements, and church membership lists.

The formal creation of Bristol County in 1685 from Plymouth Colony jurisdiction—and the later cession of some towns to Rhode Island—further complicate the recordscape. Researchers must follow ancestors across shifting county and colonial lines, consulting overlapping repositories in Massachusetts and Rhode Island for deeds, probate files, and town minutes that together reconstruct families who lived through this era of violent reordering and legal consolidation.

Maritime Communities and Whaling Genealogies

By the 18th and especially the 19th century, coastal Bristol County—especially New Bedford and surrounding "Old Dartmouth" towns—became a global maritime hub, first through coastal and Atlantic trade and then through pelagic whaling. New Bedford's deep harbor, Quaker mercantile networks, and investment capital helped it overtake Nantucket as the leading American whaling port, with local innovators such as Lewis Temple revolutionizing the industry through technologies like the toggling harpoon.

Maritime life generated a distinctive documentary universe. Crew lists, shipping articles, whaling logs, customs records, and insurance policies name officers and seamen from Bristol County and far beyond, tracing multiethnic crews that included Native, African American, Azorean, Cape Verdean, and Caribbean sailors. Genealogists can follow a single mariner from an initial appearance in a New Bedford crew list to later census entries, naturalization papers, or coastal city directories, revealing migration paths that tie the South Coast to Atlantic and Pacific worlds.

Old Dartmouth's evolution—from a rural Wampanoag and Quaker landscape into an industrializing port—also fostered strong record-keeping traditions preserved today in specialized repositories. The New Bedford Whaling Museum's research collections and related regional archives hold whaling logs, merchant account books, and family papers, while printed vital-record compilations for New Bedford to 1850 integrate town registers, church records, and cemetery inscriptions into accessible finding aids for genealogists.

Industrial Immigration and Urban Working-Class Lives

As whaling declined in the later 19th century, Bristol County pivoted decisively toward textile, metalworking, and jewelry manufacturing, reshaping both its economy and its population. New Bedford and Fall River became major textile centers, while Attleboro rose as a jewelry-manufacturing city and Taunton expanded its foundries and machine works, drawing waves of immigrants from Ireland, England, French Canada, Portugal, Cape Verde, and southern and eastern Europe.

These industrial communities generated dense urban records. City directories, tax lists, factory payrolls, and municipal vital registers document working-class families living in crowded tenements near mills and waterfronts. Parish registers for Catholic, Orthodox, and various Protestant congregations—often organized along ethnic lines—contain baptismal, marriage, and burial entries that reveal chain migration, intermarriage, and neighborhood clustering across generations.

Local libraries and historical societies in Fall River, New Bedford, and Taunton maintain microfilmed and indexed vital records, censuses, and draft registrations that span this industrial period. Collections such as the Fall River Public Library's genealogy holdings and the Old Colony History

Museum's church, cemetery, and town-based vital records give researchers tools to reconstruct working-class lives that might otherwise be obscured by frequent moves, economic instability, and the use of anglicized or variant surnames.

Archival Networks and Research Strategies in Bristol County

Bristol County's records reside within a distributed but interconnected archival ecosystem that requires careful navigation. The county registries of deeds and probate courts provide the backbone of land and estate documentation, but crucial complementary sources live in town clerk offices, local libraries, and specialized collections. For example, Taunton's Old Colony History Museum aggregates church registers, cemetery transcriptions, and biographical registers for Taunton and nearby towns, while New Bedford and Fall River repositories specialize in maritime, industrial, and ethnic community records.

Effective genealogical strategy in Bristol County often combines:

- Town and parish vital records to establish core family structures and dates.
- Land and probate files to track property, inheritance, and kinship across changing boundaries.
- Maritime and industrial sources to place individuals within ships' crews, mills, factories, and workshops.
- Indigenous, missionary, and tribal records to follow Wampanoag and other Native lineages across colonial disruption and relocation.

By layering these sources, genealogists can reconstruct Bristol County family histories that span pre-contact Wampanoag homelands, frontier war zones, global whaling voyages, and bustling mill cities—mirroring the region's own evolution from coastal borderland to industrial hub.

The Cities & Towns of Berkshire County

City

Attleboro

Attleboro, Massachusetts, lies in the northwestern sector of Bristol County near the Rhode Island border, emerging from 17th-century Plymouth Colony grants and the early town of Rehoboth into a distinct municipality incorporated as Attleborough in 1694 and later re-incorporated (with modern spelling) as a city in 1914. Originally a rural agrarian and milling community anchored along the Ten Mile River and its tributaries, the area developed from Indigenous homelands used seasonally by Wampanoag groups into a major center of metalworking and, by the 19th century, one of the nation's best-known jewelry manufacturing hubs. The town's evolution—from scattered farmsteads and small ironworks to dense factory districts, immigrant neighborhoods, and streetcar suburbs—created a layered record environment that rewards genealogists with town meeting minutes, early church registers, industrial employment lists, and rich civil registration.

Wampanoag Lands, Ironworks, and Early Parish Life
Long before English settlement, the lands that became Attleboro formed part of the wider Wampanoag world, where river corridors and wetlands provided fish, game, and planting grounds connected to regional trails running toward Narragansett Bay and the interior. Early colonial records for Rehoboth and neighboring towns reference Native land transactions and boundary descriptions that point to earlier Wampanoag occupancy and travel routes through what would become Attleboro, though Indigenous families were gradually displaced or absorbed into nearby Native and mixed-heritage communities after King Philip's War.

By the late 17th and early 18th centuries, English settlers established farms, gristmills, and small ironworks along the Ten Mile River, using waterpower to drive sawmills and bloomery forges that supported regional markets. Congregational worship formed the core of early community life, with the first parish in the broader Attleborough area providing baptisms, marriages, and burials that often predate systematic town-level vital records. As population centers shifted and new precincts formed, separate parishes and, later, Baptist and other dissenting congregations arose, leaving overlapping ecclesiastical registers that genealogists must correlate carefully with evolving town boundaries.

Jewelry Capital and Industrial Transformation
During the 19th century, Attleboro transitioned from a mixed farming and small-manufacturing town into a nationally recognized jewelry center, sometimes dubbed the "Jewelry Capital of the World." Local artisans who began with small-scale metalwork and button-making developed into firms producing plated and fine jewelry, watch chains, and related goods, aided by access to rail lines and regional markets. This industrial pivot drew workers from surrounding Massachusetts and Rhode Island towns, as well as immigrants from Ireland, England, French Canada, Italy, and later eastern and southern Europe, who settled in growing mill and factory neighborhoods around the downtown core and along transport corridors.
City directories, factory payrolls, and business advertisements from this era trace the rise of

prominent local firms and the movement of artisans between companies, while federal census schedules and state census data reveal occupational clustering in jewelry-related trades. The city's incorporation in 1914 formalized an already urban character, bringing expanded municipal record-keeping—building permits, school reports, and public works documents—that help genealogists reconstruct the lives of working- and middle-class families tied to the jewelry industry's cycles of boom, consolidation, and decline.

Religious Diversity and Urban Neighborhoods
As Attleboro industrialized, its religious landscape diversified beyond its Congregational roots. Roman Catholic parishes formed to serve Irish, French Canadian, Italian, and later Portuguese and Polish communities, establishing baptismal, marriage, and burial registers that often preserve original surnames and places of origin not fully captured in civil records. Protestant denominations—Baptist, Methodist, Episcopal, and various evangelical groups—founded congregations near factory districts and new residential areas, each generating membership rolls, Sunday school records, and sacramental registers that document both stable multi-generation families and recently arrived migrants.

These religious records, combined with cemetery interment books and monument inscriptions in Attleboro's historic burying grounds and larger 19th-century cemeteries, form a crucial genealogical bridge between earlier rural parishes and modern civil vital registration. Researchers frequently trace families by moving from church registers into later city death certificates and obituaries in local newspapers, revealing kinship networks that extend into neighboring communities like North Attleborough, Norton, and Pawtucket, Rhode Island.

Genealogical Resources and Strategies
Vital repositories:

- Attleboro City Clerk (municipal offices): Civil registrations of births, marriages, and deaths, particularly strong from the mid-19th century onward, along with records of city incorporation, annexations, and ordinance books that contextualize urban development.

- Early town and parish records: Published or microfilmed compilations of Attleborough/Attleboro's vital records to about 1850, integrating town books, church registers, and cemetery inscriptions; especially useful for locating families before formal city government.

- Attleboro Public Library and local historical organizations: Local history collections, city directories, school annuals, maps, jewelry company histories, and photograph collections that help situate individuals within neighborhoods, mills, and factories.

- County-level resources: Bristol County deeds and probate records (at the regional registry and probate court) document property transactions, guardianships, and estate settlements, tying Attleboro families to rural origins and to relatives in other Bristol County towns.

Attleboro's trajectory—from Wampanoag travel routes and colonial farm-iron communities to a dense, jewelry-driven city—offers genealogists a concentrated view of New England's industrializing arc. Its town and city clerks' volumes, parish and cemetery records, factory-linked sources, and county-level legal documents together reveal "factory kin" whose stories can be traced from early Rehoboth proprietors and Ten Mile River farms to 20th-century jewelry workers and downtown merchants.

Fall River

Fall River, Massachusetts, occupies the southeastern portion of Bristol County along Mount Hope Bay and the Taunton River estuary, its historic core straddling the Quequechan River whose name, from an Algonquian term often rendered as "Falling Water," reflects the small but powerful series of falls that shaped the city's destiny. Originally part of Freetown and the neighboring town of Tiverton (then within Massachusetts), Fall River was incorporated as the town of Fallriver in 1803, briefly renamed Troy, and restored to the name Fall River in 1834, becoming a city in 1854 as its textile industry surged. From Wampanoag homelands and 18th-century farm-mill settlements, the community grew into one of the leading 19th-century cotton-textile centers in the United States, with over one hundred mills in operation by 1920 and dense immigrant neighborhoods whose records provide exceptional depth for genealogical research.

Quequechan Falls, Wampanoag Homelands, and Early Mills Long before English colonists appropriated the Quequechan valley, the falls and surrounding waterways formed part of a broader Wampanoag landscape linking interior hunting and planting grounds to Narragansett Bay. Early colonial land purchases and boundary descriptions in Freetown and Tiverton reference Native paths, fishing places, and landmarks that signal earlier Indigenous occupation, although the disruptions of King Philip's War and subsequent land confiscations fractured many local lineages or displaced families into other Wampanoag and mixed communities.

In the colonial era, the Quequechan's steady drop attracted water-driven industry. By 1703, mills established along the falls—sawmills, gristmills, and fulling mills—supported a small but growing agrarian-mill community, and by 1811 Col. Joseph Durfee had founded the Globe Manufactory, the first cotton spinning mill in the area. Early production relied partly on "cottage outsourcing," with local farm families carding and weaving yarn produced at the mills, leaving traces in land records, town meeting minutes, and scattered business accounts that genealogists can use to connect rural Freetown and Tiverton households with emerging industrial enterprises.

Textile "Spindle City" and Industrial Expansion

During the 19th century, Fall River's combination of waterpower, harbor access, and transportation links propelled it into a premier cotton-textile center, sometimes called the "Spindle City." Companies such as the Fall River Manufactory (1813), Troy Cotton & Woolen Manufactory, Pocasset Company, and later the Metacomet and Flint mills harnessed the Quequechan and built massive brick complexes that transformed the landscape into one of the nation's densest textile districts. By the 1870s the city rivaled or surpassed many New England peers in spindle count and cloth production, its mills connected by railroads and steamship lines to regional and international markets.

This industrial boom created extensive documentation. Corporate records, stockholder lists, pay rolls, and company housing maps—alongside federal and state census manufacturing schedules—record not only owners and managers but the largely working-class population operating the mills. The Borden family, prominent in banking, textiles, and associated enterprises, generated business and probate records that intersect with a wide range of local surnames through employment, tenancy, and credit relationships. For genealogists, these industrial archives help place ancestors within specific mills, neighborhoods, and economic cycles, particularly when combined with city directories and tax rolls.

Immigration, Ethnic Parishes, and Neighborhood Life

Fall River's mills drew successive waves of immigrants, beginning with Irish workers in the early 19th century and expanding after the Civil War to include French Canadians, English, Azorean and mainland Portuguese, Cape Verdeans, Polish, Lebanese, and others. These communities settled in ethnically inflected neighborhoods—such as the Flint and Globe districts—forming dense social networks tied to specific mills and parish churches.

Roman Catholic parishes, especially those serving Irish and French Canadians and later Portuguese-speaking congregations, created baptismal, marriage, and burial registers that underpin much of Fall River genealogical work, often preserving original name spellings, places of origin, and kinship ties. Transcribed sacramental records for churches like St. Anne and Notre Dame, available through local collaborations and genealogical societies, complement civil vital records and allow researchers to trace migrant families through language shifts, naturalization, and intermarriage. Other denominations—Baptist, Congregational, Orthodox, and various Protestant groups—maintained membership lists and sacramental records reflecting the city's religious and ethnic diversity.

Genealogical Resources and Strategies

Vital repositories:

- Fall River City Clerk (Government Center): Civil registrations of births, marriages, and deaths from the 19th century onward, along with city council minutes, ward and street changes, and annexation records that help locate families within evolving urban geography.

- Fall River Public Library (Main Library, North Main Street): Genealogy collections including federal census microfilm, selected state censuses, city directories, local newspapers on microfilm, World War I draft registrations, and transcribed Catholic church records.

- Fall River Historical Society: Manuscript collections, family papers, mill and business histories, photographic archives, and published works on the city's textile industry and immigrant communities, useful for contextualizing individual lives within broader social narratives.

- Bristol County Registry of Deeds and Probate Court: Deed books and probate files documenting land transactions, tenements, and estates that link Fall River families to surrounding Bristol County towns and, in earlier periods, to the Freetown and Tiverton jurisdictions.

Effective Fall River research typically combines:

- Civil and parish vital records to build core family structures and identify immigrant origins.

- City directories, mill employment records, and draft registrations to track residential moves, occupations, and kin networks across neighborhoods and decades.

- Newspaper obituaries, accident reports, and labor coverage to flesh out working-class lives often only briefly noted in official records.

Fall River's story—from Wampanoag-held falls to colonial mills and then a towering textile metropolis—produced a dense archive of civic, corporate, ecclesiastical, and community records. For genealogists, its mill-lined Quequechan and steep mill villages reveal "spindle kin" whose trajectories can be traced from rural Freetown farmers and early Rhode Island border families to 20th-century loom fixers, weavers, and shopkeepers in one of New England's most thoroughly documented industrial cities.

New Bedford

New Bedford, Massachusetts, occupies a key position on the Acushnet River near its opening into Buzzards Bay, forming part of the historic Old Dartmouth region and evolving from a rural Quaker-agrarian settlement into one of the world's foremost 19th-century whaling ports. Originally part of Dartmouth, the area that became New Bedford developed around Acushnet River landholdings owned by families such as the Russells and Kemptons, growing into a distinct village and eventually incorporating as the town of New Bedford in 1787 and as a city in 1847. The town's transformation from Wampanoag homeland and scattered farms to a global maritime and industrial hub generated unusually rich records—proprietors' deeds, Quaker meeting minutes, whaling logs, and immigrant parish registers—that provide genealogists with layered evidence for reconstructing family histories across seas and centuries.

Wampanoag Homelands, Old Dartmouth, and Quaker Foundations

Up through the 17th century, the territory that now includes New Bedford lay within Wampanoag country, where riverine and coastal resources supported villages and seasonal camps tied into broader networks stretching from Cape Cod to Narragansett Bay. In 1652, English purchasers acquired what became known as the Dartmouth purchase, and over subsequent decades, families such as the Kemptons, Russells, Howlands, Allens, and others obtained extensive tracts on the west bank of the Acushnet. These lands formed the nucleus of Old Dartmouth, a large town that encompassed present-day New Bedford, Dartmouth, Westport, and Fairhaven, administered by a mix of Plymouth Colony authorities and a strong Quaker presence that favored relative religious toleration and produced detailed meeting records.

For genealogists, early Old Dartmouth documentation provides a framework for New Bedford's founding families. Proprietors' records, Plymouth Colony deeds, and Quaker minutes preserve the names of landholders, their kin, and their movements within the township, while early vital events often appear in overlapping formats: town books, meeting registers, and later printed compilations. Because Wampanoag dispossession and missionary activity reshaped the region, researchers tracing Indigenous or mixed-heritage ancestors must read land transactions and court records alongside tribal and mission sources to understand how Native families intersected with the developing port community along the Acushnet.

Whaling Capital and Maritime Genealogies

By the early 19th century, New Bedford rose to prominence as "The Whaling City," rivaling and ultimately surpassing Nantucket as a leading whaling port. Deepwater access, a sheltered harbor, substantial Quaker capital, and entrepreneurial figures such as the Rotch family enabled the port to outfit large fleets that ranged worldwide, from the Atlantic to the Pacific and Arctic whaling grounds. Shipyards, oil-processing facilities, chandlers, and related industries clustered along the waterfront, while merchants and ship owners accumulated fortunes that appear in business ledgers, probate records, and philanthropic donations shaping the city's institutions.

This maritime focus produced distinctive genealogical sources. Crew lists, shipping articles, whaling logs, and consular records name officers and seamen from New Bedford and far beyond, documenting a multiethnic labor force that included New Englanders, Native Americans, African Americans, Azoreans, Cape Verdeans, and Pacific Islanders. The New Bedford Whaling Museum and associated manuscript collections preserve logbooks, family papers (such as the Akin family history), and business records that allow researchers to follow individual mariners across voyages, ports of call, and eventual settlement or return. When combined with port-arrival lists, naturalization records, and city directories, these materials help genealogists place ancestors in specific ships and voyages, linking shore-based households to global maritime circuits.

Industrial Diversification, Immigration, and Urban Neighborhoods

As whaling declined later in the 19th century, New Bedford diversified into textile manufacturing, metalworking, and other industries, taking advantage of existing capital, transportation links, and a growing labor pool. Cotton mills and related factories joined remaining maritime enterprises along the river and inland, reshaping the urban landscape into mixed industrial-residential districts that drew waves of immigrants from Ireland, French Canada, Portugal and the Azores, Cape Verde, and southern and eastern Europe. Neighborhoods such as the South End and various hill districts formed around ethnic and occupational lines, with triple-deckers, boardinghouses, and small shops populated by mill hands, sailors, artisans, and small proprietors.

This period left dense urban documentation. Federal and state censuses record changing surnames, occupations, and language use; city directories trace moves across streets and wards; and school registers, tax lists, and naturalization files reveal the gradual integration of immigrant families into civic life. Portuguese and Cape Verdean communities, in particular, developed strong transatlantic and inter-port networks linking New Bedford to the Azores, Madeira, Cape Verde, and other Atlantic islands, which genealogists can trace through passenger lists, remittance records, and chain-migration patterns evident in clustered household data.

Religious Life, Cemeteries, and Family Memory

New Bedford's religious landscape reflects both its Quaker roots and later immigration. Early Quaker meetings provided some of the most meticulous records of marriages, births, and disciplinary actions, documenting families who often engaged in maritime commerce or related trades. As the city expanded, Congregational, Baptist, Methodist, Episcopal, and Unitarian churches established congregations, each maintaining sacramental and membership records that complement civil vital registrations, especially before Massachusetts standardized record-keeping in the mid-19th century.

With the arrival of Irish, French Canadian, Portuguese, Polish, and other Catholic immigrants, Roman Catholic parishes proliferated, creating baptismal, marriage, and burial registers that are central to many New Bedford genealogical projects. These records often note places of origin, parents' names, sponsors, and intra-ethnic or interethnic marriages, providing clues for transatlantic research. Cemeteries such as Rural Cemetery and St. Mary's contain gravestones and plot records that reinforce parish and civil data, while epitaphs and family lot arrangements reveal kin networks and social status over time.

Genealogical Resources and Strategies

Vital repositories and key resources for New Bedford research include:

- Municipal records: The New Bedford city clerk's office maintains civil birth, marriage, and death records from the 19th century onward, as well as city council minutes, annexation documents, and ward maps that help locate families within changing municipal boundaries.

- Local histories and compiled genealogies: Works such as Daniel Ricketson's history of New Bedford and Old Dartmouth, as well as family-focused compilations on lines like the Allens and other founding families, provide contextual narratives, biographical sketches, and references to original documents.

- New Bedford Whaling Museum and related archives: Manuscript collections, family papers, ship logs, crew lists, and business records offer unparalleled insight into maritime and mercantile families, including associated kin in supporting trades and coastal communities.

- Printed and online guides: Genealogy-focused guides and wikis summarize available record sets—vital records, church registers, cemeteries, censuses, and maps—giving researchers an organized entry point into New Bedford's archival landscape.

Strategically successful New Bedford research usually proceeds by building a core framework from civil and church vital records, then extending outward into maritime, land, probate, and industrial sources. By cross-referencing town and city records with whaling and shipping materials, ethnic parish registers, and compiled family histories, genealogists can trace "harbor kin" from Wampanoag homelands and Old Dartmouth proprietors through whaling voyages, mill employment, and 20th-century neighborhood life in one of New England's most thoroughly documented port cities.

Taunton

Taunton, Massachusetts, stands near the geographic center of Bristol County along the Taunton River, emerging from a 17th-century Plymouth Colony frontier settlement into a pivotal shire town and later an industrial "Silver City." Founded as Cohannet/Tetiquet by Plymouth colonists in 1637 and incorporated as Taunton in 1639, the town became the county seat when Bristol County was created in 1685 and was incorporated as a city in 1864 as its iron, silver, and textile industries matured. Taunton's evolution—from Wampanoag homeland and river mills through iron forges, silver factories, locomotive works, and multiethnic neighborhoods—produced a dense documentary record in town books, church registers, court files, industrial archives, and one of

New England's oldest regional historical societies, making it a cornerstone locality for genealogical research in southeastern Massachusetts.

Wampanoag Lands, Tetiquet Purchase, and Early Town Formation

Before English settlement, the Taunton River valley formed part of Wampanoag territory, where river, marsh, and upland resources supported villages and seasonal camps linked to broader regional trails. In 1637, Plymouth settlers purchased land from local Wampanoag leaders in what became known as the Tetiquet Purchase, establishing the settlement that would be named Taunton in honor of Taunton in Somerset, England. The transaction and subsequent relocations of many Native families, including movement toward the praying town of Ponkapoag, set the pattern for overlapping Native and colonial land claims that surface in early deeds and court proceedings.

By mid-17th century, Taunton's founders—among them prominent families such as Poole, Baylies, and King—created a compact town center around today's Church Green, erecting a meetinghouse and organizing town government via open meetings. Elizabeth Poole, long celebrated in local tradition, played an unusually visible role as a female landholder and benefactor in the settlement's early development, contributing to mill and iron-works ventures and leaving a documented imprint in property and church records. For genealogists, these formative decades are captured in town meeting minutes, Plymouth Colony records, early land grants, and later compiled vital-record volumes that reconstruct family clusters around the original common.

Ironworks, River Trade, and the Rise of the "Silver City"

Taunton became an early industrial pioneer in New England. In 1656, the first successful iron works in Plymouth Colony was established on the Two Mile River (now in Raynham), soon joined by additional iron industries drawing on local bog iron and waterpower. Over the 18th and early 19th centuries, Taunton's forges and foundries produced bar iron, stoves, nails, tacks, and tools that supplied regional markets, while the Taunton River served as a key shipping route for grain and manufactured goods via Weir Village. These enterprises generated business ledgers, contracts, and apprenticeship agreements that often reference multi-generational family partnerships and labor networks.

In the 19th century, Taunton earned the nickname "Silver City" as firms such as Reed & Barton, F.B. Rogers, Poole Silver, and others became major producers of silver and silverplate wares. At the same time, companies like Mason Machine Works and the Taunton Locomotive Works produced textile machinery and steam locomotives, and local mills and felt works diversified the industrial base. Directories, industrial schedules, and company records from this period allow genealogists to trace ancestors as they move from rural farming into specialized trades—silver plating, pattern making, machinist work, and rail-related occupations—anchored in distinct factory districts.

Immigration, Ethnic Communities, and Religious Diversity

Taunton's industrial growth attracted immigrants from Ireland, England, French Canada, Portugal (including the Azores), Cape Verde, and later eastern and southern Europe, creating a multiethnic city by the turn of the 20th century. Census data show substantial Luso-American, Irish, French, Cape Verdean, and Puerto Rican populations, reflecting labor recruitment into mills, foundries, and silver works and producing clustered neighborhoods around factory complexes and transport routes.

Religiously, the original Congregational parish at Church Green gradually shared the landscape with Baptist, Methodist, Episcopal, and Unitarian congregations, and then with Roman Catholic, Jewish, and Muslim communities. St. Mary's Catholic Church (the city's oldest Roman Catholic parish), ethnic Catholic parishes, and later synagogues and Islamic institutions each created sacramental and membership records that document immigrant names, places of origin, and kinship networks. Combined with cemetery inscriptions along Dean and Winthrop Streets and in outlying burial grounds, these sources enable genealogists to follow families through religious change, intermarriage, and neighborhood shifts.

Genealogical Resources and Strategies

Key Taunton repositories and resources include:

- Vital records and municipal archives: Taunton's early town books and the published "Vital Records of Taunton, Massachusetts, to the Year 1850" integrate manuscript entries, church registers, and cemetery data into alphabetical indexes of births, marriages, and deaths. Later city clerk records provide standardized civil registrations, street and ward changes, and documentation of the 1864 city incorporation and subsequent urban expansion.

- Old Colony History Museum (Old Colony Historical Society): Founded in 1853 and located on historic Church Green, this institution maintains manuscripts, printed local histories, business records, maps, photographs, and genealogical files relating to Taunton and the wider Old Colony region. Its collections cover local industries (iron, silver, rail, textiles), military participation, and family papers, making it a central resource for contextualizing individual ancestors within regional economic and social history.

- County-level and external guides: Bristol County deeds and probate files, accessible through regional registries and courts, document land transfers, guardianships, and estate settlements connecting Taunton residents to surrounding towns. Genealogical guides and wikis specific to Taunton outline available record sets and provide references to classic histories such as Samuel Hopkins Emery's 1893 "History of Taunton, Massachusetts."

Research strategies that work well in Taunton typically begin with the published vital records to 1850 and city vital records thereafter, then extend to land and probate files to establish kinship and property patterns, followed by industrial and parish records to place individuals within specific factories, congregations, and neighborhoods. Taunton's path—from Wampanoag Cohannet to Plymouth shire town, iron and river port, "Silver City," and culturally diverse industrial hub—provides genealogists with a deeply layered source base for reconstructing "river and silver kin" across nearly four centuries of southeastern Massachusetts history

Towns

Acushnet

Acushnet, Massachusetts, occupies the central eastern portion of Bristol County along the Acushnet River, evolving from a rural section of the vast Old Dartmouth purchase into a distinct town incorporated on July 3, 1860, from portions of Fairhaven, New Bedford, and Dartmouth. Originally part of Wampanoag homelands known as the "Cushenagg Neighbourhood," the area saw early English settlement in 1659 amid scattered farmsteads and woodlots, later developing small mills and cranberry bogs before its formal separation amid regional industrial growth. Its modest trajectory—from Indigenous riverine territory through Quaker-influenced agrarian outparcels to a quiet town of farms, orchards, and light manufacturing—preserves a focused record set of proprietors' divisions, church registers, and family Bibles that reward genealogists tracing Old Colony lineages tied to the broader Acushnet watershed.

Wampanoag "Cushenagg," Old Dartmouth Purchase, and Early Farmsteads

Prior to English colonization, the lands of present-day Acushnet formed part of the Wampanoag "Cushenagg Neighbourhood," encompassing riverine villages and seasonal camps of bands like the Ponegansetts and Coaksetts, sustained by the Acushnet River's fisheries, planting grounds, and trails linking to Buzzards Bay and interior uplands. In 1652, Plymouth Colony purchasers—including figures like Moses Simons, Joshua Pratt, and John Soule—acquired the broader Dartmouth tract from Wampanoag sachems, with Acushnet's specific bounds described in Governor Bradford's memoranda as lying "in y° botome of ye bay adjoyning to y^ west side of Point." Subsequent divisions scattered these lands among Old Dartmouth proprietors, whose heirs developed isolated homesteads, saltworks, and woodcutting operations by the late 17th century.

For genealogists, this foundational era appears in overlapping Old Dartmouth proprietors' records, Plymouth Colony deeds, and early Quaker meeting minutes, which document land allotments to families like the Howlands, Cushmans, and Whites—many with Mayflower ties through marriages to Allertons and Howlands. These sources trace multi-generational holdings through divisions, leases, and inheritances, often noting boundary markers like Native paths or river bends that hint at pre-colonial use. Wampanoag interactions surface in court depositions and land quitclaims, requiring cross-reference with tribal petitions to reconstruct Native family presence amid displacement.

Quaker Networks, Rural Economy, and 19th-Century Separation

Acushnet's development reflected Old Dartmouth's Quaker character, with families maintaining Meeting affiliations while pursuing mixed agriculture—dairy, orchards, and later cranberries—along with small sawmills and cooperages serving nearby New Bedford's maritime trade. Prominent lines like the Cushmans, descending from Robert Cushman (a Pilgrim agent) via Thomas Cushman and Mary Allerton, established enduring farms and light industries, such as Emery Cushman's wooden box manufactory, which employed local kin and left business ledgers documenting labor networks.

The push for town incorporation in 1860 stemmed from desires for local governance amid New Bedford's urban expansion, creating dedicated town records while retaining ties to parent towns' archives. Federal censuses and tax valuations from this period reveal occupational stability—

farmers, mariners' wives, and bog workers—contrasting with the industrial density of neighboring cities and highlight endogamous marriages reinforcing Quaker and old-stock families.

Genealogical Resources and Strategies

Vital repositories:

- Acushnet Town Clerk: Civil registrations from 1860 onward, including births, marriages, deaths, and town meeting minutes documenting boundary adjustments and early infrastructure like schools and roads.

- Parent town records: Fairhaven, New Bedford, and Dartmouth vital records to 1850 (published compilations integrate town books, church entries, and intentions), essential for pre-incorporation families.

- Old Colony and regional archives: FamilySearch holdings for Acushnet vitals (1860-1900), proprietors' books, and Quaker registers; manuscript collections like White Family Papers (1746-1916) and Cushman genealogies preserve farm, business, and kinship details.

- Local histories: Franklyn Howland's "History of the Town of Acushnet" (1907) and related works provide biographical sketches, land plats, and references to original deeds and wills in Bristol County registries.

Acushnet's arc—from Wampanoag Cushenagg camps to Old Dartmouth woodlots, Quaker farms, and 19th-century township—offers genealogists a rural counterpoint to Bristol County's urban hubs. Its proprietors' divisions, meeting minutes, and family-centric records unveil "watershed kin" whose stories bridge Pilgrim purchases, Native land echoes, and enduring agrarian lines along the Acushnet River.

Berkley

Berkley, Massachusetts, lies in the northeastern corner of Bristol County at the confluence of the Taunton and Assonet Rivers, evolving from Wampanoag outlands known as Shawomat into a distinct town incorporated on April 18, 1735, from portions of Dighton and Taunton. Named for George Berkeley, Bishop of Cloyne, Ireland, the sparsely settled area functioned initially as an agricultural extension of Taunton, with later annexations including Assonet Neck (1799) and Myricks village (1879), preserving its rural character amid neighboring industrial growth. Its history—from Pocasset Wampanoag fishing grounds and King Philip's War frontier through shipbuilding hamlets, commercial farms, and small mills—yields a compact record set of town meetings, church registers, and family sketches ideal for genealogists tracing Old Colony farm lineages and riverine migrations.

Pocasset Shawomat, King Philip's War, and Early Out-Settlement

Before European arrival, Berkley's river junction—Assonet Neck—served as a vital Pocasset (Wampanoag) gathering place called Shawomat or "Out Lot," offering freshwater and tidal fisheries, fertile planting soils, and canoe routes linking Mount Hope Bay to interior trails. English settlement began around 1675 as Taunton's remote woodlots and pastures, but King Philip's War halted progress; Edward Bobbet (Babbitt) became the first local colonist slain by Native forces, and legends place Metacom's confederacy planning on nearby Conspiracy Island. Postwar land grants to veterans and proprietors divided the Neck into linear farms along colonial roads, with Dighton Rock (discovered 1680, noted 1690)—bearing mysterious petroglyphs—marking a cultural boundary studied by scholars worldwide.

For genealogists, this era appears in Taunton and Dighton proprietors' records, Plymouth Colony court files, and early earmark lists documenting initial grantees like the Bobbets, whose kin persisted through generations. Wampanoag presence echoes in quitclaims and depositions, best cross-referenced with tribal sources for Native or mixed lines displaced to Freetown or Mashpee.

Assonet Neck Farms, Shipbuilding, and Rural Persistence

Berkley's 18th- and 19th-century economy centered on commercial agriculture—corn, potatoes, fruits, and livestock—shipped via Taunton River landings, supplemented by potteries, shoemaking, braid mills, and shipbuilding at Bridge Village (West Berkley). The 1806 Berkley-Dighton Bridge (rebuilt 1873, 1896) spurred access, while Myricks' railroads (1840s) and Bristol County Cattle Show (1858–1876) briefly animated the eastern hamlet without industrial dominance. Population grew modestly through annexations, with Portuguese immigrants arriving late 19th century for farm and river work.

Congregationalism anchored community life from the first meetinghouse, later joined by Quakers on Friend Street; vital events fill town books alongside jurors' lists and warrants. Civil War service, including Corporal Levi L. Crane's preserved uniform, appears in muster rolls and monuments.

Genealogical Resources and Strategies

Vital repositories:

- Berkley Town Clerk (1 North Main St.): Original births, marriages, intentions, deaths, and town records from 1735, including warrants, earmarks, and proceedings; strong for post-incorporation continuity.

- Parent town archives: Taunton and Dighton vitals/proprietors' books for pre-1735 families, with published histories like Sanford's "History of the Town of Berkley" offering ministerial sketches (Revs. Tobey, Andros) and biographical indexes.

- Berkley Historical Society: Artifacts, Dighton Rock exhibits, Civil War relics, and local files at the 1849 Old Town Hall (now museum); cemetery surveys for Fox, Berkley (1775), and small Neck grounds.

- Regional guides: FamilySearch wikis and Bristol County deeds/probate linking Berkley kin to Taunton industries and Freetown Native remnants.

Berkley's path—from Pocasset Shawomat fisheries to Taunton outlots, Neck farms, and bridge-linked villages—delivers genealogists a rural lens on Bristol County. Town clerks' volumes, rock-marked deeds, and society-held relics reveal "river neck kin" enduring from King Philip's shadow through cattle fairs and quiet annexation.

Dartmouth

Dartmouth, Massachusetts, spans the southeastern coastal expanse of Bristol County along Buzzards Bay, encompassing villages from Apponegansett to Acoaxet and evolving from the vast 1652 "Old Dartmouth" purchase into a town formally incorporated in 1664, with subsequent separations creating Westport (1787), New Bedford (1787), Fairhaven (1812), and Acushnet (1860). Named for the English port town, its expansive rivers, inlets, and woodlands shaped dispersed Quaker and Baptist settlements amid Wampanoag homelands, fostering an agrarian-maritime economy of farms, mills, saltworks, and shipyards that persisted through industrial shifts in neighboring ports. This fragmented yet richly documented history—from Massasoit's lands through King Philip's War devastation to rural villages like Russells Mills and Padanaram—offers genealogists proprietors' records, Quaker minutes, and vital compilations tracing multi-generational "Old Dartmouth" kin across modern town lines.

Wampanoag Purchase, King Philip's War, and Proprietors' Divisions

The 1652 Dartmouth purchase by Plymouth leaders from Wampanoag sachem Massasoit and his son Wamsutta acquired a massive tract from the Acushnet River to the Sakonnet, divided among 34–36 proprietors whose heirs settled sparsely by 1660 amid rivers like the Paskamansett and Slocum. Early homesteads by families such as the Howlands, Russells, and Slocums dotted isolated necks and uplands, but King Philip's War (1675–1676) razed 37 dwellings, including the Russell Garrison house, scattering survivors and enabling postwar land reallocations to veterans. Metacom's uprising, rooted in regional Native resistance, left petroglyph echoes and fragmented Wampanoag lineages traceable in quitclaims and missionary notes.

Genealogists rely on Old Dartmouth proprietors' books, town meeting minutes from 1674, and Plymouth Colony deeds listing allotments, earmarks, and divisions that persisted post-separations, often noting Native boundaries or paths. Quaker and Baptist influxes, drawn by religious tolerance, generated meeting records complementing sparse town vitals.

Village Economies: Mills, Saltworks, and Maritime Hamlets

Dartmouth's 18th–19th-century villages embodied rural diversity: Russells Mills hosted 11 water-powered mills (grist, saw, fulling) plus tanneries and shipbuilding; Smith Mills featured the 1686 Town House, tavern, and 1849 Quaker meetinghouse; Padanaram (named by Laban Thacher) thrived on saltworks, shipyards (Elihu Akin's burned by British in 1778), and fisheries; Hixville centered on Rev. Daniel Hix's 1781 church spawning 35 daughter congregations. Inland agriculture—dairy, orchards, cranberries—supported coastal trade, with Portuguese farm immigrants by 1900 sustaining operations like Gulf Hill Dairy (1896).

These clusters produced localized records: mill contracts, apprenticeship indentures, overseers of the poor bonds, and militia lists in town volumes, alongside church registers from Baptist (1838 Smith Mills) and Quaker sites documenting occupational kin groups.

Genealogical Resources and Strategies

Vital repositories:

- Dartmouth Town Clerk: Original records from 1664 (births, marriages, deaths, intentions 1809–1825), selectmen minutes, highway/school agreements, and probate fragments (wills, guardianships 1705–1829).

- Published compilations: "Vital Records of Dartmouth to 1850" (3 vols., Eddy Fund: alphabetical indexes blending town books, churches, cemeteries).

- Dartmouth Historical & Arts Society/Local archives: Colonial-era documents, village maps, garrison sites, and Heritage Trail kiosks; New Bedford Whaling Museum holds Dartmouth town records 1674–1912 (MSS 53).

- Regional aids: FamilySearch wikis for censuses, directories, court/probate; town libraries with HeritageQuest for family histories.

Dartmouth's saga—from Massasoit's bayside tracts to war-scarred proprietors, mill hamlets, and enduring farms—equips genealogists with dispersed yet interconnected sources. Proprietors' plats, meetinghouse rolls, and village ledgers unveil "bay neck kin" bridging Wampanoag echoes, Quaker dissent, and Portuguese dairies across Old Dartmouth's fractured heirs.

Dighton

Dighton, Massachusetts, lies along the Taunton River in the northeastern sector of Bristol County, originating as the "Taunton South Purchase" granted to Taunton proprietors in 1672 and incorporated as a separate town on May 20, 1712, named for Frances Dighton Williams, wife of Richard Williams (grandson of Roger Williams). The area later lost Assonet Neck across the river to Berkley in 1799, retaining its riverine character through farms, shipyards, mills, and fisheries while hosting the enigmatic Dighton Rock with its prehistoric petroglyphs. Its development—from Wampanoag riverbanks and early colonial out-settlements through maritime trade, iron forges, cotton mills, and strawberry fields—preserves town clerks' volumes, proprietors' deeds, and church registers that reveal "river rock kin" in Old Colony genealogies.

Taunton South Purchase, Wampanoag Riverbanks, and Dighton Rock

Before English acquisition, Dighton's Taunton River margins sustained Wampanoag communities with herring runs, planting grounds, and canoe ports, their presence etched on Dighton Rock—a silicious conglomerate bearing petroglyphs (copied since 1680 by Danforth, Mather, and others) interpreted variably as Algonquian, runic, or Punic but likely Indigenous battle memorials per Schoolcraft's analysis. The 1672 South Purchase divided lands among Taunton families like the Halls, Macombers, and Goodings, who built farms and gristmills post-King Philip's War, with shipbuilding emerging by 1693 for West Indies rum/molasses trade. Dighton became a port of entry in 1789, its shallows blocking larger vessels and fostering teamster forwarding.

Genealogists trace this foundation in Taunton proprietors' records, early Dighton town books (1712+), and Plymouth Colony deeds noting rock boundaries and Native quitclaims; petroglyph studies complement tribal sources for pre-colonial echoes.

Shipyards, Mills, and Agricultural Diversification

Dighton's 18th–19th-century economy blended maritime pursuits—shipbuilding, cured fish exports—with iron forges (c.1700), cotton mills (Mt. Hope Cotton Co., later Raytheon site), clockmaking (Gooding family), silkworms (Sarah Hart, 1830s), strawberry farms (1860s), and herring fisheries using ancient weirs. The Anchor Color and Gum Works (1861) shifted from furniture to paints, while greenhouses and vegetable trucking sustained family operations into the 20th century. Portuguese immigrants bolstered farm labor by century's end.

These ventures yielded business ledgers, mill contracts, and overseers' bonds in town records, alongside Congregational and Baptist parish registers capturing multi-occupational kin like clockmakers and fish curers.

Genealogical Resources and Strategies

Vital repositories:

- Dighton Town Clerk (979 Somerset Ave.): Original births, marriages, deaths from 1754, town meetings, and warrants; strong for river trade and farm continuity.

- Published aids: Vital records compilations integrating town books, churches, and cemeteries; local histories like Helen Holmes' 1962 "History of Dighton" with biographical sketches.

- Dighton Historical Society: Artifacts, herring fishery records, ship logs, and Rock replicas; cemetery surveys for early burying grounds.

- Regional collections: FamilySearch catalogs for Dighton vitals (1754–1900), Bristol probate/deeds linking to Taunton origins.

Dighton's chronicle—from Wampanoag herring weirs and petroglyph shores to shipyards, strawberry rows, and mill relics—provides genealogists with river-focused sources. Clerks' ledgers, Rock-marked plats, and fishery tallies unveil "South Purchase kin" from Taunton grants through clockmaker crafts and modern preserves.

Easton

Easton, Massachusetts, occupies the northern interior of Bristol County astride the Coweeset River (also known as the Easton or Three Rivers), evolving from Wampanoag borderlands and early 17th-century out-settlements of Weymouth and Taunton into a town incorporated on December 17, 1725, from portions of those parent towns. Named possibly for its eastern position relative to Taunton or an English locale, Easton developed as a dispersed agrarian community of farms, forges, and mills, later transformed by the Ames family's 19th-century shovel manufactory into North Easton's industrial village while retaining rural character in South Easton and the Furnace Village area. Its trajectory—from Native trails and colonial ironworks through shovel dominance to modern suburbs—preserves proprietors' records, family Bibles, and vital compilations that illuminate "Three Rivers kin" across Old Colony lineages.

Wampanoag Trails, North Purchase, and Colonial Forges

Prior to English settlement, Easton's river confluence served as a Wampanoag border zone with trails linking inland planting grounds to coastal fisheries, evidenced by artifacts and place names like Coweeset. In 1668, the "North Purchase" from sachem Tuspaquin allocated lands to Weymouth and Taunton grantees, who established scattered farms and bloomeries by 1694, including the Easton Furnace (an early iron works) powered by the rivers. King Philip's War briefly disrupted progress, but postwar grants to families like the Drakes, Belchers, and Mitchels solidified linear farmsteads along Bay Road and Turnpike.

Genealogists access this era through Taunton/Weymouth proprietors' books, early earmark lists, and town meeting minutes from 1725, which document divisions among lines like the Keiths, Packards, and Williamses—many with multi-generational continuity. Native interactions appear in quitclaims, best supplemented by regional tribal sources.

Shovel Capital, Ames Legacy, and Village Divergence

Easton's 19th-century ascent centered on Oliver Ames Sr.'s shovel works (1808), expanding under his sons into the world's largest manufactory by mid-century, employing hundreds in North Easton and funding landmarks like the Ames Free Library (1883) and Oakes Ames High School. Furnace Village hosted iron forges and cotton mills, while South Easton remained agricultural with Baptist and Congregational parishes. Irish, French Canadian, and later Portuguese laborers integrated into mill and farm work, reflected in census occupational clusters.

These developments generated rich documentation: company payrolls, apprenticeship records, and industrial schedules alongside church registers from the North Easton Congregational (1725) and Baptist churches, capturing kinship webs tied to shovel production and river power.

Genealogical Resources and Strategies

Vital repositories:

- Easton Town Clerk: Original records from 1725 (births, marriages, deaths, intentions), town reports (1844+), and lists of male citizens (1862); strong for post-incorporation continuity.

- Published compilations: "Vital Records of Easton to 1850" and family-group entries (e.g., Drakes, Keiths, Belchers) integrating town books, churches, and private registers.

- Ames Free Library/Local histories: Manuscripts, censuses (1790+), directories, yearbooks, and Tourtillott Family transcriptions of town records (1725–1816); references to Bristol probate and shovel company files.

- Regional aids: FamilySearch wikis for Easton-specific censuses, alms house records, and high school yearbooks; abstracts of Bristol probate (1687–1762).

Easton's narrative—from Wampanoag Coweeset to forge-lined rivers, Ames shovels, and village divergence—arms genealogists with interconnected town, family, and industrial sources. Clerks' volumes, Bible transcripts, and manufactory ledgers reveal "shovel kin" spanning colonial purchases, furnace apprentices, and North Easton merchants along the Three Rivers.

Fairhaven

Fairhaven, Massachusetts, occupies the eastern bank of the Acushnet River along Buzzards Bay in southeastern Bristol County, emerging from the 1652 "Old Dartmouth" purchase as the easternmost section known as "Cushnea" and incorporating as a separate town on April 29, 1812, from northern Dartmouth lands. Originally encompassing what became Acushnet (1860), Fairhaven developed as a maritime support community to New Bedford's whaling dominance, with shipwrights, chandlers, ropemakers, and captains' homes clustered around Oxford Village and the waterfront. Its path—from Wampanoag Cushenagg settlements and John Cooke's garrison through King Philip's War raids, Quaker maritime networks, and 19th-century shipbuilding to Riverside Cemetery's Delano legacy—preserves proprietors' records, church registers, and vital compilations tracing "Acushnet east bank kin" across fractured Dartmouth heirs.

Wampanoag Cushenagg, Cooke Garrison, and King Philip's War

Prior to 1652, Fairhaven's riverside and bayside formed the Wampanoag "Cushenagg" (head of the river) neighborhood with villages, fisheries, and contact-period sites along waterways, including Nukkeekumanset reservation (1700s) and burials near Cooke lands; early epidemics and King Philip's War further disrupted Native continuity. John Cooke (Mayflower passenger) held extensive tracts near Coggeshall Street, building a garrison house that served as a 1676 rendezvous for Capt. Benjamin Church's rangers pursuing Metacom; early attacks killed families like the Popes and Mitchells fleeing to it. Postwar reallocations solidified English farms amid Quaker influx.

Genealogists consult Old Dartmouth proprietors' books, Plymouth deeds, and Church's war narratives listing Cooke, Delano, and Taber kin; Native echoes appear in quitclaims and missionary notes like William Simon's preaching.

Maritime Villages, Shipbuilding, and Delano-Rogers Legacy

Fairhaven's 18th–19th-century economy supported New Bedford via shipyards (Elihu Akin's burned 1778), saltworks, mills, and captain homes; Warren Delano Jr. (FDR grandfather) traded opium in China, while Henry Huttleston Rogers (Standard Oil magnate) funded libraries and academies. Riverside Cemetery (1850, Delano-founded) holds family tombs; Portuguese immigrants aided fisheries and farms by 1900. Villages like Oxford (oldest core) and Sconticut Neck hosted ferries and trade.

These pursuits generated crew lists, chandlery ledgers, and First Congregational records (1794+), capturing multiethnic maritime kin alongside census occupational clusters.

Genealogical Resources and Strategies

Vital repositories:

- Fairhaven Town Clerk: Original births, marriages, deaths from 1812, intentions, and town meetings; strong for post-separation continuity.

- Published compilations: "Vital Records of Fairhaven to 1850" blending town books, churches (Congregational), and cemeteries like Riverside.

- Millicent Library/Local histories: Manuscripts, censuses, directories, Delano/Rogers papers, and Harris' "Old-Time Fairhaven" with biographical sketches.

- Regional aids: FamilySearch wikis for Fairhaven vitals (1636–1924 births), Bristol probate/deeds, and whaling museum Dartmouth records.

Fairhaven's chronicle—from Cushenagg villages and Cooke garrisons to Delano voyages and Rogers philanthropy—equips genealogists with waterfront sources. Proprietors' plats, church rolls, and cemetery lots unveil "wharf kin" bridging Native sites, war refugees, and global traders along Buzzards Bay.

Freetown

Freetown, Massachusetts, spans the central-eastern expanse of Bristol County along the Assonet River and Profile Rock, originating as a 1659–1660 proprietary purchase from Wampanoag sachem Massasoit and incorporating as a town in 1683—one of New England's oldest continuous communities. Named for its "free" status outside Plymouth Colony's stricter governance, Freetown later yielded Fall River (1803), East Freetown portions to Middleboro, and Assonet to Berkley, retaining its rural core of farms, mills, and woodlands amid the "Bridgewater Triangle" folklore. Its layered history—from Native "Assonet" lands through King Philip's War strongholds, proprietary divisions, and 19th-century agrarian persistence—preserves town clerks' volumes from 1683, proprietors' records, and vital compilations tracing "free purchase kin" across Old Colony frontiers.

Wampanoag Assonet, Proprietary Purchase, and King Philip's War

Prior to English claims, Freetown's river valleys and Profile Rock (a natural sachem profile) anchored Wampanoag Assonet bands with fisheries, planting fields, and trails to Mount Hope, disrupted by epidemics and King Philip's War (1675–76), where Capt. Benjamin Church's rangers used the area as a base against Metacom. The 1660 purchase divided 20 lots among 36 proprietors like Ralph Earl, Humphrey Turner, and Henry Howland, yielding scattered farms by 1670s amid Quaker and Baptist settlers; postwar grants rewarded veterans, with legends of Native holdouts at "Indian Burying Hill." Early earmarks and divisions fixed family clusters like the Bordens and Hathaways.

Genealogists access this era via lost proprietors' books (reconstructed in histories), Plymouth Colony deeds, and town records from 1685 listing grantees, quitclaims, and Native interactions best supplemented by tribal petitions.

Farm Divisions, Mills, and Rural Continuity

Freetown's 18th–19th-century economy emphasized mixed agriculture—corn, livestock, orchards—alongside gristmills, sawmills, and potash works at Assonet Village, with shipbuilding and iron forges emerging briefly; Fall River's separation (1803) refocused the remnant on dairy, cranberries, and woodlots. Baptist and Congregational parishes anchored villages, drawing modest Irish and Portuguese farm labor by 1900. Civil War service and temperance societies appear in muster rolls and meeting minutes.

These pursuits generated overseers' bonds, poor farm lists, and church registers in town volumes, capturing enduring kin like the Earls and Brightmans across lot divisions.

Genealogical Resources and Strategies

Vital repositories:

- Freetown Town Clerk (3 North Main St., Assonet): Original records from 1683 (births, marriages, deaths to 1840), intentions, and proprietary fragments; Massachusetts Archives holds 1841–1930.

- Published compilations: "Vital Records of Freetown, 1686–1795" and histories like Ballou's "History of Freetown" with purchaser sketches (Earl, Turner, Howland lots).

- Freetown Historical Society: Census abstracts, military lists, cemetery surveys (to 1996 via Find A Grave), and Profile Rock artifacts; private burying grounds tracked.

- Regional aids: FamilySearch wikis for Bristol probate/deeds linking Freetown to Fall River industries.

Freetown's legacy—from Assonet sachem profiles to proprietary farms and mill hamlets—delivers genealogists frontier sources. Clerks' ledgers, lot plats, and society files unveil "free lot kin" from Massasoit's grants through war veterans and enduring woodlot heirs.

Mansfield

Mansfield, Massachusetts, occupies the northern interior of Bristol County along the Canoe River, originating from the 1640 Titiquet Purchase surveyed by Captain Miles Standish and evolving through Norton North Precinct (1731) into a town incorporated on August 23, 1775, named for William Murray, Earl of Mansfield. First settled around 1685 by families like Thomas Brintnell and John Caswell, Mansfield developed as an agrarian outpost with ironworks, cotton mills, straw hat manufactories, and foundries, anchored by landmarks such as the Fisher-Richardson House (c.1743–1751, NRHP). Its path—from Wampanoag woodlots and Taunton North Purchase through colonial forges, 19th-century bonnet and knife industries, to rural persistence—preserves town clerks' volumes, proprietors' records, and vital compilations tracing "Canoe River kin" across Old Colony divisions.

Titiquet Outlands, North Precinct, and Early Ironworks

Prior to sustained English settlement, Mansfield's Canoe River lowlands formed peripheral Wampanoag hunting and bog-iron grounds tied to Taunton trails, with Cobbler's Corner marking Standish's 1640 survey point. The Taunton North Purchase (post-1707 petitions led by Nicholas White) yielded Norton in 1711, whose north precinct separated in 1731 amid 30–35 families; Col. Ephraim Leonard's 1734 ironworks on Canoe River exploited local bog ore, producing tools and establishing him as the precinct's wealthiest resident and slaveholder. Early earmarks and divisions fixed clusters like the Whites, Skinners, and Leonards.

Genealogists trace this foundation in Taunton/Norton proprietors' books, precinct meeting minutes from 1731, and Plymouth deeds noting furnace sites and Native boundaries, best cross-referenced with regional quitclaims.

Bonnet Mills, Foundries, and Industrial Hamlets

Mansfield's 19th-century economy diversified with Solomon Pratt's cotton mill (1811, rebuilt post-1830 fire), John Rogers' straw hat shop (1835, Park Street), McMoran-Fulton knife works (1835), and Rider foundries (1874); these employed farm kin in bonnet braiding, pattern-making, and casting, while Orthodox Congregational (1839) and Methodist societies reflected theological splits. Anti-slavery activism surged post-1830s, with 300 members by 1840. Civil War service drew from muster rolls.

These ventures produced payrolls, apprenticeship indentures, and church registers in town records, capturing multi-generational trades alongside agricultural continuity.

Genealogical Resources and Strategies

Vital repositories:

- Mansfield Town Clerk (6 Park Row): Original births, marriages, deaths to 1849+, town reports, and citizen lists (1862); strong post-1775 continuity.

- Published compilations: "Vital Records of Mansfield to 1849" integrating town books, churches, and private registers; Jennie Copeland's histories with settler sketches (White, Leonard, Pratt).

- Mansfield Historical Society/Fisher-Richardson House: Manuscripts, censuses, directories, and artifacts at the 1743 house museum; cemetery surveys for early grounds.

- Regional aids: FamilySearch wikis for Bristol probate/deeds linking Mansfield to Norton/Taunton origins.

Mansfield's chronicle—from Titiquet surveys and bog forges to bonnet lanes and foundry heirs—provides genealogists with riverine sources. Clerks' ledgers, precinct plats, and society files unveil "North Purchase kin" spanning Standish's corner, Leonard's iron, and Pratt's mills along Canoe Brook.

North Attleboro

North Attleborough, Massachusetts, forms the northwestern corner of Bristol County adjacent to Rhode Island, originating as the North Purchase from Rehoboth in 1694 and incorporating as a separate town on July 3, 1887, from northern Attleborough lands. Centered around John Woodcock's 1669 garrison and tavern—destroyed during King Philip's War—the area evolved from colonial farmsteads and ironworks into a 19th-century jewelry and button manufacturing hub, with villages like Dodgeville and Hebronville hosting mills and factories. Its development—from Wampanoag trails through Rehoboth out-settlements, brass forges, and immigrant workshops to modern suburbs—preserves town clerks' volumes, proprietors' records, and Catholic parish registers tracing "North Purchase kin" across Attleborough separations.

Rehoboth North Purchase, Woodcock Garrison, and King Philip's War

Prior to English settlement, North Attleborough's Ten Mile River and uplands served as Wampanoag hunting paths linking Rehoboth to Narragansett Bay, with early contact disrupted by epidemics and 1675–76 war raids that razed Woodcock's isolated homestead, killing settlers and prompting garrison reconstructions. The 1694 North Purchase divided lands among Rehoboth families like the Woods, Caprons, and Daggetts, yielding linear farms by 1700; a 1714 Congregational meetinghouse anchored the precinct, later spawning St. Mary's Catholic parish (1857) for Irish mill hands.

Genealogists access this era through Rehoboth/Attleborough proprietors' books, early precinct minutes, and Plymouth deeds noting garrison sites and Native boundaries, complemented by tribal quitclaims.

Jewelry Forges, Mills, and Industrial Villages

North Attleborough's 1780s brass forge by "the Frenchman" birthed button and jewelry trades, expanding with Dodgeville cotton mills (1809), Hebronville textiles (1812), and firms producing medals, watchcases, and plated ware by 1855; these drew French Canadian, Irish, and Italian laborers into tenement clusters. Anti-slavery and Civil War service (7th–58th regiments) filled muster rolls, while 1919–20 "Little World Series" baseball drew stars like Babe Ruth.

These industries generated payrolls, apprenticeship lists, and St. Joseph's/St. Stephen's baptismal records (1880s–1980s) in town volumes, capturing multiethnic kin shifts.

Genealogical Resources and Strategies

Vital repositories:

- North Attleborough Town Clerk: Original records from 1887 (births, marriages, deaths), ward lists, and annexation documents; pre-1887 in Attleborough volumes.

- Published compilations: "Vital Records of Attleboro to 1849" and Attleboro Library transcriptions (St. Mary's baptisms, St. Stephen's Dodgeville); Sherman's "North Attleboro, An Affectionate History."

- North Attleborough Historical Society/Richards Memorial Library: Manuscripts, directories (1875+), censuses, and jewelry firm files at the 1927 society; cemetery surveys.

- Regional aids: Attleboro Public Library local history room with Franco-American burials, probate abstracts, and city directories spanning both towns.

North Attleborough's arc—from Woodcock's razed tavern and brass forges to Dodgeville mills and medal shops—equips genealogists with borderland sources. Clerks' ledgers, parish rolls, and society artifacts unveil "garrison kin" bridging Rehoboth purchases, war survivors, and jewelry immigrants along Ten Mile River.

Norton

Norton, Massachusetts, lies in the northern interior of Bristol County astride the Wrentham border, originating as the Taunton North Purchase (1669) from Wampanoag sachem Tuspaquin and incorporating as a town on March 20, 1711, from northern Taunton lands. Named possibly for Norton, England, or its "northern" position, Norton developed as a dispersed agrarian precinct with iron forges, tanneries, and mills, later spawning Mansfield (1770) and Wheaton College (1834) amid rural persistence. Its evolution—from Native trails and Leonard ironworks through precinct controversies, Baptist schisms, and 19th-century academies—preserves town clerks' volumes, church admissions, and vital compilations tracing "North Purchase kin" across Taunton heirs.

Wampanoag Hinterlands, Taunton North Purchase, and Leonard Forges

Before English grants, Norton's uplands and streams formed Wampanoag backcountry tied to Taunton trails, with the Leonards (arr. 1669) repairing King Philip's guns under truce orders sparing Taunton during 1675–76 war raids. The North Purchase divided 40 lots among 90+ grantees like Thomas Briggs, John Brintnell, and George Leonard, yielding farms by 1680s; Rev. Joseph Avery's 1711–1749 ministry amid "precinct troubles" anchored the new town with meetinghouse (1716) and church admissions from 1714.

Genealogists consult Taunton proprietors' books, Norton town records from 1711, and Plymouth deeds listing divisions among Briggs, Leonard, and White kin; Native ties echo in Leonard lore and quitclaims.

Ironworks, Tanneries, and Baptist Schisms

Norton's 18th–19th-century economy blended agriculture with George Leonard's Taunton Iron Works outpost, Hopestill Leonard's tannery (1790s), and mills at Barrowsville; Baptist separations (1770s) formed Second Church, while anti-slavery activism and Wheaton Female Seminary (1834, now college) drew educators. Civil War service filled regimental rolls from farm families.

These pursuits yielded overseers' bonds, church rolls (Avery/Palmer/Clerke eras), and industrial schedules capturing kin clusters.

Genealogical Resources and Strategies

Vital repositories:

- Norton Town Clerk: Original births, marriages, deaths to 1850+, town reports, and almshouse records (1837); strong continuity from 1711.

- Published compilations: "Vital Records of Norton to 1850" (3 vols., alphabetical town/church/cemetery indexes); Clark's "History of Norton, 1669–1859" with admissions and biographies.

- Norton Historical Society/Public Library: Manuscripts, censuses, yearbooks (1925+), family genealogies (Perry, Rogers), and Leonard iron files at Local History Room.

- Regional aids: FamilySearch wikis for Bristol probate/deeds linking Norton to Taunton/Mansfield.

Norton's saga—from Tuspaquin grants and Leonard forges to precinct pulpits and Wheaton halls—arms genealogists with ecclesiastical sources. Clerks' ledgers, admission rolls, and library stacks unveil "iron kin" spanning Brintnells, Averys, and seminary daughters along North Purchase brooks.

Raynham

Raynham, Massachusetts, occupies the northeastern corner of Bristol County adjacent to Bridgewater and Taunton, originating as the eastern precinct of Taunton centered on the Taunton Iron Works along the Two Mile (Forge) River and incorporated as a separate town on April 2, 1731. Named for Raynham Hall in Norfolk, England, Raynham developed from bog-iron forges and farmsteads into a rural manufacturing hamlet with anchor works, ship hulls, and railroads, retaining agrarian roots amid Leonard family dominance. Its trajectory—from Wampanoag Cohannet fringes through Elizabeth Poole's Titiquet settlement, revolutionary forges, and 19th-century rail spurs—preserves town clerks' volumes, iron ledgers, and church admissions tracing "forge kin" across Taunton separations.

Cohannet Iron Precinct, Leonard Forges, and Precinct Petitions

Prior to separation, Raynham's Forge Riverbanks formed Cohannet (Taunton) iron grounds where James and Henry Leonard established Plymouth Colony's first successful iron works (1652–1656), predated only by Saugus but enduring over 200 years producing anchors, nails, and naval fittings. Elizabeth Poole's 1639 settlement yielded linear farms among Leonard, Washburn, King, Shaw, Dean, Hall, Gushee, Williams, Gilmore, Andrews, Hathaway, White, Tracy, and Knapp families: King Philip's War idled forges amid collier fears, resuming postwar. Three petitions (1726–1730) secured independence upon settling a minister and schoolmaster.

Genealogists trace origins in Taunton proprietors' books, precinct minutes from 1726, and Plymouth deeds listing forge sites and earmarks; Leonard lore and quitclaims echo Native ties.

Anchor Forges, Shipbuilding, and Rural Rail Links

Raynham's 18th–19th-century economy centered on iron evolution—Josiah Dean's anchors (to 1873), ship hulls floated to Fall River, and mills—bolstered by 1840s railroads (Boston-New Bedford line through North Raynham). First Congregational Church (1731) records baptisms from 1738; modest Irish/Portuguese farm labor integrated by 1900. Revolutionary service and town seals proclaim 1652 forge legacy.

These industries generated contracts, church rolls (1738–1822), and overseers' bonds capturing multi-generational smiths.

Genealogical Resources and Strategies

Vital repositories:

- Raynham Town Clerk: Original births, marriages, deaths from 1731, precinct warrants, and iron-related proceedings.

- Published compilations: Church records (First Congregational, Vol. 1: baptisms/marriages 1738–1822); local histories with Leonard/Dean sketches.

- Raynham Historical Society/Public Library: Manuscripts, censuses, Gushee House artifacts (1779), and cemetery surveys.

- Regional aids: FamilySearch/Taunton archives for pre-1731 vitals and Bristol probate linking forge families.

Raynham's forge-born chronicle—from Leonard bellows and precinct pleas to anchor rivers and rail hamlets—provides genealogists with industrial sources. Clerks' ledgers, church admissions, and seal-stamped deeds unveil "iron precinct kin" spanning Titiquet grants, Dean anchors, and enduring Hall heirs along Two-Mile waters.

Rehoboth

Rehoboth, Massachusetts, anchors the northeastern corner of Bristol County near the Rhode Island line, originating as one of Plymouth Colony's earliest settlements established in 1643 by Rev. Samuel Newman and his Weymouth congregation on Seacunck Plain, with formal incorporation in 1645 following the 1641 land purchase from sachem Massasoit. Encompassing a vast "Original Rehoboth" that later yielded Seekonk (1812), Pawtucket and East Providence RI, Barrington RI, and parts of Attleboro and Cumberland RI, the remnant town retained its agrarian core of farms, mills, and the expansive "Ring of the Green" common. Its foundational history—from Wampanoag Seacunck through Newman's covenant, King Philip's War garrisons, and proprietary divisions—preserves town records from 1643, church admissions, and vital compilations tracing "enlargement kin" across fractured colonial bounds.

Seacunck Purchase, Newman Covenant, and King Philip's War Garrisons

Prior to English planting, Rehoboth's plains and rivers formed Wampanoag Seacunck territory with trails and planting grounds, purchased in 1641 by Edward Winslow and John Brown for wampum and coats from Massasoit. Rev. Newman's 1643 migration established the "Ring of the Green" palisaded common, formalized by the 1644 Rehoboth Covenant signed by 30 proprietors including William Sabin, with Newman naming it for Genesis 26:22 ("the Lord hath made room"). King Philip's War (1675–76) saw Newman's Fort and four other garrisons sheltering families like the Carpenters, Pecks, and Perrys amid raids, postwar reallocations solidifying farms.

Genealogists access this era through "Early Rehoboth Documents," proprietors' books from 1645, and Plymouth deeds listing Newman followers (Sabin, Peck, Perry, Millard); Native echoes in quitclaims complement tribal sources.

Proprietary Farms, Mills, and Baptist Dissent

Rehoboth's 18th–19th-century economy centered on dispersed farms radiating from the Green, with gristmills, sawmills, and ironworks at Newman's Pond; Baptist separations (Lot Bliss, 1740s) formed dissenting churches, while anti-slavery activism and Civil War service filled rolls from Perry, Carpenter, and Wright kin. Modest Irish farm labor arrived late century.

These yielded earmark lists, church rolls (Newman to Bliss eras), and overseers' bonds capturing proprietary clusters.

Genealogical Resources and Strategies

Vital repositories:

- Rehoboth Town Clerk (148 Peck St.): Original records from 1643 (births, marriages, deaths, earmarks), town meetings, and proprietary fragments; strong for "Original Rehoboth" continuity.

- Published compilations: "Vital Records of Rehoboth" integrating town books, churches, and cemeteries; Blanchard's biographies (Perry, Pierce, Reed lines).

- Rehoboth Historical Association: Manuscripts, censuses, Green plats, and garrison sites; cemetery surveys for early grounds.

- Regional aids: FamilySearch wikis for Bristol probate/deeds linking to Seekonk/RI separations.

Rehoboth's covenant-born legacy—from Seacunck wampum to Green-ringed farms and mill brooks—delivers genealogists pioneer sources. Clerks' volumes, covenant rolls, and bio sketches unveil "Newman kin" spanning Sabins, Pecks, and Bliss Baptists across Original Rehoboth's heirs.

Seekonk

Seekonk, Massachusetts, forms the northeastern tip of Bristol County along the Rhode Island border, carved from the western half of "Old Rehoboth" and incorporated as a separate town on February 26, 1812, with subsequent losses of Pawtucket (1828) and East Providence (1862) leaving a compact remnant of farms and mills. Emerging as a fringe of Rev. Samuel Newman's 1643 Seacunck settlement, Seekonk functioned as Rehoboth's agricultural hinterland with scattered ironworks, tanneries, and the Newman Congregational meetinghouse, its riverine bounds along the Blackstone and Seekonk marked by Native trails and postwar garrisons. Its diminished path—from Wampanoag contact zones through Rehoboth proprietors, King Philip's War refugees, and 19th-century boundary disputes—preserves Rehoboth-derived town records, church admissions, and vital compilations tracing "fringe Rehoboth kin" across state lines.

Old Rehoboth Fringe, King Philip's War, and Postwar Farms

Prior to 1812 separation, Seekonk's sandy-gravelly soils and brooks like Run Brook and Torrey Creek supported peripheral Wampanoag settlement with conjectured sites along conjectured trails paralleling modern Route 152 and Arcade Avenue, tied to pre-1620 trade near Mount Hope and Narragansett Bays. As Rehoboth's western expanse, Seekonk settlers fled to garrisons in Swansea, East Providence, and North Attleborough during 1675–76 war raids, resuming postwar amid Newman Congregational influence; a pre-1795 meetinghouse and 1758 cemetery at Lake/Lincoln streets anchored an early node, with taverns near Jacob Street c.1670–80. Proprietors like those from Rehoboth's 1641 purchase (wampum and coat to Massasoit) divided fringe lots.

Genealogists trace this via Rehoboth town books (1643+), early Seekonk vitals (1773–1883), and Plymouth deeds noting garrison refugees and Native paths; tribal sources complement contact-period echoes.

Mills, Grange, and Boundary Losses

Seekonk's 19th-century economy featured small mills on Ten Mile and Running Rivers, 166 farms by 1865, and institutions like the Seekonk Grange (Italianate, late 19th c.); 1862 RI-MA border arbitration halved the town, shifting industrial focus (e.g., Slater's mill) eastward while farms persisted. Electric trolleys spurred modest growth without urbanization.

These yielded poor farm lists, Grange rolls, and Newman Church records (births/marriages/deaths) capturing enduring kin amid separations.

Genealogical Resources and Strategies

Vital repositories:

- Seekonk Town Clerk (100 Peck St.): Original births, marriages, deaths ca.1773–1883 (indexed), town meetings post-1812; pre-1812 in Rehoboth.

- Published compilations: "Seekonk Including East Providence, Pawtucket" vital abstracts; "Historical Seekonk" Vols.1–5 with biographies.

- Seekonk Public Library/Historical Commission: Local histories, Cyndi's List links, HeritageQuest (via BPL ecard), cemetery surveys.

- Regional aids: FamilySearch wikis for Rehoboth/Pawtucket overlaps, Bristol probate/deeds.

Seekonk's remnant chronicle—from Rehoboth fringe trails and war garrisons to halved farms and Grange halls—provides genealogists border sources. Clerks' indexes, church abstracts, and library stacks unveil "western Rehoboth kin" spanning Newman proprietors, 1862 exiles, and trolley-era villagers.

Somerset

Somerset, Massachusetts, lies along the Taunton River in the northeastern sector of Bristol County, originating as the 1677 Shawomet Purchase from Wampanoag sachems and incorporating as a separate town on March 22, 1790, from Swansea lands. Named to honor Mary Shelburne Bowers (born in Somerset Square, Boston), wife of first moderator Jerathmel Bowers, Somerset developed from ferry crossings and shipbuilding hamlets into a manufacturing center with ironworks, potteries, and stove foundries, its riverine bounds preserving early Quaker and Native echoes. Its path—from Wampanoag Shawomet village through colonial ferries, Revolutionary guards, and 19th-century nail factories—yields town clerks' volumes, Swansea-derived records, and vital compilations tracing "Shawomet kin" across Swansea separations.

Shawomet Purchase, Ferry Crossings, and Bowers Shipbuilding

Before English acquisition, Somerset's Taunton River shores anchored Wampanoag Shawomet with fisheries, planting fields, and trails to Mt. Hope, ravaged by 1610s epidemics leaving "skulls and bones" noted by Pilgrims; the 1677 purchase divided 31 shares among Swansea proprietors like Jonathan Bowers (1694 settler, shipwright). Ferry service began 1690 linking to Fall River, with homes on Water (now Main) Street; Henry Bowers owned Toussaint L'Ouverture (later Haitian leader) briefly c.1760. Post-King Philip's War farms solidified amid Quaker meetings.

Genealogists trace this via Swansea proprietors' books, early Somerset town meetings (1790), and Plymouth deeds noting ferry sites and Native quitclaims; tribal sources complement Shawomet village lore.

Ironworks, Potteries, and Industrial River Hamlets

Somerset's 19th-century economy featured Mt. Hope Iron Works (1815, nails/shovels), Somerset Pottery Co. (nine potters 1705–1918, Pottersville), stove foundries (Hood family), and Montaup Electric (1925); fires (1875) and Octagon House (1860) marked growth, with Irish settlers in nail works. Revolutionary guards at the ferry and Assonet Raid appear in rosters.

These generated payrolls, pottery ledgers, and church registers capturing Bowers, Tripp, and Leonard kin.

Genealogical Resources and Strategies

Vital repositories:

- Somerset Town Clerk (140 Wood St.): Original births, marriages, deaths 1790–1900 (indexed), town reports; pre-1790 in Swansea.

- Published compilations: "History of Somerset" (Hart, 1940) with purchaser maps, Revolutionary rosters, and family sketches (Bowers, Hood).

- Somerset Historical Society/Public Library: Manuscripts, censuses (1880–1899 vitals), Pottersville artifacts, and cemetery surveys.

- Regional aids: FamilySearch catalogs for Swansea overlaps, Bristol probate/deeds.

Somerset's riverine chronicle—from Shawomet epidemics and ferry guards to pottery wheels and nail hammers—provides genealogists maritime sources. Clerks' ledgers, purchaser plats, and society trunks unveil "ferry kin" spanning Jonathan Bowers, Toussaint echoes, and Hood foundry heirs along Taunton shores.

Swansea

Swansea, Massachusetts, occupies the northeastern coastal corner of Bristol County along Mount Hope Bay, originating as the 1667 Wannamoisett Purchase from Wampanoag sachems and incorporating as Plymouth Colony's first town west of Narragansett Bay on March 20, 1668—America's first Baptist settlement after Roger Williams' Providence. Named for Swansea, Wales, Swansea later yielded Somerset (1790) and parts of Warren and Barrington RI, retaining its agrarian-maritime core amid King Philip's War devastation that killed 13 of 55 original signers. Its foundational path—from Pokanoket contact lands through John Myles' Baptist church, postwar rebuilds, and 19th-century farms—preserves town records from 1667, church admissions, and vital compilations tracing "first signer kin" across Baptist frontiers.

Wannamoisett Purchase, Myles Church, and King Philip's War Massacre

Prior to English claims, Swansea's bay shores and Palmer River formed Pokanoket Wannamoisett with villages and fisheries tied to Massasoit's Mount Hope; the 1667 purchase by Capt. Thomas Willett and 54 signers (Allen, Bowen, Butterworth, Cole) divided shares amid Baptist exodus from Rehoboth. Rev. John Myles established the second Baptist church in America (1663 house-meetings), formalized 1671; war erupted June 1675 with John Salisbury's wounding of a warrior, ambushing/killing nine settlers at Swazey Corner and sparking regional conflict, razing homes and slaying signers like Sampson Mason in Pierce's Fight.

Genealogists access this via original signer lists (55 men: Alby, Aldrich, Allen, Barnes...), Plymouth deeds, and town books from 1668 noting allotments and Native boundaries; tribal petitions complement Pokanoket echoes.

Proprietary Farms, Luther's Corner, and Rural Persistence

Swansea's 18th–19th-century economy centered on dispersed farms, gristmills, and Luther's Store (1815, post office/library to 1903) at economic heart; Baptist continuity (Myles to successors) and Quaker meetings persisted amid modest Irish farm labor. Civil War service filled rolls from Allen, Bowen, and Wheaton kin.

These yielded earmark lists, church rolls, and overseers' bonds capturing signer descendants.

Genealogical Resources and Strategies

Vital repositories:

- Swansea Town Clerk: Original records from 1668 (births, marriages, deaths to 1850), signer admissions, and proprietary fragments.

- Published compilations: "Vital Records of Swansea to 1850" and Wright's "History of Swansea, 1667-1917" with signer biographies (Butterworth, Cole, Mason).

- Swansea Historical Society: Manuscripts, censuses, Luther Store artifacts, and cemetery surveys (Kickemuit, Tyler Point).

- Regional aids: FamilySearch wikis for Bristol probate/deeds linking to Somerset/RI.

Swansea's Baptist-born legacy—from Wannamoisett wampum and Myles pulpits to war-ravaged signers and Luther corners—delivers genealogists pioneer sources. Clerks' volumes, 55-signer rolls, and society files unveil "Willett kin" spanning Allens, Bowens, and Butterworth Baptists across bayfront heirs.

Westport

Westport, Massachusetts, spans the southeastern coastal reaches of Bristol County along Buzzards Bay and the Westport River, evolving from the southwestern precinct of Old Dartmouth into a town incorporated on February 28, 1787, with later annexations from Dartmouth in 1793, 1795, and 1805. Named as the westernmost port of the Massachusetts Bay Colony grant, Westport developed dispersed villages around Acoaxet, Central Village, Head of Westport, and Hix Bridge amid Wampanoag Coaksett homelands, sustaining Quaker farms, mills, saltworks, and Paul Cuffee's shipyard. Its maritime-agrarian path—from Native Coaksett through King Philip's War disruptions, postwar Quaker networks, and 19th-century cotton mills—preserves Dartmouth-derived proprietors' records, vital compilations, and Quaker minutes tracing "river neck kin" across Old Dartmouth separations.

Coaksett Homelands, Old Dartmouth Precinct, and Paul Cuffee's Shipyard

Prior to English division, Westport's rivers and necks formed Wampanoag Coaksett with villages, fisheries, and trails to Sakonnet Point, disrupted by epidemics and King Philip's War raids that scattered Native bands; postwar Quaker influx from Nantucket settled farms along the Westport River. Dartmouth proprietors divided southwestern tracts among Sisson, Howland, and Macomber families by 1670, yielding saltworks and small mills; Paul Cuffee (Wampanoag-Ashanti, 1759–1817), philanthropist and abolitionist, built a shipyard c.1800, launching the Traveller for Sierra Leone voyages and employing mixed-heritage kin.

Genealogists consult Old Dartmouth proprietors' books, Westport town records from 1787, and Plymouth deeds listing neck allotments and Native boundaries; Cuffee papers and tribal sources illuminate mixed lineages.

Village Mills, Quaker Continuity, and Rural Maritime Economy
Westport's 18th–19th-century villages featured gristmills at Hix Bridge, cotton mills at Noquochoke Lake (Dartmouth line), and saltworks supporting coastal trade; Central Village hosted Quaker meetings, while Acoaxet farms grew Macomber turnips from 1876 Centennial seeds. Border disputes with RI (1861) and Fall River (1894) refined bounds amid modest Irish/Portuguese labor. Civil War service drew from Howland and Tripp kin.

These clusters produced meeting minutes, mill contracts, and church registers capturing endogamous Quaker lines.

Genealogical Resources and Strategies
Vital repositories:

- Westport Town Clerk: Original births, marriages, deaths from 1787 (to 1850 published), town meetings, and annexation records.

- Published compilations: "Vital Records of Westport to 1850" integrating town books, Quaker registers, and cemeteries.

- Westport Historical Society: Manuscripts, Cuffee papers, family registries (130 early settlers), censuses, and village maps.

- Regional aids: FamilySearch wikis for Dartmouth overlaps, Bristol probate/deeds.

Westport's bayfront chronicle—from Coaksett necks and Cuffee keels to mill hamlets and turnip fields—equips genealogists with Quaker sources. Proprietors' plats, vital indexes, and society files unveil "western port kin" spanning Sissons, Cuffees, and Macombers across Buzzards Bay villages.

Census-Designated Places

Acushnet Center

Acushnet Center, Massachusetts, serves as the principal Census-Designated Place (CDP) and historic village core of the Town of Acushnet, located along the Acushnet River in central-eastern Bristol County and evolving from the "Cushenagg Neighbourhood" within Old Dartmouth's 1652 purchase into Acushnet's municipal heart post-1860 incorporation. Anchoring the town's rural-industrial transition with early mills, Quaker farmsteads, and the Emery Cushman wooden box manufactory, Acushnet Center represents the concentrated settlement nucleus amid dispersed cranberry bogs and orchards, its records intertwined with parent-town Fairhaven, New Bedford, and Dartmouth archives tracing "Cushenagg kin" through Mayflower-descended lines like the Cushmans.

Cushenagg Core, Old Dartmouth Proprietors, and Cushman Mayflower Descent
Prior to town separation, Acushnet Center's river headwaters formed the Wampanoag "Cushenagg" (head of Acushnet) with Ponegansett villages and seasonal camps tied to Buzzards Bay fisheries,

acquired 1652 by Plymouth purchasers including Moses Simons, Joshua Pratt, and John Soule whose heirs divided tracts by 1659. Quaker settlers like the Howlands and Cushmans—descending from Robert Cushman (Fortune 1621) via Thomas and Mary Allerton (Mayflower)—established nucleated farms around what became the village center, with Emery Cushman (1814–1884) founding a box manufactory employing local kin.

Genealogists access this via Old Dartmouth proprietors' books, Fairhaven/New Bedford vitals pre-1860, and Cushman family compilations listing George (1759), David (1774), and Emery lines; Native echoes in boundary deeds complement tribal sources.

Village Mills, Box Manufactory, and Rural Town Nucleus

Acushnet Center's 19th-century focus included small grist/sawmills, the Cushman box works (successors Henry W. and Emery Jr. incorporating 1905), and modest commerce serving surrounding cranberry operations; post-1860 town records formalized the center as civic hub with Congregational ties and school districts. Irish/Portuguese bog labor integrated by 1900, reflected in census clusters.

These yielded manufactory ledgers, school rolls, and church registers capturing endogamous old-stock families.

Genealogical Resources and Strategies

Vital repositories:

- Acushnet Town Clerk: Post-1860 births, marriages, deaths centered on village families; pre-1860 in Fairhaven/Dartmouth/New Bedford.

- Published compilations: "History of Acushnet" (Howland, 1907) with Cushman genealogy (Robert to Emery), proprietors' plats.

- Acushnet Historical Society/Library: Manuscripts, censuses, box company files, and cemetery surveys for center burying grounds.

- Regional aids: FamilySearch wikis for Old Dartmouth overlaps, Bristol probate/deeds.

Acushnet Center's riverhead chronicle—from Cushenagg purchasers and Mayflower boxes to manufactory heirs—provides genealogists village sources. Proprietors' divisions, family Bibles, and society files unveil "box kin" spanning Soules, Howlands, and Cushmans along Acushnet's agrarian core.

Bliss Corner

Bliss Corner, Massachusetts, comprises a residential Census-Designated Place (CDP) within the town of Dartmouth along the southwestern coastal fringe of Bristol County, emerging mid-18th century from Old Dartmouth's Smith Neck vicinity as a Quaker-Baptist farm and mill neighborhood named for the Bliss family of Seventh Day Baptists migrating from Rhode Island. Centered near Clark's Cove with small family trades—grocery stores, cobblers, dairies, cafes, lumberyards, and spindle makers—Bliss Corner supported Dartmouth's maritime economy without developing into a commercial hub, its records embedded in town-wide Dartmouth proprietors' divisions and church registers tracing "Bliss kin" through intermarriages with Howlands, Russells, and Kirbys.

Seventh Day Baptist Settlement, Bliss Preachers, and Family Trades

Prior to Bliss arrival (mid-1700s), the vicinity formed peripheral Wampanoag lands within Old Dartmouth's 1652 purchase, with scattered Quaker farms along coastal necks; Rev. William Bliss from Rhode Island established preaching, farming, and sawmilling, followed by son Arnold (Middleton RI preacher) whose son William shifted to milling. John Bliss (Rev. William's son, Freewill Baptist preacher, Revolutionary soldier under Col. Crary) married Deborah Howland and Ruhamah Kirby, fathering 13 children marrying into Russell/Howland lines, anchoring the neighborhood's religious and agrarian core.

Genealogists access this via Old Dartmouth proprietors' books, Dartmouth vital records pre-1850, and Bliss family genealogies noting Rhode Island migrations and Howland Unions, Native echoes minimal in coastal deeds.

Clark's Cove Guano, Trolley Growth, and Residential Persistence

Bliss Corner's 19th-century economy featured family businesses and the Clark's Cove Guano Company (late 1800s, processing bird guano for fertilizer on cove's south side), bolstered by late-1800s trolley from Padanaram driving modest residential expansion without industrialization; small dairies, lumberyards, and spindle makers served local needs amid farm continuity.

These yielded census occupational clusters, trolley-era directories, and church rolls capturing endogamous Bliss-Howland kin.

Genealogical Resources and Strategies

Vital repositories:

- Dartmouth Town Clerk: Original births, marriages, deaths encompassing Bliss Corner families within town records from 1664.

- Published compilations: "Vital Records of Dartmouth to 1850" integrating town books, Seventh Day Baptist/Freewill registers, and coastal cemeteries.

- Dartmouth Historical & Arts Society/Local libraries: Manuscripts, guano company files, family sketches (Bliss, Howland), and neighborhood maps.

- Regional aids: FamilySearch wikis for Old Dartmouth overlaps, Bristol probate/deeds.

Bliss Corner's neck-side chronicle—from RI Baptist preachers and sawmills to guano coves and trolley homes—provides genealogists neighborhood sources. Proprietors' plats, family Bibles, and church rolls unveil "preacher kin" spanning Williams, Arnolds, and John Blisses across Howland-Russell coastal lines.

Mansfield Center

Mansfield Center, Massachusetts, constitutes the principal Census-Designated Place (CDP) and historic civic core of the Town of Mansfield, situated along the Canoe River in northern Bristol County and developing from the Norton North Precinct's central nucleus post-1775 incorporation as a speculative rail village around the 1880s town common. Emerging amid Ephraim Leonard's colonial ironworks and Nicholas White's statesman farm, Mansfield Center anchored town governance with the Victorian Town Hall, Soldier's Memorial Library (1901), and Orthodox Congregational meetinghouse (1839), its grid layout reflecting 19th-century ambitions fueled by the Boston-Providence Railroad junction serving jewelry, furnaces, and chocolate industries. Its concentrated trajectory—from Taunton North Purchase outlots through precinct meetinghouses and anti-slavery pulpits to rail-era commons—embeds records within Mansfield town clerks' volumes tracing "common kin" across Leonard-White kinships.

Cobbler's Corner Precinct, White-Leonard Nucleus, and Rail Grid

Prior to town formation, Mansfield Center's riverside formed Taunton North Purchase fringes surveyed 1640 by Miles Standish at Cobbler's Corner, with Nicholas White (first deacon/treasurer) and Ephraim Leonard (iron capitalist) establishing the 1731 Norton North Precinct hub; Rev. Roland Green's 1761 ministry spanned 47 years from West Street parsonage. The 1839 Orthodox split from anti-slavery Congregationalists built the West Street meetinghouse, while 1880s rail speculation laid the central grid around South Common, attracting Chilson furnaces and Lowney chocolate opposite the 1901 Soldier's Memorial Library honoring Civil War veterans.

Genealogists access this via Norton/Mansfield precinct minutes (1731+), town books from 1775, and proprietors' deeds listing White-Fisher homes (Willow Street) and Leonard forges; church admissions complement.

Common Trades, Memorial Hall, and Civic Persistence

Mansfield Center's 19th-century commerce clustered around the common with jewelry plating, Bailey bake ovens, knife factories (McMoran-Fulton), and Rider foundries employing Irish/Canadian kin; Mulberry Tavern hosted early services, evolving into Methodist and storefronts. Trolley and auto eras sustained the Victorian core without suburban sprawl.

These yielded directories, school rolls, and library catalogs capturing central occupational webs.

Genealogical Resources and Strategies

Vital repositories:

- Mansfield Town Clerk (6 Park Row): Original births, marriages, deaths to 1849+ centered on common families; strong post-1775 continuity.

- Published compilations: "Vital Records of Mansfield to 1849" integrating town books, Orthodox Congregational registers, and common cemeteries.

- Mansfield Historical Society/Public Library: Manuscripts, censuses, Chilson/Rider files, Fisher-Richardson House (1743) artifacts at Local History Room.

- Regional aids: FamilySearch wikis for Norton/Taunton overlaps, Bristol probate/deeds.

Mansfield Center's grid-common chronicle—from Standish surveys and White pulpits to rail halls and furnace heirs—provides genealogists civic sources. Clerks' ledgers, church rolls, and society stacks unveil "precinct kin" spanning Leonards, Greens, and Chilson platers along Canoe River commons.

North Seekonk

North Seekonk, Massachusetts, represents a residential Census-Designated Place (CDP) straddling the northern fringe of Seekonk town along the Massachusetts-Rhode Island border in northeastern Bristol County, evolving as a peripheral extension of "Old Rehoboth" post-1812 Seekonk incorporation and further diminished by the 1862 boundary arbitration that ceded industrial cores to East Providence RI. Anchoring rural farmsteads and small mills amid Rehoboth's expansive proprietary lots, North Seekonk sustained agricultural outliers with tanneries, slaughterhouses, and iron forges near modern County Street and Route 118, its scattered records embedded within Seekonk and Rehoboth town books tracing "northern fringe kin" across wartime garrisons and border realignments.

Rehoboth Northern Fringe, King Philip's War Garrisons, and Border Mills

Prior to Seekonk separation, North Seekonk's uplands and brooks like Runnins River formed Rehoboth's remote agricultural hinterland with conjectured Wampanoag sites tied to pre-1675 trails paralleling Arcade Avenue; during King Philip's War, settlers fled to Swansea and East Providence garrisons, resuming postwar amid Newman Congregational influence. Early 18th-century nodes included a pre-1795 meetinghouse and 1758 cemetery at Lake/Lincoln streets junction, with taverns c.1670–80 near Jacob Street; 19th-century tanneries, slaughterhouses (Locust Avenue), and iron forges (County/Route 118) supported farm economies.

Genealogists access this via Rehoboth town records (1643+), Seekonk vitals from 1773, and Plymouth deeds noting garrison refugees; 1862 RI-MA arbitration scattered families across jurisdictions.

Farm Persistence, Trolley Expansion, and Suburban Transition

North Seekonk's 19th–20th-century character emphasized 166 farms (1865 census) with grist/sawmills on Runnins and Ten Mile Rivers, evolving via electric trolleys into modest residential clusters without heavy industry; Grange halls and poor farms documented kin networks amid Hall, Kent, and Peck families noted in land transactions.

These yielded census occupations, Grange rolls, and church abstracts capturing enduring farm lines.

Genealogical Resources and Strategies

Vital repositories:

- Seekonk Town Clerk (100 Peck St.): Post-1812 births, marriages, deaths encompassing North Seekonk; pre-1812 in Rehoboth, 1773–1883 indexed.
- Published compilations: Seekonk vital abstracts blending town/church/cemetery data; Rehoboth histories with northern proprietor sketches.

- Seekonk Public Library/Historical Commission: Local histories, HeritageQuest censuses, and border arbitration maps for fringe families.
- Regional aids: FamilySearch wikis for Rehoboth/Pawtucket overlaps, Bristol probate/deeds.

North Seekonk's border chronicle—from Rehoboth garrison fringes and Runnins mills to halved farms and trolley homes—provides genealogists peripheral sources. Clerks' indexes, land rolls, and library files unveil "fringe kin" spanning wartime Pecks, 1862 Halls, and Kent grantees across Seekonk's northern heirs.

North Westport

North Westport, Massachusetts, designates an interior Census-Designated Place (CDP) within the Town of Westport along the northern shores of South Watuppa Pond in southeastern Bristol County, characterized by 19th- and 20th-century residential clusters rather than a singular colonial core, developing post-1787 town incorporation amid Old Dartmouth's southwestern proprietary tracts. Emerging around crossroads like Old Bedford and Blossom Roads with dispersed agrarian nodes—Borden family homesteads, Gershon-Wordell Farm (c.1850), and Sampson potato operations—North Westport anchored rural commerce via the Old Colony Railroad's 1870s bridge creating "The Narrows" recreational hamlet on Middle Pond, later filled by Route 195, its fragmented records woven into Westport town volumes tracing "pondside kin" through Bordens, Lassondes, and Ouellettes.

Watuppa Crossroads, Borden Farms, and Narrows Recreation

Prior to rail arrival, North Westport's pond margins and upland farms formed peripheral Wampanoag Coaksett extensions within Old Dartmouth, with postwar Quaker proprietors dividing lots among Bordens (from 1630s) yielding linear homesteads along Sanford and Blossom Roads by early 1800s. The 1870s Old Colony bridge bifurcated South Watuppa Pond into Middle Pond ("The Narrows"), spawning boathouses, casinos, ice houses (Lassonde/Ouellette families), and winter skating venues that magnetized nightlife through 1940s; Brownell Corner Historic District (1840 cemetery, 1858 Baptist church, 1871 school) formalized the crossroads cluster.

Genealogists access this via Old Dartmouth/Westport proprietors' books, town vitals from 1787, and census farm schedules listing Borden/Sampson kin, Native echoes sparse in pond deeds.

Ice Houses, Rail Hamlets, and Suburban Corridors

North Westport's late-19th-century economy blended agriculture—potatoes, cattle, vegetables—with ice harvesting for year-round delivery and Route 6/I-195 corridors fostering residential growth; Beulah camp meetings (Gifford Road) and Sampson Farm (Blossom/Old Bedford) exemplified large operations, with 1960s highway filling Middle Pond ending the social hub.

These yielded ice ledgers, Grange rolls, and church registers capturing multi-generational pond families.

Genealogical Resources and Strategies

Vital repositories:

- Westport Town Clerk: Post-1787 births, marriages, deaths encompassing North Westport farms; pre-1787 in Dartmouth.

- Published compilations: "Vital Records of Westport to 1850" integrating town books, Baptist registers, and crossroads cemeteries.

- Westport Historical Society: Manuscripts, Borden/Sampson files, Narrows photos, and pond plats.

- Regional aids: FamilySearch wikis for Dartmouth overlaps, Bristol probate/deeds.

North Westport's pond-crossroads chronicle—from Borden outlots and ice stacks to filled Narrows and Route 6 homes—provides genealogists rural sources. Proprietors' divisions, census farms, and society trunks unveil "Watuppa kin" spanning Bordens, Lassondes, and Sampson spudders across interior heirs.

Norton Center

Norton Center, Massachusetts, designates the central Census-Designated Place (CDP) and historic village core of the Town of Norton in northern Bristol County, coalescing around the Taunton North Purchase's 1711 town common and fortified by the Norton Center Historic District encompassing 19th-century civic buildings adjacent to Wheaton College. Developing from Rev. Joseph Avery's 1716 meetinghouse amid Leonard ironworks and White statesman farms, Norton Center anchored precinct governance with the 1826 Town Hall, Greek Revival churches, and Wheaton Seminary (1834) drawing educators and anti-slavery reformers, its compact grid reflecting rural-academic ambitions sustained by trolleys and rail. Its nucleated trajectory—from Wampanoag hinterlands through Baptist schisms and almshouse farms to college-bordered commons—embeds records in Norton town clerks' volumes tracing "seminary kin" across Briggs-Avery lineages.

North Purchase Common, Avery Ministry, and Wheaton Nucleus

Prior to 19th-century expansion, Norton Center's uplands formed Taunton North Purchase core with Tuspaquin grants divided among 90+ proprietors like Thomas Briggs and George Leonard by 1669; Rev. Joseph Avery's 1711–1749 pastorate built the first meetinghouse (1716, replaced 1826) amid "precinct troubles," spawning Baptist separations and the 1837 almshouse farm on Reservoir Street. Wheaton Female Seminary (1834, Judge Laban Wheaton founder) clustered faculty housing and students around East Main Street, intersecting with anti-slavery activism and Civil War musters from central kin.

Genealogists access this via Taunton/Norton proprietors' books, town records from 1711, and church admissions (Avery/Palmer eras); Mayflower ties via Wetherell/Briggs lines noted in vital indexes.

Trolley Commons, Historic District, and Academic-Residential Core

Norton Center's late-19th-century commerce featured rail depots, Lowney chocolate works, and trolley barns (N.T.&A. line to Attleboro), evolving into the Norton Center Historic District (NRHP

1981) with Town Hall, libraries, and college gates; Baptist/Methodist parishes documented occupational webs of educators, iron agents, and farm overseers.

These yielded yearbooks, directories, and library catalogs capturing seminary-forged kin.

Genealogical Resources and Strategies

Vital repositories:

- Norton Town Clerk: Original births, marriages, deaths to 1850+ centered on common families; almshouse/precinct minutes from 1711.

- Published compilations: "Vital Records of Norton to 1850" (3 vols., town/church/cemetery indexes); Clark's "History of Norton" with admissions/biographies.

- Norton Historical Society/Public Library: Hiltz Room manuscripts, Wheaton yearbooks (1925+), Leonard files, and Local History Room genealogies (Perry, Rogers).

- Regional aids: FamilySearch wikis for Taunton overlaps, Bristol probate/deeds.

Norton Center's common-seminary chronicle—from Avery pulpits and almshouse fields to trolley gates and historic halls—provides genealogists academic sources. Clerks' ledgers, church rolls, and library stacks unveil "precinct kin" spanning Leonards, Averys, and Wheaton daughters along North Purchase mains.

Ocean Grove

Ocean Grove, Massachusetts, comprises a residential and recreational Census-Designated Place (CDP) within the town of Swansea along the eastern shore of Narragansett Bay in northeastern Bristol County, developing in the late 19th century as a summer resort extension of Swansea village amid the Shawomet Purchase's coastal fringes. Named for its oceanfront groves and beach cottages, Ocean Grove clustered around St. Michael Catholic Church (1922) and the Plains along Wilbur Avenue, evolving from post-King Philip's War farmsteads into a seasonal enclave with bathhouses, stores, and Italianate homes serving mill workers from Fall River and Swansea proper. Its resort trajectory—from Wampanoag coastal sites through colonial ferries and 20th-century ethnic parishes—embeds records within Swansea town volumes tracing "bay grove kin" across Bowers-Tripp shorelines.

Shawomet Shores, Resort Cottages, and St. Michael Parish

Prior to resort development, Ocean Grove's bayfront formed peripheral Wampanoag Shawomet with fisheries and trails noted in 1677 purchase deeds, yielding postwar Swansea farms by Cole and Bowers families: late 19th-century speculation erected beach cottages and the Plains commercial strip amid Long Point and Touisset Neck nodes. St. Michael Catholic Church (1922–1995 records) served Portuguese/Irish mill families, anchoring baptisms amid summer visitors.

Genealogists access this via Swansea proprietors' books, town vitals from 1668, and church registers noting shore occupations, Native echoes in coastal quitclaims.

Plains Commerce, Bathhouses, and Seasonal Persistence

Ocean Grove's early 20th-century economy featured grocery stores, cafes, and bathhouses along Wilbur Avenue serving day-trippers, sustained by auto access without heavy industry; Italianate homes and cemeteries documented kin networks of Tripp, Hood, and immigrant lines.

These yielded directories, parish rolls, and census beach clusters capturing multi-generational vacationers.

Genealogical Resources and Strategies

Vital repositories:

- Swansea Town Clerk: Post-1668 births, marriages, deaths encompassing Ocean Grove; strong coastal continuity.
- Published compilations: "Vital Records of Swansea to 1850" integrating town books, St. Michael abstracts (1922+).
- Swansea Historical Society/Public Library: Photo archives, Plains postcards, cottage plats, and shore cemetery surveys.
- Regional aids: FamilySearch wikis for Swansea/Fall River overlaps, Bristol probate/deeds.

Ocean Grove's bay-resort chronicle—from Shawomet fisheries and cottage rows to parish beaches—provides genealogists seasonal sources. Clerks' ledgers, church baptisms, and society photos unveil "Plains kin" spanning Coles, Trips, and St. Michael Portuguese along Narragansett shores.

Raynham Center

Raynham Center, Massachusetts, forms the principal Census-Designated Place (CDP) and civic nucleus of the Town of Raynham in northeastern Bristol County, centered on the town common where Taunton's eastern precinct formalized independence in 1731 amid the enduring Leonard ironworks along the Two Mile River. Developing from Elizabeth Poole's Titiquet settlement and Rev. Enoch Sanford's 1731 Congregational meetinghouse, Raynham Center anchored governance with the 1873 Town Hall, Gushee Library (private since 1872), and rail depots serving anchor forges and ship cradles, its compact green reflecting forge-born prosperity sustained by founding families like Leonard, Hall, and Washburn. Its common-focused arc—from Cohannet iron precinct through three petitions for separation to rail-trolley commons—preserves town clerks' volumes tracing "forge common kin" across Taunton heirs.

Titiquet Precinct Common, Sanford Pulpit, and Leonard Dominance

Prior to town status, Raynham Center's riverside formed Taunton's eastern core with James/Henry Leonard's 1652 ironworks (Plymouth Colony's first enduring manufactory), Elizabeth Poole's 1639 farm yielding linear lots among Washburn, King, Shaw, Dean, Hall, Gushee, Williams, Gilmore, Andrews, Hathaway, White, Tracy, and Knapp by 1726 petitions; Rev. Enoch Sanford's 1870 history documented the 1731 meetinghouse amid Court-mandated minister/schoolmaster. Postwar ship cradles on Taunton Riverbanks (Hall property) floated schooners to Berkley.

Genealogists access this via Taunton proprietors' books, Raynham precinct minutes (1726+), and church records (1738 baptisms); Leonard wills note iron kin.

Rail Commons, Gushee Library, and Cottage Industries

Raynham Center's 19th-century hub featured Boston-New Bedford rail (1840s North Raynham), tack/grist/straw hat factories, shoe shops, and Williams box mill (Richmond Street, fish crates to New Bedford), with 1931 bicentennial at Weonit Hall; private Gushee Library sustained literacy amid fruit farms (39 apple varieties).

These yielded directories, church rolls, and overseers' bonds capturing multi-generational smiths/farmers.

Genealogical Resources and Strategies

Vital repositories:

- Raynham Town Clerk: Original births, marriages, deaths from 1731, precinct warrants, and iron proceedings.

- Published compilations: First Congregational records (1731–1822 baptisms/marriages), Sanford's "History of Raynham" with family sketches.

- Raynham Historical Society/Public Library: Digitized anniversary histories (1931/1976), Fallen Heroes bios, Gushee House artifacts.

- Regional aids: FamilySearch wikis for Taunton overlaps, Bristol probate/deeds.

Raynham Center's forge-green chronicle—from Leonard bellows and Poole plats to rail commons and Gushee stacks—provides genealogists industrial sources. Clerks' ledgers, church admissions, and society files unveil "precinct kin" spanning Halls, Deans, and Williams boxmakers along Two Mile forges.

Smith Mills

Smith Mills, Massachusetts, designates a historic village and Census-Designated Place (CDP) within the Town of Dartmouth along the eastern inland fringe of Bristol County, coalescing in the late 17th century around water-powered mills at the intersection of Hixville and State Roads (Route 6) from Old Dartmouth's proprietary divisions. Named for the Smith family—John Smith (1618 England, arr. Plymouth c.1630s) whose son Eliashib acquired grist/sawmill privileges in 1707—the neighborhood served as an early civic hub with Dartmouth's first "town house" (1686), taverns, and crossroads commerce supporting maritime outlots. Its mill-centered trajectory—from Wampanoag inland paths through Quaker mills and Revolutionary musters to 20th-century residential persistence—embeds records in Dartmouth town volumes tracing "mill kin" across Smith-Howland generations.

Old Dartmouth Crossroads, Eliashib Smith Mills, and Town House

Prior to Smith tenure, the mill privilege site formed interior Wampanoag trails linking coastal necks to Acushnet; Henry Tucker's 1684 gristmill grant passed to Eliashib Smith (John's son, m. Dinah Allen 1704 Quaker), who operated 60 years yielding the neighborhood name, with seven Smith generations buried in adjacent Homestead Hill (from 1692). The 1686 Town House hosted town meetings pre-Pittsfield relocation, amid taverns for Swansea/Dartmouth travelers; Gershom Smith (John's son) farmed adjacent Smith's Neck.

Genealogists access this via Old Dartmouth proprietors' books (1710 survey), Dartmouth vitals to 1850 noting Smith-Ripley/Russell marriages, and Taunton probates (John's 1694 will); Quaker minutes complement.

Cummings Expansion, Inns, and Village Persistence
Smith Mills' 19th-century growth featured Cummings family mills/stores (four mills, two shops), inns/taverns at crossroads, and spindle production serving New Bedford; post-trolley residential clusters sustained without industrialization, with Pine Island Road cemetery anchoring kin.

These yielded directories, tavern licenses, and church rolls capturing multi-occupational Smith descendants.

Genealogical Resources and Strategies
Vital repositories:

- Dartmouth Town Clerk: Original births, marriages, deaths from 1664 encompassing Smith Mills; strong Quaker continuity.

- Published compilations: "Vital Records of Dartmouth to 1850" (3 vols., town/church/cemetery indexes incl. G.R. Smith family grounds).

- Dartmouth Historical & Arts Society: Manuscripts, mill deeds, town house sketches, and neighborhood maps.

- Regional aids: FamilySearch wikis for Old Dartmouth overlaps, Bristol probate (Taunton).

Smith Mills' crossroads chronicle—from Eliashib bellows and town house to Cummings shops—provides genealogists village sources. Proprietors' surveys, vital Bibles, and society files unveil "grist kin" spanning Johns, Eliashibs, and Gershoms across inland Howland lines.

Villages

Assonet

Assonet, Massachusetts, constitutes a historic village and Census-Designated Place (CDP) within the Town of Freetown along the Assonet River in central Bristol County, settled in 1659 as part of the Freemen's Purchase from Wampanoag sachem Massasoit and developing as Freetown's industrious northern core with gristmills, sawmills, and the N.R. Davis Gun Manufactory. Named from the Algonquian "place of rocks" or "song of praise," Assonet anchored commerce via the Green Dragon Tavern on the Boston-Rhode Island stagecoach route, later featuring railroads, shipbuilding, and the Crystal Springs Bleachery amid the Assonet Historic District (NRHP 1999). Its riverine trajectory—from Wampanoag Assonet bands through King Philip's War skirmishes, Revolutionary ferries, and Civil War arms production—preserves Freetown town records tracing "mill rock kin" across proprietary lots.

Freemen's Purchase, Profile Rock, and Green Dragon Crossroads

Prior to English division, Assonet's rocky riverbanks and Profile Rock (natural Massasoit profile) sustained Wampanoag villages with fisheries and trails to Mount Hope, sold 1659 yielding Freetown incorporation (1683); postwar farms clustered around South/North Churches (1795/1809) with Paul Revere bell and river baptisms. The Green Dragon Tavern (South Main Street) hosted stagecoaches/mail, while Village School (1794) served lawyers and mill agents.

Genealogists access this via Freetown proprietors' books (1680s lost, reconstructed), town vitals from 1686, and church records (South/North alternating services); Native echoes in Profile lore and quitclaims.

Gun Manufactory, Bleachery, and Industrial Revival

Assonet's 19th-century boom included N.R. Davis Gun Works (Hathaway Park site, Union arms), Crystal Springs Bleachery/Dyeing (Mill Pond remnants), and Monument Manufacturing (WWII sleeping bags on Mill/Locust); railroads and Route 79 (old stage path) spurred mills employing Fall River commuters, with white-black-ring chimneys marking Tory homes.

These yielded payrolls, overseers' bonds, and parish rolls capturing multi-occupational kin.

Genealogical Resources and Strategies

Vital repositories:

- Freetown Town Clerk (Assonet): Original births, marriages, deaths from 1686 (to 1795 published), tavern licenses, and mill proceedings.
- Published compilations: "Vital Records of Freetown, 1686–1795"; Assonet Historic District surveys with church abstracts (South/North).
- Freetown Historical Society: Manuscripts, Davis gun files, Profile Rock artifacts, and village cemetery surveys.
- Regional aids: FamilySearch wikis for Fall River overlaps, Bristol probate/deeds.

Assonet's rocky chronicle—from Freemen's mills and Profile gaze to gun forges and bleach ponds—provides genealogists industrial sources. Clerks' ledgers, church bells, and society trunks unveil "stage kin" spanning taverns, Tories, and Davis gunners along Assonet waters.

Bowensville

Bowensville, Massachusetts, represents a small historic village and former mill hamlet within the Town of Somerset along the Taunton River in northeastern Bristol County, emerging in the early 19th century from the Shawomet Purchase's eastern fringes as a cotton and woolen manufactory settlement named for the locally prominent Bowen family. Centered around the Bowensville Mill (c.1810s, water-powered by Brightman Cove tributaries) and associated tenements, the village supported Swansea and Fall River laborers with boardinghouses, stores, and a Baptist meetinghouse, its compact industrial core later declining amid textile shifts yet preserving mill ledgers and family Bibles tracing "cove mill kin" across Shawomet proprietors like the Bowens and Hoods.

Shawomet Cove Mills, Bowen Manufactory, and Labor Hamlets

Prior to mill era, Bowensville's cove and uplands formed peripheral Wampanoag Shawomet with fisheries tied to 1677 Swansea purchase deeds, yielding postwar farms by Bowen descendants (from Jonathan, 1694 shipwright); early 1800s cotton factory harnessed tidal streams for carding/spinning, employing daughters and Irish hands in tenement rows amid Brightman family commerce. Baptist prayer meetings and simple burying grounds anchored spiritual life for operatives.

Genealogists access this via Swansea proprietors' books, Somerset vitals post-1790 noting mill births, and Taunton probates (Bowen wills); Native echoes sparse in cove quitclaims.

Tenement Labor, Textile Decline, and Residential Remnant

Bowensville's mid-19th-century peak featured expanded woolen production and store/post office serving Fall River commuters, sustained briefly by rail access before relocation and fires scattered operations; surviving mill houses document kin networks of Hood, Tripp, and immigrant lines through census boarders.

These yielded payrolls, overseers' bonds, and church rolls capturing multi-generational operatives.

Genealogical Resources and Strategies

Vital repositories:

- Somerset Town Clerk: Post-1790 births, marriages, deaths encompassing Bowensville mills; pre-1790 in Swansea.
- Published compilations: "History of Somerset" with Bowen mill sketches and Shawomet purchaser maps.
- Somerset Historical Society: Manuscripts, textile ledgers, tenement plats, and cove cemetery surveys.
- Regional aids: FamilySearch wikis for Swansea/Fall River overlaps, Bristol probate/deeds.

Bowensville's cove chronicle—from Shawomet tides and Bowen looms to tenement echoes—provides genealogists mill sources. Clerks' ledgers, family rolls, and society trunks unveil "factory kin" spanning Jonathans, Hoods, and Irish spinners along Brightman waters.

Britania

Britannia, Massachusetts, refers to a small historic mill hamlet and neighborhood within the Town of Fall River in southeastern Bristol County, developing in the mid-19th century around cotton textile factories powered by the Quequechan River's lower falls amid the city's industrial expansion. Named possibly for British immigrant workers or patriotic fervor during the era's textile boom, Britannia clustered tenement housing, boardinghouses, and mill operations near modern Brayton Avenue and President Avenue, serving as a working-class enclave for Irish, English, and French-Canadian laborers feeding Fall River's "Spindle City" economy. Its compact factory trajectory—from post-Revolutionary farmsteads through 1840s mill construction to labor strikes and urban assimilation—embeds records within Fall River city volumes tracing "spindle kin" across immigrant mill hands and boarding clusters.

Quequechan Lower Falls, Mill Tenements, and Immigrant Labor

Prior to industrialization, Britannia's riverside formed peripheral Wampanoag lands within Freetown/Tiverton tracts, yielding early 19th-century farmsteads displaced by Fall River's 1803 incorporation; by 1840s, cotton mills harnessed the Quequechan's falls for carding/spinning, erecting brick tenements housing Irish famine arrivals and English overseers amid company stores and Catholic prayer groups. Ethnic boardinghouses documented chain migration patterns.

Genealogists access this via Fall River city directories (1840s+), ward censuses noting mill occupations, and parish registers (St. Roch/Notre Dame); Native echoes absent in urban deeds.

Boardinghouse Clusters, Labor Strikes, and Residential Remnant

Britannia's peak featured dense tenements supporting 100+ operatives per mill, sustained by rail/steamboat access before 1920s decline scattered families; surviving triple-deckers preserve kin networks of Murphy, O'Brien, and Canadian lines through draft registrations.

These yielded payrolls, poor relief rolls, and church baptisms capturing multi-generational weavers.

Genealogical Resources and Strategies

Vital repositories:

- Fall River City Clerk: Post-1803 births, marriages, deaths centered on Britannia wards; strong mill-era continuity.

- Published compilations: City directories integrating mill addresses, ward maps, and ethnic parish abstracts.

- Fall River Historical Society/Public Library: Manuscripts, tenement censuses, labor strike files, and neighborhood photos.

- Regional aids: FamilySearch wikis for Freetown overlaps, Bristol probate/deeds.

Britannia's fallside chronicle—from Quequechan tenements and immigrant looms to strike echoes—provides genealogists labor sources. Clerks' ledgers, directory pages, and society trunks unveil "factory kin" spanning Irish Murphys, English overseers, and Canadian spinners along Brayton waters.

East Freetown

East Freetown, Massachusetts, forms a rural village and historic hamlet within the Town of Freetown along the eastern uplands bordering Middleboro in central Bristol County, developing from the proprietary lots of the 1659–1660 Freemen's Purchase as an agricultural outlier with Braley, Chace, and Mason family cemeteries marking early clusters. Named for its eastern position relative to Assonet Village, East Freetown sustained dispersed farms, sawmills, and Quanapoag No. IX burying ground amid Profile Rock's shadow, its agrarian persistence contrasting Freetown's northern mills while embedding records in town-wide Freetown clerks' volumes tracing "eastern lot kin" across Earl, Hathaway, and Brightman lineages.

Freemen's Eastern Lots, Quanapoag Cemeteries, and Farm Outliers

Prior to dense settlement, East Freetown's wooded uplands formed Wampanoag extensions of Assonet with conjectured planting grounds tied to Profile Rock trails, divided among eastern proprietary lots like No. IX (Quanapoag, Slab Bridge), No. X (Braley), No. XI (Mason's), and No. XIII (Furnace) settled by Ralph Earl descendants, Henry Brightman, and John Hathaway heirs post-1683 incorporation. Private cemeteries—Braley's East/West, Chace, Dr. Braley—preserve 18th-century markers for farm kin, with Slab Bridge mill serving isolated steads.

Genealogists access this via reconstructed Freetown proprietors' books (originals lost), town vitals from 1686 noting eastern earmarks, and cemetery surveys, Native echoes in lot boundaries.

Slab Bridge Mills, Dairy Farms, and Rural Continuity

East Freetown's 19th-century economy emphasized dairy, orchards, and small sawmills at Slab Bridge, with Braley/Noquochoke operations and private grounds documenting kin amid Civil War musters; Find A Grave listings track abandoned sites like East Freetown Cemetery.

These yielded tax valuations, overseers' bonds, and church rolls capturing enduring farm clusters.

Genealogical Resources and Strategies

Vital repositories:

- Freetown Town Clerk (3 North Main St., Assonet): Original births, marriages, deaths 1683–1840 (family lists), 1841–1930 Massachusetts Archives; eastern farm continuity.
- Published compilations: "Vital Records of Freetown, 1686–1795"; Ballou's "History of Freetown" with eastern lot sketches (Quanapoag, Braley).
- Freetown Historical Society: Cemetery listings (to 1996, incl. private/abandoned), censuses, and eastern farm files.
- Regional aids: FamilySearch wikis, Find A Grave for Braley/Chace surveys.

East Freetown's upland chronicle—from Freemen's lots and Slab mills to Braley stones—provides genealogists farm sources. Clerks' lists, cemetery transcripts, and society files unveil "eastern kin" spanning Earls, Brightmans, and Mason steadholders across Freetown's fringe.

East Taunton

East Taunton, Massachusetts, comprises a rural village and historic hamlet within the Town of Taunton along the eastern fringes bordering Raynham in northeastern Bristol County, emerging from the Taunton North Purchase's eastern outlots as an agricultural extension with Reed, Caswell, and Hall family farms clustered around East and Bay Roads. Developing post-1731 Raynham separation as Taunton's remote eastern precinct with small mills on the Three Mile River and the East Taunton Fire District (1871), the neighborhood sustained dispersed steadings, tanneries, and the Congregational East Parish (1802) amid Leonard forge influence, its farm-centric trajectory—from Wampanoag Cohannet trails through proprietary divisions to dairy persistence—embeds records in Taunton town volumes tracing "eastern stead kin" across Reed-Hall lineages.

Cohannet Eastern Outlots, East Parish, and Reed Farms

Prior to dense settlement, East Taunton's uplands formed Wampanoag Cohannet fringes with trails paralleling Three Mile River tied to Taunton River systems, divided among North Purchase grantees like Oliver Reed (arr. 1660s) whose descendants farmed linear lots by 1700s; the East Parish Congregational (Church Green extension) formalized 1802 with Rev. Isaac Safford amid Raynham separation debates. Private cemeteries and fire district records mark kin clusters.

Genealogists access this via Taunton proprietors' books, East Parish registers, and town vitals noting earmarks, Native echoes in boundary deeds.

Tanneries, Dairy Farms, and Fire District Continuity

East Taunton's 19th-century economy blended agriculture—dairy, orchards—with Three Mile tanneries and small sawmills, evolving into the 1871 East Taunton Fire District serving steadholders; Civil War musters from Reed-Caswell kin documented service.

These yielded tax rolls, parish rolls, and fire records capturing multi-generational farmers.

Genealogical Resources and Strategies

Vital repositories:

- Taunton City Clerk: Original births, marriages, deaths encompassing East Taunton; East Parish abstracts from 1802.
- Published compilations: Emery's "History of Taunton" with eastern farm sketches (Reed, Hall).
- Old Colony History Museum: Manuscripts, East Parish files, and cemetery surveys for stead grounds.
- Regional aids: FamilySearch wikis for Raynham overlaps, Bristol probate/deeds.

East Taunton's outlot chronicle—from Cohannet trails and Reed plats to fire district dairies—provides genealogists farm sources. Clerks' ledgers, parish admissions, and museum files unveil "North Purchase kin" spanning Olivers, Caswells, and Safford parishioners across eastern heirs.

Fall River Station

Fall River Station, Massachusetts, designates the historic railroad neighborhood and vicinity of the Fall River MBTA Commuter Rail station (opened 1845, rebuilt 1891 by Bradford Gilbert, modernized 2024 for South Coast Rail) within central Fall River, serving as a transportation nexus amid the city's 19th-century textile boom along the Quequechan River. Emerging from Freetown/Tiverton lands as the eastern terminus of the Fall River Railroad connecting to Old Colony lines, the station area clustered boardinghouses, rail yards, and immigrant tenements supporting mill workers commuting from Taunton and Boston, its rail-centric trajectory—from 1840s boat trains to 1958 passenger decline and 2025 revival—embeds records in Fall River city volumes tracing "depot kin" across Durfee-Borden rail laborers.

Quequechan Terminus, Boat Trains, and Pearce Street Yards

Prior to station construction, the area formed Freetown's southern falls with early sawmills (Benjamin Church 1690); Fall River Railroad's 1845 terminus at Central Street tunnel spurred Pearce Street yards and Bowenville station (1867), evolving to granite Richardsonian Romanesque depot (1891) handling 2,000–3,000 daily riders amid Fall River Line steamers from New York. Irish/French Canadian boarding clusters documented chain migration near tracks.

Genealogists access this via Fall River city directories (1845+), ward censuses noting rail occupations, and passenger manifests; Native echoes absent in urban plats.

Commuter Yards, Decline, and Rail Revival

Fall River Station's peak featured Old Colony expansions (Newport line 1864), trolley connections, and WWII freight before 1958 passenger end: 2020s reconstruction revived service, sustaining neighborhood tenements with Borden/Durfee kin in muster rolls and naturalizations.

These yielded employee lists, draft registrations, and church rolls capturing multi-generational brakemen.

Genealogical Resources and Strategies

Vital repositories:

- Fall River City Clerk: Post-1803 births, marriages, deaths near station wards; strong rail-era continuity.
- Published compilations: City directories with depot addresses, ward maps, ethnic parish abstracts.
- Fall River Historical Society/Public Library: Rail manifests, Pearce Street photos, labor files.
- Regional aids: FamilySearch wikis for Old Colony overlaps, Bristol probate.

Fall River Station's rail chronicle—from Quequechan trains and Pearce yards to commuter revival—provides genealogists transport sources. Clerks' ledgers, directory pages, and society trunks unveil "depot kin" spanning Irish loaders, Durfee engineers, and Borden commuters along Quequechan lines.

Five Corners

Five Corners, Massachusetts, designates a rural crossroads village and historic neighborhood within the Town of Rehoboth in northeastern Bristol County, emerging from the "Original Rehoboth" proprietary divisions as a 17th-century intersection of five colonial roads (Bay Road, Homestead Avenue, and spurs) serving as a Wampanoag trail junction and early English farm hub named for its pentagonal layout. Developing amid Newman Congregational outliers with scattered homesteads, taverns, and small mills by the 18th century, Five Corners anchored dispersed steadings for Peck, Perry, and Carpenter kin, its simple trajectory—from Seacunck paths through King Philip's War refugees to agrarian persistence—embeds records in Rehoboth town volumes tracing "crossroad kin" across covenant signers.

Seacunck Crossroads, Newman Outliers, and Perry Homesteads

Prior to dense settlement, Five Corners' junction formed Rehoboth's northern Wampanoag trail nexus linking Seacunck Plain to Swansea ferries, divided among 1644 covenant proprietors like William Sabin and James Peck whose heirs farmed linear lots by 1670s; postwar garrisons sheltered Carpenter-Perry families amid Newman church admissions, with simple markers in adjacent private grounds.

Genealogists access this via Rehoboth proprietors' books from 1645, town vitals noting earmarks at crossroads, and church rolls, Native paths in boundary deeds.

Tavern Hamlets, Farm Clusters, and Road Persistence

Five Corners' 18th–19th-century role featured way taverns for Boston-Providence travelers, small sawmills, and Perry-Carpenter steadings sustained by town meetings; Civil War musters from junction kin documented service without industrialization.

These yielded overseers' bonds, earmark lists, and parish rolls capturing multi-generational wayfarers.

Genealogical Resources and Strategies

Vital repositories:

- Rehoboth Town Clerk: Original births, marriages, deaths from 1643 encompassing crossroads; strong proprietary continuity.

- Published compilations: "Vital Records of Rehoboth" integrating town books and private grounds.

- Rehoboth Historical Association: Manuscripts, junction plats, tavern licenses, cemetery surveys.

- Regional aids: FamilySearch wikis for Swansea overlaps, Bristol probate/deeds.

Five Corners' junction chronicle—from Seacunck trails and garrison crossroads to Perry taverns—provides genealogists way sources. Clerks' volumes, covenant rolls, and association files unveil "pentagon kin" spanning Sabins, Pecks, and Carpenter steadholders across Rehoboth lanes.

Flint Village

Flint Village, Massachusetts, comprises a densely settled industrial neighborhood and historic mill district within the City of Fall River along the eastern banks of the Quequechan River, emerging in the 1870s around the Flint Mills complex (incorporated 1872, rebuilt 1883 after fire) named for President John D. Flint amid the city's textile ascendancy. Extending from County Street to the river and northward from Alden Street, Flint Village clustered brick tenements, boardinghouses, and company stores housing Irish, French Canadian, and Portuguese operatives feeding the Flint Mills' cotton production, its factory-centric path—from Freetown farmlands through 1880s mill expansions to labor enclaves—embeds records in Fall River city volumes tracing "spindle kin" across Flint-Borden mill hands.

Quequechan East Mills, Flint Reconstruction, and Tenement Clusters

Prior to Flint tenure, the riverside formed Freetown's southern periphery with early sawmills within Tiverton bounds, acquired 1872 by John D. Flint and shareholders (Samuel C. Wrightington, Simeon Borden) for $500,000 capital yielding the original granite mill (300x94 ft., mansard tower) destroyed 1882 and rebuilt wider; 62 surrounding acres developed into operative housing amid Fall River Line rail access. Ethnic boarding documented chain migration patterns.

Genealogists access this via Fall River city directories (1870s+), ward censuses noting mill occupations, and parish registers (St. Michael/Notre Dame); Freetown echoes in pre-1862 deeds.

Mill Expansions, Labor Districts, and NRHP Legacy

Flint Village's growth included 1909 second mill/addition and detached granite office, sustained by rail yards before 1920s decline; National Register listing (1983) preserves complex amid surviving triple-deckers housing Tripp, Murphy, and Canadian lines through draft rolls.

These yielded payrolls, poor relief lists, and church baptisms capturing multi-generational weavers.

Genealogical Resources and Strategies

Vital repositories:

- Fall River City Clerk: Post-1803 births, marriages, deaths in Flint wards; strong textile continuity.
- Published compilations: City directories with mill addresses, ward maps, ethnic abstracts.
- Fall River Historical Society: Flint ledgers, tenement censuses, labor photos.
- Regional aids: FamilySearch for Freetown overlaps, Bristol probate.

Flint Village's riverside chronicle—from Flint granite and Quequechan looms to tenement districts—provides genealogists factory sources. Clerks' ledgers, directory pages, and society files unveil "mill kin" spanning John D. Flints, Borden shareholders, and Portuguese spinners along Alden waters.

Four Corners

Four Corners, Bristol County, Massachusetts: A Detailed Historical and Genealogical Overview

Four Corners, Massachusetts, marks a historic rural crossroads village within the Town of Rehoboth in northeastern Bristol County, formed at the pentagonal intersection of Bay Road, Homestead Avenue, and three minor spurs serving as a key junction in the "Original Rehoboth" proprietary layout from the 1640s. Named for its distinctive five-way configuration linking Seacunck Plain to Swansea ferries and Taunton trails, Four Corners anchored dispersed farmsteads, early taverns, and town meeting outliers for Peck, Perry, and Sabin kin amid Newman Congregational influence, its simple wayfaring role—from Wampanoag path nexus through King Philip's War refugees to 19th-century stage stops—embeds records in Rehoboth town volumes tracing "junction kin" across covenant proprietors.

Rehoboth Junction, Postwar Taverns, and Perry Steadings

Prior to European roads, Four Corners' site formed a Wampanoag trail crossroads connecting interior planting grounds to coastal paths, surveyed within 1641 Seacunck purchase and divided among Newman followers like James Peck and William Sabin whose heirs established linear farms by 1670s; postwar garrisons sheltered Perry-Carpenter families, with a mid-18th-century tavern hosting Boston-Providence travelers near private burying grounds.

Genealogists access this via Rehoboth proprietors' books (1645+), town vitals noting earmarks at the corners, and church admissions, Native trails in boundary markers.

Stage Stops, Farm Hamlets, and Road Continuity

Four Corners' 18th–19th-century function emphasized taverns for stagecoaches, small blacksmith shops, and Perry steadings sustained by town pounds and muster fields; Civil War service from junction kin appears in regimental rolls without mills or commerce.

This yielded way taxes, overseers' lists, and parish rolls capturing multi-generational teamsters.

Genealogical Resources and Strategies

Vital repositories:

- Rehoboth Town Clerk: Original births, marriages, deaths from 1643 encompassing crossroads steadings; proprietary fragments strong.

- Published compilations: "Vital Records of Rehoboth" integrating town books and corner grounds.

- Rehoboth Historical Association: Manuscripts, junction sketches, tavern deeds, cemetery surveys.

- Regional aids: FamilySearch wikis for Swansea/Taunton overlaps, Bristol probate/deeds.

Four Corners' pentagon chronicle—from Seacunck paths and garrison taverns to Perry stages—provides genealogists crossroads sources. Clerks' volumes, earmark rolls, and association files unveil "way kin" spanning Pecks, Sabins, and Carpenter junction holders across Rehoboth radials.

Globe Village

Globe Village, Massachusetts, designates a densely populated historic mill neighborhood and village within the City of Fall River in southeastern Bristol County, originating from the 1811 Globe Manufactory (Col. Joseph Durfee's cotton spinning mill at Cook Pond outlet) and expanding as the city's southernmost textile district amid 19th-century boundary disputes with Tiverton RI. Centered around Globe Street, Spring Street, and Laurel Lake with tenements, boardinghouses, and print works (Globe Print Works 1829–1839), Globe Village housed Irish, French Canadian, and Portuguese operatives feeding the Quequechan's southern falls, its factory-centric path—from Freetown farmlands through Durfee's pioneering mill to labor enclaves—embeds records in Fall River city volumes tracing "cotton kin" across Borden-Durfee mill hands.

Cook Pond Outlet, Durfee Manufactory, and Print Works

Prior to textile dominance, Globe Village's pond and streams formed Freetown's southern periphery with early sawmills within Tiverton bounds until 1824 boundary settlement; Col. Joseph Durfee (Battle of Freetown hero) established the 1811 Globe Manufactory (first Fall River cotton mill), succeeded by Oliver Chace's 1813 reorganization and Riverton Print Works (1835), yielding operative tenements amid Laurel Lake mills. Ethnic boarding documented famine-era migration.

Genealogists access this via Fall River city directories (1810s+), ward censuses noting print occupations, and parish registers (St. Roch); Freetown echoes in pre-1803 deeds.

Tenement Districts, Labor Expansion, and Urban Assimilation

Globe Village's growth included Laurel Lake Mills and Bay State Print Works expansions, sustained by rail before 1920s decline; surviving triple-deckers preserve Tripp, Borden, and immigrant lines through draft rolls.

These yielded payrolls, poor lists, and church baptisms capturing multi-generational printers.

Genealogical Resources and Strategies

Vital repositories:

- Fall River City Clerk: Post-1803 births, marriages, deaths in Globe wards; strong cotton continuity.
- Published compilations: City directories with village addresses, ward maps, ethnic abstracts.
- Fall River Historical Society: Globe ledgers, tenement censuses, Durfee files.
- Regional aids: FamilySearch for Freetown/Tiverton overlaps, Bristol probate.

Globe Village's pond chronicle—from Durfee spindles and Laurel looms to tenement districts—provides genealogists factory sources. Clerks' ledgers, directory pages, and society trunks unveil "print kin" spanning Durfees, Bordens, and Irish operatives along Cook waters.

Gushee Pond

Gushee Pond, Massachusetts, refers to a rural pondside neighborhood and historic farm cluster within the Town of Raynham in northeastern Bristol County, named for the prominent Gushee family among the town's 1731 founding proprietors and situated along the pond's wooded shores amid Taunton's eastern precinct. Emerging from the Cohannet ironworks vicinity with Wampanoag trails converging on the pond for fishing and fowling, Gushee Pond anchored dispersed steadings of the Gushee, Hall, and Leonard kin supporting subsistence agriculture and small mills, its pond-centric trajectory—from Native lifeways through proprietary lots to private library legacy—embeds records in Raynham town volumes tracing "pond kin" across Washburn-Gushee lineages.

Cohannet Pond Trails, Gushee Proprietors, and Fowling Grounds

Prior to English settlement, Gushee Pond's margins formed Wampanoag Cohannet gathering sites with trails to Titicut and Plymouth noted in indigenous lore, allocated among 1726 petition signers including the Gushees whose heirs farmed linear lots by 1731 incorporation; the pond supplied fish/fowl for Leonard ironworkers, with private Gushee homesteads marking family continuity.

Genealogists access this via Taunton/Raynham proprietors' books, town vitals noting pond earmarks, and church admissions, Native paths in boundary surveys.

Subsistence Farms, Private Library, and Pond Persistence

Gushee Pond's 19th-century role featured family farms, small mills, and the private Gushee Library (est. 1872) sustaining literacy amid dairy operations; Civil War service from pond kin documented in muster rolls without industrialization.

These yielded tax valuations, library catalogs, and parish rolls capturing multi-generational fowlers.

Genealogical Resources and Strategies
Vital repositories:

- Raynham Town Clerk: Original births, marriages, deaths from 1731 encompassing pond families; precinct continuity strong.

- Published compilations: Congregational records with Gushee sketches; Sanford's "History of Raynham."

- Raynham Historical Society: Manuscripts, pond plats, library files, cemetery surveys.

- Regional aids: FamilySearch wikis for Taunton overlaps, Bristol probate/deeds.

Gushee Pond's watery chronicle—from Cohannet trails and fowling reeds to Gushee stacks—provides genealogists pond sources. Clerks' ledgers, proprietor rolls, and society files unveil "forge kin" spanning Halls, Leonards, and library heirs along Raynham waters.

Highlands

Highlands, Massachusetts, comprises a residential neighborhood and historic residential district within the City of Fall River in southeastern Bristol County, developing in the late 19th century on elevated terrain east of the Quequechan River as an upscale suburb for mill owners, managers, and professionals amid the city's textile prosperity. Extending from Rock Street to President Avenue with Victorian homes and granite churches, the Highlands offered respite from crowded mill villages like Flint and Globe, attracting Borden and Durfee kin through Prospect Hill Cemetery (1855) and St. Roch's parish (1871), its elevated trajectory—from Tiverton farmlands through post-Civil War subdivisions to streetcar enclaves—embeds records in Fall River city volumes tracing "hill kin" across managerial lines.

Quequechan Heights, Victorian Subdivisions, and St. Roch Parish
Prior to suburban growth, the Highlands' slopes formed Tiverton's eastern uplands with scattered farms acquired post-1812 boundary settlement, subdivided 1870s–1890s yielding Queen Anne and Stick Style homes for textile elites; St. Roch Catholic Church (French Canadian, 1871) and Prospect Hill Cemetery anchored spiritual life amid boarding school conversions.

Genealogists access this via Fall River city directories (1870s+), ward censuses noting professional occupations, and parish registers; Tiverton echoes in pre-1803 deeds.

Streetcar Heights, Cemetery Clusters, and Managerial Persistence

Highlands' expansion featured electric trolleys connecting to downtown mills, sustaining elite residences before 1920s assimilation: Prospect Hill interments document Borden-Durfee kin through lot ownership.

These yielded tax valuations, school rolls, and church baptisms capturing multi-generational managers.

Genealogical Resources and Strategies

Vital repositories:

- Fall River City Clerk: Post-1803 births, marriages, deaths in Highlands wards; strong suburban continuity.

- Published compilations: City directories with hill addresses, Prospect Hill surveys.

- Fall River Historical Society: Subdivision plats, St. Roch files, cemetery lot records.

- Regional aids: FamilySearch for Tiverton overlaps, Bristol probate.

Highlands' slope chronicle—from Tiverton plats and Roch spires to Prospect elites—provides genealogists suburb sources. Clerks' ledgers, directory pages, and society files unveil "manager kin" spanning Bordens, Durfees, and French overseers along Quequechan heights.

Hixville

Highlands, Massachusetts, forms an elevated residential neighborhood and historic suburb within Fall River along the eastern slopes above the Quequechan River, developing post-Civil War from Tiverton farmlands into a Victorian enclave for mill managers and professionals with Prospect Hill Cemetery (1853) and St. Roch parish (1871). Named for its commanding heights overlooking the city's textile core, the Highlands clustered Queen Anne homes and granite churches from Rock to President Streets, attracting Borden-Durfee kin via streetcar access, its upscale trajectory—from boundary farmlands through 1870s subdivisions to elite persistence—embeds records in Fall River city volumes tracing "hill kin" across managerial lines.

Tiverton Heights, Prospect Cemetery, and St. Roch Enclave

Prior to suburbanization, Highlands' slopes lay within Tiverton's eastern uplands acquired post-1812 settlement, subdivided 1870s yielding elite residences around Prospect Hill Cemetery (Borden family tombs) and St. Roch Catholic Church serving French Canadian elites; boarding schools and physicians' homes documented professional kin.

Genealogists access this via Fall River directories (1870s+), ward censuses noting occupations, and parish registers; Tiverton deeds pre-1803.

Streetcar Suburbs, Elite Persistence, and Hill Legacy

Highlands' growth featured trolleys to mills, sustaining managerial homes before assimilation; Prospect interments track Durfee-Borden lots through ownership.

These yielded tax rolls, school lists, and baptisms capturing multi-generational overseers.

Genealogical Resources and Strategies

Vital repositories:

- Fall River City Clerk: Post-1803 births, marriages, deaths in Highlands wards.
- Published compilations: Directories with hill addresses, Prospect surveys.
- Fall River Historical Society: Plats, St. Roch files, cemetery records.
- Regional aids: FamilySearch for Tiverton, Bristol probate.

Highlands' height chronicle—from Tiverton slopes and Roch spires to Prospect elites—provides suburb sources. Clerks' ledgers, directory pages, and society files unveil "manager kin" spanning Bordens, Durfees, and French professionals along Quequechan crests.

Hixville

Hixville, Massachusetts, constitutes a historic rural village and Census-Designated Place within the Town of Dartmouth along the inland eastern fringe of Bristol County, centered on the 1781 Congregational Meetinghouse founded by Rev. Daniel Hix and encompassing the Hixville Village Historic District with farmsteads, crossroads commerce, and mill privileges from Old Dartmouth's proprietary divisions. Named for the Hix family whose parsonage and 35 daughter congregations radiated influence, Hixville anchored agricultural outliers amid maritime necks with saltworks, tanneries, and small sawmills serving New Bedford trade, its ecclesiastical trajectory—from Wampanoag interior paths through postwar Quaker farms to 19th-century village persistence—embeds records in Dartmouth town volumes tracing "meetinghouse kin" across Hix-Akin lineages.

Interior Dartmouth, Hix Meetinghouse, and Parsonage Farms

Prior to Hix tenure, Hixville's brooks and uplands formed Wampanoag inland extensions within 1652 Dartmouth purchase, with postwar proprietors dividing tracts among Akins, Tabers, and Howlands yielding isolated farms by 1700s; Rev. Daniel Hix's 1781 church on Hixville Road formalized the nucleus with parsonage, school, and 35 satellite congregations, anchoring spiritual life amid saltworks on adjacent ponds.

Genealogists access this via Old Dartmouth proprietors' books, Dartmouth vitals pre-1850 noting Hix baptisms, and church admissions, Native paths in boundary deeds.

Saltworks, Crossroads Commerce, and Rural Nucleus

Hixville's 19th-century economy featured small mills, tanneries, and stores at village crossroads, sustained by New Bedford trolleys without industrialization; private cemeteries document multi-generational Hix-Akin kin.

These yielded overseers' bonds, school rolls, and parish registers capturing farm clusters.

Genealogical Resources and Strategies

Vital repositories:

- Dartmouth Town Clerk: Original births, marriages, deaths from 1664 encompassing Hixville; strong church continuity.

- Published compilations: "Vital Records of Dartmouth to 1850" integrating meetinghouse abstracts and village grounds.

- Dartmouth Historical & Arts Society: Manuscripts, Hix parsonage files, district surveys.

- Regional aids: FamilySearch wikis for Old Dartmouth overlaps, Bristol probate/deeds.

Hixville's brookside chronicle—from postwar tracts and Hix pulpits to crossroads saltworks—provides genealogists village sources. Proprietors' plats, church rolls, and society files unveil "parsonage kin" spanning Daniels, Akins, and 35-congregation heirs across Dartmouth interiors.

Holbrook Village

Holbrook Village, Massachusetts, originally the southern precinct of Braintree in Bristol County before annexation to Norfolk County—constituted the historic core of what became the Town of Holbrook, incorporated February 29, 1872, from East Randolph lands amid shoe manufactory expansion and Old Colony Railroad division. Emerging from 1710 British colonial farms with Native Cochato precedents, Holbrook Village anchored cottage shoemaking that industrialized during the Civil War, yielding Union Cemetery (54th Massachusetts burials) and Holbrook Square Historic District with Gothic Revival town hall (1878), Winthrop Church (1880), and fire station post-1877 blaze. Its shoe-centric path—from Braintree outlots through Randolph schisms to leap-year independence—preserves Randolph-derived records tracing "East Parish kin" across Holbrook-Thayer lineages.

Braintree South Farms, East Parish Schism, and Shoe Cottages

Prior to separation, Holbrook Village's uplands formed southern Braintree (Bristol Co.) steadings with Wampanoag Cochato sites noted 1634, divided among Thayer, Holbrook, and Bass proprietors by 1710 yielding linear farms; 1818 Second Randolph Church (East Parish) formalized the nucleus amid cupola disputes sparking 1871 independence petition, with Elisha N. Holbrook funding town hall/library. Civil War boot factories shifted home production to Stetson Hall shops.

Genealogists access this via Braintree/Randolph proprietors' books, East Parish registers pre-1872, and vital abstracts; county shifts complicate Bristol/Norfolk deeds.

Holbrook Square, Factory Boom, and Suburban Transition

Holbrook Village's post-incorporation core featured shoe factories along rail tracks, Gothic Hall/church/fire station arrayed on Mary Wales Holbrook Park, evolving via WWII service to commuter suburbia; Union Cemetery preserves 54th Regiment markers amid Thayer kin.

These yielded payrolls, parish rolls, and tax lists capturing multi-generational cordwainers.

Genealogical Resources and Strategies

Vital repositories:

- Holbrook Town Clerk: Post-1872 births, marriages, deaths; pre-1872 in Randolph/Braintree (Bristol Co. origins).

- Published compilations: "Holbrook and Allied Families"; vital records blending East Parish abstracts and Union surveys.

- Holbrook Historical Society/Library: Manuscripts, shoe ledgers, square plats, 54th bios.

- Regional aids: FamilySearch wikis for Braintree/Randolph overlaps, Norfolk/Bristol probate transitions.

Holbrook Village's leap-year chronicle—from Cochato farms and parish vents to shoe squares—provides genealogists boundary sources. Clerks' ledgers, church admissions, and society files unveil "East Randolph kin" spanning Thayers, Holbrooks, and 54th bootmakers across county lines.

Horbine

Hornbine, Massachusetts, designates a rural historic district and school/church hamlet within the Town of Rehoboth in northeastern Bristol County, coalescing around the one-room Hornbine School (c.1840s–1862, NRHP 1983) and adjacent Hornbine Baptist Church (1753) at the intersection of Hornbine Road and Baker Street amid "Old Rehoboth" proprietary farmsteads. Named possibly for local hornbeam trees or phonetic Wampanoag place names, Hornbine anchored District #10 education from 1847–1937 with 49 peak pupils, serving scattered Peck, Medberry, and Wheaton kin through Greek Revival architecture and stone-walled fields, its scholastic trajectory—from Seacunck outliers through Baptist separations to museum preservation—embeds records in Rehoboth town volumes tracing "district kin" across Newman covenant descendants.

Rehoboth District #10, Hornbine Schoolhouse, and Baptist Meeting

Prior to school construction, Hornbine's crossroads formed Rehoboth's southern agricultural fringe with Wampanoag trails noted in 1643 Seacunck purchase, divided among proprietary lots yielding postwar Baptist farms by 1753 when the vernacular Hornbine Baptist Church formalized separations from Newman Congregational; the Greek Revival schoolhouse (clapboard, gable roof, 1923 rear extension) educated district children until consolidation, now museum with outhouse.

Genealogists access this via Rehoboth town books (1645+), district school committees, and Baptist admissions noting pupil rosters, Native echoes in lot surveys.

One-Room Persistence, Consolidation, and Museum Revival

Hornbine's 19th–20th-century role emphasized farm children walking stone walls to school, sustained until 1937 closure and 1968 restoration for Rehoboth's 325th anniversary by Hornbine School Association (summer openings); church continuity documents Wheaton-Peck kin.

These yielded attendance rolls, committee minutes, and parish registers capturing multi-generational scholars.

Genealogical Resources and Strategies

Vital repositories:

- Rehoboth Town Clerk: Original births, marriages, deaths from 1643 encompassing Hornbine district; school fragments strong.

- Published compilations: "Vital Records of Rehoboth" integrating Baptist abstracts and school grounds.

- Hornbine School Association/Rehoboth Historical: Pupil lists, church rolls, museum artifacts, cemetery surveys.

- Regional aids: FamilySearch wikis for Swansea overlaps, Bristol probate/deeds.

Hornbine's district chronicle—from Seacunck farms and Baptist gables to one-room slates—provides genealogists school sources. Clerks' volumes, pupil rolls, and museum files unveil "district kin" spanning Medberrys, Wheaton scholars, and Peck parishioners across Rehoboth fields.

Hortonville

Hortonville, Massachusetts, forms a linear rural village and historic district (NRHP 1990) within northern Swansea along Cole's River near the Rehoboth border, settled in the 18th century by Hale, Martin, and Eddy families amid the 1677 Shawomet Purchase's northern farms with 19th-century saw, grist, and cotton mills powering early industry. Named for local Horton proprietors or phonetic Native terms, Hortonville clustered around Locust Street with schoolhouse, post office (1885), Universalist chapel, and Swansea Cotton Manufacturing Co. (1806–1836, Oliver Chace), its riverine path—from Wampanoag Cole's River fisheries through postwar rebuilds to mill decline—preserves Swansea town records tracing "northern farm kin" across Eddy-Slade lineages.

Shawomet Northern Farms, Cole's River Mills, and Chace Cotton

Prior to mill era, Hortonville's river bends sustained Wampanoag fisheries tied to Wannamoisett trails, yielding postwar Swansea steadings by Eddys and Martins; Nathaniel/Dexter Wheeler and Oliver Chace established cotton spinning (1806) with dam remnants, employing farm daughters until 1836 fire ended operations amid grist/saw persistence. Universalist Society and school formalized community life.

Genealogists access this via Swansea proprietors' books, town vitals noting mill births, and church abstracts, Native echoes in river quitclaims.

Post Office Clusters, Mill Remnants, and Agricultural Reversion

Hortonville's late 19th-century nodes included stores, post office, and chapel at Locust/Hortonville Road serving rail-distant farms, reverting post-mill closure to residential agriculture with family grounds like Peleg Slade Burying Ground documenting kin.

These yielded census occupations, school rolls, and overseers' bonds capturing multi-generational millers.

Genealogical Resources and Strategies

Vital repositories:

- Swansea Town Clerk: Post-1668 births, marriages, deaths encompassing Hortonville; pre-1790 overlaps strong.

- Published compilations: "Vital Records of Swansea to 1850" integrating Universalist abstracts and river cemeteries.

- Swansea Historical Society: District surveys, Chace mill files, Hale-Eddy homestead plats.

- Regional aids: FamilySearch wikis for Rehoboth overlaps, Bristol probate/deeds.

Hortonville's river chronicle—from Shawomet wheels and Chace dams to Locust posts—provides genealogists mill sources. Clerks' ledgers, family grounds, and society files unveil "cotton kin" spanning Wheelers, Eddys, and Slade northerners along Cole's heirs.

Kingmans Corner

Kingsman Corner, Massachusetts, refers to a rural crossroads hamlet within the Town of Mansfield in northern Bristol County, emerging at the intersection of Bay Road and Kingman Street amid the Taunton North Purchase's northern outlots as a farm and tavern nexus named for the locally prominent Kingman family of early proprietors and Revolutionary soldiers. Situated near Cobbler's Corner and Rumford River mills, Kingsman Corner anchored dispersed steadings with small shops, forges, and stagecoach stops serving Norton and Attleboro travelers, its wayfaring trajectory—from Wampanoag Cohannet trails through proprietary divisions to 19th-century persistence—embeds records in Mansfield town volumes tracing "bay road kin" across Kingman-Leonard lineages.

North Purchase Crossroads, Kingman Taverns, and Bay Road Junction

Prior to dense settlement, Kingsman Corner's junction formed Wampanoag trails paralleling Bay Road (Captain Miles Standish survey 1640), allocated among Taunton grantees like Henry Kingman (arr. 1652 Weymouth, Norton settler) whose heirs farmed linear lots by 1700s; Revolutionary taverns hosted musters amid Norton North Precinct debates, with private grounds marking family continuity.

Genealogists access this via Taunton/Mansfield proprietors' books, town vitals noting earmarks at corners, and church admissions, Native paths in boundary deeds.

Stage Stops, Forge Hamlets, and Road Continuity

Kingsman Corner's 19th-century role featured family forges, stores, and Bay Road taverns for Boston-Providence coaches, sustained by rail proximity without industrialization; Civil War service from Kingman kin documented in rolls.

This yielded way taxes, overseers' lists, and parish rolls capturing multi-generational teamsters.

Genealogical Resources and Strategies

Vital repositories:

- Mansfield Town Clerk: Original births, marriages, deaths from 1775 encompassing corners; Norton overlaps strong.

- Published compilations: "Vital Records of Mansfield to 1849" integrating corner grounds.

- Mansfield Historical Society: Manuscripts, Kingman tavern files, Bay Road plats.

- Regional aids: FamilySearch wikis for Norton/Taunton, Bristol probate/deeds.

Kingsman Corner's junction chronicle—from Cohannet paths and Kingman signs to Bay stages—provides genealogists way sources. Clerks' ledgers, earmark rolls, and society files unveil "purchase kin" spanning Henrys, Leonards, and corner steadholders across Mansfield radials.

Myricks

Myricks, Massachusetts, designates a rural railroad village and historic hamlet straddling the Berkley-Freetown line in central Bristol County, originating c.1713 as a farming settlement named for the Myrick (Merrick) family among early Dighton/Taunton proprietors and transforming post-1870 with the Old Colony Railroad station serving dispersed steadings along the Assonet River. Emerging amid Freemen's Purchase fringes with small mills and the Myricks post office (1875), the neighborhood anchored agricultural outliers for Myrick, Reed, and Hathaway kin through one-room schools and Methodist prayer meetings, its rail-farm trajectory—from Wampanoag Assonet paths through postwar rebuilds to commuter persistence—embeds records in Berkley town volumes tracing "station kin" across Merrick lineages.

Assonet Farms, Myrick Steadings, and Railroad Junction

Prior to rail arrival, Myricks' riverine farms formed Wampanoag extensions within Freetown/Dighton tracts divided among Myricks (from 1636 Merrick arrivals) yielding linear homesteads by 1700s; the 1870 Old Colony station formalized the nucleus with platform, store, and Methodist outpost amid small sawmills, employing farm sons as brakemen. Private grounds preserved family markers.

Genealogists access this via Berkley/Freetown proprietors' books, town vitals noting station births, and Merrick compilations, Native echoes in river deeds.

Station Commerce, Farm Persistence, and Commuter Transition

Myricks' late 19th-century economy blended dairy/orchards with rail freight and post office serving Fall River/Taunton commuters, sustained without heavy industry; Civil War service from Myrick-Reed kin documented in rolls.

These yielded census occupations, school rolls, and Methodist registers capturing multi-generational farmers.

Genealogical Resources and Strategies

Vital repositories:

- Berkley Town Clerk: Post-1734 births, marriages, deaths encompassing Myricks; Freetown overlaps pre-1760.

- Published compilations: "Genealogy of the Merrick-Myrick Family, 1636–1902"; Berkley vitals integrating station cemeteries.

- Berkley Historical Society: Manuscripts, Myrick homestead files, rail timetables.

- Regional aids: FamilySearch wikis for Dighton/Freetown, Bristol probate/deeds.

Myricks' station chronicle—from Assonet steadings and Merrick plats to rail platforms—provides genealogists farm sources. Clerks' ledgers, family genealogies, and society files unveil "Myrick kin" spanning 1713 settlers and station heirs across Berkley lanes.

North Attleboro Center

North Attleboro Center, Massachusetts, serves as the historic civic core and principal Census-Designated Place (CDP) of North Attleborough town in northern Bristol County, evolving from John Woodcock's 1669 North Purchase tavern settlement within "Old Attleborough" into a jewelry manufacturing hub post-1887 town separation from Attleboro. Anchoring the 1694 Rehoboth North Purchase with the First Congregational meetinghouse (1714), North Attleboro Center developed around Washington Street with Richardsonian Romanesque town hall (1891), Richards Memorial Library, and brass/jewelry factories like Evans & Richardson amid French Canadian immigration, its commercial trajectory—from Wampanoag Ten Mile River farms through King Philip's War garrison to rail-era commons—preserves Attleborough-derived records tracing "garrison kin" across Woodcock-Richardson lineages.

North Purchase Tavern, Woodcock Garrison, and Congregational Nucleus

Prior to separation, North Attleboro Center's riverside formed Rehoboth North Purchase with John Woodcock's 1669 farm/tavern (attacked 1675 King Philip's War) yielding the 1714 First Congregational meetinghouse amid Dodgeville and Hebronville mill outliers; 1780 French brass forge birthed jewelry trade employing Capron and Sweet kin.

Genealogists access this via Rehoboth/Attleborough proprietors' books, church admissions from 1714, and vital abstracts, Native attacks in garrison rosters.

Jewelry Commons, Rail Districts, and Civic Persistence

North Attleboro Center's 19th-century commerce clustered brass/jewelry factories, rail depots, and ethnic parishes (St. Stephen's Catholic 1880) around the common, sustained by Dodgeville mills; Civil War service filled rolls from center kin.

These yielded directories, parish rolls, and overseers' bonds capturing multi-occupational jewelers.

Genealogical Resources and Strategies

Vital repositories:

- North Attleborough Town Clerk: Post-1887 births, marriages, deaths centered on common families; pre-1887 in Attleboro.

- Published compilations: "Vital Records of Attleborough to 1849"; St. Stephen's baptisms/marriages (1880–1986).

- North Attleborough Historical Society/Public Library: Manuscripts, Richards Room censuses, jewelry ledgers, Woodcock files.

- Regional aids: FamilySearch wikis for Rehoboth/Attleboro overlaps, Bristol probate/deeds.

North Attleboro Center's garrison chronicle—from Woodcock signs and Ten Mile forges to jewelry commons—provides genealogists commercial sources. Clerks' ledgers, church rolls, and society stacks unveil "North Purchase kin" spanning Caprons, Sweets, and Richardson casters along Washington mains.

North Raynham

North Raynham Village, Massachusetts, constitutes the northern rail hamlet and historic outlier within the Town of Raynham in northeastern Bristol County, developing post-1840s around the Boston-New Bedford Railroad station amid Taunton North Purchase farms with King, Williams, and Stetson family steadings powering small mills on the Three Mile River. Named for its position above Raynham Center, the village anchored dispersed agriculture and cottage industries—tack factories, straw hats, and Williams box mills—with the North Raynham post office (1848) and Methodist outpost serving Leonard forge descendants, its rail-farm trajectory—from Cohannet trails through proprietary divisions to commuter persistence—embeds records in Raynham town volumes tracing "northern stead kin" across King-Williams lineages.

North Purchase Outlots, Rail Station, and Williams Boxes

Prior to rail arrival, North Raynham's uplands formed Taunton's northern fringes with Wampanoag paths paralleling Three Mile River, divided among 1726 petitioners like John King (1680 arrival) whose heirs farmed linear lots by 1731; the 1840s Old Colony depot formalized the nucleus with platform, store, and Richmond Street box mill (fish crates for New Bedford), employing farm kin amid tack production.

Genealogists access this via Taunton/Raynham proprietors' books, town vitals noting station births, and King family compilations, Native echoes in river deeds.

Tack Factories, Straw Hats, and Commuter Farms

North Raynham Village's 19th-century economy blended orchards/dairy with rail freight and small manufactories, sustained by Taunton trolleys; Civil War service from Williams-Stetson kin filled rolls without dense settlement.

These yielded census occupations, school rolls, and Methodist registers capturing multi-generational boxmakers.

Genealogical Resources and Strategies

Vital repositories:

- Raynham Town Clerk: Original births, marriages, deaths from 1731 encompassing North Raynham; precinct continuity strong.

- Published compilations: "Genealogy of the Kings of Raynham, 1680+"; vital records integrating station cemeteries.

- Raynham Historical Society: Manuscripts, rail timetables, Williams mill files.

- Regional aids: FamilySearch wikis for Taunton overlaps, Bristol probate/deeds.

North Raynham Village's rail chronicle—from King outlots and Three Mile boxes to station orchards—provides genealogists farm sources. Clerks' ledgers, family genealogies, and society files unveil "purchase kin" spanning Johns, Williams, and Stetson commuters across Raynham northlands.

North Rehoboth Village, Massachusetts, represents a rural northern outlier and farm hamlet within the Town of Rehoboth along the Massachusetts-Rhode Island border in northeastern Bristol County, emerging from the expansive "Old Rehoboth" proprietary lots post-1812 Seekonk separation as a dispersed cluster of Millard, Perry, and Wheaton steadings near modern Route 44. Named for its position above Rehoboth Center amid Seacunck Plain extensions, North Rehoboth anchored agricultural fringes with small mills on the Palmer River and Baptist prayer meetings serving Newman Congregational outliers, its peripheral trajectory—from Wampanoag northern trails through King Philip's War refugees to 19th-century farm persistence—embeds records in Rehoboth town volumes tracing "plain kin" across Millard-Perry lineages.

Seacunck Northern Fringe, Millard Farms, and Palmer Mills

Prior to dense settlement, North Rehoboth's plains formed Rehoboth's remote Wampanoag contact zones with trails to Providence, divided among 1643 proprietors like John Millard Sr. (d.1688/9) whose descendants (Robert, Samuel) farmed linear lots by 1670s; postwar refugees rebuilt amid Baptist separations, with Palmer River gristmills employing Perry kin.

Genealogists access this via Rehoboth proprietors' books (1645+), town vitals noting northern earmarks, and Millard compilations, Native paths in boundary deeds.

Baptist Outposts, Farm Clusters, and Border Persistence

North Rehoboth Village's 18th–19th-century economy emphasized dairy/orchards and small mills, sustained by Seekonk commerce without rail; Civil War musters from Millard-Wheaton kin documented service.

These yielded tax rolls, overseers' bonds, and church rolls capturing multi-generational plain dwellers.

Genealogical Resources and Strategies

Vital repositories:

- Rehoboth Town Clerk (148 Peck St.): Original births, marriages, deaths from 1643 encompassing northern farms; proprietary fragments strong.
- Published compilations: "Vital Records of Rehoboth" integrating Millard abstracts and plain cemeteries.
- Rehoboth Historical Association: Manuscripts, northern plats, Perry-Millard files.
- Regional aids: FamilySearch wikis for Seekonk/RI overlaps, Bristol probate/deeds.

North Rehoboth Village's plain chronicle—from Millard lots and Palmer wheels to border farms—provides genealogists fringe sources. Clerks' volumes, proprietor rolls, and association files unveil "northern kin" spanning Johns, Roberts, and Perry refugees across Rehoboth frontiers.

North Taunton

North Taunton Village, Bristol County, Massachusetts, functions as a northern industrial hamlet within the City of Taunton, originating from 19th-century mill expansions along the Mill River amid proprietary divisions from George Hall's 1639 Cohannet settlement, with Hall, Leonard, and Williams descendants powering iron forges and cotton factories. Positioned above Taunton Center near modern Route 140, the village clustered around North Main Street with the Hopewell and Whittenton mills employing Irish and French-Canadian laborers, alongside Baptist meetinghouses serving forge kin, its manufacturing arc—from Wampanoag river sites through King Philip's War bloomeries to rail-era persistence—preserves Taunton records tracing "northern forge kin" across Hall-Leonard lineages.

Cohannet Northern Forges, Hall Proprietors, and Mill River Bloomeries

Early North Taunton's riverbanks formed Taunton North Purchase outliers with George Hall (d.1669) lots extending to iron works founded 1652 by Leonards, where sons John and Joseph Hall clerked amid 1675 garrison rebuilds; 19th-century dams powered Hopewell cotton (1820s) and Whittenton print works.

Genealogists access this via Taunton proprietors' books, vital records noting forge births, and Hall compilations, Native sachem deeds in land grants.

Cotton Mills, Irish Parishes, and Rail Districts

North Taunton Village's economy fused iron/cotton with rail depots by 1870s, sustained by Fall River trolleys; Civil War rolls document Leonard-Hall service from mill families.

These produced directories, overseers' bonds, and parish registers capturing multi-occupational operatives.

Genealogical Resources and Strategies

Vital repositories:

- Taunton City Clerk: Original births, marriages, deaths from 1638 covering northern mills; continuity robust.

- Published compilations: "Vital Records of Taunton to 1850" with Hall abstracts and mill cemeteries.

- Taunton Historical Society: Manuscripts, forge ledgers, Leonard files.

- Regional aids: FamilySearch wikis for Bristol probate/deeds.

North Taunton Village's forge chronicle—from Hall bloomeries and Mill River dams to cotton districts—provides genealogists industrial sources. Clerks' ledgers, vital volumes, and society archives unveil "Cohannet kin" spanning Georges, Johns, and Leonard casters across Taunton northlands.

Oakland

Oakland, Massachusetts, operates as a small residential neighborhood and historic farm enclave within the town of Norton in central Bristol County, tracing origins to 19th-century subdivisions of Wampanoag-derived pasture lands from the 1669 North Purchase amid Norton Academy outliers and Wheaton College fringes. Positioned north of Norton Center near modern Route 140 and the Rumford River, Oakland clustered modest homesteads with Baptist prayer groups and small dairy operations serving academy students, its peripheral farm arc—from proprietary divisions through King Philip's War remnants to commuter persistence—integrates into Norton town records tracing "pasture kin" across Richardson-Horton lineages from earlier Attleborough overlaps.

North Purchase Pastures, Academy Outliers, and Rumford Farms

North of Norton village, Oakland's uplands formed extended lots from 1669 proprietors like Benjamin Richardson whose heirs grazed amid 1675 garrison rebuilds: 1830s academy growth spurred farm supplies with Horton kin milking for dormitories by Rumford mills.

Genealogists access this via Norton proprietors' books, town vitals noting pasture earmarks, and academy ledgers, Native trails in boundary surveys.

Dairy Clusters, Baptist Groups, and Commuter Lots

Oakland's 19th–20th-century focus blended orchards/dairy with Providence trolleys, without dense industry; Civil War rolls capture Richardson-Horton service from farm families.

These produced census farms, school rolls, and church admissions for multi-generational yeomen.

Genealogical Resources and Strategies

Vital repositories:

- Norton Town Clerk: Original births, marriages, deaths from 1711 covering Oakland farms; academy continuity aids.

- Published compilations: "Vital Records of Norton" with pasture abstracts and hill cemeteries.

- Norton Historical Society: Manuscripts, farm plats, Richardson files.

- Regional aids: FamilySearch wikis for Bristol probate/deeds, Wheaton overlaps.

Oakland's pasture chronicle—from Richardson lots and Rumford barns to academy suppliers—provides genealogists farm sources. Clerks' volumes, vital rolls, and society stacks unveil "North Purchase kin" spanning Benjamins, Hortons, and dairy hands across Norton enclaves.

Padanaram

Padanaram, Massachusetts, forms a historic maritime village in South Dartmouth within the Town of Dartmouth along Buzzards Bay in southeastern Bristol County, originating from 1652 Wampanoag land purchases at the Apponagansett River mouth where early houses burned during King Philip's War (1675) and British raids (1778), later renamed by Laban Thatcher around 1817 after the biblical Padanaram for his wharf, shipyard, saltworks, and magnesia factory serving Akin and Rotch kin. Evolving from Ponaganset garrison sites through shipbuilding and whaling to a National Register Historic District (1985) with Elm-to-Bridge Street homes, Padanaram's waterfront arc—from Native trails and Russell stockade to Federal-era commerce—preserves Dartmouth records tracing "river mouth kin" across Thatcher-Akin lineages.

Apponagansett Garrisons, Laban Wharves, and Saltworks

Pre-naming, Padanaram's shores hosted Russell Garrison defenses amid 1675 fires, with Captain John Akin (Church's company) resettling post-war; 1805 arrival of Laban Thatcher from Harwich built infrastructure employing Slocum and Howland descendants by 1828 deeds.

Genealogists access this via Dartmouth proprietors' books, town vitals noting river births, and Thatcher abstracts, Wampanoag deeds in Plymouth grants.

Shipyards, Whaling Outfits, and Resort Shift

Padanaram Village's 19th-century economy thrived on shipbuilding, salt evaporation, and New Bedford provisioning, sustained by street railways; Civil War service from Akin-Rotch kin filled maritime rolls.

These yielded directories, private Bibles (Howland, Wing), and gravestone records (G.R.20-22) capturing multi-occupational mariners.

Genealogical Resources and Strategies

Vital repositories:

- Dartmouth Town Clerk: Original births, marriages, deaths from 1652 covering Padanaram; garrison continuity strong.

- Published compilations: "Vital Records of Dartmouth to 1850" with 40+ private records (P.R.1-40) and Apponagansett cemeteries.

- Dartmouth Historical Society/Old Dartmouth Society: Manuscripts, ship logs, Akin-Thatcher files.

- Regional aids: FamilySearch catalogs for Bristol probate/deeds, New Bedford overlaps.

Padanaram's river chronicle—from Ponaganset stockades and Thatcher wharves to historic homes—provides genealogists maritime sources. Clerks' volumes, Bible registers, and society stacks unveil "Apponagansett kin" spanning Johns, Labans, and Rotch shipwrights across Dartmouth shores.

Peck's Corner

Peck's Corner, Massachusetts, stands as a rural historic crossroads and farm hamlet in northwestern Rehoboth within the Town of Rehoboth in northeastern Bristol County, named for the early Peck family settlers from the 1638 Diligent voyage including Joseph Peck and descendants like Nicholas and Hezekiah who held proprietary lots amid Wampanoag trails near the Seekonk border. Emerging from "Old Rehoboth" divisions post-King Philip's War with garrison rebuilds, Peck's Corner clustered homesteads of Peck, Bosworth, and Carder kin around modern Summer Street with Baptist prayer meetings and small orchards, its peripheral farm trajectory—from 1643 proprietary allotments through 18th-century persistence to modern quiet—embeds records in Rehoboth town volumes tracing "crossroads kin" across Peck-Bosworth lineages.

Proprietary Crossroads, Peck Garrisons, and Bosworth Lots

Early Peck's Corner formed at Rehoboth's northwest fringes with Joseph Peck (1587–1663) heirs like Nicholas Peck (d.1710) farming linear lots divided 1645, defended by family garrisons during 1675 attacks; Hezekiah Peck Jr. (b.1695) married Elizabeth Carder amid postwar expansions employing Bosworth descendants.

Genealogists access this via Rehoboth proprietors' books, town vitals noting corner earmarks, and Peck compilations, Native paths in boundary deeds.

Baptist Prayer Sites, Orchard Farms, and Border Yeomen

Peck's Corner's 18th–19th-century economy centered on dairy/orchards and Seekonk commerce without industry, sustained by Swansea paths; Revolutionary and Civil War rolls capture Peck-Carder service from farm kin.

These yielded tax lists, overseers' bonds, and church admissions for multi-generational husbandmen.

Genealogical Resources and Strategies

Vital repositories:

- Rehoboth Town Clerk: Original births, marriages, deaths from 1643 covering Peck's Corner; proprietary continuity strong.

- Published compilations: "Vital Records of Rehoboth" with Peck abstracts and corner cemeteries.

- Rehoboth Historical Association: Manuscripts, plats, Peck-Bosworth files.

- Regional aids: FamilySearch wikis for Seekonk/RI overlaps, Bristol probate/deeds.

Peck's Corner's crossroads chronicle—from Joseph allotments and garrison homes to orchard steadings—provides genealogists farm sources. Clerks' volumes, proprietor rolls, and association files unveil "Diligent kin" spanning Nicholases, Hezekiahs, and Bosworth tillers across Rehoboth corners.

Perry's Corner

Perry's Corner, Massachusetts, emerges as a rural historic crossroads and farm hamlet likely within Rehoboth or Swansea in northeastern Bristol County, named for early Perry family settlers from the 1650s including Ezra Perry (d.1688/9) and descendants like Benjamin Perry who built steadings amid Wampanoag trails near the Seekonk Plains border. Developing from "Old Rehoboth" proprietary divisions post-King Philip's War with garrison defenses, Perry's Corner clustered homesteads of Perry, Reed, and Walker kin around period roads with Baptist outposts and orchards, its peripheral trajectory—from 1645 land allotments through 18th-century farm persistence to quiet modern use—embeds records in Rehoboth or Swansea town volumes tracing "plains kin" across Perry-Reed lineages.

Proprietary Crossroads, Perry Garrisons, and Reed Lots

Early Perry's Corner lay at Rehoboth's fringes with Ezra Perry heirs farming linear lots post-1676 rebuilds after Native attacks; Benjamin Perry (b. ca.1665) constructed homes by 1690s employing Reed descendants amid Swansea paths.

Genealogists access this via Rehoboth/Swansea proprietors' books, town vitals noting corner earmarks, and Perry abstracts, Native boundaries in deeds.

Baptist Sites, Orchard Farms, and Border Husbandry

Perry's Corner's 18th–19th-century focus centered on dairy/orchards without industry, sustained by Seekonk commerce; Revolutionary rolls capture Perry-Walker service from farm families.

These produced tax lists, church admissions, and overseers' bonds for multi-generational yeomen.

Genealogical Resources and Strategies

Vital repositories:

- Rehoboth/Swansea Town Clerks: Original births, marriages, deaths from 1640s covering corners; proprietary strong.
- Published compilations: "Vital Records of Rehoboth/Swansea" with Perry cemeteries.
- Local Historical Associations: Manuscripts, plats, Perry-Reed files.
- Regional aids: FamilySearch wikis for Bristol probate/deeds.

Perry's Corner's plains chronicle—from Ezra allotments and garrison homes to orchard crossroads—provides genealogists farm sources. Clerks' volumes, proprietor rolls, and association files unveil "Perry kin" spanning Benjamins, Ezras, and Reed tillers across Bristol corners.

Perryville

Perryville, Massachusetts, designates a rural mill hamlet in southern Rehoboth within the Town of Rehoboth in northeastern Bristol County, originating from late-1600s Butterworth Falls where John Butterworth built a sawmill before 1690, later acquired by Ezra Perry and descendants who shifted operations from Ash Street sites to produce wood bobbins for Pawtucket cotton factories amid Wampanoag Palmer River branches. Positioned at Danforth Street and Perryville Road near modern Route 118, Perryville clustered mill tenements with Perry, Cole, and Bliss kin around the dam, its industrial-farm trajectory—from proprietary saws through King Philip's War rebuilds to 19th-century flood litigation—preserves Rehoboth records tracing "falls kin" across Perry-Butterworth lineages.

Butterworth Falls, Perry Sawmills, and Bobbin Works

Early Perryville formed at Palmer River west branch with Butterworth's pre-1690 sawmill on large farm tracts, bought out by Ezra Perry (early 1800s) from Aaron Cole partnership; 1820 spring flood sparked neighbor suits, prompting site shifts while bobbins fed Slater mills.

Genealogists access this via Rehoboth proprietors' books, town vitals noting falls births, and Perry abstracts, Native echoes in river deeds.

Grist Dams, Flood Suits, and Farm-Mill Hybrids

Perryville's 19th-century economy blended saw/grist milling with orchards, sustained by Seekonk paths without rail; Civil War rolls from Perry-Cole kin documented service.

These yielded litigation bonds, mill censuses, and church rolls capturing multi-occupational turners.

Genealogical Resources and Strategies

Vital repositories:

- Rehoboth Town Clerk: Original births, marriages, deaths from 1643 covering Perryville dams; mill continuity aids.

- Published compilations: "Vital Records of Rehoboth" integrating Perry cemeteries and falls abstracts.

- Rehoboth Historical Association: Manuscripts, dam plats, Butterworth-Perry files.

- Regional aids: FamilySearch wikis for Bristol probate/deeds, Swansea overlaps.

Perryville's falls chronicle—from Butterworth saws and Perry bobbins to dam tenements—provides genealogists mill sources. Clerks' volumes, proprietor rolls, and association stacks unveil "Palmer kin" spanning Ezras, Johns, and Cole turners across Rehoboth waters.

Plesantfield

Pleasantfield, Massachusetts, serves as a quiet residential neighborhood and former farm hamlet within the town of Raynham in northeastern Bristol County, developing from 18th-century divisions of Taunton North Purchase lands amid Cohannet Wampanoag territories with early Jones, Leonard, and Dean family steadings near the Nemasket River fringes. Positioned east of Raynham Center along modern Route 104 toward Bridgewater, Pleasantfield anchored dispersed agriculture with small orchards and Baptist prayer meetings serving iron forge outliers, its rural trajectory—from proprietary allotments through King Philip's War rebuilds to 20th-century commuter persistence—integrates into Raynham town records tracing "northern plain kin" across Jones-Dean lineages.

Cohannet Plain Lots, Jones Steadings, and Nemasket Farms

Prior to Raynham incorporation (1731), Pleasantfield's uplands formed Taunton's eastern extensions with 1726 precinct petitioners like Abraham Jones farming linear lots post-1675 garrison defenses; Dean kin expanded orchards by 1750s amid forge supplies from Fowling Pond.

Genealogists access this via Taunton/Raynham proprietors' books, town vitals noting plain earmarks, and Jones abstracts, Native paths in river deeds.

Orchard Clusters, Baptist Outposts, and Trolley Farms

Pleasantfield's 19th-century economy emphasized dairy/orchards with Taunton trolleys, without dense mills; Civil War rolls from Dean-Leonard kin documented service.

These yielded census farms, school rolls, and church admissions capturing multi-generational yeomen.

Genealogical Resources and Strategies

Vital repositories:

- Raynham Town Clerk: Original births, marriages, deaths from 1731 covering Pleasantfield; Taunton continuity strong.
- Published compilations: "History of Raynham" with plain abstracts and hill cemeteries.
- Raynham Historical Society: Manuscripts, plats, Jones-Dean files.
- Regional aids: FamilySearch wikis for Taunton/Bridgewater overlaps, Bristol probate/deeds.

Pleasantfield's plain chronicle—from Jones allotments and Nemasket barns to orchard homes—provides genealogists farm sources. Clerks' volumes, vital rolls, and society stacks unveil "Cohannet kin" spanning Abrahams, Deans, and Leonard tillers across Raynham fields.

Pleasant Street

Pleasant Street, Massachusetts, functions as a historic rural thoroughfare and farm corridor traversing central Raynham within the Town of Raynham in northeastern Bristol County, laid out amid 18th-century Taunton North Purchase divisions from Cohannet Wampanoag lands with early Williams, Hall, and Leonard steadings paralleling Nemasket River tributaries. Extending from Raynham Center eastward toward Bridgewater along modern alignments, Pleasant Street anchored linear agriculture with Baptist meeting outposts and small forges serving Taunton ironworks outliers, its linear trajectory—from proprietary paths through King Philip's War remnants to trolley-era persistence—embeds records in Raynham town volumes tracing "plain corridor kin" across Williams-Hall lineages.

North Purchase Paths, Williams Corridors, and Nemasket Lanes

Prior to formal roads, Pleasant Street's trace formed Taunton's eastern bridle paths with 1726 petitioners like Samuel Williams farming adjacent lots post-1675 rebuilds; Hall kin expanded steadings by 1750s amid Fowling Pond supplies.

Genealogists access this via Taunton/Raynham proprietors' books, town vitals noting street earmarks, and Williams abstracts, Native trails in boundary surveys.

Forge Outliers, Trolley Farms, and Linear Yeomen

Pleasant Street's 19th-century economy blended dairy/orchards with Taunton streetcars, without clustered mills; Civil War rolls from Hall-Leonard kin filled service lists.

These yielded census occupations, school rolls, and church admissions capturing multi-generational farmers.

Genealogical Resources and Strategies

Vital repositories:

- Raynham Town Clerk: Original births, marriages, deaths from 1731 covering Pleasant Street farms; continuity robust.

- Published compilations: "History of Raynham" integrating street abstracts and plain cemeteries.

- Raynham Historical Society: Manuscripts, road plats, Williams-Hall files.

- Regional aids: FamilySearch wikis for Taunton/Bridgewater overlaps, Bristol probate/deeds.

Pleasant Street's corridor chronicle—from Williams paths and Nemasket lanes to trolley steadings—provides genealogists linear sources. Clerks' ledgers, vital rolls, and society stacks unveil "Cohannet kin" spanning Samuels, Halls, and Leonard tillers across Raynham thoroughfares.

Pottersville

Pottersville, Massachusetts, designates the central pottery manufacturing village within the Town of Somerset in eastern Bristol County, emerging around 1815 from Swansea proprietary lands at the Egypt trading outpost where Chace Pottery and subsequent stoneware/earthenware kilns employed Buffinton, Slade, and Reed kin amid Lee River clay deposits from Wampanoag coastal sites. Positioned along County Street between Somerset Village and Brayton Point near modern Route 6, Pottersville clustered kilns, tenements, and Baptist meetinghouses serving potter families, its industrial trajectory—from 1701 church sites through 19th-century production peaks to bungalow persistence—preserves Somerset records tracing "clay kin" across Chace-Buffinton lineages.

Egypt Trading Outpost, Chace Kilns, and Stoneware Clusters

Prior to naming, Pottersville's clay flats hosted Swansea's Egypt section with 1701 meetinghouse remnants, formalized by 1815 Chace operations producing redware for Fall River provisioning; Buffinton heirs expanded kilns by 1830s amid Slade capital.

Genealogists access this via Swansea/Somerset proprietors' books, town vitals noting kiln births, and Chace abstracts, Native pottery in coastal deeds.

Earthenware Peaks, Bungalow Districts, and Pottery Decline

Pottersville's 19th-century economy dominated stoneware supply to central New England, sustained by Providence ferries without rail; Civil War rolls from Reed-Slade kin documented service.

These yielded directories, overseers' bonds, and gravestone records capturing multi-occupational throwers.

Genealogical Resources and Strategies

Vital repositories:

- Somerset Town Clerk: Original births, marriages, deaths from 1790 covering Pottersville kilns; Swansea continuity strong.

- Published compilations: "History of Somerset" with pottery abstracts and central cemeteries.

- Somerset Historical Society: Manuscripts, kiln plats, Chace-Buffinton files.

- Regional aids: FamilySearch wikis for Swansea/Fall River overlaps, Bristol probate/deeds.

Pottersville's clay chronicle—from Egypt outposts and Chace wheels to bungalow kilns—provides genealogists industrial sources. Clerks' volumes, vital rolls, and society stacks unveil "Swansea kin" spanning Chaunceys, Buffintons, and Slade potters across Somerset centers.

Prattville

Prattville, Massachusetts, constitutes a historic northwestern neighborhood within the City of Chelsea along the Mystic River fringes in Suffolk County (historic Norfolk extensions), originating from 1695 inheritance by Thomas Pratt of the 390-acre Ireland-Way Farm where generations of Pratts farmed, hosted George Washington during the 1775 Siege of Boston, and built tide mills amid Pawtucket Native paths. Centered around Washington Avenue with Prattville School (1897), Whidden Hospital site, and remnants of the 1660 Ireland-Way-Pratt House (demolished 1954), Prattville evolved from agricultural enclave through Revolutionary barracks to dense urban persistence, its farm-to-city trajectory—from 1641 native footpaths through colonial estates to civic legacy—preserves Chelsea records tracing "Pratt kin" across Thomas-Hermon lineages.

Ireland-Way Farm, Thomas Mills, and Washington Barracks

Early Prattville formed on Mill Hill (62 ft.) with Thomas Pratt (1699–1780) constructing 1734 tide-water grist mill powering Chelsea outskirts, defended as Colonel Gerrish barracks 1775–76; Caleb Pratt IV (1847 house) piped water from Charlestown by 1868 amid elm plantings.

Genealogists access this via Chelsea proprietors' books, vital records noting farm births, and Pratt compilations, Native paths in early surveys.

Prattville School, Park Developments, and Civic Houses

Prattville's 19th-century landscape blended farms with Hermon Pratt's (mayor) advocacy yielding 1897 school, Washington Park (1885), and Ladies' Relief Society (1885/1897); Civil War service from Pratt kin filled rolls.

These yielded directories, school rolls, and gravestone records capturing multi-occupational builders.

Genealogical Resources and Strategies

Vital repositories:

- Chelsea City Clerk: Original births, marriages, deaths from 1629 covering Prattville farms; continuity robust.

- Published compilations: "Slade Genealogy" and Pratt histories with mill abstracts and hill cemeteries.

- Chelsea Historical Society: Manuscripts, farm plats, Thomas-Hermon files.

- Regional aids: FamilySearch wikis for Suffolk probate/deeds, Revere overlaps.

Prattville's hill chronicle—from Ireland-Way estates and tide mills to Washington parks—provides genealogists farm sources. Clerks' volumes, vital rolls, and society stacks unveil "Pawtucket kin" spanning Thomases, Calebs, and Hermon Pratts across Chelsea enclaves.

Ramblewood

Ramblewood, Massachusetts, comprises a modern residential apartment complex and late-20th-century suburban development within the town of Holbrook in central Norfolk County (historic extensions from Plymouth/Braintree purchases), constructed amid post-WWII housing expansions on former pasture lands tracing to 1645 Braintree North Precinct divisions with early Hayward, Thayer, and Wildes farmstead remnants near the Cochato River. Situated off Longmeadow Drive south of Route 37 between Braintree and Randolph, Ramblewood anchors commuter enclaves with 1–3-bedroom units serving Red Line and rail proximity, its suburban trajectory—from Wampanoag woodland trails through colonial grazing commons to 1970s garden apartments—integrates into Holbrook town records tracing "pasture kin" across Hayward-Thayer lineages.

Braintree North Pastures, Hayward Farms, and Cochato Lanes

Prior to development, Ramblewood's site formed Braintree outliers with Hayward proprietors farming linear lots post-1675 garrison rebuilds; Thayer kin expanded pastures by 1750s amid Randolph paths supplying Boston markets.

Genealogists access this via Braintree/Holbrook proprietors' books, town vitals noting pasture earmarks, and Hayward abstracts, Native trails in boundary deeds.

Commuter Apartments, Red Line Districts, and Suburban Clusters

Ramblewood's contemporary landscape features landscaped grounds with pool/clubhouse amenities, sustained by Routes 3/93/128 access; recent censuses capture diverse renters from regional kin.

These yield directories and school rolls for multi-generational commuters.

Genealogical Resources and Strategies

Vital repositories:

- Holbrook Town Clerk: Original births, marriages, deaths from 1872 covering Ramblewood sites; Braintree continuity strong.

- Published compilations: "Vital Records of Braintree" with pasture abstracts and hill cemeteries.

- Holbrook Historical Society: Manuscripts, plats, Hayward-Thayer files.

- Regional aids: FamilySearch wikis for Norfolk/Plymouth probate/deeds.

Ramblewood's pasture chronicle—from Hayward commons and Cochato barns to apartment homes—provides genealogists suburban sources. Clerks' volumes, vital rolls, and society stacks unveil "North Precinct kin" spanning Haywards, Thayers, and Wildes renters across Holbrook enclaves.

Rehoboth Village

Rehoboth Village, Massachusetts, anchors the historic civic core of the Town of Rehoboth in northeastern Bristol County, founded 1643 on Seacunck Plain after Rev. Samuel Newman's Weymouth group purchased 12-square-mile tract from Massasoit for wampum and coat, encompassing modern Rehoboth, Seekonk, East Providence, Barrington, and Pawtucket portions with early proprietors like John Brown, Edward Winslow, Anthony Perry, and Thomas Bliss dividing home lots amid Wampanoag trails. Centered at Anawan Rock and Palmer River with 1651 Newman meetinghouse (burned 1675), the village developed around County Road with Baptist separations (1690s), garrison defenses, and post-war rebuilds serving Perry, Reed, and Pierce kin, its proprietary trajectory—from 1641 scouting through King Philip's War refugees to 1812 Seekonk division—preserves town records tracing "Seacunck kin" across Newman-Perry lineages.

Seacunck Plain Purchase, Newman Meetinghouse, and Proprietors' Lots

Prior to war, Rehoboth Village's central plain hosted 1643 home lots with Rev. Newman's 1651 frame church, defended by 10 garrisons during 1675–76 attacks where Capt. Michael Pierce fell; postwar lots rebuilt by Perry-Millard heirs amid Baptist splits.

Genealogists access this via Rehoboth proprietors' books (1645+), town vitals from 1642, and Newman abstracts, sachem deeds in Plymouth grants.

Baptist Divisions, Pierce Garrisons, and Farm Nucleus

Rehoboth Village's 18th-century economy centered dairy/orchards with Swansea paths, sustained by Attleborough commerce; Revolutionary rolls from Reed-Bliss kin filled musters.

These yielded tax lists, church admissions (Newman/Palmer River), and overseers' bonds capturing multi-generational planters.

Genealogical Resources and Strategies

Vital repositories:

- Rehoboth Town Clerk (148 Peck St.): Original births, marriages, deaths from 1642; "Tan Book" (Arnold index) and directories 1896+.

- Published compilations: "Vital Records of Rehoboth, 1642-1896" with 40+ private records and central cemeteries.

- Carpenter Museum/Rehoboth Antiquarian Society: Manuscripts, Trim collection, Perry-Pierce files.

- Regional aids: FamilySearch wikis for Seekonk/Pawtucket overlaps, Bristol probate/deeds.

Rehoboth Village's plain chronicle—from Massasoit purchases and Newman pulpits to Baptist steadings—provides genealogists proprietary sources. Clerks' volumes, Arnold indexes, and museum stacks unveil "Old Rehoboth kin" spanning Anthonys, Michaels, and Bliss planters across Seacunck centers.

Sassaquin

Sassaquin, Massachusetts, marks a northern residential neighborhood and historic pond hamlet within the City of New Bedford in southeastern Bristol County, centered on Sassaquin Pond (also Myle's Pond) named for a Wampanoag sachem amid the 1652 Dartmouth Proprietors' Purchase tracts where early Russell and Tripp families farmed alongside Acushnet River outliers before whaling dominance. Positioned along Sassaquin Avenue north of downtown near Route 18/195 interchanges and the former Sassaquin Sanatorium (1910 tuberculosis facility), the area clustered recreational picnics, mills, and multi-ethnic tenements serving Wamsutta cotton operatives, its pondside trajectory—from Native fishing grounds through 19th-century sanatorium isolation to urban persistence—preserves New Bedford records tracing "pond kin" across Russell-Tripp lineages.

Dartmouth Pond Sites, Russell Farms, and Sachem Namesakes

Prior to city growth, Sassaquin's pond shores formed Dartmouth fringes with Joseph Russell III (1750 tryworks) steadings and open-air schools amid 1675 garrison echoes; 19th-century recreation drew buggies for swimming as mills emerged nearby.

Genealogists access this via Dartmouth/New Bedford proprietors' books, town vitals noting pond births, and Russell abstracts, sachem references in Plymouth deeds.

Sanatorium Isolation, Mill Tenements, and Highway Fragments

Sassaquin's 20th-century landscape featured the 1910–1960s Sassaquin Sanatorium (1924 admin building by Hammond) and Wamsutta mill housing for Portuguese/Irish kin, fragmented by I-195/Route 18 construction; recent censuses capture diverse residents.

These yielded patient rolls, mill directories, and gravestone records for multi-occupational laborers.

Genealogical Resources and Strategies

Vital repositories:

- New Bedford City Clerk: Original births, marriages, deaths from 1760 covering Sassaquin; Dartmouth continuity strong.

- Published compilations: "Vital Records of New Bedford/Dartmouth" with pond cemeteries and sanatorium abstracts.

- New Bedford Whaling Museum/Standard-Times Archives: Manuscripts, mill files, Russell-Tripp ledgers.

- Regional aids: FamilySearch wikis for Acushnet/Freetown overlaps, Bristol probate/deeds.

Sassaquin's pond chronicle—from sachem waters and Russell farms to sanatorium homes—provides genealogists residential sources. Clerks' volumes, vital rolls, and museum stacks unveil "Acushnet kin" spanning Josephs, Tripps, and operative hands across New Bedford northlands.

South Attleboro

South Attleboro, Massachusetts, comprises the southern industrial village and commercial district within the City of Attleboro in northern Bristol County, developing from 18th-century Rehoboth North Purchase fringes post-1694 incorporation where Capron, Sweet, and Richardson families farmed amid Ten Mile River meadows before jewelry manufactories clustered around Washington Street and Route 1A. Formerly known as Southgate with its own early telephone exchange, South Attleboro anchored brass rolling mills, watch chain factories (Everett & Stanley 1831), and ethnic tenements serving French Canadian operatives near Rhode Island borders, its manufacturing trajectory—from proprietary meadows through King Philip's War garrison outliers to interstate commerce—preserves Attleboro records tracing "southern mill kin" across Capron-Richardson lineages.

North Purchase Meadows, Capron Farms, and Ten Mile Forges

Prior to industry, South Attleboro's river flats formed Attleborough's southern extensions with Capron steadings divided 1694, defended by Sweet garrisons during 1676 attacks: 1780s brass forges birthed jewelry trade employing Richardson heirs.

Genealogists access this via Attleboro proprietors' books, town vitals noting meadow births, and Capron abstracts, Native paths in river deeds.

Jewelry Mills, Ethnic Districts, and Route 1 Commerce

South Attleboro's 19th-century economy dominated chain/die production with rail depots, sustained by Providence trolleys; Civil War rolls from Sweet-Richardson kin filled infantry lists.

These yielded directories, overseers' bonds, and parish registers capturing multi-occupational casters.

Genealogical Resources and Strategies

Vital repositories:

- Attleboro City Clerk: Original births, marriages, deaths from 1694 covering South Attleboro; Rehoboth continuity strong.

- Published compilations: "Vital Records of Attleborough to 1849" with mill cemeteries and southern abstracts.

- Attleboro Public Library/Historical Society: Manuscripts, jewelry ledgers, Capron-Sweet files.

- Regional aids: FamilySearch wikis for Rehoboth/Pawtucket overlaps, Bristol probate/deeds.

South Attleboro's meadow chronicle—from Capron lots and Ten Mile forges to chain districts—provides genealogists industrial sources. Clerks' volumes, vital rolls, and library stacks unveil "North Purchase kin" spanning Sweets, Richardsons, and operative hands across Attleboro southlands.

South Rehoboth

South Rehoboth, Massachusetts, represents a rural southern farm hamlet and proprietary outlier within the Town of Rehoboth in northeastern Bristol County, emerging from the 1643 Seacunck Plain purchase extensions along Palmer River southern branches where Carpenter, Bowen, and Walker families received linear lots amid Wampanoag coastal trails post-1675 King Philip's War garrison rebuilds. Positioned below Rehoboth Village near modern Route 118 and Swansea borders with Baptist prayer sites and small gristmills, South Rehoboth anchored dispersed agriculture serving Swansea commerce, its peripheral trajectory—from 1645 allotments through Revolutionary farm musters to 19th-century persistence—embeds records in Rehoboth town volumes tracing "southern plain kin" across Carpenter-Bowen lineages.

Seacunck Southern Lots, Carpenter Garrisons, and Palmer Branches

Early South Rehoboth's river fringes formed Rehoboth's southern proprietary divisions with William Carpenter (Gen. 2, d.1658/9) heirs farming amid 10 garrisons during Native attacks; Bowen descendants like Richard (1640 arrival) expanded steadings by 1700s employing Walker kin at grist sites.

Genealogists access this via Rehoboth proprietors' books, town vitals noting southern earmarks, Carpenter abstracts, sachem paths in Plymouth deeds.

Baptist Outposts, Grist Farms, and Swansea Borders

South Rehoboth's 18th–19th-century economy emphasized dairy/orchards and Swansea paths without dense settlement; Civil War rolls from Bowen-Walker kin documented service.

These yielded tax rolls, church admissions, and overseers' bonds capturing multi-generational planters.

Genealogical Resources and Strategies

Vital repositories:

- Rehoboth Town Clerk: Original births, marriages, deaths from 1642 covering South Rehoboth; proprietary continuity strong.

- Published compilations: "Vital Records of Rehoboth" with Carpenter cemeteries and southern abstracts.

- Rehoboth Antiquarian Society: Manuscripts, plats, Bowen-Carpenter files.

- Regional aids: FamilySearch wikis for Swansea/Pawtucket overlaps, Bristol probate/deeds.

South Rehoboth's plain chronicle—from Carpenter allotments and Palmer garrisons to border farms—provides genealogists fringe sources. Clerks' volumes, proprietor rolls, and society stacks unveil "Seacunck kin" spanning Williams, Richards, and Walker tillers across Rehoboth southlands.

Squawbetty

Squawbetty, Massachusetts, identifies a historic rural hill and farm enclave in eastern Taunton within the City of Taunton in northeastern Bristol County, named for a Wampanoag woman ("Squaw Betty") associated with local Native paths amid Cohannet proprietary divisions from 1639 purchases where Hall, Williams, and Leonard families grazed uplands near the Three Mile River before iron forge expansions. Positioned along modern West Street east of Taunton Center with period maps marking "Squawbetty Hill," the area anchored dispersed pastures with Baptist prayer outposts serving Cohannet outliers, its elevated trajectory—from sachem trails through King Philip's War remnants to 19th-century farm persistence—integrates into Taunton records tracing "hill kin" across Hall-Williams lineages.

Cohannet Hill Pastures, Hall Steadings, and Native Namesakes

Prior to naming, Squawbetty's rise formed Taunton's eastern fringes with George Hall (d.1669) heirs farming post-1675 garrison rebuilds; Williams kin expanded by 1700s amid Betty path traditions supplying forge hamlets.

Genealogists access this via Taunton proprietors' books, town vitals noting hill earmarks, and Hall abstracts, Wampanoag references in early surveys.

Pasture Clusters, Forge Supplies, and Trolley Farms

Squawbetty's 19th-century economy emphasized dairy/orchards with Fall River trolleys, without dense industry; Civil War rolls from Leonard-Williams kin documented service.

These yielded census farms, school rolls, and church admissions capturing multi-generational yeomen.

Genealogical Resources and Strategies

Vital repositories:

- Taunton City Clerk: Original births, marriages, deaths from 1638 covering Squawbetty hills; continuity robust.

- Published compilations: "Vital Records of Taunton to 1850" with hill abstracts and pasture cemeteries.
- Taunton Historical Society: Manuscripts, plats, Hall-Williams files.
- Regional aids: FamilySearch wikis for Bristol probate/deeds, Raynham overlaps.

Squawbetty's hill chronicle—from Native paths and Hall pastures to forge suppliers—provides genealogists elevated sources. Clerks' ledgers, vital volumes, and society archives unveil "Cohannet kin" spanning Georges, Williams, and Leonard grazers across Taunton uplands.

Steep Brook

Steep Brook, Massachusetts, designates a northern residential neighborhood and early farm hamlet within the City of Fall River in southeastern Bristol County, originating from late-1700s house clusters at North Main Street and Wilson Road junction amid Freetown proprietary outliers where Turner, Durfee, and Valentine families farmed near Quequechan River tributaries before cotton mill expansions. Positioned along Highland Avenue east of downtown with Steep Brook Corners marking the historic core, the area anchored dispersed homesteads with Friends' meeting outposts and ice ponds serving early industry, its brookside trajectory—from Pocasset Native displacements through King Philip's War remnants to 19th-century mill persistence—preserves Fall River records tracing "northern farm kin" across Turner-Durfee lineages.

Freetown Brook Farms, Turner Lots, and Valentine Houses

Prior to city incorporation, Steep Brook's slopes formed Freetown fringes with Joseph Turner (d. post-1671) heirs building houses 1780–1799 amid 1704 Pocasset reservations nearby; Durfee kin expanded by 1800 with burial grounds on Hood Street.

Genealogists access this via Freetown/Fall River proprietors' books, town vitals noting brook births, and Turner abstracts, Native lots in colony deeds.

Ice Ponds, Mill Supplies, and Ethnic Districts

Steep Brook's 19th-century economy blended orchards with cotton provisioning via streetcars, sustained by Portuguese/French immigration; Civil War rolls from Valentine-Durfee kin filled musters.

These yielded directories, school rolls, and gravestone records capturing multi-occupational laborers.

Genealogical Resources and Strategies

Vital repositories:

- Fall River City Clerk: Original births, marriages, deaths from 1803 covering Steep Brook; Freetown continuity strong.
- Published compilations: "Phillips History of Fall River" with brook abstracts and northern cemeteries.
- Fall River Historical Society: Manuscripts, plats, Turner-Durfee files.

- Regional aids: FamilySearch wikis for Freetown/Tiverton overlaps, Bristol probate/deeds.

Steep Brook's valley chronicle—from Turner houses and ice ponds to mill homes—provides genealogists farm sources. Clerks' volumes, vital rolls, and society stacks unveil "Pocasset kin" spanning Josephs, Durfees, and Valentine hands across Fall River northlands.

Titicut

Titicut, Massachusetts, constitutes a historic rural village and Wampanoag-derived hamlet straddling the Titicut River within the Town of Bridgewater in central Plymouth County, originating from 1649 Satucket land grants extending into Native settlement territories purchased from Massasoit and later Pompanuh where Edson, Byram, and Keith families established mills amid sachem villages before precinct formation. Positioned along modern Central Street and Route 106 with Titicut Parish Cemetery (1750 from James Thomas land), the area anchored dispersed farms, shipyards (early 19th century), and summer camps serving Edson-Leonard kin, its riverine trajectory—from prehistoric artifacts through King Philip's War displacements to conservation persistence—preserves Bridgewater records tracing "Satucket kin" across Edson-Byram lineages.

Satucket Purchases, Edson Mills, and Sachem Villages

Prior to precincts, Titicut's shores formed Bridgewater's southern extensions with 1650 house lots near Town River, confirmed 1685 by Governor Hinckley; Samuel Edson built early mills while Native James Thomas gifted cemetery land 1750 amid Byram expansions.

Genealogists access this via Bridgewater proprietors' books, town vitals noting river births, and Edson abstracts, Wampanoag deeds in Plymouth colony grants.

Shipyards, Parish Farms, and Camp Outliers

Titicut's 19th-century economy blended grist/shipbuilding with orchards, sustained by Taunton paths; Civil War rolls from Keith-Leonard kin documented service without dense industry.

These yielded tax rolls, parish admissions, and gravestone records capturing multi-generational millers.

Genealogical Resources and Strategies

Vital repositories:

- Bridgewater Town Clerk: Original births, marriages, deaths from 1656 covering Titicut; Satucket continuity strong.

- Published compilations: "History of Bridgewater" with parish abstracts and river cemeteries.

- Bridgewater Historical Society: Manuscripts, plats, Edson-Byram files.

- Regional aids: FamilySearch wikis for Middleborough/Taunton overlaps, Plymouth probate/deeds.

Titicut's river chronicle—from sachem sites and Edson wheels to parish farms—provides genealogists Native-adjacent sources. Clerks' volumes, proprietor rolls, and society stacks unveil "Old Colony kin" spanning Samuels, Jameses, and Leonard planters across Bridgewater waters.

Tracy Corner

Tracy Corner, Massachusetts, serves as a rural historic crossroads and farm hamlet within the Town of Raynham in northeastern Bristol County, named for early Tracy family settlers amid Taunton North Purchase divisions from Cohannet Wampanoag lands where Williams, Leonard, and Dean kin farmed linear lots near Nemasket River outliers before small mill expansions. Positioned at the intersection of modern routes paralleling Raynham Center with transitional Greek Revival/Italianate cottages, Tracy Corner anchored dispersed agriculture and Baptist prayer meetings serving forge outliers, its crossroads trajectory—from proprietary paths through King Philip's War remnants to 19th-century persistence—embeds records in Raynham town volumes tracing "northern plain kin" across Tracy-Williams lineages.

North Purchase Crossroads, Tracy Steadings, and Nemasket Lanes

Prior to naming, Tracy Corner's site formed Taunton's eastern bridle paths with 1726 petitioners like Tracy heirs farming post-1675 garrison rebuilds; Williams kin expanded orchards by 1750s amid Fowling Pond supplies.

Genealogists access this via Taunton/Raynham proprietors' books, town vitals noting corner earmarks, and Tracy abstracts, Native trails in boundary surveys.

Orchard Clusters, Forge Outposts, and Trolley Farms

Tracy Corner's 19th-century economy emphasized dairy/orchards with Taunton trolleys, featuring sidehall cottages without dense industry; Civil War rolls from Leonard-Dean kin documented service.

These yielded census occupations, school rolls, and church admissions capturing multi-generational yeomen.

Genealogical Resources and Strategies

Vital repositories:

- Raynham Town Clerk: Original births, marriages, deaths from 1731 covering Tracy Corner; Taunton continuity strong.
- Published compilations: "History of Raynham" with corner abstracts and plain cemeteries.
- Raynham Historical Society: Manuscripts, plats, Tracy-Williams files.
- Regional aids: FamilySearch wikis for Taunton/Bridgewater overlaps, Bristol probate/deeds.

Tracy Corner's crossroads chronicle—from proprietary lanes and Tracy barns to cottage farms—provides genealogists rural sources. Clerks' volumes, vital rolls, and society stacks unveil "Cohannet kin" spanning Tracys, Williams, and Leonard tillers across Raynham intersections.

Wade's Corner

Wade's Corner, Massachusetts, functions as a residential neighborhood and historic crossroads within the City of Taunton in northeastern Bristol County, named for early Wade family settlers amid Cohannet proprietary divisions from 1639 purchases where Hall, Leonard, and Williams kin farmed uplands near Three Mile River tributaries before small forge expansions. Positioned at the junction of modern Route 44 and Westville fringes west of Taunton Center with Greek Revival cottages, Wade's Corner anchored dispersed agriculture and Baptist prayer outposts serving ironworks outliers, its intersection trajectory—from Wampanoag paths through King Philip's War remnants to 19th-century trolley persistence—embeds records in Taunton volumes tracing "western plain kin" across Wade-Hall lineages.

Cohannet Crossroads, Wade Steadings, and Forge Lanes

Prior to naming, Wade's Corner formed Taunton's western bridle paths with Wade proprietors farming linear lots post-1675 garrison rebuilds; Hall kin expanded orchards by 1750s amid Cohannet supplies.

Genealogists access this via Taunton proprietors' books, town vitals noting corner earmarks, and Wade abstracts, Native trails in boundary surveys.

Orchard Clusters, Trolley Districts, and Westville Borders

Wade's Corner's 19th-century economy emphasized dairy/orchards with Fall River streetcars, without dense mills; Civil War rolls from Leonard-Williams kin documented service.

These yielded census farms, school rolls, and church admissions capturing multi-generational yeomen.

Genealogical Resources and Strategies

Vital repositories:

- Taunton City Clerk: Original births, marriages, deaths from 1638 covering Wade's Corner; continuity robust.

- Published compilations: "Vital Records of Taunton to 1850" with corner abstracts and western cemeteries.

- Taunton Historical Society: Manuscripts, plats, Wade-Hall files.

- Regional aids: FamilySearch wikis for Raynham/Berkley overlaps, Bristol probate/deeds.

Wade's Corner's crossroads chronicle—from proprietary lanes and Wade barns to trolley homes—provides genealogists rural sources. Clerks' volumes, vital rolls, and society stacks unveil "Cohannet kin" spanning Wades, Halls, and Leonard tillers across Taunton intersections.

Weir Village

Weir Village, Massachusetts, forms a historic riverfront industrial neighborhood within the City of Taunton in northeastern Bristol County, named for pre-colonial Wampanoag fishing weirs across the Taunton River where herring runs supported early Cohannet settlements before English proprietors like Hall and Leonard developed shipyards and copper mills amid 1639 land purchases. Positioned along Weir Street from Plain to Berkley streets near modern Riverfront Park with East Weir Cemetery (1797) and remnants of Weir Grammar School (1870), the village clustered tenements, stove foundries (Weir Stove Co. 1902), and rail junctions serving French Canadian and Irish operatives, its port trajectory—from Native fish traps through 19th-century Crockers' copper rolling to 20th-century persistence—preserves Taunton records tracing "river kin" across Hall-Leonard lineages.

Cohannet Weirs, Shipyards, and Copper Docks

Prior to naming, Weir Village's shores hosted Massasoit-era herring weirs with 1700s shipbuilding by Cobb captains; Crocker Brothers relocated Norton copper mills here by 1838 for Taunton Branch Railroad export, employing Leonard heirs amid tidewater docks.

Genealogists access this via Taunton proprietors' books, town vitals noting weir births, and Hall abstracts, Wampanoag references in Plymouth deeds.

Stove Foundries, Ethnic Districts, and Rail Hubs

Weir Village's 19th-century economy dominated silverware/stoves with F.B. Rogers factories and grain shipping, sustained by Fall River ferries; Civil War rolls from Irish-Leonard kin filled musters.

These yielded directories, parish registers, and gravestone records (East Weir) capturing multi-occupational founders.

Genealogical Resources and Strategies

Vital repositories:

- Taunton City Clerk: Original births, marriages, deaths from 1638 covering Weir Village; Cohannet continuity robust.

- Published compilations: "Vital Records of Taunton to 1850" with river cemeteries and weir abstracts.

- Taunton Historical Society: Manuscripts, Crockers' ledgers, Hall-Leonard files.

- Regional aids: FamilySearch wikis for Berkley/Somerset overlaps, Bristol probate/deeds.

Weir Village's river chronicle—from Wampanoag traps and Crocker docks to stove tenements—provides genealogists port sources. Clerks' volumes, vital rolls, and society stacks unveil "Cohannet kin" spanning Halls, Leonards, and operative hands across Taunton waters.

Westerville

Westerville, Massachusetts, designates a rural western farm hamlet and proprietary outlier within the Town of Raynham in northeastern Bristol County, emerging from 18th-century Taunton North Purchase uplands along Three Mile River heads where King, Stetson, and Williams families farmed linear lots amid Cohannet Wampanoag territories post-1731 town separation. Positioned west of Raynham Center near modern Route 24 corridors toward Taunton with Baptist prayer sites and dispersed orchards, Westerville anchored agricultural fringes supplying Leonard forge outliers, its upland trajectory—from 1726 precinct petitions through King Philip's War remnants to trolley-era persistence—embeds records in Raynham town volumes tracing "western plain kin" across King-Williams lineages.

North Purchase Uplands, King Steadings, and Forge Supplies

Prior to dense settlement, Westerville's hills formed Taunton's northwestern extensions with John King (1680 arrival) heirs grazing post-1675 garrison rebuilds; Stetson kin expanded by 1750s amid Williams tack mills paralleling Forge River ironworks.

Genealogists access this via Taunton/Raynham proprietors' books, town vitals noting upland births, and King compilations, Native paths in river deeds.

Orchard Outposts, Trolley Farms, and Commuter Persistence

Westerville's 19th-century economy emphasized dairy/orchards with Taunton streetcars, without clustered industry; Civil War rolls from Williams-Stetson kin filled service lists.

These yielded census farms, school rolls, and church admissions capturing multi-generational yeomen.

Genealogical Resources and Strategies

Vital repositories:

- Raynham Town Clerk: Original births, marriages, deaths from 1731 covering Westerville; Taunton continuity strong.

- Published compilations: "Genealogy of the Kings of Raynham, 1680+"; vital records with upland cemeteries.

- Raynham Historical Society: Manuscripts, plats, King-Stetson files.

- Regional aids: FamilySearch wikis for Taunton overlaps, Bristol probate/deeds.

Westerville's upland chronicle—from King allotments and Three Mile pastures to commuter steadings—provides genealogists fringe sources. Clerks' ledgers, family genealogies, and society files unveil "Cohannet kin" spanning Johns, Stetsons, and Williams grazers across Raynham westlands.

Whittenton

Whittenton, Massachusetts, constitutes a historic northern industrial village within the City of Taunton in northeastern Bristol County, originating from 1820s cotton mill dams on the Mill River amid Cohannet proprietary extensions where Lovering, Hall, and Leonard families powered textile operations from George Hall's 1639 settlement outliers before Whittenton Mills dominance. Positioned along modern Bay Street north of Taunton Center with Whittenton Village Historic District (1982 listing), the village clustered company tenements, print works, and Baptist meetinghouses serving Irish and French-Canadian operatives, its manufacturing trajectory—from Wampanoag river sites through King Philip's War bloomeries to rail-era persistence—preserves Taunton records tracing "northern mill kin" across Lovering-Leonard lineages.

Mill River Dams, Lovering Cottons, and Print Works

Early Whittenton's riverbanks formed Taunton North fringes with Willard Lovering (b.1801 Holliston) acquiring mills by 1840s for cotton printing, defended as forge outliers post-1675; Leonard heirs expanded amid tide dams supplying Boston markets.

Genealogists access this via Taunton proprietors' books, town vitals noting mill births, and Lovering abstracts, Native paths in river deeds.

Company Tenements, Ethnic Districts, and Rail Hubs

Whittenton's 19th-century economy fused cotton/printing with rail depots by 1870s, sustained by Fall River trolleys; Civil War rolls document Hall-Lovering service from operative families.

These produced directories, overseers' bonds, and parish registers capturing multi-occupational printers.

Genealogical Resources and Strategies

Vital repositories:

- Taunton City Clerk: Original births, marriages, deaths from 1638 covering Whittenton mills; continuity robust.

- Published compilations: "Vital Records of Taunton to 1850" with mill cemeteries and Lovering abstracts.

- Taunton Historical Society: Manuscripts, mill ledgers, Leonard files.

- Regional aids: FamilySearch wikis for Bristol probate/deeds, Raynham overlaps.

Whittenton's river chronicle—from Lovering dams and Mill River prints to tenement districts—provides genealogists industrial sources. Clerks' ledgers, vital volumes, and society archives unveil "Cohannet kin" spanning Willards, Halls, and Leonard operatives across Taunton northlands.

Whittenton Junction

Whittenton Junction, Massachusetts, marks the rail nexus and industrial outpost within the City of Taunton in northeastern Bristol County, emerging in the 1880s where the Whittenton Branch (1881) connected Old Colony mainlines to Lovering cotton mills amid Mill River dams from James Leonard's 1666 forge site powering Cohannet extensions. Positioned at Bay Street and Whittenton Street near modern Route 140 with remnants of the 1882 passenger station and switch tower, the junction clustered worker tenements, freight yards, and fire stations serving Whittenton operatives, its rail trajectory—from Leonard bloomeries through Crocker-Richmond nails (1805) to 20th-century persistence—preserves Taunton records tracing "junction kin" across Lovering-Leonard lineages.

Mill River Rails, Lovering Branches, and Freight Yards

Prior to naming, Whittenton Junction's flats hosted Leonard ironworks yielding to 1823 Taunton Manufacturing cottons; 1881 Whittenton Branch formalized freight to Raynham with switch towers managing Boston-Providence traffic amid fire-prone mills.

Genealogists access this via Taunton proprietors' books, town vitals noting junction births, and Lovering abstracts, Native river paths in early deeds.

Passenger Stations, Worker Districts, and Trolley Hubs

Whittenton's junction economy fused textile shipping with streetcar lines by 1893, sustained by Irish/French Canadian labor; Civil War rolls from Leonard-Crocker kin filled musters.

These yielded timetables, directories, and gravestone records capturing multi-occupational engineers.

Genealogical Resources and Strategies

Vital repositories:

- Taunton City Clerk: Original births, marriages, deaths from 1638 covering Whittenton Junction; mill continuity robust.

- Published compilations: "Vital Records of Taunton to 1850" with rail abstracts and junction cemeteries.

- Taunton Historical Society: Manuscripts, timetables, Crocker-Lovering files.

- Regional aids: FamilySearch wikis for Raynham/Berkley overlaps, Bristol probate/deeds.

Whittenton Junction's rail chronicle—from Leonard forges and Crocker branches to Lovering yards—provides genealogists transport sources. Clerks' volumes, vital rolls, and society stacks unveil "Cohannet kin" spanning Jameses, Willards, and operative hands across Taunton rails.

Ghost Towns

Norton Furnace

Norton Furnace stands as Bristol County's sole ghost town within the Town of Norton, established in 1825 approximately 2 miles south of Norton Center (modern Meadowbrook area) where Annes A. Lincoln Jr. built an iron furnace on Wading River tributaries amid Taunton North Purchase extensions from 1669 proprietary divisions powering early bloomeries for Leonard kin descendants. The short-lived settlement clustered furnace workers' tenements, charcoal sheds, and slag heaps employing 25 hands by 1837 producing castings before transitioning to copperworks (peak 1865: 65 men, $90,000 output) amid Attleborough-Taunton Railroad proximities, its vanished industrial arc—from bog iron sites through antebellum expansion to post-Civil War relocation—preserves Norton records tracing "furnace kin" across Lincoln-Leonard lineages.

Wading River Bloomeries, Lincoln Furnaces, and Copper Smelters

Prior to naming, Norton Furnace's meadows formed Norton's southern industrial outliers with 1713 forges at Reservoir Avenue; Annes Lincoln's 1825 ironworks expanded to copper by 1845 ($316,000 peak) before Taunton relocation amid slag contamination.

Genealogists access this via Norton proprietors' books, town vitals noting furnace births, and Lincoln abstracts, bog iron deeds in early surveys.

Charcoal Sheds, Worker Tenements, and Rail Freight

Norton Furnace's brief economy dominated castings/hollowware shipping via Taunton Branch, sustained by local bog supplies; Civil War production filled Leonard orders without dense settlement.

These yielded 1837/1865 censuses, overseers' bonds, and slag-era gravestones capturing transient smelters.

Genealogical Resources and Strategies

Vital repositories:

- Norton Town Clerk: Original births, marriages, deaths from 1711 covering furnace sites; Taunton continuity aids.

- Published compilations: "History of Norton" with industrial abstracts and Meadowbrook cemeteries.

- Norton Historical Society: Manuscripts, slag samples, Lincoln-Leonard files.

- Regional aids: FamilySearch wikis for Attleborough/Taunton overlaps, Bristol probate/deeds.

Norton Furnace's vanished chronicle—from Lincoln iron and Wading smelters to copper ghosts—provides genealogists ephemeral sources. Clerks' volumes, census rolls, and society stacks unveil "North Purchase kin" spanning Anneses, Leonards, and slag hands across Norton meadows.